CORPORATE FRAUD INVESTIGATIONS
AND
COMPLIANCE PROGRAMS

Eugene M. Propper
Holland & Knight LLP

OCEANA PUBLICATIONS, INC.
DOBBS FERRY, NY

Information contained in this work has been obtained by Oceana Publications from sources believed to be reliable. However, neither the Publisher nor its authors guarantee the accuracy or completeness of any information published herein, and neither Oceana nor its authors shall be responsible for any errors, omissions or damages arising from the use of this information. This work is published with the understanding that Oceana and its authors are supplying information, but are not attempting to render legal or other professional services. If such services are required, the assistance of an appropriate professional should be sought.

You may order this or any other Oceana publications by visiting Oceana's website at http://www.oceanalaw.com

Library of Congress Cataloging-in-Publication Data

Propper, Eugene M.
   Corporate fraud investigations and compliance programs / by Eugene M. Propper.
     p. cm.
  Includes bibliographical references.
  ISBN 0-379-21410-5 (cloth : alk. paper)
   1. Fraud—Prevention. 2. Employee crimes—Prevention. 3. Fraud investigation.
  4. Auditing, Internal. 5. Corporations—Corrupt practices. I. Title.

HV6691.P76 1999
658.4'73—dc21

99-55585

© 2000 by Oceana Publications, Inc. and Eugene M. Propper.

All rights reserved. No part of this publication may be reproduced or transmitted in any way or by any means, electronic or mechanical, including photocopy, recording, xerography, or any information storage and retrieval system, without permission in writing from the publisher.

Manufactured in the United States of America on acid-free paper.

TABLE OF CONTENTS

ABOUT THE AUTHOR	ix
ACKNOWLEDGEMENTS	xi
INTRODUCTION	xv
CHAPTER 1: CORPORATE CRIMINAL LIABILITY	1
I. Criminal Liability of the Corporation	1
A. Liability for Subsidiaries' Acts	2
B. Collective Knowledge	2
C. Punishment of Corporations for Criminal Offenses	3
II. Corporate Civil Liability for Criminal Conduct	3
III. Criminal Liability of Corporate Officers and Directors	4
A. The "Responsible Corporate Officer" Doctrine	5
IV. Civil Liability of Corporate Officers and Directors for Corporate Misconduct	7
CHAPTER 2: THE CORPORATE DUTY TO INVESTIGATE	9
I. Background and Introduction	9
II. Recent Trends	10
A. The Corporate Sentencing Guidelines	11
B. The Caremark Decision	12
C. Securities Law Developments	15
1. The Blue Ribbon Committee Report	16
2. The SEC's Grace Report	18
D. Healthcare and Other Regulatory Developments	19
E. The Benefits of Corporate Investigation and Compliance Programs	20
CHAPTER 3: ATTORNEY-CLIENT PRIVILEGE AND WORK-PRODUCT DOCTRINE	23
I. Attorney-Client Privilege	23
II. Purpose of the Attorney-Client Privilege	24
III. When Does the Privilege Apply	24
A. Privilege in the Context of Corporate Investigations	24
B. What Does Upjohn Cover?	26
IV. When Does the Privilege Not Apply?	27
V. Exceptions to the Privilege	29
VI. Work-Product Doctrine	31
VII. Waiver of the Attorney-Client Privilege and Work-Product Doctrine in the Conduct of an Internal Corporate Investigation	35
A. Intentional Disclosures	37

B. Partial Disclosures	37
VIII. Considerations Attending the Waiver of the Attorney-Client Privilege Differ from those Attending the Waiver of the Work-Product Doctrine	37
IX. Waiver in the Context of an Internal Corporate Investigation	41
A. Waiver by Voluntary Disclosure of the Investigative Report or Information to the Government	42
X. Reminders to Consider	47
XI. Other specialized Privileges and Legal Theories for Protecting Documents	47
XII. Self-Evaluative Privilege	47

CHAPTER 4: HOW THE INVESTIGATION STARTS — 51

I. Introduction	51
II. Should an Internal Investigation be Conducted	51
III. Benefits of an Internal Investigation	52
IV. Type of Investigation	53
V. Choice of Counsel for the Investigation	53
VI. Early Analysis by Counsel	56
VII. Press Coverage	58
VIII. Statements that may Affect Stock Price	58
IX. Get Control of the Documents and Computer Files	59
X. Notices to Employees	59
XI. Product or Brand Name Harm	59
XII. Plan in Advance	60

CHAPTER 5: CONDUCTING THE INVESTIGATION — 61

I. Interviewing Employees	61
II. Preparing for Employee Interviews	62
III. Conducting the Interviews	63
IV. Ethical Concerns	63
V. Retaining Separate Counsel for Employees	64
VI. Termination of Non-Cooperative and Culpable Employees	65
A. Non-Cooperative Employees	65
B. Placing the Blame on Employees	66
C. Precautions in Terminating Guilty or Non-Cooperative Employees	67
VII. Preparation of Employees and Other Witnesses for Interviews by Government Agents or Grand Jury Appearances	68
VIII. Obstruction of Justice	70
A. The Statutes	70
1. Section 1503	70
2. Section 1505	71
3. Section 1512	72
B. Application of Obstruction of Justice Statutes to Attorneys	73
C. Obstruction Concerns When Interviewing Witnesses	74
D. Preparing Witnesses	75

E. Federal Agents	76
IX. Preparation of a Script	77
X. Creating a Record	79
XI. Documents	80
A. The Importance of Document Gathering and Production	80
B. Finding and Reviewing the Documents	81
C. Organization of Documents	82
XII. Report of the Investigation	82
A. Content of the Report	83
B. Dissemination of a Written Report	84
C. Oral Report	84
D. Protecting the Company from Suits Arising from the Report	84
E. Maintaining Confidentiality after Disclosure of the Report (Waiver)	85
XIII. Guidelines for Protecting Investigative Materials from Disclosure	87
XIV. Other Steps to Establish and Preserve Attorney-Client Privilege and the Work-Product Doctrine in the Context of an Internal Company Investigation	90
XV. Additional Protection	91
XVI. Dealing with the Prosecutor	92
CHAPTER 6: PARALLEL CIVIL, CRIMINAL & ADMINISTRATIVE PROCEEDINGS	99
I. The Significance of Parallel Proceedings	99
II. The Preclusive Impact of One Proceeding upon a Parallel Proceeding	100
III. The Discovery Issue	101
IV. The Government's Use of Parallel Proceedings as an Enforcement Tool	103
V. The Government's Right to Proceed on Multiple Fronts	104
VI. The Use of Protective Orders to Resolve Parallel Proceedings Issues	107
VII. The Use of Stays to Resolve Parallel Proceedings Issues	108
VIII. A Balancing Act	110
CHAPTER 7: MULTIPLE REPRESENTATION	113
I. Introduction	113
II. Conflicts and Disqualification	113
III. Permissible Multiple Representation	116
IV. Preventing Unintended Formations of Attorney-Client Relationships	117
V. Identifying Conflicts	118
VI. Indemnification	120
VII. Joint Defense Agreements	121
CHAPTER 8: CORPORATE SENTENCING GUIDELINES AND COMPLIANCE PROGRAMS	127
I. The Sentencing Guidelines	127
A. Remedying Harm from Criminal Conduct	128
B. Imposing a Fine as Punishment	128

1. The "Base Fine"	128
2. The "Culpability Score"	128
3. Increasing the "Culpability Score"	129
4. Decreasing the "Culpability Score"	130
C. Probation	131
II. Compliance Programs	131
A. An Effective Compliance Program	132
1. The Sentencing Guidelines	132
2. The Defense Industry Initiative	133
3. Identifying Compliance Risk Issues	135
4. Codes of Conduct	140
5. Administration and Enforcement of the Compliance Program	141
B. Responding to Suspected Offenses	144
CHAPTER 9: CONDUCTING AN INTERNAL INVESTIGATION OVERSEAS	147
I. Background	147
II. The Foreign Corrupt Practices Act	150
CHAPTER 10: INVESTIGATIONS IN THE HEALTH CARE INDUSTRY	153
Introduction	153
The Primary Weapons of the Government in Health Care Fraud Investigations	155
I. Federal False Claims Statutes	155
A. Civil False Claims Act	156
1. Background	156
2. Elements of the Civil FCA	157
3. *Qui Tam* Actions	159
B. Criminal False Claim Statutes	161
II. Application of Civil False Claims Act in the Health Care Industry	162
A. Physician Billings—"Upcoding"	162
B. Hospital Cost Reimbursement—Cost Report Fraud	165
C. Skilled Nursing Facilities—Quality of Care	168
III. Enforcement Initiatives—Results and Outlook	169
A. Legislative Reform of the FCA	169
B. HHS—Comprehensive Strategy on Waste, Fraud, and Abuse	171
1. Improper Payments Reduced by 50%	171
2. Operation Restore Trust	171
3. Increased Enforcement Funding Through HIPAA	172
4. OIG Presence in New States	172
5. Beneficiary Rewards for Fraud and Abuse Reporting	172
6. "Fraud Buster" Initiatives	172
C. HCFA—Comprehensive Plan for Program Integrity	173
1. Inpatient Hospital Services	173
2. Congregate Care	173
3. Managed Care Plans	174
4. Community Mental Health Centers	174
5. Skilled Nursing Facilities	175

Table of Contents

IV. The Federal Anti-Kickback Statute	175
A. The Statute	175
B. History of the Statute	178
C. Intent Requirement	179
1. Intent to Induce	180
2. "Knowingly and Willfully"	181
D. Safe Harbor Regulations	182
E. Scope of Enforcement	184
V. The Prohibitions Against Self-Referrals—The Stark Law	185
A. The Stark Law: Prohibition on Physician Self-Referrals	185
VI. The Health Insurance Portability and Accountability Act of 1996	190
A. Fraud and Abuse after HIPAA	190
B. HIPAA Provisions	191
1. Section 201. Fraud and Abuse Control Program	191
2. Section 202. Medicare Integrity Program	192
3. Section 203. Beneficiary Incentive Programs	192
4. Section 204. Application of Fraud and Abuse Penalties to All Federal Health Care Programs	192
5. Section 205. Guidance Regarding Application of Fraud and Abuse Sanctions	193
6. Revisions to Current Administrative Sanctions for Fraud and Abuse	193
7. Changes in Civil Monetary Penalties Under the Social Security Act	194
8. Criminal Law Revisions	195
VII. The Balanced Budget Act of 1997	196
A. Section 4301: Permanent Exclusion for Those Convicted of Three Healthcare Related Crimes	196
B. Section 4302: Authority to Refuse to Enter into Medicare Agreements with Individuals or Entities Convicted of Felonies	197
C. Section 4303: Exclusion of Entity Controlled by a Family Member of a Sanctioned Individual	197
D. Section 4304: Imposition of Civil Money Penalties	197
E. Section 4311: Improving Information to Medicare Beneficiaries	198
F. Section 4312: Disclosure of Information and Surety Bonds	198
G. Section 4313: Provision of Certain Identification Numbers	199
H. Section 4314: Advisory Opinions Regarding Certain Physician Self-Referral Matters	199
I. Section 4317: Requirement to Furnish Diagnostic Information	199
J. Section 4320: Definitions of Reasonable Costs	199
K. Section 4321: Nondiscrimination in Post Hospital Referral to Home Health Agencies and Other Entities	200
VIII. Exclusion and Other Administrative Penalties Related to Federal Health Care Programs	200
A. Introduction	200
B. History of Exclusionary Authority	201
C. Grounds for Exclusion	203
1. Mandatory Exclusion	203

2. Permissive Exclusion	203
3. Permanent Exclusion for Three Program Convictions	204
4. Exclusion In Other Statutory Provisions	205
D. Due Process Protections in the Exclusion Process	206
1. Mandatory Exclusion Requiring No Hearing	206
2. Permissive Exclusion by Judicial or Agency Determination	207
3. Allegations Requiring Hearing Before Exclusion	207
E. Reinstatement into Federal Health Care Programs	209
IX. Compliance Programs Are a Virtual Requirement in the Health Care Industry	209
X. Special Considerations In Health Care Investigations	212
A. Potential Duty to Self-Report	212
B. Conduct of Internal Investigations	215
C. Parallel Proceedings	217
XI. Conclusion	219

CHAPTER 11: ENVIRONMENTAL CRIMES & ENVIRONMENTAL COMPLIANCE — 221

I. Environmental Criminal Statutes	222
A. Resource Conservation and Recovery Act (42 U.S.C. §§ 6901-6992k)	223
B. Clean Water Act (33 U.S.C. §§ 1251-1387)	224
C. Clean Air Act (42 U.S.C. §§ 7401-7671g)	225
D. Comprehensive Environmental Response, Compensation and Liability Act (42 U.S.C. §§ 9601-9675)	226
E. Additional Environmental Criminal Statutes	227
II. Nontraditional "Environmental" Crimes	228
A. Conspiracy to Commit Offense or to Defraud the United States, 18 U.S.C. § 371	228
B. False Statements, 18 U.S.C. § 1001	229
C. Mail and Wire Fraud, 18 U.S.C. §§ 1341, 1343	229
D. Money Laundering Control Act , 18 U.S.C. §§ 1956, 1957	229
III. The Basis of Environmental Criminal Liability	230
IV. Environmental Criminal Prosecutions Target the Responsible Corporate Official	234
V. Responsible Corporate Officer and Strict Liability	235
VI. Negligent Violations of the CWA and CAA	237
VII. Environmental Compliance Programs Are Essential for Avoiding Criminal Liability	238

CHAPTER 12: ENVIRONMENTAL CRIMINAL PROSECUTIONS IN THE MARITIME INDUSTRY — 241

I. Background	241
II. Threat of Criminal Prosecution	243
A. Criminal Negligence and No-Fault Crimes	243
B. Compliance Programs	245
III. Oversight Programs Generally	245

IV. ISM Code	246
V. ISO 9000	247
VI. ISO 14001	247
VII. Comparison: ISM Code, ISO 9000, ISO 14001, and Maritime Compliance Program	249
CHAPTER 13: FORENSIC ACCOUNTING	251
I. The Forensic Accounting Process	255
II. Computer Fraud	256
III. Accounting Conventions	256
IV. Money Laundering	257
V. Government Investigations	258
APPENDIX 1. JULY 28, 1997 OFFICE OF THE ATTORNEY GENERAL MEMO	261
APPENDIX 2. CHAPTER EIGHT—SENTENCING OF ORGANIZATIONS	263
APPENDIX 3. 31 U.S.C. § 3729 THROUGH U.S.C. § 3733	301
APPENDIX 4. PROVIDER SELF-DISCLOSURE PROTOCOL	327
APPENDIX 5. U.S. DEPARTMENT OF JUSTICE POLICY STATEMENT	337
APPENDIX 6. ENVIRONMENTAL PROTECTION AGENCY POLICY STATEMENT	345
APPENDIX 7. EXAMPLES OF NO-FAULT ENVIRONMENTAL CRIMES	351
APPENDIX 8. COMPARISON: ISM CODE, ISO 9000, ISO 14001, AND MARITIME COMPLIANCE PROGRAM	355
LIST OF SOURCES OF ADDITIONAL INFORMATION	361

ABOUT THE AUTHOR

Eugene M. Propper represents clients in the areas of complex civil and criminal fraud investigations. Mr. Propper has handled internal fraud investigations for domestic and foreign corporations, both in the United States and overseas, as well as for foreign governments. He has assisted clients in implementing compliance programs and systems to deter and prevent fraud. Mr. Propper also represents individual and corporate clients in complex civil and criminal trials and he counsels clients on litigation and pre-litigation strategy.

Mr. Propper began his career at the Department of Justice in 1971 and spent eight years as an Assistant United States Attorney in Washington, D.C. During his career there, he was the lead prosecutor in the international investigation and trial of the persons responsible for the political assassination of former Chilean Ambassador to the United States Orlando Letelier. The Department of Justice awarded Mr. Propper a Special Achievement Award "in appreciation and recognition of Sustained Superior Performance of Duty." Mr. Propper is the co-author of "Labyrinth", a book written about the investigation of that case. Mr. Propper is a partner in Holland & Knight's Washington, D.C. office. Prior to joining Holland & Knight, Mr. Propper was the head of the Litigation Department at two Washington, D.C. law firms.

ACKNOWLEDGEMENTS

The author gratefully acknowledges the contributions of his colleagues in several Holland & Knight offices, without which this book could not have been written. In addition to the chapters written by Mr. Propper, the following lawyers contributed chapters or portions thereof:

Steven D. Gordon practices in the areas of white collar criminal defense and civil litigation, representing both corporations and individual clients. He conducts internal investigations for corporate clients, and advises them on issues relating to compliance programs and voluntary disclosure. Mr. Gordon is a former Assistant United States Attorney and is a partner in the Washington, D.C. office of Holland & Knight. He authored the chapter on Corporate Criminal Liability and co-authored the chapters on Parallel Proceedings and Corporate Sentencing Guidelines and Compliance Programs.

Christopher Myers is the co-chair of Holland & Knight's White Collar and Corporate Compliance National Practice Group. His practice is focused on representing clients, particularly those in the health care and other highly regulated industries, in complex criminal and civil fraud investigations and litigation. He also works with clients on the development and implementation of corporate compliance programs. Mr. Myers is a former Assistant United States Attorney for the District of Columbia and is a partner in Holland & Knight's Washington, D.C. office. He co-authored the chapter on Investigations in the Health Care Industry.

John P. Rowley III practices in the areas of white collar criminal defense and complex civil litigation, with an emphasis on cases for health care and high-technology companies. Before joining Holland & Knight, Mr. Rowley spent 8 years with the United States Attorney's Office in Alexandria, Virginia, where he was a criminal unit supervisor. Mr. Rowley is a partner in Holland & Knight's Northern Virginia office. He co-authored the chapter on Parallel Proceedings and the section on Dealing with the Prosecutor.

James H. Rodio practices in the areas of white collar criminal defense and complex civil litigation with a focus on fraud and false claims cases. Mr. Rodio spent 11 years with the Criminal Section, Tax Division, United States Department of Justice, prosecuting criminal tax, money laundering and related fraud cases prior to joining Holland & Knight where he is a partner in the Northern Virginia office. He co-authored the chapter on Parallel Proceedings.

Brian Albritton practices in the area of white collar criminal defense and he devotes a substantial portion of his practice to defending individuals and companies accused of environmental offenses. In addition to being a partner in Holland & Knight's Tampa office, Mr. Albritton currently teaches Federal Criminal Law Seminar at Stetson University College of Law in St. Petersburg, Florida. He authored the chapter on Environmental Crimes.

Dennis Bryant focuses on federal and international maritime and environmental matters. Prior to joining Holland & Knight, Mr. Bryant served on active duty with the U.S. Coast Guard for 27 years, retiring as a Captain. While on active duty, he supervised the writing of regulations to implement the Oil Pollution Act of 1990. Mr. Bryant is a Senior Counsel in Holland & Knight's Washington, D.C. office. He authored the chapter on Criminal Prosecutions in the Maritime Industry.

Leonard Kleinman's practice includes representation in federal and state tax investigations and disputes, both civil and criminal, from the administrative level through trial. Mr. Kleinman also practices in the transactional area involving tax and business, sports and entertainment and mergers and acquisitions. Mr. Kleinman has served as the Executive Vice President and Chief Operating Officer of the New York Yankees, Vice Chairman of the American Shipbuilding Company and Branch Chief of the Audit Division of the Internal Revenue Service. Mr. Kleinman is a Senior Counsel at Holland & Knight's Tampa office. Mr. Kleinman's co-authored the chapter on The Corporation's Duty to Investigate.

Richard Moore practices in the areas of civil litigation and appellate representation and has participated in a wide variety of commercial and other civil litigation matters in both state and federal courts at the trial and appellate levels, and in arbitration proceedings. Prior to joining Holland & Knight, in its northern Virginia office, Mr. Moore practiced with law firms in both northern Virginia and San Diego, California. Mr. Moore served on active duty with the U.S. Marine Corps for twenty seven years. At the time of his retirement in 1981, as a Brigadier General, Mr. Moore was the Assistant Judge Advocate General of the Navy (Military Law). He co-authored the chapter on the Attorney-Client Privilege and Work-Product Doctrine.

Christopher Margand practices in the area of complex civil and criminal fraud litigation, and commercial litigation in the Washington D.C. office of Holland & Knight. Prior to entering the practice of law Mr. Margand served for almost seven years as a D.C. Metropolitan Police officer. He authored the chapter on multiple representation.

Jonathan Greenberg specializes in complex commercial litigation and arbitration. Prior to joining Holland & Knight, Mr. Greenberg was a litigator in New York for five years, focusing on general commercial, securities, antitrust and intellectual property litigation. Mr. Greenberg is a partner in Holland & Knight's Washington, D.C. office. He co-authored the chapters on Investigations in the Health Care Industry and Duty of Management to Address Corporate Misconduct.

Scott M. Pritchett practices in the Health Care Group, focusing in the areas of regulatory compliance, federal and state survey processes, defense under federal and state false claims, anti-kickback, and self-referral statutes, and provider financing and acquisitions. Mr. Pritchett has advised clients on the design and operation of their corporate compliance programs and in conducting pre-acquisition due diligence. His practice includes representing clients in multi-jurisdictional civil and criminal investigations of long-term care providers and related entities. Mr. Pritchett is an associate in Holland & Knight's Washington, D.C. office. He co-authored the chapter on Investigations in the Health Care Industry.

Leslie McAdoo practices in the area of white collar criminal defense and general criminal defense in Holland & Knight's Washington, D.C. office. Ms. McAdoo is a member of the National Criminal Defense Attorneys Association and the Maryland Criminal Defense Attorneys Association. Ms. McAdoo is a former Special Agent for the Department of Defense. She authored the section on Obstruction of Justice.

Marc B. Sherman is a forensic accountant and the National Partner in Charge for KPMG's Forensic and Litigation Services and Intellectual Property Services practice. He is resident in the Washington, D.C. and Baltimore offices. Mr. Sherman has conducted civil and criminal fraud investigations both domestically and internationally across a wide range of industries. He has testified as an expert witness in fraud cases and lectures frequently across the U.S. and internationally on fraud and forensic investigations. Mr. Sherman is a certified public accountant, a certified fraud examiner, a certified reorganization and insolvency accountant and a lawyer. Mr. Sherman wrote the chapter on forensic accounting and was assisted by Greg Donovan, a senior consultant at KPMG. Mr. Sherman co-authored the chapter on Conducting an Internal Investigation Overseas with Mr. Propper.

Special thanks go to John E. Schwarz, a former colleague with whom I have worked for nearly 15 years for his editing of portions of this book and to Pat Saylor, my administrative assistant of over 8 years for her assistance in proof reading and cite checking. Thanks also go to Ethan Arenson, who assisted with preliminary research of this book. Mr. Arenson will join the Holland & Knight office in Washington, D.C. in the Fall of 2000.

INTRODUCTION

Companies that do business in the United States, both domestic and foreign, increasingly find themselves under scrutiny by government agencies and federal and state prosecutors for a wide range of regulatory violations or criminal wrongdoing. More and more often, the government seeks to regulate corporate behavior through punitive legal actions, such as administrative sanctions and criminal prosecutions. In many instances, corporate officers and employees are being targeted, in addition to their corporate employers. The amounts that have been paid in judgments, settlements and fines grows at a geometric rate, and an increasing number of business executives have been prosecuted, convicted, and even imprisoned.

Every company is a potential subject of a government investigation. In certain highly regulated areas, such as health care and the environment, investigations and prosecutions happen more frequently. Today, every corporate general counsel and business executive must be aware of the risks of governmental investigations and be prepared how to best deal with such events when they arise.

An internal corporate investigation is the primary mechanism for responding to a governmental investigation and developing the facts essential to formulating the strategy for defending the company and its officers or employees. A well conducted internal investigation may enable a company to avoid administrative sanctions or a criminal prosecution, or else to minimize the damage; it can make the difference whether a company can remain in business, or whether an executive goes to jail.

The utility and significance of internal investigations is not limited to dealing with government investigations or enforcement actions. Internal investigations are equally essential in responding to threatened or pending civil litigation, or in ferreting out suspected internal fraud or misconduct. Furthermore, companies increasingly seek to be proactive and conduct internal investigations to ensure the absence of any corporate wrongdoing and to ensure, if the company has a compliance program in place, that it is working effectively. Internal investigations are invaluable to companies both in dealing with problems and in seeking to prevent them.

It is essential, however, that an internal investigation be conducted properly, and that the requisite steps be taken to preserve the confidentiality of the process and its results. A poorly conducted investigation can produce misleading results that cause the corporation to make flawed strategic decisions. In some instances, a defective investigative process may actually worsen the company's position if it is later deemed a whitewash or cover-up. And failure to safeguard the confidentiality of an investigation could result in it becoming a "roadmap" for the company's adversaries, including the government, to use in pursuing claims against the company.

Compliance programs are another important tool that companies should employ to protect themselves and to keep the government and civil litigants at bay. A well conceived compliance program, that is carried out effectively, gives management the ability to forestall many potential problems before they occur or before they get out of control. An effective compliance program also demonstrates good corporate citizenship and is useful to help defend the company should a problem arise. It may dissuade a prosecutor from charging the company for the misdeeds of an errant employee. And, under the Federal Sentencing Guidelines, a good compliance program can lighten significantly the punishment that a company receives if it is prosecuted. Indeed, in many industries, it now is nothing short of negligent for a company not to have an active and effective compliance program in place.

Once again, however, it is worthless to a company to have a compliance program that is poorly conceived, ineffective, or mere "window dressing." The only sort of compliance program that is worth having is one that is carefully thought out, properly structured, and diligently enforced.

The purpose of this book is to provide corporate counsel, private practitioners, and business executives with insight into the benefits and pitfalls of internal investigations and compliance programs, and a basic working knowledge of how to conduct such investigations and to structure an effective compliance program.

The book includes chapters on health care fraud and environmental enforcement, two areas of high interest to governmental regulators and investigators. There is also a chapter on criminal enforcement of environmental laws in the maritime industry, something that strongly affects businesses of many nations whose vessels travel into U.S. waters.

Additionally, just as foreign companies who do business in the U.S. must become familiar with internal investigations and compliance programs, so too U.S. businesses must know how to conduct such investigations overseas. There is, therefore, a chapter on conducting investigations outside the United States. Finally, because so many investigations have complicated financial components to them, the book also has a chapter on forensic accounting for internal investigations.

CHAPTER 1:
CORPORATE CRIMINAL LIABILITY

I. Criminal Liability of the Corporation

The general rule is that a corporation is vicariously liable for the criminal acts of its employees or agents under the doctrine of *respondeat superior*, just as it would be liable in tort for their tortious acts. Thus, a corporation may be held criminally liable for violations committed by its employees or agents, including low level employees, if those employees or agents (i) were acting within the scope of their authority, or apparent authority; and (ii) were acting, at least in part, with intent to benefit the business.[1] A corporation is not liable for an employee's criminal acts which were undertaken solely to advance the employee's own interests or those of a third party.[2] However, the corporation is liable where its employee acted both for his own benefit and for the benefit of the employer.[3] Indeed, an employee's criminal conduct which is actually or potentially detrimental to the company may nonetheless be imputed to the corporation if the conduct was motivated, at least in part, by an intent to benefit the company.[4]

Moreover, as a general rule a corporation may be held liable for the criminal violations of its employees committed within the scope of their authority even though such acts were against company policy or express instructions to the employees.[5] Although the existence of company policies or instructions

---

[1] *E.g., United States v. Automated Medical Laboratories. Inc.*, 770 F.2d 399, 406-08 (4th Cir. 1985); *United States v. Cincotta*, 689 F.2d 238, 241-42 (1st Cir.), *cert. denied*, 459 U.S. 991 (1982).

[2] *United States v. Cincotta*, 689 F.2d at 241-42; *Standard Oil Company of Texas v. United States*, 307 F.2d 120, 128-29 (5th Cir. 1962).

[3] *United States v. Automated Medical Laboratories. Inc.*, 770 F.2d at 406-08; *United States v. Gold*, 743 F.2d 800, 823 (11th Cir. 1984), *cert. denied*, 469 U.S. 1217 (1985).

[4] *United States v. Sun-Diamond Growers of Calif.*, 138 F.3d 961, 970-71 (D.C. Cir. 1998), *aff'd*, ___ U.S. ___, 119 S. Ct. 1402 (1999).

[5] *E.g., Hanlester Network v. Shalala*, 51 F.3d 1390, 1400 (9th Cir. 1995); *United States v. Automated Medical Laboratories, Inc.*, 770 F.2d at 406 n.5; *United States v. Cadillac Overall Supply Co.*, 568 F.2d 1078, 1090 (5th Cir. 1978); *United States v. Hilton Hotels Corp.*, 467 F.2d 1000, 1004-07 (9th Cir. 1972), *cert. denied*, 409 U.S. 1125 (1973).

prohibiting the conduct in issue does not provide a *legal* defense to criminal liability, it may provide a *factual* defense in some instances if the company can persuade the jury that it was sufficiently diligent in enforcing such policies or instructions.[6] Some courts, however, have indicated that the existence of a corporate compliance program is irrelevant to determining a company's criminal liability.[7]

Thus, as a practical matter, a corporation comes close to being strictly liable for the criminal acts of its employees or agents committed (even arguably) within the scope of their employment. The corporation can attempt to insulate itself from liability by creating a strong compliance program and enforcing that program vigorously. These steps should help to prevent criminal conduct in the first instance and thereby reduce the company's exposure to criminal sanctions. Should an employee nonetheless commit a crime, the existence of an effective compliance program may persuade a prosecutor not to bring criminal charges against a corporation for an employee's criminal act. If the compliance program does not dissuade the prosecutor from charging the corporation, it may still furnish a potential defense at trial. In any event, the existence of an effective compliance program will reduce the sentence that a corporation faces under the Federal Sentencing Guidelines even if it does not prevent prosecution or conviction.

A. Liability for Subsidiaries' Acts

A corporation may be held liable for criminal acts committed by a subsidiary or division of the corporation, just as it would be liable for the acts of an individual agent. A parent corporation has an obligation to supervise the subsidiary's conduct and assure that it complies with all applicable law.[8]

B. Collective Knowledge

In some instances a corporation may be criminally liable for its conduct, even though no individual employee is culpable, as a result of the doctrine of "collective knowledge." This doctrine holds that a corporation's knowledge consists of the totality of what all of its employees know within the scope of their employment. *United States v. Bank of New England*, 821 F.2d 844 (1st Cir. 1987), is the leading case applying this doctrine. In that case, the defendant bank faced felony charges for failing to file Currency Transaction Reports with the government for certain customer transactions exceeding $10,000. Part of the bank's defense was that the employees who handled the transactions in issue were not aware of the

---

6   *See United States v. Beusch*, 596 F.2d 871, 878 (9th Cir. 1979); *United States v. Basic Construction Co.*, 711 F.2d 570, 573 (4th Cir.), *cert. denied*, 464 U.S. 956 (1983).

7   *See United States v. Twentieth Century Fox Film Corp.*, 882 F.2d 656, 660-61 (2d Cir. 1989), *cert. denied*, 493 US 1021 (1990)(evidence regarding the corporate defendant's compliance program properly excluded as irrelevant to the company's liability).

8   *United States v. Wilshire Oil Co.*, 427 F.2d 969, 974-74 (10th Cir.), *cert. denied* 400 U.S. 829 (1970).

currency reporting requirement. Other employees, however, were aware of the requirement and the court allowed all of the employees' knowledge to be aggregated to establish a knowing violation by the bank.

The ramifications of the "collective knowledge" doctrine upon corporate criminal liability are potentially huge. If pushed to its limits, the doctrine could transform episodes of innocent error on the part of corporate employees into criminal conduct on the part of the corporation. Fortunately, the "collective knowledge" doctrine has been invoked only infrequently in criminal cases. Prosecutors apparently have been reluctant to use the doctrine to prosecute a corporation when no individual employee engaged in criminal conduct. Furthermore, the courts sometimes have rejected the doctrine in cases where the Government does attempt to invoke it.[9]

C . Punishment of Corporations for Criminal Offenses

What are the consequences for a corporation that is convicted of a federal criminal offense? Although the organization cannot be incarcerated, nonetheless, it is subject to potentially severe sanctions. First, it will be ordered to make restitution to the victim(s) of the offense.[10] As for punishment, the company can be fined or placed on probation, or both.[11] The maximum fine for a felony normally is the greatest of (i) $500,000, (ii) twice the gross pecuniary gain from the offense, or (iii) twice the gross pecuniary loss caused by the offense.[12] The fine can be still higher if the law setting forth the particular offense provides for a greater amount.[13] In addition, a special assessment is imposed on convicted defendants for the purpose of funding the Crime Victims Fund.[14] Currently, the assessment for organizations is $400 if convicted of a felony and $125 or less if convicted of a misdemeanor.[15]

Furthermore, a corporation may be placed on probation for up to five years and subjected to potentially onerous requirements regarding reporting and accounting for its operations and finances, and subjecting itself to outside examinations.[16]

II. Corporate Civil Liability for Criminal Conduct

In addition to criminal liability, the misconduct of an employee can expose the corporation to substantial civil liability. To start with, the company faces liability to the victim of the crime. For example, where an employee commits a fraud, the

---

9   *See United States v. United Technologies Corp.*, 51 F. Supp. 2d 167 (D.Conn. 1999) at 195-99 (refusing to apply "collective knowledge" doctrine in civil False Claims action).

10   18 U.S.C. §§ 2327, 3556, 3663, 3663A.

11   18 U.S.C. § 3551(c).

12   18 U.S.C. § 3571(c).

13   18 U.S.C. § 3571(c)(1).

14   18 U.S.C. § 3013.

15   *Id.*

16   *See* 18 U.S.C. §§ 3561, 3551(c); U.S.S.G. § 8D1.1, *et seq.*

corporation may be held liable not only for the victim's actual damages but for punitive damages, too.[17]

If the corporation is a government contractor and the misconduct results in a false claim being presented to the government, the company faces liability under various antifraud statutes.[18] The False Claims Act,[19] for example, provides for treble damages and a civil money penalty of $5,000-$10,000 per claim to be recovered from the company. Further, it permits whistleblowers (disgruntled employees or others) to institute such actions and to prosecute them in the name of the federal government if the Department of Justice declines to intervene and take over prosecution of the suit.

In addition, where the corporation is a government contractor or operates in a highly regulated industry, it may face severe administrative sanctions for criminal conduct. Indeed, these sanctions may dwarf the civil or criminal penalties that the company faces. For instance, federal agencies can debar or exclude contractors who have engaged in misconduct from doing business with the federal government for years or even indefinitely.[20] And health care providers who are convicted of health care fraud face a mandatory exclusion for participating in any federal health care program for a minimum of five years.[21]

III. Criminal Liability of Corporate Officers and Directors

The general rule, subject to some very limited exceptions, is that an officer or director of a corporation cannot be criminally prosecuted for the company's misconduct unless he personally participated in that misconduct. An officer must be an "active and knowing" participant in the criminal scheme in order to be held individually liable.[22]

The personal participation necessary to make someone individually liable for a crime does not require direct, "hands on" involvement in the offense. The law provides that an individual is liable for a criminal offense committed by another person if he aided, abetted, commanded, induced or procured its commission.[23] This requires some affirmative conduct by the individual designed to aid the criminal venture.[24] In the corporate context, an officer becomes liable if he or she

---

17 *Pacific Mut. Life Ins. Co. v. Haslip*, 499 U.S. 1, 12-15 (1991).

18 *See UMC Electronics Co. v. United States*, 43 Fed. Cl. 776 (1999) (discussing three different antifraud provisions: the False Claims Act, 31 U.S.C. § 3729, the claim forfeiture statute, 28 U.S.C. § 2514, and the Contract Disputes Act, 41 U.S.C. § 604).

19 31 U.S.C. §§ 3729 *et seq.*

20 *See* 48 C.F.R. §§ 9.400 *et seq.*

21 42 U.S.C. § 1320a-7.

22 *E.g., United States v. Gibson*, 690 F.2d 697, 701 (9th Cir. 1982), *cert. denied*, 460 U.S. 1046 (1983).

23 18 U.S.C. § 2.

24 *United States v. Vasquez*, 953 F.2d 176, 183 (5th Cir.), *cert. denied*, 504 U.S. 946 (1992).

expressly or impliedly authorized or ratified criminal conduct by corporate employees or agents.[25]

Mere knowledge of criminal conduct committed by corporate employees, without more, does not make an officer or director personally subject to prosecution. The offense of "misprision of felony" imposes liability upon any person who, knowing that a crime has been committed, conceals that offense.[26] However, misprision of a felony requires an affirmative step to conceal the underlying offense; mere failure to make it known does not suffice.[27]

A. The "Responsible Corporate Officer" Doctrine

Most criminal offenses have a *scienter* (state of mind) requirement that penalizes only knowing or deliberate violations. There is, however, a narrow class of cases in which corporate officers have been held criminally liable for offenses committed by the company even though the officer did not know of or personally participate in the criminal act. The principal example is prosecutions of corporate managers for corporate violations of statutes designed to ensure the safety of food and drugs sold for public consumption. The courts have ruled that Congress intended to impose a form of criminal strict liability for corporate managers with respect to violations of these statutes.

The Federal Food, Drug, and Cosmetic Act, for example, forbids the introduction of misbranded and adulterated articles into interstate commerce. The Supreme Court twice has issued decisions upholding convictions of corporate mangers for violations of this Act based solely on their position of responsibility.[28] The Court ruled that the Act placed "the burden of acting at hazard upon a person otherwise innocent but standing in responsible relation to a public danger."[29] In other words, the Act imposed a form of strict liability. "Congress has seen fit to enforce the accountability of responsible corporate agents dealing with products which may affect the health of consumers by penal sanctions cast in rigorous terms. . . .".[30] The Court reasoned that the onerous requirements of the Act "are no more stringent than the public has a right to expect of those who voluntarily assume positions of authority in business enterprises whose services and products affect the health and well-being of the public that supports them."[31]

---

25 *United States v. Cattle King Packing Co., Inc.*, 793 F.2d 232, 240 (10th Cir.), *cert. denied*, 479 U.S. 985 (1986); *United States v. Gibson*, 690 F.2d 697, 701 (9th Cir. 1982), *cert. denied*, 460 U.S. 1046 (1983).

26 18 U.S.C. § 4.

27 *United States v. Warters*, 885 F.2d 1266, 1275 (5th Cir. 1989).

28 *United States v. Dotterweich*, 320 U.S. 277 (1943); *United States v. Park*, 421 U.S. 658 (1975).

29 *United States v. Dotterweich*, 320 U.S. at 277.

30 *United States v. Park*, 421 U.S. at 673

31 *Id.* at 672.

This strict liability rationale likewise has been applied to prosecutions of responsible corporate officers for violations of the Federal Meat Inspection Act.[32]

Prosecutors have attempted to expand the "responsible corporate officer" doctrine to reach other sorts of offenses. Currently, the principal battleground is criminal prosecutions for violations of the environmental statutes such as the Resource Conservation and Recovery Act ("RCRA") and the Clean Water Act ("CWA"). In prosecutions under RCRA, the courts so far have refused to apply the doctrine, ruling that a mere showing of official responsibility is not an adequate substitute for proof of actual guilty knowledge on the officer's part.[33]

Cases under the CWA have presented a somewhat more difficult issue because Congress has explicitly defined a "person" within the scope of the statute's criminal sanctions to include "any responsible corporate officer."[34] Courts have agreed that Congress added this language to apply the principle enunciated by the Supreme Court in the food and drug cases to cases arising under the CWA.[35] However, the courts have differed in their articulations of what that principle is and how it should be applied.

One court has suggested that the "responsible corporate officer" doctrine can be used in a CWA prosecution to impute the requisite criminal state of mind to an officer by virtue of his position of responsibility, even though the officer personally lacks consciousness of any wrongdoing.[36] A different—and more palatable—application of the doctrine was articulated recently by another federal court. In that case, the court ruled that a corporate officer could be found criminally liable for the company's violation of the CWA if (1) he had knowledge that pollutants were being discharged by company employees; (2) he had the authority and capacity to prevent the discharge; and (3) he failed to prevent the discharge.[37] The court did not utilize the "responsible corporate officer" doctrine as a substitute for proving that the officer had guilty knowledge of the offense. Instead, the concept was employed to impose liability on officers who do know that an offense is being committed by the company and fail to stop it. In other words, the concept was used to negate the rule normally applied in cases of misprision of a felony that

---

32 *United States v. Cattle King Packing Co., Inc.*, 793 F.2d 232, 240 (10th Cir.), *cert. denied*, 479 U.S. 985 (1986).

33 *United States v. MacDonald & Watson Waste Oil Co.*, 933 F.2d 35, 50-55 (1st Cir. 1991); *United States v. White*, 766 F. Supp. 873, 894-95 (E.D. Wash. 1991).

34 33 U.S.C. § 1319(c)(6).

35 *United States v. Iverson*, 162 F.3d 1015, 1023-24 (9th Cir. 1998); *United States v. Brittain*, 931 F.2d 1413, 1419 (10th Cir. 1991).

36 *United States v. Brittain*, 931 F.2d 1413, 1419 (10th Cir. 1991).

37 *United States v. Iverson*, 162 F.3d at 1022-26.

mere knowledge of an offense committed by another is not sufficient to impose criminal liability on a person absent an affirmative step to conceal the offense.[38]

In summary, the courts generally have exhibited a deep reluctance to impose criminal liability upon corporate officials simply by virtue of their position, absent knowledge of the wrongdoing. And most federal criminal offenses, unlike the CWA, do not explicitly include "any responsible corporate officers" within their scope. Nonetheless, the courts agree that a corporate official's actual guilty knowledge may be inferred from circumstantial evidence, including the position and responsibility of the defendant. Furthermore, a defendant's willful blindness (*i.e.*, ostrich-like behavior) to the facts constituting the offense may be sufficient to establish knowledge.[39]

As a practical matter, most responsible corporate officials who learn of criminal wrongdoing by their company will take appropriate steps to put an end to it, simply as a matter of law abiding good citizenship. Should they fail to do so, they risk prosecution either under the "responsible corporate officer" doctrine or under the more traditional notion that they have impliedly authorized the ongoing offense through their failure to act.

IV. Civil Liability of Corporate Officers and Directors for Corporate Misconduct

The potential for personal criminal liability is not the only concern of corporate officers and directors with respect to corporate misconduct. In addition, there are substantial risks of civil liability to the individual officer or director.

In the first place, an officer or director may become personally liable to the victim of corporate misconduct. When corporate officers directly participate in or authorize the commission of a wrongful act, even if the act is done on behalf of the corporation, they may be personally liable.[40]

Second, an officer or director who is involved in misconduct or who fails to remedy it may face a "derivative" suit brought by a shareholder on behalf of the corporation for breach of his fiduciary duty to the company.[41] Some states recognize three distinct bases for imposing personal liability on officers or directors for corporate misconduct: participation in the misconduct, knowledge amounting to

---

38　A more detailed explanation of criminal liability under the environmental laws is set forth in Chapter 11.

39　*United States v. MacDonald & Watson Waste Oil Co.*, 933 F.2d at 53-55; *see also United States v. Johnson & Towers, Inc.*, 741 F.2d 662, 669-70 (3d Cir. 1984), *cert. denied*, 469 U.S. 1208 (1985).

40　*General Motors Acceptance Corp. v. Bates*, 954 F.2d 1081, 1085 (5th Cir. 1992); *Delong Equip. Co. v. Washington Mills Abrasive Co.*, 840 F.2d 843, 851 (11th Cir. 1988), *cert. denied*, 494 U.S. 1081 (1990).

41　*See generally Cohen v. Beneficial Industrial Loan Corp.*, 337 U.S. 541, 549 (1949).

acquiescence, or negligent management and supervision.[42] The Delaware Chancery Court has held that senior managers and directors must make a good faith effort to ensure that the company has an adequate system to internally detect illegal activity in a timely manner.[43] Failure to establish such a detection system, or failure to investigate possible misconduct after warning signs appear, could expose officers and directors to personal liability even though they, individually, have no involvement in or knowledge of the misconduct.[44]

In the case of public companies, failure to disclose corporate misconduct that materially impacts the company's financial position may create a distinct basis for personal liability on the part of officers and directors. The Securities and Exchange Commission ("SEC") has imposed a duty of disclosure in circumstances where the misconduct would have an impact on the company's public statements. "If an officer or director knows or should know that his company's statements concerning particular issues are inadequate or incomplete, he or she has an obligation to correct that failure."[45]

Congress recently created a similar disclosure duty when it enacted the Private Securities Litigation Reform Act. The Act requires auditors of public companies to detect illegal acts that would have a direct and material effect on the financial statements of the corporation and to inform management and the board of directors of any such illegal act. If the auditor concludes that (1) the illegal act has a material effect on the company's financial statements, (2) the directors and/or management have failed to take timely and appropriate remedial actions, and (3) the failure to take remedial action is reasonably expected to cause the auditor to depart from a "standard" report, then the auditor must deliver a special report to the board. The company then must notify the SEC within one business day and furnish the auditor with a copy of the notice given to the SEC. The auditor must deliver a copy of his report directly to the SEC if he does not receive back a copy of the company's notice within one business day.[46]

Officers or directors who fail to comply with these disclosure obligations may face enforcement actions by the SEC, or suits by disgruntled investors.[47] And individuals, like companies, can be excluded from doing business with the government or from participating in federal programs.

---

42   *Keams v. Tempe Tech. Institute, Inc.*, 993 F. Supp. 714, 725 (D. Ariz. 1997) (construing Arizona law).

43   *In re Caremark Int'l Inc. Derivative Litig.*, 698 A.2d 959, 970 (Del. Ch. 1996).

44   *See Bates v. Dresser*, 251 U.S. 524, 529-31 (1920).

45   *In re W.R. Grace & Co.*, Securities Exchange Act Release No. 39157 (Report of Investigation).

46   15 U.S.C. § 78j-1.

47   *See, e.g., Magna Investment Corp. v. John Does One Through Two Hundred*, 931 F.2d 38, 39 (11th Cir. 1991)(discussing shareholder's action against management, under the securities laws, for making a material misstatement or omission in a document filed with the SEC).

CHAPTER 2:
THE CORPORATE DUTY TO INVESTIGATE

I. Background and Introduction

For decades, under the "business judgment" presumption, management had limited responsibility to assure corporate compliance with the law. Corporate boards were "management-dominated, passive, and generally inert. . . . [and] were not expected to do much more than rubber-stamp management's decisions."[1] Companies were required to react only when an actual or potential illegality came to the attention of senior executives or directors. Those instances aside, management could presume that the corporation and its employees were acting lawfully. As the Delaware Supreme Court stated, "absent cause for suspicion there is no duty upon the directors to install and operate a corporate system of espionage to ferret out wrongdoing which they have no reason to suspect exists."[2] Management's duty, at bottom, was *reactive*: to throw water on the flames once the fire had been detected.

Against this backdrop, the federal government historically required that only a few heavily regulated industries "ferret out wrongdoing" of one type or another. This was based on the recognition that certain lines of business merit greater vigilance and oversight, because they present more opportunities for fraud and abuse. Thus, under the Securities Exchange Act of 1934, securities dealers must ensure that their brokers and other employees are not violating the securities laws.[3] Government contractors are charged with the duty of reporting bribes to the

---

1   Ira M. Millstein, "Introduction to the Report and Recommendations of the Blue Ribbon Committee on Improving the Effectiveness of Audit Committees", 54 *Bus. Law.* 1057 (May 1999) (hereinafter, "Blue Ribbon Introduction"). Mr. Millstein served as co-chair of the Blue Ribbon Committee on audit committees, discussed *infra*.

2   *Graham v. Allis-Chalmers Mfg. Co.*, 188 A.2d 125, 130 (Del. 1963).

3   *See, e.g.*, "Supervisory Responsibilities of Broker-Dealer Management", Exchange Act Release No. 34-8404, 33 *Fed. Reg.* 14,286 (Sept. 11, 1968) ("Clearly, the primary responsibility of assuring that the firm's operation complies with sound business practices and the rules and regulations of all regulatory bodies rests with the firm's management").

appropriate authorities.[4] Federally insured banks must report instances in which their institution may have been defrauded.[5] Companies working overseas have adopted compliance programs in connection with the Foreign Corrupt Practices Act, which Congress enacted in 1977.[6]

The last 15 years has seen a steady erosion of the once formidable legal and regulatory divide between these specially regulated industries and the general business community. Today, as one commentator put it succinctly, "the presumption of business regularity may be giving way to a belated assumption of failed oversight in the face of misconduct."[7] Corporations in every industry are increasingly being subjected to a host of statutes and regulations governing their conduct. The penalties associated with corporate non-compliance have risen astronomically—as have the benefits associated with a vigorous compliance program, and active and vigilant managerial oversight. Management now has the duty to think and behave *proactively*: to institute a program of detection, prevention and monitoring that is designed to prevent fires from starting in the first place.

Employees at even the best-run firms may still find ways to break the law. However, corporate executives and directors who are attuned to their duties in this new legal landscape will be able to avoid potential disaster. The business judgment rule will continue to protect managerial decisions—no matter how "wrong" or seemingly irrational—as long as these decisions were made in good faith, after consideration of all available evidence, in an environment that demonstrates the company's commitment to legal compliance. Conversely, companies that continue to adopt a "see no evil, hear no evil" approach may be shocked at the tremendous costs that can arise from violations committed by even the lowest-level employees. The business judgment rule is alive and well—but now its protection must be "earned" through active investigation, querying and compliance.

II. Recent Trends

In the 1990's, five major developments have accelerated the trend towards a *de facto* corporate duty of investigation:

- The 1991 adoption of the United States Sentencing Commission Guidelines for Organizations ("Sentencing Guidelines");
- The landmark 1996 decision in *Caremark*;[8]

---

4   *See* 41 U.S.C. § 57.

5   *See* 12 C.F.R. § 21.10.

6   Pub. L. No. 95-213, 91 Stat. 1494 (1977).

7   "When Reasonable Reliance Isn't Enough: the Evolving Standards for Board Oversight", *Insights*, January, 1998.

8   *In Re Caremark International, Inc.*, 698 A. 2d 959 (Del. Ch. 1996).

- Expansion of securities laws and regulations to require more managerial investigation and disclosure, with particular focus on the role of the corporate audit committee;

- A vigorous federal enforcement campaign in the healthcare field, combined with more aggressive antitrust, environmental, civil rights, and general regulatory enforcement by the federal government in the 1990's; and

- Broad recognition—from judges, prosecutors, legislators, and commentators—that corporate management should be rewarded for its good faith investigative and compliance efforts.

A. The Corporate Sentencing Guidelines

On November 1, 1991, the United States Sentencing Guidelines for Organizational Defendants became effective.[9] The importance of the Guidelines has become increasingly clear in the years since then; they have effected dramatic changes in the sentencing of business entities. The Guidelines prescribe far stiffer penalties than the norms previously imposed. Companies can be punished through substantial fines and/or probation of up to five years. The fines now being imposed upon transgressing businesses can reach into millions or even hundreds of millions of dollars.[10] And probation under the Guidelines is no mere slap on the wrist. Typically, a condition of probation will be acceptance of highly intrusive and expensive auditing, reporting and compliance programs.

The punishment imposed upon businesses convicted of a crime is determined by a complicated formula based on the gravity of the offense and the company's culpability as an organization. The Guidelines introduce a novel mechanism for assessing a company's "culpability score" from a series of aggravating and mitigating circumstances. "Points" are accrued for aggravating factors, and deducted for mitigating circumstances. Depending on the culpability score, the potential fine can be reduced to as little as 5 percent of the base fine or increased to as much as 400 percent of the base fine. For example, in a situation where the base fine is $10 million, a company could either be fined $500,000 or $40 million—a differential of $39.5 million.

The aggravating factors under the Guidelines include: (1) a high level employee was involved in (or tolerant of) the criminal activity; (2) the organization obstructed justice; (3) the organization previously committed similar offenses; and (4) the misconduct violated a judicial order or injunction, or terms of probation.[11]

---

9   These Sentencing Guidelines are discussed in detail in Chapter 8. A copy of the Guidelines, as they relate to organizations, is attached as Appendix 2 to this book.

10   Notable examples of fines assessed under the Sentencing Guidelines include a $340 million criminal fine paid by Daiwa Bank and $100 million paid by Archer Daniels Midland. *See* Paul Fiorelli, "Why Comply? Directors Face Heightened Personal Liability After *Caremark*," *Business Horizons*, July 17, 1998.

11   U.S.S.G. § 8C2.5.

Mitigating circumstances include (1) the presence of an effective corporate compliance program prior to the criminal conduct in question; (2) voluntary self-reporting to the authorities; (3) cooperation with the government's investigation; and (4) acknowledgment of responsibility.[12]

Thus the Guidelines are designed to encourage companies to engage in self-policing and self-reporting, especially through the use of corporate compliance programs. Indeed, the Guidelines even set forth criteria for an "effective" compliance program.[13] The Guidelines do not explicitly create a corporate duty to investigate, but they do create strong incentives for a corporation to do so.

B. The Caremark Decision

A recent decision that has focused much attention on both the Sentencing Guidelines and compliance in general is *In Re Caremark International Inc.*[14]

Caremark International, Inc. ("Caremark") is a large healthcare provider that was indicted in 1994 on false claim and kickback violations of the healthcare laws. In settlements with the federal government and private parties, Caremark was required to pay out approximately $250 million.[15] Caremark's shareholders sued the company's board of directors, alleging that they had breached their duty of care by failing to detect and prevent violations of the law by Caremark employees.

In approving the settlement of the action, Chancellor Allen wrote a thoughtful—and increasingly influential—overview of directors' duties to monitor corporate operations. Allen began by observing the "increasing tendency, especially under federal law, to employ the criminal law to assure corporate compliance with external legal requirements."[16] Allen focused special attention on the Sentencing Guidelines, noting that they provide penalties that "equal or often massively exceed those previously imposed on corporations" as well as important compliance incentives:

> The Guidelines offer powerful incentives for corporations today to have in place compliance programs to detect violations of law, promptly to report violations to appropriate public officials when discovered, and to take prompt, voluntary remedial efforts.
>
> . . . .
>
> Any rational person attempting in good faith to meet an organizational governance responsibility would be bound to take into account this

---

12   *Id.*

13   Compliance programs and a full discussion of the sentencing guidelines are discussed in Chapter 8.

14   698 A.2d 959 (Del. Ch. 1996).

15   *Caremark*, 698 A.2d at 960.

16   *Id.* at 969.

development and the enhanced penalties and the opportunities for reduced sanctions that it offers.[17]

In light of these developments, corporate boards must assure themselves that "information and reporting systems exist in the organization that are reasonably designed to provide to senior management and to the board itself timely, accurate information sufficient. . . to reach informed judgments concerning both the corporation's compliance with law and its business performance."[18] Failure to assure the existence of an adequate corporate information and reporting system "may, in theory at least, render a director liable for losses caused by non-compliance with applicable legal standards."[19]

By any measure, *Caremark* is a benchmark legal decision. It elucidates, for the first time, the fact that a corporate board of directors faces personal liability to shareholders if it does not take measures to ensure an effective reporting and information system within the company. No longer can a board sit back and presume that management, or consultants hired by the company, will take care of all legal and compliance issues. The board members themselves must make active inquiries of management and gain a level of comfort regarding the information systems that are in place at the company. If the current reporting scheme is deemed inadequate, the board must take corrective measures.[20]

Chancellor Allen took pains to note that, once the board has satisfied its duty to ensure adequate reporting systems, the business judgment rule kicks in with all of its vigor.[21] *Caremark* also makes it clear that breach of duty cases premised on a failure of oversight face some steep hurdles. The "level of detail" that is required for a corporate information system is itself a question of business judgment.[22] Moreover, the fact that the corporate controls in question failed, thereby permitting a violation of the law, does not in itself establish a director's breach of duty.[23]

Yet the boundaries of the decision are still unclear. Does *Caremark* in effect impose a corporate "compliance duty", or does the duty of care literally only extend to ensuring adequate information systems? If such a "compliance duty" exists, by

---

17   *Id.* at 969-970.

18   *Id.* at 970.

19   *Id.*

20   Some have divined from *Caremark* a new rule that "it may be a per se breach of fiduciary duty for the board and management of a corporation in a highly regulated industry, such as health care, to fail to implement an effective compliance program." "Corporate Compliance Programs: the Benefits Extend Far Beyond the Criminal Prosecution Context," *The Metropolitan Corporate Counsel* (Mid-Atlantic Ed.), July 1999.

21   As the court noted, whether a board decision is "substantively wrong, or degrees of wrong extending through 'stupid' to 'egregious' or 'irrational', provides no ground for director liability, so long as the court determines that the process employed was either rational or employed in a good faith effort to advance corporate interests." *Id.* at 967.

22   698 A.2d at 970.

23   *Id.*

what measure should it be judged—the Sentencing Guidelines or a more general standard of reasonableness? What about directors or executives that have access to a functioning reporting system, but choose to ignore warning signals about possible violations?

The plaintiffs' securities bar will obviously seek to answer these questions in a manner that greatly expand the boundaries of directorial oversight and responsibility. Already, plaintiffs in securities cases have relied upon *Caremark* in asserting breach of duty claims against corporate boards.[24] Companies, by contrast, will seek to limit *Caremark* to its precise holding.

For all these reasons, *Caremark* has generated intense scrutiny amongst the legal, business and accounting communities. The decision has begun to reverberate in U.S. courts.[25] Although the Delaware Supreme Court has yet to explicitly affirm the principles set forth in *Caremark*, it seems likely that it will head that way.[26] *Caremark* is even having an impact overseas—with Canada, England, and even countries in Asia noting the potential changes it heralds.[27]

Surprisingly, there appears to be almost uniform agreement that Chancellor Allen was right, and that corporate boards really must focus more attention on assuring company compliance with the law. As SEC Chairman Arthur Levitt recently remarked in a speech extolling the reasoning behind *Caremark*, directors now have a

---

24 In 1997, shareholders of Columbia/HCA sued the company's directors on the theory that they failed to adopt proper information reporting and compliance procedures, leading to a wide-scale and highly damaging federal healthcare fraud investigation. *See* "The Crime of the Nineties," *Trustee*, April 1998.

25 *See Benjamin v. Kim*, 1999 U.S. Dist. LEXIS 6089 at *46-*47 (S.D.N.Y. Apr. 28, 1999) (citing *Caremark* for the proposition that "a director does have a duty to be reasonably informed about the company and must make sure that appropriate information and reporting systems are in place").

26 Remarks by Chief Justice E. Norman Veasey suggest that the Delaware Supreme Court is aligned with Chancellor Allen's views on corporate governance. As Veasey noted in a speech in March 1999, "a modern compliance system is a good corporate practice whether or not the failure to do so in a given case may result in liability." *See* "History and Recent Developments Implicating the Interaction Between the Delaware Court of Chancery and the Supreme Court," *Metropolitan Corporate Counsel* (N.Y. ed. May 1999). Veasey has also remarked that "it would be unwise for a board to adopt an ostrich attitude and do nothing" and that "boards should establish—and monitor—reasonable law compliance programs." Veasey, "The Director and the Dynamic Corporation Law," Address to the Corporate and Securities Law Institute in Chicago (Apr. 24, 1997).

27 *See, e.g.*, "Directors Must Pay Closer Attention to Day-to-Day Affairs," *Directors Briefing* (June 1999) (Canadian publication citing *Caremark* for the proposition that directors may avoid liability by establishing "appropriate systems to constantly monitor delegated responsibilities"); "Model of Compliance; U.S. Corporate Governance Standards Go Global," *New York Law Journal*, Apr. 9, 1998 (noting the "internationalization" of *Caremark* in meetings between foreign companies in Asia and U.S. compliance experts "to develop codes of conduct and compliance programs with penalties, and to establish clear responsibilities for corporate directors"). The latter notes an "increasing recognition that global commerce requires rules that are more alike than different" and that U.S. corporate governance and disclosure rules "are serving as models for nations around the world."

duty to look beyond the presumption of business regularity: "Today, that increasingly means they must act to prevent management wrongdoing."[28] Nobody seems to pine for the days when corporate boards consisted of "a group of old guys named George who get together every few months to drink coffee."[29]

C. Securities Law Developments

Since the 1970's, corporate governance has increasingly been shaped by new requirements from the SEC and the stock exchanges.[30] These have included mandating special, independent committees to monitor securities laws compliance as a condition to settling SEC enforcement actions, as well as the SEC's approval in 1977 of a NYSE rule requiring all listed domestic companies to establish audit committees consisting of only independent directors.[31]

At the same time, corporate boards increasingly have been charged with responsibility for ensuring accurate financial disclosures. The Delaware Supreme Court recently held that "[d]irectors who knowingly disseminate false information that results in corporate injury or damage to an individual stockholder violate their fiduciary duty and may be held accountable."[32] A majority of the board must now sign a company's annual Form 10-K report, which includes annual financial statements.

The SEC would like to go further and (1) require that a majority of the board sign, and certify that they have read, each quarterly Form 10-Q filed by a company;[33] and (2) render any officer or director liable under Section 10(b) of the 1934 Securities and Exchange Act (the general antifraud provision) if they sign a public filing "with scienter"—regardless of whether that individual was involved in daily management or played any role in generating the document in question.[34] The SEC

---

28   *See* "Audit Committees Need to Serve as 'Watchdogs,'" *The National Law Journal*, June 28, 1999.

29   Ralph Ward, "Corporate Accountability: 10 Things You Know About Corporate Boards That are Wrong," *Vital Speeches of the Day*, April 15, 1998.

30   *See generally*, Blue Ribbon Introduction.

31   *See* Blue Ribbon Introduction. The NYSE rule requiring completely independent audit committees is in the Listed Company Manual, Section 303.00. The American Stock Exchange (ASE) and the NASDAQ require audit committees in which a majority of directors are independent. *See* ASE Company Guide at Section 121; NASD Marketplace Rules at 4460.

32   *Malone v. Brincat*, 755 A.2d 5 (Del. 1998). Under previous rulings, the board of directors only had a fiduciary duty to disclose material information when seeking shareholder action. *See* John C. Coffee, "Disclosure Duties: New Law and New Issues," *New York Law Journal*, Jan. 21, 1999 at 5.

33   One commentator has criticized this SEC proposal as springing from "the unrealistic notion that an outside director who is not engaged in day-to-day operations can 'cold read' a disclosure document and make meaningful judgments as to whether it meets standards." Curtis Barnette, "Realistic Expectations for Audit Committees," *Directors & Boards*, Jan. 1, 1999.

34   *See* "Liability for Persons Signing SEC Disclosure Documents," *New York Law Journal*, Aug. 26, 1999 at 5.

apparently wants to "require officers and directors to take 'steps' to 'ensure' a document's accuracy, thus constraining their ability to rely on a corporation's internal disclosure processes."[35]

These developments have not gone unnoticed by shareholders and the plaintiffs' securities bar. Increasingly, large institutional shareholders have been taking a sharp look at the way their investments are being managed. Companies with lax enforcement and compliance policies, and whose stock has suffered as a result, might find their largest shareholders taking an active interest in overhauling corporate management. In 1997, for example, the nation's largest pension fund (the California Public Employees Retirement System or CalPERS) joined a shareholder lawsuit alleging that the officers and directors of Columbia HCA Healthcare Corp. breached their fiduciary duties by permitting widespread fraud and abuse at their hospitals.[36]

1. The Blue Ribbon Committee Report

Corporate audit committees have been described as the "link between the board of directors, as representatives of the shareholders, and the corporation's independent auditors."[37] Audit committees have come under considerable scrutiny recently, reflecting the trend towards increased corporate compliance, as well as the SEC's stepped-up enforcement efforts.

Recently, at the prompting of the SEC, the NYSE and NASD formed a Blue Ribbon Committee on Improving the Effectiveness of Corporate Audit Committees ("Blue Ribbon Committee"). The Blue Ribbon Committee was formed with the goal of improving the overall quality of financial reporting—specifically by ensuring that "independence, awareness, diligence, and care were the primary principles governing the [board of director's] unavoidable exercise of discretion" in overseeing the financial reporting process.[38]

On February 8, 1999, the committee issued a report (the "Blue Ribbon Report")[39] that made recommendations in three key areas:

> (1) improving audit committee independence through a more stringent definition of independence than is currently required by the NYSE and NASD;

---

35   *Id.* The author characterizes the SEC's stance as creating "an implicit shift in the burden of proof in securities cases, requiring officers and directors to prove that they took appropriate steps to ensure a document's accuracy." *Id.*

36   *See* "Largest Pension Fund Throws Weight Behind Columbia Suit," *Pension Fund Litigation Reporter,* Nov. 21, 1997. CalPERS explained that "it had to take an active role in the reformation of Columbia's corporate governance after watching the value of its 3.7 million Columbia shares drop by $50 million since three company executives were indicted in July [1997]." *Id.*

37   *See,* Black, *Corporate Internal Investigations,* Vol. C5, Business Law Monographs, Release No. 52 (1998) at § 3.03[1][c].

38   *See,* Blue Ribbon Introduction.

39   Report and Recommendations of the Blue Ribbon Committee on Improving the Effectiveness of Corporate Audit Committees (1999), reprinted in 54 *Bus. Law.* 1067 (1999).

(2) improving audit committee effectiveness by requiring certain members to establish "financial literacy"; and

(3) ensuring the accountability of the audit committee, management and outside auditors, through such measures as (a) adopting a charter of formal responsibilities; (b) amending Generally Accepted Auditing Standards to require accountants to discuss with the committee the "quality" of the company's financial reporting (as opposed to simply the acceptability of such records); and (c) requiring the audit committee to file a letter with the company's annual report detailing the substance of communications with outside auditors, as well as the committee's belief as to whether the financial statements comply with GAAP.[40]

The Blue Ribbon Report recommendations have yet to be formally implemented by the SEC, NYSE and NASD. In recent remarks, however, SEC Chairman Arthur Levitt described the report as a "solid, action-worthy roadmap from which to move forward."[41] Moreover, following *Caremark*, the Blue Ribbon Report recommendations "may well become key elements in litigation that challenges directors on the point of whether the corporate audit committee has functioned adequately as part of the company's system of internal controls."[42] Accordingly, it might make sense for companies to begin measuring their own management practices against the best practices advocated in the Blue Ribbon Report. Some companies already have taken the initiative and engaged in voluntary "self-improvement" designed to permit closer monitoring of corporate affairs by independent board members.[43]

The Blue Ribbon Report has already begun to generate controversy. Some commentators have been strongly supportive of the report's proposals, declaring them to be "on target", "pragmatic", and an effective means to reduce fraud and improve the quality of financial reporting.[44]

Critics, on the other hand, have charged that the recommendations will burden audit committees with detailed, technical financial responsibilities and analyses that are better suited to outside accountants or company management.[45] Commentators are also concerned that audit committee members may face increased liability

---

40 *See generally* "Blue Ribbon Audit Committee Report: A Mixed Bag," *Insights*, July 1999.

41 *See* "Assurance Forum: Now is the Time to do What's Right by Investors," *Accounting Today*, Aug. 23, 1999 (Levitt remarks at the Audit Committee Symposium in New York on June 29, 1999).

42 John F. Olson, "Corporate Governance Symposium: How to Really Make Audit Committees More Effective," 54 *Bus. Law.* 1097, May 1999.

43 *See* Blue Ribbon Introduction.

44 *E.g.,* "Financial Fraud and Audit Committee Reform", *Insights*, July 1999, "Audit Committees Need to Serve as 'Watchdogs,'" *The National Law Journal*, June 28, 1999.

45 *See* "Blue Ribbon Audit Committee Report: A Mixed Bag," *Insights*, July 1999.

exposure as a result of the new responsibilities proposed in the report.[46] Coming on top of the report's more stringent independence and "financial literacy" requirements, corporations could "find it more and more difficult to attract qualified and willing candidates to serve on audit committees."[47]

Criticisms aside, it seems likely that many of the proposals in the Blue Ribbon Report will eventually be endorsed by the SEC, NYSE, NASD and perhaps other organizations as well. Indeed, the Blue Ribbon Report exemplifies the global trend towards recognizing the important governance role of corporate audit committees, as shown by recent audit committee studies in Canada and the United Kingdom.[48] There appears to be an emerging consensus that "audit committee members must equip themselves for adequate surveillance of management in all matters of legal and financial compliance."[49] Having done so, corporate boards "may have difficulty dealing with what they discover, but they at least must be able to say they have looked."[50]

2. The SEC's Grace Report

On September 30, 1997, the SEC issued an administrative Cease-and-Desist Order and a Report of Investigation of W.R. Grace & Co. (the "Grace Report").[51]

The specific transgressions in Grace seemed relatively minor. Certain corporate officers and directors were alleged to have known about a proposed related-party transaction, as well as retirement benefits for an outgoing CEO. The related-party transaction was not described, and the retirement benefits only partially described, in company filings.[52] The officers and directors argued that they had relied on the judgment of the company's securities counsel, who was involved with both matters and whom they assumed had properly evaluated disclosure issues.[53]

The SEC nonetheless found that Grace had violated the periodic reporting and proxy solicitation disclosure requirements of the Securities and Exchange Act of

---

46 *See* John F. Olson, "Corporate Governance Symposium: How to Really Make Audit Committees More Effective," 54 *Bus. Law.* 1097, May 1999. The Blue Ribbon Committee, anticipating this concern, advocated an SEC "safe harbor" for audit committee disclosures concerning GAAP and GAAS compliance. Further, the committee suggested that compliance with the report's recommended practices should shield audit committee members from liability under state law. *See* Blue Ribbon Report, 54 *Bus. Law* 1083, 1088.

47 *See* "Blue Ribbon Audit Committee Report: A Mixed Bag," *Insights*, July 1999.

48 *See* "Audit Committee Composition and Interaction with Internal Auditing: Canadian Evidence," *Accounting Horizons*, March 1998.

49 "Audit Committees Need to Serve as 'Watchdogs,'" *The National Law Journal*, June 28, 1999.

50 *Id.*

51 *See* Cease and Desist Order, Release No. 34-39, 156, 65 SEC Docket 1236 (Sept. 30, 1997); Report of Investigation, Release No. 39157, 65 SEC Docket at 1240 (1997).

52 65 SEC Docket at 1236.

53 65 SEC Docket at 1243-44.

1934. The SEC held that when an officer or director "knows or should know that his or her company's statements concerning particular issues are inadequate or incomplete, he or she has an obligation to correct that failure."[54] Given their particular knowledge of the two events, the officers should have sought "the specific and fully informed advice of counsel" regarding the company's disclosure obligations.

The Grace Report is significant because it suggests a whole new area of inquiry and vigilance for company executives and directors—namely, "an obligation to question and take affirmative steps to ensure that the corporation's public disclosures are complete and accurate" and comply with federal securities laws.[55] Grace is a reminder that corporate boards cannot always rely on the mere existence of "internal corporate procedures and on determinations made by securities counsel as to the propriety of such disclosures."[56]

The Grace Report echoes the *Caremark* decision on the crucial issue of a board's affirmative obligations. Once again, the board cannot blindly assume that management (or even securities counsel) has done its job properly. On matters of personal knowledge, the board is charged with making an independent assessment of what should be disclosed in public filings, and to make specific inquiries of counsel to ensure adequate disclosure.

D. Healthcare and Other Regulatory Developments

In recent years, the Office of the Inspector General ("OIG") of the U.S. Department of Health and Human Services ("HHS") has been at the forefront of the federal government's campaign against healthcare fraud and abuse. In fiscal 1997, the OIG collected more than $1 billion in fines and settlements.[57]

The OIG has repeatedly underscored its desire for healthcare providers in virtually every field to voluntarily implement effective compliance programs. Compliance program guidance "is a major initiative of the OIG in its effort to engage the private health care community in combating fraud and abuse."[58]

Recently, the OIG issued draft compliance guidelines for nursing facilities.[59] To date, the OIG has issued detailed guidance programs for six healthcare industry sectors: hospitals, clinical laboratories, home health agencies, durable medical equipment suppliers, third-party medical billing companies, and hospices.[60] The

---

54   Report of Investigation, 65 SEC Docket at 1240.

55   *See* "Amazing Grace: SEC Suggests Expanded Disclosure Duties," *New York Law Journal*, Jan. 22, 1998.

56   *Id.*

57   OIG Semiannual Report for Oct. 1, 1997—March 31, 1998 at i (1998).

58   *See* 64 *Fed. Reg.* at 58420 (October 29, 1999).

59   *See* 64 *Fed. Reg.* at 58419 (October 29, 1999).

60   *Id.* at 58420 & n.1.

OIG intends to issue, in the near future, additional guidelines for coordinated care plans, ambulance companies, and small group physician practices.[61] In each instance, the OIG guidelines reflect the basic compliance themes set forth in the Sentencing Guidelines.[62]

The healthcare field is not the only area of government regulation that has seen a renewed emphasis on investigation, compliance and enforcement programs. In areas as diverse as antitrust and civil rights enforcement, the federal government has begun to insist on the creation of compliance programs as a condition to the settlement of claims.[63] Compliance programs are playing an increasingly prominent role in Bureau of Export Administration customs investigations.[64] In 1995, the United States Environmental Protection Agency ("EPA") began a "self-audit" policy that encourages companies to conduct their own, internal environmental review.[65] For companies that promptly disclose and correct environmental violations, the EPA "will forgo punitive penalties and generally will not recommend criminal prosecution."[66] The EPA might also expedite environmental permits for companies with trustworthy compliance plans.[67]

E. The Benefits of Corporate Investigation and Compliance Programs

Perhaps the "ultimate benefit" of an effective corporate investigative and compliance program is that it can provide defense counsel with "powerful ammunition to persuade prosecutors or regulators to decline filing charges" in the first place.[68] These benefits extend to the civil arena as well—DOJ treats compliance-friendly civil defendants more leniently, and is more likely to decline prosecution of civil *qui tam* actions if the defendant has an effective compliance program.[69]

---

61   *Id.*

62   *See* Chapter 8 on Sentencing Guidelines.

63   *See* "Choosing a Company Compliance Officer," *Metropolitan Corporate Counsel*, (Mid-Atlantic Ed. May 1999).

64   *See* "Two Experts Clarify Key Trade Compliance Issues and Programs," *Managing Exports*, March 1999.

65   *See* Chapter 11 on Environmental Crimes.

66   "The Case for Implementing a Corporate Compliance Program," *Metropolitan Corporate Counsel* (Mid-Atlantic Ed. Feb. 1998).

67   *See* "For Any Lawyer Trying to Keep an Honest Company Straight," 85 A.B.A.J. 64, June 1999.

68   Robert Tarun, "Unlucky Side Effects: 13 Common Problems With Compliance Programs," *The Corporate Counsellor* (Nov. 1998).

69   Jerome Levy, "Use of Compliance Programs," *New York Law Journal*, Aug. 3, 1998. *See* "When Reasonable Reliance Isn't Enough," *Insights*, January, 1998 (describing how prosecutors and regulators utilize compliance programs in "evaluating whether prosecution is necessary at all, as well as the imposition of civil or administrative penalties").

The HHS OIG views voluntary compliance agreements as a key component of its efforts to regulate the healthcare industry.[70] Other government agencies view compliance programs (particularly insofar as they conform with the Sentencing Guidelines standards) as ameliorative factors in conducting settlement negotiations "for civil matters, whether formally filed or not."[71] The SEC, for example, "has been more lenient toward broker dealers and public companies which have taken initiatives to prevent and report serious problems."[72]

Put simply, compliance programs give companies and their managers credibility—a key tool for convincing the government that a company can self-police without the need for criminal or civil prosecution. Burdensome government-mandated compliance programs are increasingly becoming a standard part of administrative actions and settlements.[73] By having an effective program in place, a company can avoid or substantially curtail the intrusiveness and cost of a government-mandated program.

If a company has an advanced detection and reporting system, and an active and informed board of directors that has focused on potential compliance issues, this will go a long way towards showing that the board has not violated its duty of care under *Caremark*. SEC Chairman Arthur Levitt recently remarked that "an active, involved and educated committee or board can rest more easily at night than a board composed of directors who merely go through the motions and watch the clock."[74] Indeed, some commentators suggest that effective compliance programs "may very well insulate directors from shareholder derivative suits," while the absence of such a program might indicate a breach of the duty of care.[75]

---

70 The OIG recently set forth this policy pronouncement regarding compliance programs:

> The OIG believes a comprehensive compliance program provides a mechanism that brings the public and private sectors together to reach mutual goals of reducing fraud and abuse, improving operational functions, improving the quality of health care services, and reducing the cost of health care. . . . In addition to fulfilling its legal duty to ensure that it is not submitting false or inaccurate claims to Government and private payers, a [healthcare provider] may gain numerous additional benefits by voluntarily implementing a compliance program.

64 *Fed. Reg.* at 58421, Oct. 29, 1999. The OIG further noted that a compliance program could reduce a company's "exposure to civil damages and penalties, criminal sanctions, and administrative remedies." *Id.*

71 "U.S. Sets its Sights on Serial Billers to Fight Medicare Fraud," *Chicago Daily Law Bulletin*, Aug. 3, 1998.

72 "The Case for Implementing a Corporate Compliance Program," *Metropolitan Corporate Counsel* (Mid-Atlantic Ed. Feb. 1998).

73 *See* "When Reasonable Reliance Isn't Enough," *Insights*, January, 1998.

74 *See* "Assurance Forum: Now is the Time to do What's Right by Investors," *Accounting Today*, Aug. 23, 1999 (remarks by Arthur Levitt at the Audit Committee Symposium in New York on June 29, 1999).

75 "Covering Corporate Compliance: What You Can Learn from the Organizational Sentencing Guidelines and Caremark," 150 N.J.L.J. 1120 (Dec. 22, 1997). *See* Paul Fiorelli, "Why Comply? Directors Face Heightened Personal Liability After *Caremark*," *Business Horizons,* July 17, 1998 (commenting that "a board of directors composed of "integrity advocates.... will avoid

There is recent precedent for the notion that an effective compliance program can actually absolve a company from underlying liability. In *Faragher v. Boca Raton*, 524 U.S. 775, 806-07 (1998), the Supreme Court held—in the context of a "hostile atmosphere" sexual harassment claim under Title VII of the Civil Rights Act of 1964[76]—that employers may raise "an affirmative defense to liability or damages" of providing a "proven, effective mechanism for reporting and resolving complaints of sexual harassment, available to the employee without undue risk or expense."[77]

In the future, companies might also benefit from proposals to exempt them from any punitive damages liability for violations encompassed by effective compliance programs.[78] As one commentator observed, it is anomalous for a company to have its punishment "effectively reduced to zero" under the Sentencing Guidelines, yet face the prospect of virtually unlimited punitive damages before a jury for the very same conduct.[79] Indeed, eliminating punitive damages liability seems to be a natural extension of the *Faragher* Court's elimination of Title VII liability in situations where a company has made serious efforts at compliance.

In many instances, an effective compliance program can contribute to a company's financial and ethical bottom line. From the financial standpoint, it is estimated that U.S. industry loses about $400 billion a year to criminal and unethical behavior.[80] Early detection and prevention could help reduce direct theft or other losses attributable to violations of the law, help eliminate wasteful and inefficient practices, and even help reduce insurance premiums.[81]

---

personal liability, even if their organizations engage in improper activity").

76   42 U.S.C. § 2000e2(a)(1).

77   The defense only applies if (1) "no tangible employment action" (*e.g.,* dismissal) was taken; and (2) the plaintiff employee "unreasonably failed to take advantage" of the company's harassment reporting program, or otherwise failed to avoid harm. 524 U.S. at 807.

78   *See "Caremark* Impact Continues to Grow, Board Oversight Duty Expands," *Corporate Officers and Directors Liability Litigation Reporter,* June 22, 1998.

79   *See* "Voluntary Compliance Efforts Should Be Considered When Judging Punitive Damages," *Legal Backgrounder,* June 25, 1999.

80   *See* "For Any Lawyer Trying to Help Keep an Honest Company Straight," 85 A.B.A.J. 64, June 1999 (quoting loss estimate by The Association of Certified Fraud Examiners).

81   *See* "For Any Lawyer Trying to Keep an Honest Company Straight," 85 A.B.A.J. 64, June 1999.

CHAPTER 3:
ATTORNEY-CLIENT PRIVILEGE AND WORK-PRODUCT DOCTRINE

I. Attorney-Client Privilege

It is critical for counsel to be aware of the parameters of the legal privileges and protections available to a company—particularly when the company is under active investigation or is likely to be in the near future. A corporate internal investigation must be structured to take advantage of the protections the law offers. Those protections include the attorney-client privilege,[1] attorney work-product doctrine and, under some circumstances, the "self-evaluative" privileges.

The scope of the attorney-client privilege and work-product doctrine may vary, depending upon whether litigation in which they are at issue is commenced in state or federal court. State law may, however, control, even in federal court, where federal jurisdiction is dependent upon diversity. In federal cases involving a federal question, the federal common law controls on the issue of attorney-client privilege, even if there are pendent state law claims.[2] The federal work-product doctrine, originating in *Hickman v. Taylor*, 329 U.S. 495 (1947), is codified in Fed. R. Civ. P. 26 (b) (3),[3] and Fed. R. Crim. P. 16 (a)(2) and 16 (b)(2). This discussion of waiver of the attorney-client privilege and work-product doctrine will be limited to applicable federal law.

---

1   Although not a natural person, a corporation is treated as such for purposes of the attorney-client privilege. This contrasts with the Fifth Amendment privilege against self-incrimination, which may not be asserted by a corporation. *Radiant Burners, Inc. v. American Gas Ass'n*, 320 F.2d 314, 322-23 (7th Cir.), *cert. denied*, 375 U.S. 929 (1963).

2   *See Religious Tech. Center v. Wottersheim*, 971 F.2d 364, 367 n. 10 (9th Cir. 1992).

3   *But see* James Wm. Moore, 6 Moore's Federal Practice (3d ed. 1999) § 26.70 [2][c], taking the position that the work-product doctrine articulated in *Hickman* is only partially codified in Fed. R. Civ. P. 26 (b)(3), and continues to have vitality outside of the Rule. *Accord: Sporck v. Peil*, 759 F.2d 312, 316 (3d Cir.), *cert. denied*, 474 U.S. 903 (1985).

II. Purpose of the Attorney-Client Privilege

In order to protect internal investigations from compelled disclosure, it is essential that the investigations be conducted under the umbrella of attorney-client privilege. The purpose of the privilege is to encourage full and frank communications between attorneys and their clients and to thereby promote broader public interests in the observation of law and the administration of justice.[4] "The lawyer-client privilege rests on the need for the advocate and counselor to know all that relates to the client's reasons for seeking representation if the professional mission is to be carried out."[5] The privilege applies to all confidential communications between a company's employees and counsel during an internal review, and any communications between counsel and management reporting the results of the review.[6] The communication must occur in the context of legal advice provided by counsel and must be intended to be confidential. It must be "primarily or predominantly" legal in nature,[7] and must above all else be intended to be confidential.[8] However, the privilege, where it applies, belongs to the company itself, not the shareholders, officers, directors or employees.[9]

III. When Does the Privilege Apply

A. Privilege in the Context of Corporate Investigations[10]

Upjohn Co. v. United States, 449 U.S. 383 (1981) is the principal case defining the privilege in the context of corporate investigations. *Upjohn* demonstrates the importance of possessing a thorough understanding of the parameters of the attorney-client privilege in structuring an internal review. Prior to *Upjohn*, the lower courts had developed various criteria to determine whether the company's privilege should be extended only to communications with members of senior management (the so-called "Control Group Test") or more broadly to communications with other employees. *Upjohn* determined that the issue should be decided on a case by case basis, and declined to establish a "bright line" rule for determining when the privilege will apply to communications between counsel and the

---

4   *Upjohn Co. v. United States*, 449 U.S. 383, 389 (1981).

5   *Trammel v. United States*, 445 U.S. 40, 51 (1980).

6   *Upjohn Co. v. United States*, 449 U.S. 383 (1981).

7   Spectrum Systems International, Corp. v. Chemical Bank, 78 N.Y.2d 371, 378, 581 N.E.2d 1055, 1060 (1991); *ABB Kent-Taylor, Inc. v. Stallings and Co., Inc.*, 172 F.R.D. 53, 55 (W.D.N.Y. 1996).

8   *See Upjohn*, 449 U.S. at 395 (1981).

9   *United States v. Int'l Brotherhood of Teamsters, Chauffeurs, Warehousemen and Helpers of America, AFL-CIO*, 119 F.3d 210, 215 (2d Cir. 1997); *Diversified Industries v. Meredith*, 572 F.2d 596, 611 n.5 (8th Cir. 1978) (*en banc*).

10 With respect to the report of the investigation prepared by counsel, there are serious issues regarding potential waiver of attorney-client and work-product privilege. They are discussed in Chapter 5.

Attorney-Client Privilege and Work-Product Doctrine

company's employees.[11] But the Court did give some guidance. Citing factors in *Diversified Industries, Inc. v. Meredith*,[12] the Court in *Upjohn*[13] stated that the privilege applies to an employee's communication if:

1. the communication was made for the purpose of securing legal advice;

2. the employee making the communication did so at the direction of his corporate superior;

3. the superior made the request so that the company could secure legal advice;

4. the subject matter of the communication is within the scope of the employee's corporate duties; and

5. the communication is not disseminated beyond those persons who, because of the corporate structure, need to know its contents.

In *Upjohn*, an auditor of one of Upjohn's foreign subsidiaries discovered that the subsidiary made payments to foreign government officials in order to secure business. When this information was communicated to Upjohn's management, the company retained outside counsel to assist its in-house general counsel in conducting an internal review of the circumstances of the payments and to examine their legality. As part of that review, counsel prepared a questionnaire to all foreign managers of the company which was sent out by Upjohn's chairman. The letter stated that the company had recently discovered the payment of "possibly illegal" sums to foreign government officials, indicated that the company's general counsel had been asked to conduct an internal investigation of the matter, and requested that the investigation be treated as "highly confidential." Recipients were instructed to return the completed questionnaires to the general counsel, and employees were subsequently interviewed by both the in-house counsel and the retained outside counsel. Upjohn submitted a report to the Securities & Exchange Commission, with a copy simultaneously filed with the IRS, disclosing the questionable payments. Soon thereafter, it received an IRS summons demanding production of all files relating to the company's internal review of the matter, including the completed questionnaires and notes of employee interviews.[14] The company refused to produce these documents on the grounds that they were protected from disclosure by the attorney-client privilege and constituted the work-product of its attorneys in anticipation of litigation.[15]

The government sought to enforce the summons and, for different reasons, the district court and the appellate court ordered Upjohn to produce the review. When *Upjohn* reached the Supreme Court, the government argued, as it did below, that

---

11   449 U.S. at 397.

12   572 F.2d 596, 609 (8th Cir.), *rev'd on reh'g en banc*, 572 F.2d 609 (8th Cir 1978)

13   *See* 449 U.S. at 394-395.

14   449 U.S. at 387-88.

15   449 U.S. at 388.

the questionnaires and notes were not privileged because they related to communications between counsel and company employees other than the senior management "control group."[16] In rejecting the government's position, the Supreme Court held that the communications reflected in the internal review were privileged. The Court's reasoning was that the communications were made by Upjohn employees to counsel, at the direction of corporate superiors, in order to secure legal advice from counsel. Further, the communications concerned matters within the scope of the employees' corporate duties, and the employees themselves were sufficiently aware that they were being questioned in order that the company could obtain legal advice."[17] Accordingly, the Court declined to allow the government access to the review.[18]

B. What Does Upjohn Cover?

The *Upjohn* principle applies to communications involving former employees as well as current ones[19] and communications involving outside retained counsel as well as in-house corporate counsel.[20] The privilege also covers communications with non-lawyers working under the control and supervision of counsel, including secretaries and other assistants, as well as accountants, other experts and private investigators.[21] Of course, the privilege exists only if the communications with the non-lawyers assisting counsel were made at the request of counsel, in connection with the matter in which counsel is representing the client, and for the purpose of assisting counsel in the rendition of legal services.[22]

A significant point, since the privilege belongs to the company, not the individuals in the company who assert it on behalf of the company, is that the company can waive a privilege to the detriment of its employees.[23] Thus, for example, if the company decides to waive the privilege and disclose a conversation between

---

16   449 U.S. at 390-92.

17   449 U.S. at 394.

18   The Court further refused to uphold the government's subpoena for the company's attorneys' notes and memoranda of interviews finding that such materials constituted attorney work product. 449 U.S. at 397.

19   *Better Gov't Bureau, Inc. v. McGraw (In re Allen)*, 106 F.3d 582, 605-607 (4th Cir. 1997).

20   *See Upjohn*, 449 U.S. 383. In *Upjohn* itself, the investigation was carried out by in-house counsel with the assistance of outside counsel, and the communications that the Court held privileged included notes of interviews conducted by both in-house and outside counsel. *Id.* at 387-88 & 397. *See also Dunn v. State Farm Fire & Cas.*, 122 F.R.D. 507, 509-510 (N.D. Miss. 1988) (internal investigation conducted entirely by outside retained counsel); *Hasso v. Retail Credit Co.*, 58 F.R.D. 425, 427 (E.D. Pa. 1973) (attorney-client privilege applies equally to in-house and outside counsel).

21   *See United States v. Schwimmer*, 892 F.2d 237, 243 (2d Cir. 1989); *United States v. Kovel*, 296 F.2d 918, 921 (2d Cir. 1961).

22   *United States v. Schwimmer*, 892 F.2d 237, 243 (2d Cir. 1989).

23   *CFTC v. Weintraub*, 471 U.S. 343, 348-49 (1985); *United States v. Int'l Brotherhood of Teamsters, Chauffeurs, Warehousemen and Helpers of America, AFL-CIO*, 119 F.3d 210, 215 (2d Cir. 1997); *Diversified Industries v. Meredith*, 572 F.2d 596, 611 n.5 (8th Cir. 1978) (*en banc*).

counsel and a corporate executive, the executive has no individual protection from having this former confidential communication disclosed.[24] In the context of an internal investigation, where counsel is interviewing corporate executives, they must understand that the company may disclose their conversations to the government if the company deems it to be in its own best interests.

IV. When Does the Privilege Not Apply?

The purpose of the privilege is to protect communications between lawyer and client. Underlying facts, even if contained in documents attached to a communication between lawyer and client, are not protected simply because they are attached to such a communication or even placed within it.[25]

In many companies, in-house counsel often spend more time with business issues than legal issues and their role is more one of business counselor than legal counsel. This often leads to communications with mixed business and legal content, and such documents are often found by courts to be unprotected for that reason. It is also much more likely that in-house counsel can be called as a witness regarding his communications with the company if counsel was playing such a dual role at the time. Accordingly, in-house counsel should not commingle business discussions or advice with legal advice in the same document, if possible, because the former are not privileged and the latter is.[26] It is particularly helpful for attorneys who also play a business role in the company, to indicate in a document when it is being written in their role as counsel.[27]

---

24   *United States v. Int'l Brotherhood of Teamsters, Chauffeurs, Warehousemen and Helpers of America, AFL-CIO*, 119 F.3d 210, 215 (2d Cir. 1997). The right to waive the privilege belongs to the present management of the company, and is normally exercised by its present officers and directors, acting in a manner consistent with their fiduciary duties. *CFTC v. Weintraub*, 471 U.S. 343, 348-49 (1985). The privilege may be waived by new management, even over the protest of former corporate managers who made the communications in their corporate capacities while in control of the company. *Id.*

25   *Upjohn*, 449 U.S. at 395-96; *Sedco Int'l, S.A. v. Cory*, 683 F.2d 1201, 1205 (8th Cir.), *cert. denied*, 459 U.S. 1017 (1982); *United States v. Doe*, 959 F.2d 1158, 1165 (2d Cir. 1992); *Fisher v. United States*, 425 U.S. 391, 403-04 (1976).

26   Documents containing both legal and business advice are accorded privilege if the client sought "primarily legal advice," or, in some courts, if the legal advice contained in the document predominates over the business advice. *Allendale Mutual Ins. Co v. Bull Data Sys., Inc.*, 152 F.R.D. 132, 137 (N.D. Ill. 1993) (legal advice must be the predominant element in the communication). *See Gould, Inc., v. Mitsui Mining & Smelting Co.*, 825 F.2d 676, 679-80 (2d Cir. 1987) [business records are not protected under the attorney-client privilege merely because they are sent to and used by counsel conducting an internal corporate investigation]. However, the inclusion of business or other non-privileged matters in a document does not necessarily render the entire document non-privileged. Many courts employ a "primary purpose test". Isolated paragraphs or sentences within the document may be privileged, despite the overall nature of the document, if the primary purpose of these discrete portions meets the test for attorney-client privilege. *See United States v. Chevron Corp.*, No. C 94-1885 SBA, 1996 WL 444597, at *2 (N.D. Cal. 1996), [collecting authorities].

27   The burden will be on the corporation to prove that the document was written by in-house counsel in his role as counsel. *See Hawkins v. Stables*, 148 F.3d 379, 383 (4th Cir. 1998) (the

Likewise, if the purpose of the investigation is purely investigatory, for the purpose of learning facts for business reasons rather than for enabling counsel to give legal advice, courts may rule that the resulting reports and other documents are not protected, even if the investigatory work is conducted by attorneys.[28] It is thus critical, not only that the investigation be conducted by lawyers, but that it be made clear in writing that the purpose of the investigation is to render legal advice. The fact that counsel intends to render legal advice should be reflected in the board resolution ordering the investigation, the retainer letter with any outside law firm and other appropriate documents.

Where a third person, who is not a party to the attorney-client relationship, often including even a spouse or close relative, is present during or at the time of the communication, no attorney-client privilege arises.[29] The absence of the required confidentiality prevents the creation of the privilege.[30]

Even where a third-party stranger is not present during the communication, not all communications with an attorney are covered by the attorney-client privilege. The communication must have been intended to be private, and the communication must have been for the purpose of obtaining legal advice.[31] Thus, purely business advice does not qualify for application of the attorney-client privilege.[32]

---

burden of showing the applicability of the privilege to a particular communication is on the proponent).

28   *Spectrum Systems International, Corp. v. Chemical Bank*, 78 N.Y.2d 371, 378-79, 581 N.E.2d 1055, 1060-61 (1991).

29   *Johnson v. United States*, 542 F.2d 941, 942 (5th Cir. 1976).

30   Accordingly, as will be discussed in the section on waiver, below, this situation is not one of waiver, but of the non-application of the attorney-client privilege. *See Federal Election Com'n v. Christian Coalition*, 178 F.R.D. 61, 71 (E.D.VA), *aff'd in part mod. in part*, 178 F.R.D. 465 (E.D. Va. 1998) ["... it is technically proper to speak of waiver only in the case where the attorney or client communicates the privileged information to a third party after the privilege came into existence. If a third party is present when the communication is made, it is not technically correct to say that the client has 'waived' the privilege because one cannot waive what never existed"].

31   The accepted definition of the attorney-client privilege normally follows that articulated in the oft-cited case of *United States v. United Shoe Mach. Corp.*, 89 F. Supp. 357, 358-59 (D. Mass. 1950), *i.e.*, the privilege applies only if the asserted holder is or sought to become a client; the communication was made to an attorney, or his subordinate, acting as an attorney in connection with the communication; the communication relates to a fact of which the attorney is informed by the client, without the presence of strangers, and for the purpose of securing primarily an opinion on law or legal services, or assistance in some legal proceeding, and not for the purpose of committing a crime or tort; and the privilege has been claimed, and not waived, by the client.

32   *See, e.g., Bowne of New York City Inc. v. AmBase Corp.*, 150 F.R.D. 465, 471 (S.D. N.Y. 1993); *SEC v. Gulf & W. Indus.*, 518 F. Supp. 675, 683 (D.D.C. 1981). However, when the communication is a combination of business and legal advice the courts normally resolve the issue by recognizing the privilege if the predominate purpose of the communication was legal advice. *See* Vincent F. Alexander, *The Corporate Attorney-Client Privilege: A Study of the Participants*, 63 St. John's L.Rev. 191, 281 (1989); *United States Postal Service v. Phelps Dodge Ref. Corp.*, 852

Accordingly, the presence of an attorney at a board of director's or other corporate meeting does not render all communications made therein privileged. Privilege will apply only if the communications involved a request for legal advice, or the giving of such advice, and were intended to be confidential and privileged.[33] It is also important to understand that the attorney-client privilege applies to the content of the communication, as opposed to the underlying facts communicated. Only the former—absent waiver, or an exception to the privilege—is protected.[34] One aspect of the principle that the attorney-client privilege extends to the communication, and not to the facts communicated, is that a disclosure of the facts communicated does not constitute a waiver of the privilege.[35]

Thus, communications between a client and attorney may be privileged, even though the facts communicated are publicly known, or have been communicated to others, so long as the substance of what was said or written remains confidential.[36]

V. Exceptions to the Privilege

In contrast to circumstances in which the attorney-client privilege is not applicable, the law recognizes certain exceptions to the privilege. These are circumstances in which the privilege would normally be expected to apply, but they do not, only because a specific exception to their application has been created as a matter of public policy. They are discussed here only briefly.

An exception to both the attorney-client privilege and the work-product doctrine is the crime-fraud exception.[37] Protection is denied to a client's communications with an attorney, made for the purpose of committing a crime or fraud.[38] For this exception to apply there must be a *prima facie* showing that the client was

---

F. Supp. 156, 160 (E.D.N.Y. 1994) [advice from counsel constituted legal advice, although incidentally involving "business advice"].

33   *See International Tel. & Tel. Co. v. United Tel. Co.*, 60 F.R.D. 177, 185 (M.D. Fla. 1973); *Diversified Industries Inc. v. Meredith*, 572 F.2d 596, 611 (8th Cir. 1978). *See also* Dennis J. Block, *Responding to a Corporate Crisis*, 1121 PLI/Corp 449, 459 (1999). Consistent with this principle, the attorney-client privilege applies to these portions of corporate board minutes reflecting the discussion of legal advice. *Welch v. Board of Directors of Wildwood Golf Club*, 146 F.R.D. 131, 139 (W.D. Pa. 1993); *Great Plains Mut. Ins. Co. v. Mutual Reinsurance Bureau*, 150 F.R.D. 193 (D. Kan. 1993).

34   *Upjohn v. United States*, 449 U.S. 383, 395-96 (1981).

35   Edna Selan Epstein, *The Attorney-Client Privilege and the Work-Product Doctrine* (3d ed. 1997), at 174-75.

36   Paul R. Rice, *Attorney-Client Privilege: The Eroding Concept of Confidentiality Should Be Abolished*, 47 Duke L.J. 853, 855-56 (1998); *Upjohn v. United States*, 449 U.S. 383, 395-96 (1981).

37   Michael J. Chepiga, *Federal Attorney-Client Privilege and Work-Product*, 601 PLI/Lit 541, 583 (1999) ["[e]very Circuit which has considered the question has either held or assumed that (the crime-fraud) exception applies to (the) work-product doctrine"].

38   *Clark v. United States*, 298 U.S. 1 (1993); *United States v. Zolin*, 491 U.S. 554 (1989).

engaged in criminal or fraudulent conduct when seeking the advice of counsel; or that the client was planning such conduct when seeking the advice of counsel; or that the client committed a crime or engaged in fraud after receiving the benefit of counsel's advice. Moreover, the exception requires a showing that the attorney's assistance was obtained in furtherance of the criminal or fraudulent activity, or was closely related to it.[39] The exception applies to future or ongoing crime or fraud. It does not apply to communications concerning past or completed crimes or frauds.[40] Thus, it is unlikely to arise as an issue in internal investigations unless a client seeks advice to criminally extend or conceal the criminal conduct under investigation.[41]

The Fifth Circuit created the so-called "fiduciary exception" to the attorney-client privilege in *Garner v. Wolfinbarger*.[42] *Garner* held that where a company is involved in a suit against its shareholders, on a charge of acting inimically to the shareholders' interests, the availability of the attorney-client privilege for the corporate client is subject to the right of the shareholders to show cause why it should not be invoked in a particular instance. After *Garner*, which has gained overwhelming acceptance,[43] but which has been rejected by some authorities,[44] the fiduciary exception to the attorney-client privilege has been expanded from shareholder litigation to ERISA fiduciary litigation.[45] Most courts, recognizing the

---

39   *See e.g., In re Grand Jury Investigation (Schroeder)*, 842 F.2d 1233, 1226 (11th Cir. 1987).

40   *See e.g., In re Sealed Case*, 754 F.2d 395 (D.C. Cir 1985).

41   For a full explication of the crime-fraud doctrine, see The Crime-Fraud Exception to the Attorney-Client Privilege in the Context of Corporate Counseling, by H. Lowell Brown, Vol. 87, Number 4 Kentucky Law Journal 1998-99.

42   430 F.2d 1093, 1103 (5th Cir. 1970), *cert. denied*, 401 U.S. 974 (1971). *See also* Craig C. Martin and Matthew H. Metcalf, *The Fiduciary Exception to the Attorney Client Privilege*, 34 Tort & Ins. L. J. 827 (1999), noting that the "fiduciary exception" is more accurately characterized as a conditional or qualified privilege.

43   *See* Robert R. Summerhayes, *The Problematic Expansion of the Garner v. Wolfinbarger Exception to the Corporate Attorney-Client Privilege*, 31 Tulsa L. J. 275, 287 (1995) [the exception created in *Garner* has gained overwhelming acceptance in federal courts].

44   *See, e.g., In re Celotext Corp. (The Asbestos Health Claimants' Committee v. Jasper Corp.)*, 196 B.R. 596, 600 n. 3 (Bankr., M.D. Fla. 1996); *Milroy v. Hanson*, 875 F. Supp. 646, 651 (D. Neb. 1995), *Shrivani v. Capital Investing Corp., Inc.*, 112 F.R.D. 389, 391 (D. Conn. 1986); *Lefkowitz v. Duquesne Light Co.*, Nos. 86-1046 and 86-2085, 1988 WL 169273, at *6 (W.D. Pa. 1988); Stephen A. Saltzburg, *Corporate Attorney-Client Privilege in Shareholder Litigation and Similar Cases: Garner Revisited*, 12 Hofstra L. Rev. 817, 840 (1984) ["*Garner* was wrong...."]. *See also* Robert R. Summerhays, *The Problematic Expansion of the Garner v. Wolfinbarger Exception to the Corporate Attorney-Client Privilege*, 31 Tulsa L. J. 275, 302 (1995) [the doctrinal underpinnings of *Garner* are frustratingly ambiguous]. *But see* Jack B. Weinstein *et al.*, Weinstein's Evidence 503 (b) [05], at 503-43-98 (1992) [approving of *Garner*].

45   *Compare In re Long Island Lighting Co.*, 129 F.3d 268, 271-73 (2d Cir. 1997), *with Donovan v. Fitzsimmons*, 90 F.R.D. 583, 587 (N.D. Ill. 1981).

policy differences behind the attorney-client privilege and work-product doctrine, have not been willing to apply *Garner* to the work-product doctrine.[46]

The foregoing discussion is not exhaustive as to the circumstances in which the attorney-client privilege does not apply in the first instance, or as to the exceptions to the privilege.[47]

VI. Work-Product Doctrine

The work-product doctrine protects documents and tangible things prepared by the attorney in anticipation of litigation[48] and is a protection separate and distinct from the attorney-client privilege. While they focus on different things, both the work-product doctrine and the attorney-client privilege focus on the same principle; i.e., that counsel cannot provide complete legal representation without keeping certain matters from opponents. But there are differences in what each is designed to protect. The attorney-client privilege protects confidential communications between lawyer and client and it focuses on that relationship. Information other than "communications" is unprotected. Additionally, voluntary disclosure by the client to a third party, or with a third party present, waives the privilege, not only as to the specific communication but, in some cases, to all other communications on the subject matter. The work-product doctrine is not limited to communications. It applies to material prepared in anticipation of litigation, so much of what it protects is broader than client communication. Moreover, it is not automatically waived because of a disclosure to a third party.[49]

The work-product doctrine protects the mental impressions, conclusions and legal theories of counsel. Traditionally, the doctrine protects from disclosure documents or other materials prepared "principally or exclusively" in anticipation of litigation.[50]

---

46 *See e.g., In re Celotex Corp.*, 196 B.R. at 600 n.3; *Donovan v. Fitzsimmons*, 90 F.R.D. at 588; *Wilbur v. ARCO Chem. Corp.*, 974 F.2d 631, 646 (5th Cir. 1992); Martin & Metcalf, *The Fiduciary Exception to the Attorney-Client Privilege*, 34 Tort & Ins. L. 827 (1999). *But see* Edna Selan Epstein, The Attorney-Client Privilege and the Work-Product Doctrine (3d ed. 1997), at 400, noting that some courts are increasingly applying the *Garner* doctrine to work-product materials, citing *Aguinaga v. John Morrell & Co.*, 112 F.R.D. 671, 682 (D. Kan. 1986), and *Nellis v. Air Line Pilots Assoc.*, 144 F.R.D. 68 (E.D. Va. 1992)

47 For example, omitted from this discussion are the "at-issue" and "self-defense" exceptions to the attorney-client privilege; the general non-applicability of the attorney-client privilege to a client's identity or fee information (and the exceptions to that non-applicability); and the "at-issue" exception to the work-product doctrine. *See* Michael J. Chepiga, *Federal Attorney-Client Privilege and Work-Product Doctrine*, 601 PLI/Lit 541, 559-60, 562-63, 584 (1999).

48 *Hickman v. Taylor*, 329 U.S. 495 (1947).

49 *In re Sealed Case*, 676 F.2d 793, 808-809 (D.C. Cir. 1982).

50 *United States v. Gulf Oil Corp.*, 760 F.2d 292, 296-97 (Temp. Emer. Ct. App. 1985); *United States v. El Paso Co.*, 682 F.2d 530, 542-43 (5th Cir. 1982), *cert. denied*, 466 U.S. 944 (1984). The Second Circuit has, however, recently rejected the traditional "principally or exclusively" requirement, and has held that a document should be protected simply if it was

The seminal work-product case, still relevant today, is *Hickman v. Taylor*, 329 U.S. 495 (1947). The Court stated:

> Historically, a lawyer is an officer of the court and is bound to work for the advancement of justice while faithfully protecting the rightful interests of his or her clients. In performing his various duties, however, it is essential that a lawyer work with a certain degree of privacy, free from unnecessary intrusion by opposing parties and their counsel. Proper preparation of a client's case demands that he assemble information, sift what he considers to be the relevant from the irrelevant facts, prepare his legal theories and plan his strategy without undue and needless interference. That is the historical and the necessary way in which lawyers act within the framework of our system of jurisprudence to promote justice and to protect their clients' interests.[51]

Hickman established a principle that has given rise to a distinction between "opinion" and "ordinary" work-product that is now long embedded in the law. If the work-product reveals the opinions, judgments, and thought processes of counsel, it receives the highest level of protection, and a party seeking discovery of this information must demonstrate extraordinary justification.[52] This principle is now codified in Federal Rule of Civil Procedure 26(b)(3), which provides in relevant part:

> Subject to the provisions of subdivision (b)(4) of this rule, a party may obtain discovery of documents and tangible things otherwise discoverable under subdivision (b)(1) of this rule and prepared in anticipation of litigation or for trial by or for another party or by or for that other party's representative (including the other party's attorney, consultant, surety, indemnitor, insurer, or agent) only upon a showing that the party seeking discovery has substantial need of the materials in the preparation of the party's case that that the party is unable without undue hardship to obtain the substantial equivalent of the materials by other means. In ordering discovery of such materials when the required showing has been made, the court shall protect against disclosure of the mental impressions, conclusions, opinions or legal theories of an attorney or other representative of a party concerning the litigation.

---

prepared "because of" the "prospect of litigation", even if the primary original purpose for creating it was business planning rather than preparation for possible litigation. *United States v. Adlman*, 134 F.3d 1194, 1197-1203 (2d Cir. 1998). Under the Second Circuit's test, however, a document will still not be protected if it is "prepared in the ordinary course of business or . . . would have been created in essentially similar form irrespective of the litigation". *Id.* at 1202. While rejecting the Fifth Circuit's *El Paso* test, *Adlman* did not perceive it was creating new doctrine, as it cited as consistent with its "because of" rule decisions of the Third, Fourth, Seventh, Eighth and D.C. Circuits, and Charles Alan Wright, Arthur R. Miller, and Richard L. Marcus, 8 Federal Practice and Procedure § 2024, at 343 (1994).

51 *Hickman*, 329 U.S. at 510-11.

52 *In re Sealed Case*, 676 F.2d 793, 809-810 (D.C. Cir. 1982); *Better Gov't Bureau, Inc. v. McGraw (In re Allen)*, 106 F.3d. 582, 606 (4th Cir. 1997).

The application of the doctrine to criminal proceedings[53] has been codified in Rule 16(b)(2) of the Federal Rules of Criminal Procedure, which states in relevant part:

> Except as to scientific or medical reports, this subdivision does not authorize the discovery or inspection of reports, memoranda, or other internal defense documents made by the defendant, or the defendant's attorneys or agents in connection with the investigation or defense of the case, or of statements made by the defendant, or by the government or defense witnesses, or by prospective government or defense witnesses, to the defendant, the defendant's agents or attorneys.[54]

The protection afforded by *Hickman v. Taylor* goes beyond the statutory protection of Fed. R. Civ. P. 26(b)(3) and Fed. R. Crim. P. 16(b)(2), which apply only to discovery procedures. Work-product protection extends to the trial of cases[55] as well as to discovery by the government through a grand jury.[56]

"Work-product" does not include only attorney-generated work. It includes documents prepared in anticipation of litigation by the client itself or by someone working for the attorney on behalf of the client. In the context of internal investigations conducted because of an ongoing governmental inquiry, as in all other cases, the work-product of all persons assisting the lawyers in the investigation, such as accountants, investigators, experts and other non-lawyers will normally be protected, just as much as that of the lawyers themselves.[57]

To be protected, however, the work-product must, according to Fed. R. Civ. P. 26(b)(3), have been "prepared in anticipation of litigation or for trial". If litigation has not started, it must be clear, at the time the document is created, that there is a real possibility that litigation will happen.[58] Clearly, any internal investigation that

---

53 While originally arising in the context of civil actions, the courts have recognized the work-product doctrine is even more important in the context of a criminal trial. *United States v. Nobles*, 422 U.S. 225, 238 (1975); ". . . the work-product doctrine not only applies in criminal cases, but . . . it plays an even more vital role in criminal than in civil cases." *In re Martin Marietta Corp.*, 856 F.2d 619, 624 (4th Cir. 1988), *cert. denied*, 490 U.S. 1011 (1989).

54 The Government has certain work-product protection as well, set forth in Rule 16(a)(2).

55 *United States v. Nobles*, 422 U.S. 225, 239 (1975).

56 *In re Grand Jury Proceedings (Duffy)*, 473 F.2d 840, 845 (8th Cir. 1973).

57 *United States v. Nobles*, 422 U.S. 225, 238-39 (1975). *See also*, Fed. R. Civ. P. 23(b)(3); Fed. R. Crim. P. 16(b)(2).

58 *See In re Grand Jury Investigation*, 599 F.2d 1224, 1228-1229 (3d Cir. 1979). As the court explained, although there is agreement that there must be at least "some possibility" of litigation, there is no agreed upon formulation of the exact test to be applied. The "variety of formulas" given by different courts and commentators include: that there must be "a substantial probability that litigation will occur and that commencement of such litigation is imminent"; that the threat of litigation must be "real and imminent"; that the prospect of litigation must be "identifiable"; that litigation must "reasonably have been anticipated or apprehended"; or simply that "the document can fairly be said to have been prepared or obtained because of the prospect of litigation." *Id.*

was generated by a governmental investigation will have been conducted "in anticipation of litigation," even though no charges may have been filed at the time the investigation began.[59] But, in other less obvious cases, to support a valid claim of work-product doctrine, it is not sufficient that there be merely an incidental and speculative possibility of litigation sometime down the road. There does not need to be imminent governmental inquiry or litigation. The company may merely know or suspect wrongdoing and believe that, once others discover it, there may be litigation down the road. But, while litigation need not be imminent, the primary motivating purpose behind the creation of a document or investigative report must be to aid in some foreseeable potential future litigation.[60]

Under the traditional rule followed by many courts, the work-product doctrine will not protect an internal review from disclosure if it was commenced principally for a reason other than assisting in preparing for anticipated or pending litigation.[61] If, for example, an internal review was initiated by in-house counsel to examine a company's operations from a compliance standpoint, but not in anticipation of pending or threatened litigation, it may be subject to subpoena during a later investigation. The coexisting presence of a business purpose is not fatal to work-product protection, unless it is the primary motivation for the internal review. It is, therefore, critical that an internal review be designed to be primarily litigation-oriented in nature.

Since the work-product doctrine protects only communications and documents prepared in anticipation of litigation, the company should make every effort to create a record which shows that it was concerned about potential litigation. Such a record can be established through the retainer letter engaging the law firm, in the resolution authorizing the investigation, and in other documents. The retainer agreement and the authorization should make note of the fact, where applicable, that the investigation is being conducted in anticipation of litigation with the government, and should set forth in as much detail and with as much breadth as possible, the anticipated nature of the litigation. The retainer and the authorization

---

59   *Martin v. Monfort*, 150 F.R.D. 172, 173 (D. Colo. 1993).

60   *United States v. El Paso Co.*, 682 F.2d 530 (5th Cir. 1982), *cert. denied*, 466 U.S. 944 (1984).

61   *See, e.g., In Re Kidder Peabody Securities Litigation*, 168 F.R.D. 459, 466 (S.D.N.Y. 1996). However, as discussed in note 50, the Second Circuit has recently rejected the traditional "principally or exclusively" requirement. *See United States v. Adlman*, 134 F.3d at 1197-203. Under *Adlman*, a study created by an attorney primarily for business planning purposes will still be protected so long as the document was also created because of the prospect of litigation, and would not have been prepared in essentially similar form irrespective of the litigation. While a number of circuits have retreated from the traditional "principally or exclusively" requirement, the traditional rule still has many adherents. Accordingly, counsel should be fully aware that documents not created principally or exclusively to assist in litigation may not be able to be protected against disclosure.

should also, if appropriate, note any civil or administrative litigation that may be possible, including debarment proceedings, *qui tam* actions and the like.

The work-product doctrine protects counsel's conclusions, opinions and mental impressions and lawyers should make every effort to include these in all documents they wish to protect. Counsel should also seek to include legal theories along with their mental impressions in the documents that they wish to protect. Taped interviews or verbatim notes of witness statements offer no protection under the doctrine.[62] Where notes contain factual information, counsel should, if possible, include legal analysis in with the factual information.

The opposing party can potentially circumvent the work-product doctrine only if it can make a showing that it has "substantial need" for the documents and will suffer "undue hardship" if the documents are not produced.[63] The government, in the context of a grand jury investigation, may be more likely to succeed in such a showing than a civil litigant.[64]

The doctrine does not prevent information from being disclosed even if it is included in a document that is protected by the doctrine. It simply protects a party from having to produce documentation containing the information. However, if available, the same information can be obtained by an opposing party through appropriate interrogatories and depositions.

VII. Waiver of the Attorney-Client Privilege and Work-Product Doctrine in the Conduct of an Internal Corporate Investigation

A condition precedent to a waiver of either the attorney-client privilege or the work-product doctrine is their prior existence. When the attorney-client privilege or the work-product has never come into existence, protective devices to guard against release of the information through waiver are worthless. Practitioners and corporate officials alike need to be aware of this, in order to protect against or prevent the occurrence of circumstances creating such non-applicability or exceptions.[65] It is frustrating and nonproductive to employ efforts to avoid waiver of the

---

62   Fed. R. Civ. P. 26(b)(3) gives a party or non-party witness a right to obtain, without any required showing of hardship or need, a copy of any statement made by them concerning the subject matter of the litigation.

63   Fed. R. Civ. P. 26(b)(3); *see also Hickman v. Taylor*; 329 U.S. 495, 511 (1947).

64   *See In re Sealed Case*, 676 F.2d 793, 806 (D.C. Cir. 1982) (stating that "[n]owhere is the public's claim to each person's evidence stronger than in the context of a valid grand jury subpoena").

65   *See* Paul R. Rice, *Corporate Attorney-Client Privilege: Study Reveals Corporate Agents Are Uniformed: What They Don't Know Can Destroy The Privilege*, American Corporate Counsel Association, August 1988. Professor Rice noted that, in a survey of selected Fortune 100 corporations, the Evidence Project of the American University Washington College of Law discovered that many corporate agents—including officers and directors—know too little about the

attorney-client privilege or work-product doctrine for information which a company needs to protect from disclosure, when the information was never protected to begin with. More importantly, just as a company may be harmed by the release of protected information through waiver, it suffers similar harm from the failure to understand and prevent the creation of circumstances in which the attorney-client privilege or work-product doctrine does not apply, or as to which exceptions to the privilege or doctrine arise.

The issue of waiver of attorney-client privilege and the work-product doctrine is very broad.[66] Thus, this discussion of waiver[67] is limited to the context of internal corporate investigations.[68] While waiver of both the privilege and the doctrine is discussed, there are some unique aspects with regard to the privilege.

---

attorney-client privilege. Only 58 percent of those surveyed knew that the confidentiality of attorney-client communications has to be subsequently maintained by allowing their distribution within the corporation only on a 'need to know' basis. As Professor Rice observed, this lack of knowledge about the requirement of confidentiality could have two significant consequences. First, the confidentiality could be destroyed, thereby losing the protection of the privilege. Second, even if the confidentiality were preserved, without established circulation procedures that are known and followed by employees and other corporate agents, the preservation of confidentiality will have to be proven for each communication through the costly and time-consuming procedure of filing affidavits from each recipient, attesting to the propriety of receipt and further distribution. Officers and directors were no better informed than other employees, with almost one-half thinking it was not necessary to either segregate privileged documents or clearly label them as "attorney-client communications," so as to alert potential readers to their confidential nature. In this regard, Professor Rice observes that, while neither procedure is theoretically required, when both are absent, there is an increased risk that unauthorized persons with access to unsegregated documents will inappropriately read them, and thus destroy the privilege. Accordingly, Professor Rice recommends, "corporations must protect themselves and their attorney-client privileges by informing employees about the privilege's requirements and of the corporation's storage and dissemination policies regarding confidential communications. This must be given immediate attention." *Id.*, at 2-3. Emphasis in original.

66   The issue of waiver with regard to the report of investigation is discussed in more detail later in this chapter and in Chapter 5.

67   The First Circuit has described "waiver" as "a loose and misleading label for what is in fact a collection of different rules addressed to different problems. Cases under this 'waiver' heading include situations as divergent as an express and voluntary surrender of the privilege, partial disclosure of a privileged document, selective disclosure to some outsiders but not to all, and inadvertent overhearings or disclosures." *United States v. Massachusetts Institute of Technology*, 129 F.3d 681, 684 (1st Cir. 1997).

68   Necessarily excluded is any discussion of the waiver of attorney-client privilege and the work-product doctrine in the myriad of circumstances attendant to pretrial and trial proceedings, including but not limited to pretrial discovery; the filing of a complaint or defense which puts the privilege or doctrine at issue; and the presentation of testimonial or documentary evidence at trial. *See, e.g.*, Richard L. Marcus, *The Perils of Privilege: Waiver and the Litigator*, 84 Mich. L. Rev. 1605 (1986); Ettie Ward, *The Litigator's Dilemma: Waiver of Core Work Product Used in Trial Preparation*, 62 St. John's L. Rev. 515 (1988); T. Maxfield Bahner and Michael L. Gallion, *Waiver of Attorney-Client Privilege Via Issue Injection: A Call for Uniformity*, 65 Defense Counsel J. 199 (1998). In general, *see* Edna Selan Epstein, The Attorney-Client Privilege and the Work-Product Doctrine (3d ed. 1997), published by the American Bar Association.

A principal requirement for the attorney-client privilege is that the communication be made in confidence for the purpose of obtaining or providing legal advice. The issue of waiver focuses on situations where the confidentiality is lost. Unlike most constitutional rights, which can only be knowingly and intentionally waived,[69] attorney-client privilege can be waived even when neither the attorney nor the client so intend. Waiver may occur from an inadvertent or negligent disclosure of privileged documents or by conduct of the client in various types of circumstances where the test is usually "fairness". Courts use a wide variety of terms to discuss waiver including "voluntary" and "involuntary"; "intentional" and "unintentional"; "total", "selective" and "partial"; "express" and "implied". The names themselves are not particularly helpful. It is more useful to look at situations where courts have ruled on the waiver issue.

A. Intentional Disclosures

If a client reveals confidential information to a third party (excluding in some instances the government), the information is deemed to be waived because it is no longer confidential. For example, parties may voluntarily provide documents to one government agency. If the party then tries to assert privilege elsewhere, fairness policies normally prevent the client from doing so; *i.e.*, the party cannot pick and choose when to assert the privilege.[70]

B. Partial Disclosures

If a client discloses part of a privileged communication, an opposing party can ask the court to require a more full disclosure on the same subject matter. This is often discussed in terms of fairness where additional material must be disclosed so that the material will not be viewed out of context.[71]

VIII. Considerations Attending the Waiver of the Attorney-Client Privilege Differ from those Attending the Waiver of the Work-Product Doctrine

In the conduct of an internal corporate investigation it is important for counsel to fully understand the attorney-client privilege and the work-product doctrine, in order to be able to ensure the broadest protection to information developed by and in the investigation, and to be able to fully appreciate the benefits and disadvantages of disclosing any of that information outside of the company. Such an understanding requires not only the knowledge of what constitutes the attorney-client privilege and work-product doctrine, and the exceptions thereto, but of the interrelationship between the two protections.

---

69   *Brewer v. Williams*, 430 U.S. 387, 404 (1977); *Johnson v. Zerbst*, 304 U.S. 458, 464 (1938).

70   *United States v. Massachusetts Institute of Technology*, 129 F.3d 681, 685 (1st Cir. 1997); *Permian Corp. v. United States*, 665 F.2d 1214, 1221-22 (D.C. Cir. 1981).

71   *United States v. Jones*, 696 F.2d 1069, 1072 (4th Cir. 1982).

Considerations attending the waiver of the attorney-client privilege differ from those attending the waiver of the work-product doctrine.

A recent judicial decision instructively observed that:

> the attorney-client privilege is like quicksilver. Initially difficult to grasp, once in one's possession it can easily slide through one's fingers. Disclosure of the communication to a third person is one of the quickest ways for one to lose the attorney-client privilege.[72]

Indeed, at common law, any disclosure, even by a thief who purloined privileged documents, operated as a waiver, on the theory that a client should carefully protect any communication claimed to be privileged.[73] While that harsh approach to waiver no longer holds full sway,[74] it is still the view of the courts that the attorney-client privilege is fragile, and easily lost. Such a conclusion is premised upon at least two factors. First, the attorney-client privilege is designed to promote full and complete disclosure between counsel and the client.[75]

---

72   *Federal Election Com'm v. Christian Coalition*, 178 F.R.D. 61, 71 (E.D. VA), *order aff'd in part, modified in part*, 178 F.R.D. 456 (E.D. VA 1998). *See also Johnson v. United States*, 542 F.2d 941, 942 (5th Cir. 1976), *cert. denied* 430 U.S. 934 (1977) [communications in the presence of third parties, not part of the attorney-client relationship, are not considered confidential, and are, therefore, not privileged]. Once the privilege is waived it is not subject to restoration. It is gone permanently. *Smith v. Armour Pharmaceutical Co.*, 838 F. Supp. 1573, 1576 (S.D. Fla. 1993).

73   8 J.Wigmore, Evidence §2325, at 633, (McNaughton, rev. ed. 1961 ["the risk of insufficient precautions is upon the client"].

74   *See, e.g., In re Grand Jury Proceedings Involving Berkley & Co.*, 466 F. Supp. 863, 869-70 (D. Minn. 1979) [delivery of employer's documents to the government by a discharged ex-employee who stole them did not constitute a waiver]. *See also* Paul R. Rice, *Attorney-Client Privilege: The Eroding Concept of Confidentiality Should Be Abolished*, 47 Duke L. J. 853,880-82 (1998), noting the tendency of the courts to overlook the loss of confidentiality when that loss was not due to any serious fault on the part of the client or the client's authorized agent.

The same divergence of opinion exists regarding the so-called "inadvertent" disclosure or production of protected information or documents. Some courts insist upon the rule that disclosure automatically results in waiver, even if the disclosure was inadvertent. *See, e.g., Wichita Land & Cattle Co. v. American Federal Bank*, 148 F.R.D. 456, 457 (D.D.C. 1992). A second view precludes waiver through inadvertent disclosure. *See, e.g., Mendenhall v. Barber-Green Co.*, 531 F. Supp. 951, 954 (N.D. Ill. 1982); *Conn. Mut. Life Ins. Co. v. Shields*, 18 F.R.D. 448, 451 (S.D. N.Y. 1955) [only a client can waive the privilege, and there must be evidence that he intended to do so]. A third position is taken by many courts, which look to a series of factors in deciding whether a given disclosure has waived an otherwise applicable privilege, all predicated upon the overriding issue of fairness. *See* Charles John Wright and Richard L. Marcus, 8 Fed. Prac & Proc. Civil 2d §2016.2 (199). *See also* Richard Marcus, *The Perils of Privilege: Waiver and the Litigator*, Mich. L. Rev. 1605, 1654-55 (1986), arguing that waivers should be always be based upon principles of fairness, rather than upon a judicial indulgence of a dislike of privileges, resulting in finding excuses to direct their withdrawal through waiver. For a general discussion of inadvertent waiver *see* John T. Hundley, "*Inadvertent Waiver" of Evidentiary Privileges: Can Reformulating the Issue Lead to More Sensible Decisions?*, 19 S. Ill. L. J. 263 (1995).

75   *Branzburg v. Hayes*, 408 U.S. 665, 690 n. 29 (1972); *Commodity Futures Trading Comm'n v. Weintraub*, 471 U.S. 343, 348 (1985).

That requires confidentiality. Accordingly, the key element of the privilege is confidentiality—clients' expectations that their communications to counsel are confidential, and will continue to be so.[76] Second, courts construe the attorney-client privilege narrowly, recognizing that privileges "obstruct the search for truth," and should apply only where "necessary to achieve (their) purpose."[77] Accordingly, the goals of the attorney-client privilege are no longer relevant or entitled to recognition when circumstances exist which demonstrate that the client's expectation of confidentiality has come to an end. This is not to say, however, that every disclosure of a confidential communication will waive the attorney-client privilege.[78] Where the disclosure is necessary to further the goal of enabling the client to seek informed legal advice, waiver may not result.[79]

The work-product doctrine, on the other hand, is in some ways broader than the attorney-client privilege.[80] The purpose of the work-product doctrine is to permit the proper development, preparation and presentation of a party's case for trial, by protecting and safeguarding the facts of an attorney's trial preparations from discovery by an actual or potential adversary.[81] Accordingly, the work-product doctrine is not waived by a disclosure to a third party made in pursuit of trial preparation, and not inconsistent with maintaining secrecy against opponents or adversaries, even though the disclosure would waive the attorney-client privilege by

---

76 *Fisher v. United States*, 425 U.S. 391, 403 (1976).

77 "[E]nforcement of a claim of privilege acts in derogation of the overriding goals of liberal discovery and adjudication of cases on their merits. It is for this reason that privileges are disfavored and generally to be narrowly construed." *Bowne of New York City, Inc. v. AmBase Corp.*, 150 F.R.D. 465, 473 (S.D.N.Y. 1993). *Accord: Univ. of Pennsylvania v. EEOC*, 493 U.S. 182, 189 (1990); *In re Grand Jury Investigation (Ocean Transp.)*, 604 F.2d 672, 675 (D.C. Cir. 1979). *See also Manna v. United States Dept. of Justice*, 815 F. Supp. 798, 814 (D.N.J. 1993), *aff'd* 541 F.3d 1158 (3d Cir.), *cert denied*, 516 U.S. 975 (1995) [the attorney-client privilege is narrowly drawn, and disclosure of any meaningful part of the privileged communication will waive the privilege as to the whole].

78 *See* James Wm. Moore, 6 Moore's Federal Practice (3d ed. 1999) §26.70[6][a]; *In re Grand Jury Proceedings*, 43 F.3d 966, 970 (5th Cir. 1994) [mere voluntary disclosure to a third person is insufficient, in and of itself, to waive work product protection].

79 *See* Nancy Horton Burke, *The Price of Cooperating With the Government: Possible Wavier of Attorney-Client and Work-Product Privileges*, 49 Baylor L. Rev. 33, 37 (1997) citing Comment, *Stuffing the Rabbit Back Into the Hat: Limited Wavier of the Attorney-Client Privilege In An Administrative Agency Investigation*, 130 U. Pa. L. Rev. 1198, 1207 (1982). *See also* 81 Am. Jur. 2d Witnesses § 348 (1992) [no waiver occurs by reason of disclosure of confidential communications to business associates to whom disclosure is reasonably necessary].

80 *See* James Wm. Moore, 6 Moore's Federal Practice (3d ed. 1999) §26.70 [8], opining that the work-product doctrine is broader than the attorney-client privilege. *Accord*: Michael J. Chapiga, *Federal Attorney-Client Privilege and Work-Product Doctrine*, 601 PLI/Lit 541, 577 (1999), citing *United States v. Nobles*, 422 U.S. 225 (1975). *See also In re Martin Marietta Corp.*, 856 F.2d 619, 624 (4th Cir. 1988), *cert. denied*, 490 U.S. 1011 (1989) ["...the work-product privilege is a broader protection (than the attorney-client privilege)"].

81 *See, e.g., Hickman v. Taylor*, 329 U.S. 495, 510-11 (1947); *United States v. American Tel. & Tel. Co.*, 642 F.2d 1285, 1299 (D.C.Cir. 1980).

destroying the concept of continued confidentiality.[82] Thus, in connection with waiver of the work-product doctrine, disclosure to a third-party will not effect a waiver unless it is to a litigation adversary, or substantially increases the likelihood that an adversary will gain access to the information.[83]

The attorney-client privilege and the work-product doctrine differ in another respect. If there has been no waiver, the attorney-client privilege is absolute, and not subject to penetration because an opposing litigant has a substantial need for the information at issue, and is unable without undue hardship to obtain the substantial equivalent thereof by other means.[84] Indeed, the privilege continues after death.[85] On the other hand, non-opinion work-product (ordinary or fact work-product),[86] is subject to discovery by a litigation opponent, pursuant to Fed. R. Civ. P. 26(b)(3), upon a showing of substantial need of the materials in the presentation of the party's case, and that the party is unable without undo hardship to obtain the substantial equivalent of the materials by other means.[87] The issue of waiver is not

---

82   *United States v. American Tel & Tel. Co.*, 642 F.2d at 1299. *In re: Steinhardt Partners, L.P.*, 9 F.3d 230, 236 (2d Cir. 1993).

83   Charles A. Wright & Arthur R. Miller, Federal Practice and Procedure § 2024 (1970); James Wm. Moore, 6 Moore's Federal Practice (3d ed. 1999) § 26.70[6][c]; *Gramm v. Horsehead Indust., Inc.*, No. 87 CIV. 5122 (MJL), 1990 WL142404, at *2 (S.D.N.Y. 1990). *See also* Michael J. Chapiga, *Federal Attorney-Client Privilege and Work-Product Doctrine*, 6091 PLI/Lit 541, 585 (1999) ["[m]ost courts hold that for waiver to occur, disclosure must enable an adversary to gain access to the information," citing *Westinghouse Electric Corp. v. Republic of the Philippines*, 951 F.2d 1414, 1428 (3d Cir. 1981), and *United States v. AT&T*, 642 F.2d 1285, 1299 (D.C. Cir. 1980)]; Edna Sedan Epstein, the Attorney-Client Privilege and the Work-Product Doctrine (3d ed. 1997), at 404 ["[t]he essential question concerning waiver of the work-product by disclosure is whether the material has been kept from adversaries"].

84   *See* Richard S. Griener, *General Counsel in an Era of Compliance Programs*, 46 Emory L. J. 1113, 1179 (1997) [the attorney-client privilege is an absolute protection, unless waived, unlike the work-product doctrine, which can be overcome by a litigant's showing of substantial need for information and undue hardship in obtaining it elsewhere]. *Accord*: Mark D. Coldiron, *Use of Experts In Environmental Litigation and Enforcement Matters*, 11-Sum Nat. Resources & Envt., 13, 15 (1996); Alex Koch, *Internal Corporate Investigations: The Wavier of Attorney-Client Privilege and Work-Product Through Voluntary Disclosures to the Government*, 34 Am. Crim. L. Rev. 347, 352 (1997). *See also* Brian M. Smith, *Be Careful How You Use It Or You May Lose It: A Modern Look At Corporate Attorney-Client Privilege And The Ease Of Waiver In Various Circuits*, 75 U. Det. Mercy L. Rev. 389, 397 (1998).

85   *Swidler v. United States*, 524 U.S. 399 (1998).

86   The work-product doctrine protects materials prepared for, in anticipation of, or because of litigation, normally divides work-product into two categories, "opinion" work product, and "fact" work product. The latter is work that recites factual matters, and the former is work which reflects an attorney's opinions, conclusions, mental impressions or legal theories. *See United States v. Weissman*, No. 81 94 Cr. 760 (CSH), 1995 WL 244522, at *5 (S.D.N.Y. 1995); Michael J. Chepiga, *Federal Attorney-Client Privilege and Work Product Doctrine*, 601 PLI /Lit 541, 577 (1999).

87   Opinion work product, however, essentially enjoys a nearly absolute immunity, and can seldom, if ever, be subject to discovery by a litigation adversary. *See* Charles Alan Wright and Victor James Gold, 28 Fed. Prac. & Proc. Evid. § 6188 [the privacy of opinion work product is essential to maintaining an attorney's effectiveness as an adversary, while ordinary fact work

relevant, and if a court finds the requisite substantial need and unavailability under Fed.R.Civ.P. 26 (b)(3), it may order production of the requested trial preparation material, even though a waiver has never occurred. In this connection, the in-some-ways hardier work-product doctrine is less protective then the attorney-client privilege, to which Fed.R.Civ.P. 26 (b)(3) has no application.

These differing considerations[88] attendant to the attorney-client privilege and work-product doctrine are important to appreciate in the context of the waiver of either in connection with an internal corporate investigation.

IX. Waiver in the Context of an Internal Corporate Investigation

The conduct of an internal corporate investigation, which may be required in certain circumstances,[89] is fraught with potential pitfalls for counsel and corporate officials attempting to protect against the waiver of corporate attorney-client privilege and the work-product doctrine.

---

product is not given absolute protection because other important policies, such as promoting the truth, may be frustrated by the concealment of work product which merely collects facts]. *Compare Duplan Corp. v. Moulinage et Retorderie de Chavanoz*, 509 F.2d 730, 734-35 (4th Cir.), *cert. denied*, 420 U.S. 997 (1974), according opinion work product close to absolute immunity, *with Office of Thrift Supervision v. Vinson & Elkins, L.L.P.*, 124 F.3d 1304, 1307-08 (D.C. Cir. 1997), merely applying a higher standard for the discovery of opinion work product than to fact work product. The Supreme Court, in *Upjohn Company v. United States*, 449 U.S. 383, 399 (1981), recognized a conflict existing between the circuits on the issue of whether opinion work product is afforded absolute protection from disclosure, but expressly left the question open.

88 Not all courts accept that there are differing considerations attendant to the attorney-client privilege and work-product doctrine. *Compare Transmirra Products Corp v. Monsanto Chemical Co.*, 26 F.R.D. 572, 578 (S.D.N.Y. 1960), recognizing that waiver of the attorney-client privilege does not imply a waiver of the work-product doctrine, *with In re Sealed Case*, 676 F.2d 793, 813 (D.C.Cir. 1982), holding that "[a]n exception or waiver of the work-product privilege will also serve as an exception or waiver of the attorney-client privilege."

89 *See, e.g., In re Caremark Int'l, Inc. Derivative Litig.*, 698 A.2d 959, (Del. Ch. 1996), requiring a good faith effort by senior managers and directors to ensure the company has an adequate system to internally detect illegal activities in a timely manner. *See also* John Gibeaut, *Getting Your House In Order*, 85-Jun A.B.A.J. 64 (1999). In the health care area, 42 U.S.C. §1320a-7(b)(a)(3) may impose a duty on providers in certain circumstances to report improper payments or overpayments received from the federal government (albeit this is somewhat uncertain), and contractual obligations with Medicare or Medicaid programs may require health care providers to disclose improper payments or over-payments. Further, the OIG, Department of Health and Human Services, requires health care providers to report as soon as possible the existence of certain misconduct or violation of federal criminal law, or material violations of applicable civil laws, rules and regulations. *See* Russell Hayman, *Voluntary Disclosure*, 1129 PLI/Corp 193, 204 (1999). Moreover, under certain state false claims acts (*e.g.*, Calif. Govt. Code §1265), a failure to disclose improper reimbursement, even if innocently obtained, may in and of itself constitute a false claim. *Id.* at 202.

A. Waiver by Voluntary Disclosure of the Investigative Report or Information to the Government

Historically, corporate officials and counsel have encountered the majority of their problems in attempting to protect against the waiver of the attorney-client privilege and work-product doctrine in connection with furnishing the government with the results of internal corporate investigations.

A number of government agencies, including the SEC, the Department of Defense, and the Department of Justice, have instituted voluntary disclosure programs, under which companies could receive more lenient treatment if they investigate themselves, disclose the results to the government, and take steps to correct deficiencies or reform wrongdoing.[90] In the arena of corporate criminal conduct, the Federal Sentencing Guidelines also provide incentives for internal corporate investigation, and disclosure to and cooperation with the government.[91]

Except in cases wherein disclosure to the government may be required, in response to a subpoena, or because of other corporate obligations,[92] a company conducting an internal investigation, and its counsel, must consider the advantages and disadvantages of disclosing the investigative results to the government. The sobering fact is that, except in the Eighth Circuit, such disclosure to the government may well waive both the attorney-client privilege and work-product doctrine.

The Eighth Circuit's opinion is *Diversified Industries, Inc. v. Meredith*, 572 F. 2d 596 (8th Cir. 1978).[93] The court's entire treatment of the issue is set out below:

> We finally address the issue of whether Diversified waived its attorney-client privilege with respect to the privileged material by voluntarily surrendering it to the SEC

---

90   *See* Beth S. Dorris, Note, *The Limited Waiver Rule: Creation of an SEC-Corporation Privilege*, 36 Stan. L. Rev. 789, 793-95 (1984) [describing the SEC Voluntary Disclosure Program]; Anton R. Valukas and Robert R. Stauffer, *Internal Corporate Investigations: The Law, Practice and Strategies of Corporate Self-Policing*, The Lawyer's Brief, April 30, 19992, at 2-3 note 4 (describing the DOD program): Gary R. Spratling, *The Corporate Leniency Policy: Answers to Recurring Questions*, 1120 PLI/Corp 325 (1999) [describing the Corporate Leniency Policy (Amnesty Program) of the Antitrust Division of the Department of Justice].

91   *See* Chapter 8.

92   *See, e.g.*, note 89, *supra*.

93   This is the *en banc* decision. The panel decision was decided in 1977. The author of the panel decision concurred in part and dissented in part to the *en banc* decision. The author of the *en banc* decision concurred in part and dissented in part to the panel decision. The *en banc* decision begins at 572 F. 2d 606.

pursuant to the agency's subpoena.[94] As Diversified disclosed these documents in a separate and nonpublic SEC investigation, we conclude that only a limited waiver of the privilege occurred (citations omitted).[95] To hold otherwise may have the effect of thwarting the developing procedure of corporations to employ independent outside counsel to investigate and advise them in order to protect stockholders, potential stockholders and customers.

572 F.2d at 611.

Despite finding early acceptance by some district courts outside of the Eighth Circuit,[96] and by some commentators,[97] *Diversified* has been rejected by every other circuit considering the issue of waiver, in the context of a voluntary surrender of privileged material to the government.

The D.C. Circuit was the first to depart from *Diversified*. In *In re Subpoenas Duces Tecum*,[98] the Court specifically rejected *Diversified* in finding implied waiver[99] of

---

94   *Diversified Industries, Inc. v. Meredith*, 572 F.2d, at 611, described the corporation's actions *vis-a-vis* the SEC as "*voluntarily surrendering* (the privileged material) to the SEC pursuant to an agency subpoena." Emphasis added. On the other hand, *In re Subpoena Duces Tecum*, 738 F.2d 1367, 1373 (D.C. Cir. 1984), discussing the provision of a corporate investigative report to the SEC, noted that there is a distinction between voluntary disclosure and disclosure by subpoena, *i.e.*, "the latter, being involuntary, lacks the self-interest which motivates the former. As such, there may be less reason to find waiver in circumstances of involuntary disclosure." *In re Steinhardt Partners, L.P.*, 9 F.3d 230, 234 (2d Cir. 1993), also noted that a voluntary disclosure of a legal memorandum to the SEC was "distinguishable from situations in which disclosure to an adversary is only obtained through compulsory legal process." *See also* Fed. R. Civ. P. 45 (c)(3)(A)(iii), requiring a court, on timely motion, to quash or modify a subpoena if it requires disclosure of privileged or other protected matter.

95   Limited waiver in this context means it was a waiver as the SEC alone.

96   This occurred primarily in the district courts of the Second Circuit, before *In re Steinhardt Partners L.P.(Salomon Bros/Treasury Lit. v. Steinhardt Partners, L.P.)*, 9 F.3d 230 (2d Cir. 1993), rejecting *Diversified.*

97   *See, e.g.,* Paul R. Rice, *Attorney-Client Privilege: The Eroding Concept of Confidentiality Should Be Abolished*, 47 Duke L. J. 853, 883-84 (1998). Professor Rice argues in favor of the limited waiver concept, noting, *inter alia*, that the Supreme Court, in *Upjohn Co. v. United States*, 449 U.S. 383, 392-94 (1981), inferentially condoned the concept of limited waiver by concluding that the communication disclosed in the report which the company had shared with the SEC remained privileged against a subpoena from the IRS.

98   738 F. 2d 1367, 1369-70, 1371-73 (D.C. Cir. 1984).

99   According to some courts, the doctrine of implied waiver is employed as a matter of objective fairness whenever a party claiming a privilege attempts to use it in a manner inconsistent with its purpose. Implied waiver of the attorney-client privilege occurs whenever disclosure is inconsistent with confidentiality. Implied waiver of the work-product doctrine occurs whenever maintenance thereof is not required to maintain a healthy adversary system. *In re Sealed Case*, 676 F.2d 793, 818 (D.C. Cir. 1982). Courts finding an implied waiver may apply it to all materials on the same subject matter. *Id.* However, that result is not required, as the scope of waiver "properly depend[s] heavily on the factual context in which the privilege is asserted." *In re Sealed Case*, 877 F. 2d 976, 981 (D.C. Cir. 1989). In the context of the attorney-client privilege, any disclosure of documents or other matters normally waives the privilege as to all documents or other matters related to the same subject matter. *Id.*, 877 F. 2d at 980-81. On the other hand, there is substantial authority for the proposition that a waiver of attorney-work product as to

both the attorney-client privilege and the work-product doctrine, when a company furnished to the SEC and a grand jury documents which were the product of a law firm's investigation of the company's alleged illegal payments to foreign officials.[100] *In re Subpoenas Duces Tecum* relied upon the D.C. Circuit's earlier decisions in *Permian Corp. v. United States*,[101] ["(a)ny voluntary disclosure by the holder of (the attorney-client) privilege is inconsistent with the confidential relationship and thus waives the privilege"], and *In re Sealed Case*,[102] [agreeing with *Permian*, and affirming that a company had waived its work-product protection for all its counsel's records on the same subject matter when it submitted counsel's investigative report and notes to the SEC under the latter's voluntary disclosure program].

The court in *Permian* took the traditional view that, as to the attorney-client privilege, any disclosure inconsistent with confidentiality waives the privilege. Accordingly, a release to the SEC of documents containing attorney-client communications waived the privilege, whether or not there was any agreement between the SEC and the company not to further disclose the communications. No waiver of the work-product doctrine was found by the district court in *Permian*, and the D.C. Circuit found this not to be clearly erroneous.

Unlike *Permian*, in *In re Sealed Case* there was no issue of a confidentiality agreement between the company and the SEC to protect against further disclosure to adversaries, and the company impliedly waived the protection of its work-product by voluntarily releasing its counsel's investigative report to the SEC. The D.C. Circuit suggested, however, that an implied waiver of the work-product doctrine may not have occurred if there had been an agreement with the SEC limiting disclosure to other agencies, consistent with its responsibilities under the law.[103]

---

particular documents does not extend to other documents addressing the same subject matter. *See e.g., In re United Mine Workers of America Employee Benefit Plans Litigation*, 159 F.R.D. 307, 310-11 (D.D.C. 1994) (collecting authorities). Some courts have determined that subject matter waivers depend upon whether the waiver occurs during litigation or is extra-judicial, holding that the former effect subject matter waiver, while the latter may not. *See, e.g., In re Von Bulow*, 828 F.2d 94, 101 (2d Cir. 1987); *United States v. Jacobs*, 117 F.3d 82, 89 (2d Cir. 1997); *Hartford Fire Ins. v. Pure Air On The Lake, Ltd.*, 154 F.R.D. 202, 211 (N.D. Ind. 1993). In this connection, the disclosure of an internal investigative report to the SEC has been found not to be extra-judicial. *See In re Kidder Peabody Sec. Litig.*, 168 F.R.D. 459, 470-71 (S.D.N.Y. 1996).

100 The specific fact situation in *Diversified*, in *In re Subpoenas Duces Tecum*, and in the other cases addressing this issue vary, as do the reasons advanced by the courts in reaching their holdings. A detailed analysis of those fact situations, and of the reasoning supporting these decisions, is beyond the scope of this discussion. Nevertheless, such an analysis should be undertaken by counsel before specific reliance thereon in supporting or resisting motions to compel production.

101 665 F. 2d 1214, 1219 (D.C. Cir. 1951).

102 676 F.2d 793, 817-18 (D.C. Cir. 1982).

103 676 F.2d at 824.

The Fourth Circuit was next to reject the doctrine of limited waiver in *In re Martin Marietta*,[104] Martin Marietta, in settling with the government, both as to criminal charges, and administratively with the Department of Defense (DOD), disclosed otherwise privileged materials to the U.S. Attorney and the DOD. Those disclosures effected an implied subject matter waiver of the company's attorney-client privilege and non-opinion work-product. No implied waiver of the company's opinion work-product occurred.[105]

The next assault upon *Diversified* came from the Third Circuit in *Westinghouse Electric Corp. v. Republic of the Philippines*, 951 F.2d 1414, (3d Cir. 1991), holding that disclosures by companies to the SEC and Department of Justice (DOJ) during investigations conducted by these agencies waived the attorney-client privilege and work-product doctrine. In rejecting *Diversified, Westinghouse* adopted the reasoning of the D.C. Circuit in *Permian. Westinghouse* agreed that there is no waiver of the attorney-client privilege where the disclosure serves the purpose of enabling clients to obtain informed legal advice.[106] However, *Westinghouse* viewed the justification for permitting selective waiver in *Diversified* (the encouragement of corporate internal investigations, and their voluntary disclosure to government agencies), as not serving the purpose of the attorney-client privilege, *i.e.*, encouraging full disclosure to one's attorney in order to obtain informed legal assistance, and promoting the attorney-client relationship. *Westinghouse* also held that there had been a waiver of the work-product doctrine as against all other adversaries by the disclosure of work-product to the SEC and the DOJ. *Westinghouse* further held that, even if the SEC and the DOJ had made an agreement to keep the documents disclosed to them confidential, there was still an implied waiver of the work-product doctrine.[107] The *Westinghouse* court applied

---

104 856 F.2d 619, 623-26 (4th Cir. 1988), *cert. denied*, 490 U.S. 1011 (1989).

105 The Fourth Circuit rejected the extension of subject matter waiver to opinion work-product for two reasons. One, opinion work-product is accorded great protection by the courts, and two, the underlying rationale for subject matter waiver has little application in the context of a pure expression of legal theory or legal opinion. The court considered that the latter is unlikely to be used both as a sword and as a shield in the trial of a case. 856 F.2d at 626.

106 For example, disclosure to an agent assisting the attorney in giving legal advice to the client, or disclosure to co-defendants or co-litigants.

107 *Westinghouse* indicated that a "different result" may have been reached if the SEC and the DOJ were not the corporation's adversaries, and had agreed to keep the material disclosed to them confidential. The adversarial relationship in *Westinghouse* did not permit such a "different result." The *Westinghouse* court thereby agreed with *In re Chrysler Motors Corp. Overnight Eval. Program Litigation*, 860 F.2d 844, 846-47 (8th Cir. 1988), that a disclosure to an adversary waives the work-product doctrine as to all other adversaries, even if the disclosure was pursuant to a confidentiality agreement. The *Westinghouse* court rejected the D.C. Circuit's "fairness" doctrine, which considers *inter alia*, the disclosing party's expectations of confidentiality, and *In re John Doe*, 662 F.2d 1073, 1081-82 (4th Cir. 1981) which also held that, to effect a forfeiture of work product by waiver, disclosure must occur in circumstances in which the attorney cannot reasonably expect to limit the future use of the otherwise protected material. In this latter connection, *see also In re M&L Business Machine Co. Inc.*, 161 B.R. 689, 696 (D.Colo. 1993), indicating that a confidentiality agreement is a factor to be considered on the issue of implied

its holding of waiver to both opinion and non-opinion work-product. *See*, 951 F.2d at 1431 n.17, finding the distinction between the two types of work-product not "to be significant on this record."

In 1993, the Second Circuit rejected *Diversified*, and aligned itself with *Westinghouse*, in *In re Steinhardt Partners, L.P. (Salomon Brothers Treasury Litigation v. Steinhardt Partners, L.P.)*,[108] *Steinhardt* found that a trader's voluntary submission of a legal memorandum to the SEC, with whom the trader stood in an adversarial position, waived the protection of the work-product doctrine. A notice reading "FOIA Confidential Treatment Requested" appeared on the memorandum, but there was no agreement that the SEC would maintain the confidentiality of the memorandum. Significantly, however, the *Steinhardt* court declined to adopt a *per se* rule that all voluntary disclosures to the government waive the work-product doctrine. Indeed, in articulating its reasons for not adopting a *per se* rule, the Second Circuit instructively stated that:

> Establishing a rigid rule would fail to anticipate situations in which the disclosing party and the government may share a common interest in developing legal theories and analyzing information, or situations in which the SEC and the disclosing party have entered into an explicit agreement that the SEC will maintain the confidentiality of the disclosed materials.

9 F.3d at 236.

The Second Circuit, therefore, has joined the D.C. Circuit in remaining open to the effectiveness of confidentiality agreements in appropriate cases to preserve the protection of work-product voluntarily disclosed to the government.

In 1997, both the First Circuit and the Federal Circuit rejected the limited waiver doctrine of *Diversified. See Genentech, Inc. v. United States International Trade Commission*,[109] and *United States v. Massachusetts Institute of Technology*.[110]

In the *MIT* case, the university, a government contractor, was found to have forfeited its attorney-client privilege and work-product protection by voluntarily disclosing documents to the Defense Contract Audit Agency, the auditing arm of the Department of Defense, and a potential adversary. However, the First Circuit went

---

waiver of the work-product doctrine. *Accord: United States v. Polichemi*, No. 94 CR 555, 1996 WL 332680, at *1 (N.D.Ill. 1996). *But see In re Worlds of Wonder Securities Litigation*, 147 F.R.D. 208, 211-12 (N.D.Cal. 1992), agreeing with *Westinghouse*, and finding waiver of work-product protection by voluntary production of documents to the SEC, even if the corporation had expressly reserved all of its rights, submitted information confidentially, and requested confidential treatment from the SEC's FOIA officer.

108   9 F.3d 230 (1993).

109   122 F.3d 1409, 1417 (Fed. Cir. 1997). *Genentech* was not a government disclosure case but, in the context of considering the issue of inadvertent disclosure during discovery, the court considered *Diversified*, and noted its rejection of the doctrine of limited waiver.

110   129 F.3d 681, 686-87 (1st Cir. 1997).

out of its way to note that its decision did not address two issues: (i) when the disclosure of one document warrants forfeiture of protection for a different but related document, and (ii) whether selective disclosure waives ordinary work-product protection, but not that for opinion work-product.

X. Reminders to Consider

Counsel and all corporate officials requesting and participating in an internal investigation should be constantly aware of and sensitive to the desirability of creating and preserving, to the fullest practicable extent, the corporate attorney-client privilege and work-product protection. In particular, before undertaking an internal corporate investigation counsel should re-familiarize themselves with both the underlying policies behind, and the legal principles attendant to, the corporate attorney-client privilege and work-product doctrine, including the circumstances in which a waiver of the privilege or doctrine may occur. Moreover, whenever the report of an internal corporate investigation is voluntarily released to any government agency it should be understood that the agency is likely to be regarded as an actual or potential adversary. Such a release will, therefore, probably waive the attorney-client privilege and the protection for at least any factual work-product. Corporate counsel should, therefore, attempt to negotiate the strongest possible confidentiality agreement with the government agency to whom the report is released. Additionally, corporate counsel should consult with the agency's FOIA officer, to ensure that the latter will accord the report the maximum protections against release available under the Freedom of Information Act.

XI. Other specialized Privileges and Legal Theories for Protecting Documents

In addition to attorney-client privilege and the work-product doctrine, counsel should also consider the possible application of other more specialized and less well-established privileges and theories for protecting investigative materials: for example, self evaluative and medical peer review privileges, statutory protections, and possible copyright protections. Only the self-evaluative privilege is discussed herein.

XII. Self-Evaluative Privilege

If a company's compliance department is doing its job, it will identify operational problems and report back to management so that those problems can be addressed. Compliance department reports can be an attractive source of information for government investigators or civil litigants. Many times these reports are prepared as part of the company's normal business operations and are not done at the direction of corporate counsel. While the state of the law remains unsettled, it may be possible to protect these reports from disclosure, at least as to private litigants, under the "self-evaluative privilege."

The qualified privilege of self-evaluation, to the extent it has been recognized, shields from discovery information:

(1) resulting from a critical self-analysis undertaken by the party seeking protection;

(2) which is representative of information in which there is a strong public interest in fostering; and

(3) which might not be generated absent restrictions on its disclosure.[111]

The self-evaluative privilege is believed to have been first recognized in *Bredice v. Doctors Hospital, Inc.*[112] There, pursuant to accreditation requirements, the hospital held staff meetings in which the professional staff evaluated the care and treatment of patients. In a medical malpractice action against the hospital, the administratrix of Bredice's estate sought discovery of the minutes of the staff meeting in which Bredice's treatment or death had been discussed. The court refused discovery of that information since review of the effectiveness of treatments was invaluable to the general quality of healthcare, and physicians would be unwilling to participate in such investigations if the candid evaluations were later subject to discovery in a subsequent malpractice action.

The self-evaluative privilege has been widely adopted in the medical peer review context[113] and has been extended by some courts to other areas, including employment discrimination litigation, where it has been used to protect the subjective, evaluative portions of employer information and affirmative action reports. The privilege also has been recognized in cases involving antitrust law, product safety, environmental compliance, and securities law.[114] However, the privilege has not been universally accepted[115] and limitations have been placed on it when it has been recognized. For example, only subjective impressions and opinions may be

---

111   Note, "The Privilege of Self-Critical Analysis," 96 Harv.L.Rev. 1083, 1086 (1983).

112   50 F.R.D. 249 (D.D.C. 1970), *aff'd*, 479 F.2d 920 (D.C. Cir. 1973).

113   *See* D. Leonard, *Codifying a Privilege of Self-Critical Analysis*, 25 Harv. J. on Legis. 113, 119-20 (1988).

114   *See, e.g., Banks v. Lockheed-Georgia Co.*, 53 F.R.D. 283 (N.D. Ga. 1971) (company's assessment of equal employment opportunity practices); *In Re Crazy Eddies Securities Litigation*, 792 F. Supp. 197 (E.D.N.Y. 1992)(securities law); *Keyes v. Lenoir Rhyne College*, 552 F.2d 579 (4th Cir.) (academic peer reviews), *cert. denied*, 434 U.S. 904 (1977); *Granger v. National R.R. Passenger Corp.*, 116 F.R.D. 507 (E.D. Pa. 1987) (railroad accident investigations); *Lloyd v. Cessna Aircraft Co.*, 74 F.R.D. 518 (E.D. Tenn. 1977) (product quality assessments). *See, also,* Jeffrey M. Kaplan, Joseph E. Murphy, and Winthrop M. Swenson, *Compliance Programs and the Corporate Sentencing Guidelines*, § 5.36 (1995)(collecting cases).

115   *See, e.g., Spencer Savings Bank, SLA v. Excell Mortgage Corp.*, 960 F. Supp. 835 (D.N.J. 1997)(collecting cases rejecting, limiting and recognizing the "self-evaluative" or "self-critical analysis" privilege); *United States v. Dexter Corp.*, 132 F.R.D. 8 (D. Conn. 1990)(rejecting corporate "self-evaluative" privilege in action brought by government to enforce Clean Water Act); Witten *v. A.H. Smith & Co.*, 100 F.R.D. 446, 449-65 (D. Md. 1984), *aff'd*, 785 F.2d 306 (4th Cir. 1986) (equal employment opportunity suit context).

privileged, not objective facts.[116] Importantly, the privilege probably is not applicable when documents have been subpoenaed by a government agency as part of an administrative or criminal proceeding.[117] Even in the case of a challenge made by a civil litigant, the privilege is qualified and can be overcome by showing of extraordinary circumstance or special need.[118]

The self-evaluative privilege may offer some means of protecting from disclosure compliance reports or other documents and information prepared by a company in an otherwise non-privileged situation. By itself, the self-evaluative privilege, even if recognized in the jurisdiction in which the company is located, will not protect it against the disclosure of documents subpoenaed by the government. Nevertheless, it may offer a basis for resisting disclosure of sensitive reports to private civil litigants. That could be extremely important if the government has not sought such reports in a concurrent proceeding. A company involved in routine "self-evaluative" practices should consider whether the reports it creates can be protected from disclosure, as well as the likely consequences disclosure can bring.

---

116   *See, e.g., Webb v. Westinghouse Electric Corp.*, 81 F.R.D. 431, 434 (E.D. Pa. 1978).

117   *See FTC v. TRW, Inc.*, 628 F.2d 207, 210 (D.C. Cir. 1980)(action to enforce FTC subpoena); *Emerson Electric Co. v. Schlesinger*, 609 F.2d 898, 907 (8th Cir. 1979)(motion to preclude sharing of information between EEOC and the Department of Labor); *United States v. Dexter Corp.*, 132 F.R.D. 8 (D. Conn. 1990)(action to enforce Clean Water Act). *See, e.g., Federal Trade Commission v. TRW, Inc.*, 628 F.2d 207, 210 (D.C. Cir. 1980). See, also, *In Re Grand Jury Proceedings*, 861 F. Supp. 386, 388-89 (D. Md. 1994).

118   *Reichhold Chemicals, Inc. v. Textron, Inc.*, 157 F.R.D. 522, 527 (N.D. Fla. 1994).

CHAPTER 4:
HOW THE INVESTIGATION STARTS

I. Introduction

While internal investigations can be performed for a variety of reasons, most typically an internal corporate investigation is generated by a governmental investigation of possible illegal corporate conduct. The company may learn of such conduct in a variety of ways, including:

- from the report or statements of government auditors;
- from third parties such as customers;
- from its own employees or on a company hotline;
- by receiving a grand jury or other governmental subpoena;
- by having federal investigators show up at the company's door with a search warrant;
- by learning that government investigators are asking questions of company employees, business associates, customers or even competitors;
- from the filing of a civil suit against the company.

II. Should an Internal Investigation be Conducted

Once the company learns of potential criminal conduct, the question arises whether to conduct an internal investigation. This decision should ultimately be made by the board of directors. Board members have a fiduciary duty to the company to insure that it is not engaged in illegal conduct and must attempt to protect the company from potential civil or criminal liability.[1]

However, the company needs to be aware of the risks of conducting an internal investigation. The potentially most serious risk is that a report of counsel, written for the company and detailing the results of the investigation, may have to be disclosed to the government and, possibly, to third party civil litigants.[2] If this occurs,

---

1   *See, e.g., Caremark Int'l Inc. Derivative Lit.*, 698 A.2d 959, 970 (Del. Ch. 1996).

2   *See* Chapters 3 and 5.

the result may be that the company will, in effect, have paid to prepare the government's case and will likely give the government the strongest case possible. In addition, an internal investigation can turn employees against the company, or make them so concerned about their own liability that they cooperate with the government and become witnesses against the company. In short, an internal investigation may well be necessary, but the company must carefully consider the reasons for doing it and how it should be done.

In considering whether to conduct an internal investigation, the company needs to consider how serious the ultimate ramifications may be. The fact that an investigation may be commenced by an agency other than the Department of Justice, or because it may not be commenced through the use of a subpoena, does not mean that the government intends the matter to be civil in nature. There are many agencies of the federal government that have statutory authority to refer matters to the Justice Department for criminal prosecution. It is really the nature of the conduct, not the identity of the agency that commences the investigation, that should be important to the company. Once there is reason to believe that there has been any conduct which may be the basis for criminal charges and/or civil liability, management should consider directing that an internal investigation be conducted in order to learn what occurred.

The need to learn the nature and extent of the problem, and the desire to remedy it, as well as the requirements of government contracts and voluntary disclosure programs, all weigh heavily in favor of conducting an internal investigation.[3] The purpose of the investigation will be to learn the nature and extent of wrongdoing to allow the company to minimize its liability, and to obtain legal advice from its counsel based on full knowledge of the facts.

III. Benefits of an Internal Investigation

An internal investigation may help the company avoid criminal proceedings completely, and avoiding a corporate indictment is of paramount importance. However, even if criminal proceedings are not entirely avoided, the fact that an internal investigation was conducted can dramatically reduce the company's exposure. For example, under the Federal Organizational Sentencing Guidelines, which went into effect on November 1, 1991, corporate self-reporting of violations may reduce criminal fines by millions of dollars. Reductions are also possible if the company has previously instituted a compliance program. Voluntary disclosure, in certain circumstances, may help convince the government not to prosecute or, at a

---

3   Board members also have a duty to investigate whether corporate assets have been or are being diverted for private use, if for no other reason than to file suit to obtain their return. The Board may learn that there is indeed a basis for filing a suit, and yet decide, nonetheless, not to file. If, prior to making this decision, an internal investigation is conducted, and there are valid reasons for not proceeding with litigation, the fact that the Board initiated an investigation may subsequently protect the Board members, in the event of a shareholder derivative suit.

minimum, may have an impact on sentencing.[4] Moreover, an internal investigation will also help the company deal with any civil litigation.

IV. Type of Investigation

The reasons for conducting the investigation will generally determine what type of investigation should be done. If an investigation is undertaken in response to government action, such as by a subpoena from an Inspector General or grand jury, or to defend against a civil suit or some other event external to the company, the investigation will normally be reactive in nature. The matters investigated will likely be limited in scope to the specific matters that are of interest to the third party.

If, however, the investigation is generated by the company, to determine whether there was a violation of company policy and procedures (or even, in some instances, government regulation), the investigation will often be more broadly focused. In this type of investigation, counsel can analyze the facts and decide on the best strategy without the pressure of the government demanding documents and interviewing employees, and without the concern that a criminal investigation generates.

In the context of a government investigation, it may not immediately be clear what conduct the government is investigating. Particularly in a regulated industry, such as healthcare, there are so many potential regulations that may have been violated, even if only in a small way, that the company is often forced to scramble just to learn precisely what is being investigated.

One way to do this is to debrief employees who have been interviewed by the government although, of course, it is preferable to interview employees prior to their being interviewed by the government. A subsequent debriefing of the employee is helpful, but not as critical as interviewing the employee in advance.[5]

Counsel can meet with the prosecutor or government agent and, depending on their willingness to talk at an early stage of the investigation, get some particularized understanding of what is being investigated. However, it is unlikely the government will provide anything significant early in an investigation. Between interviewing employees and talking to the prosecutor or government agent, and others with knowledge in the relevant areas, the company should be able to get a reasonable grasp of the government's interest if the government has not made it immediately clear.

V. Choice of Counsel for the Investigation

Whether the company should have its internal investigation guided by in-house counsel or by retained counsel, is often decided on factors such as the size of the

---

4   *See* Chapter 8 on the Corporate Sentencing Guidelines and Compliance Programs.

5   Employee interviews raise an entire range of issues, from employee rights to potential issues of obstruction of justice, which are discussed in Chapter 5.

company, its budget, the nature of the investigation, the role of the in-house counsel in the matter being investigated, his experience in conducting investigations and whether litigation of the issues is anticipated. There are some advantages to each option but, when the company is being investigated by the government, the balance clearly tilts towards using retained counsel.

It is important for the company to recognize that, over the past 20 years, conducting an internal investigation has become as much a legal specialty as any other complex area of law. Numerous issues arise in such investigations which require the lawyer conducting it to be knowledgeable in civil commercial law, white collar criminal law, parallel proceedings, and other areas of law. The dramatic expansion of criminal laws, the use of agency inspector generals and the implementation of corporate sentencing guidelines all further complicate what was already a field littered with potential landmines for any attorney who is not extremely experienced in this area.

Using in-house counsel will, of course, be less costly and in-house counsel will start out with a better knowledge of the company and its personnel as well as its policies and procedures. However, if the conduct under investigation could involve or lead to a criminal investigation or indictment, or even a civil trial, retained counsel will need to be involved in any event. To the extent the same outside counsel will be able to handle all functions from the start, the cost may be minimized.

Retained counsel normally bring certain advantages to the investigation, including:

- Greater investigative experience;
- More trial experience. This will be very important in the event of a criminal or civil trial, as the company will not have to switch horses midstream from in-house to retained counsel;
- More extensive experience dealing with criminal statutes and prosecutors;
- Prosecutors typically believe that retained counsel have more independence than in-house counsel, and may be more candid and willing to work with them.

There are, moreover, some specific disadvantages involved in using in-house counsel to conduct the investigation:

- Prosecutors may view an in-house counsel as a business rather than a legal advisor, and may try to obtain his or her investigative materials, especially if he or she is also an officer or director of the company;[6]
- In-house counsel may be viewed by employees as part of the corporate management team, a perception which can put a strain on relations between management and employees and may possibly raise a conflict between them. Additionally, there will always be concern that an in-house counsel may try

---

6   A claim of attorney-client privilege for communications between the company and in-house counsel may be susceptible to challenge on the grounds that it was undertaken for a purpose other than legal advice. *See, e.g., In Re John Doe Corp.*, 675 F.2d 482, 488 (2d Cir. 1982).

to shape testimony, even inadvertently, because of his or her close relationship with management.[7]

- An in-house counsel may become a necessary or important witness, either because he or she rendered opinions on the conduct in question prior to the investigation or because corporate employees under investigation may assert an advice-of-counsel defense.[8]

If the decision is made to use outside retained counsel, a further question is whether to use the company's regular outside counsel or specially selected investigative counsel. Regular outside counsel may have the advantage of knowing the company's business and will likely already be known to its top management. However, regular outside counsel will most likely be a corporate lawyer. For this reason, as a practical matter, even if the law firm of the regular outside counsel is retained, an investigative lawyer/litigator from the same firm will normally be brought in to actually conduct the investigation, and this lawyer will likely have little or no knowledge about how the company operates.

There are many good reasons to use specially selected counsel with experience in internal investigations. Investigative counsel have more experience dealing with prosecutors, regulators and investigators, and will be more familiar with relevant criminal statutes. Moreover, regular outside counsel may have previously given legal advice that is within the scope of the investigation and may be "conflicted out" from representing the company, or may even be subpoenaed as a witness by the government (or the opposing party in civil litigation).

As in the case of in-house counsel, prosecutors may try to obtain documents generated by regular outside counsel, claiming they contain business, not legal, advice. Prosecutors may not trust regular outside counsel because they are viewed as tied to the company by friendship as well as by fees. In fact, it may be difficult for regular outside counsel to conduct the investigation because of existing personal relationships with members of the company's management who may be under investigation.

The company's general counsel must feel comfortable with retained counsel's ability, both as investigators and, in the event of trial (either civil or criminal), as trial lawyers. The need to have lawyers who are experienced in white collar cases is obvious in the context of a criminal investigation. The investigative counsel retained by the company should be experienced in conducting internal investigations, as well as handling grand jury investigations and criminal trials. He or she should also

---

7   Of course, even the appearance of any such conduct can lead to obstruction of justice concerns. *See* Chapter 5.

8   in the absence of retaining outside counsel, an "advice of counsel" defense based upon advice provided to the company by in-house counsel may be unpersuasive. *See generally, United St. v. Beech-Nut Nutrition Corp.*, 871 F.2d 1181, 1194 (2d Cir. 1989).

be experienced in civil litigation, as civil lawsuits often follow criminal prosecutions—and sometimes proceed at the same time.[9]

As in any competitive activity—and investigations and trials are both very competitive enterprises—prosecutors look at the ability of their adversaries when investigating and deciding whether to bring criminal cases, and one factor in their decision whether to take a case to trial may be the knowledge and experience of opposing counsel.

Many lawyers believe that the retention of an attorney who formerly worked as a prosecutor can often provide subtle advantages to the company under investigation. Government prosecutors and agents may view former colleagues with less suspicion then they would an attorney who has been on the defense side of the bar for his or her entire career. While selection of even the best counsel is not a guarantee of success, selection of a former prosecutor as counsel may help influence the tenor of the investigative "relationship" between company and prosecutor.

Experienced outside counsel will be able to recommend counsel to represent employees who find themselves to be subjects or targets of the investigation. The selection of counsel for company employees is extremely important since counsel for the company and counsel for its employees will often combine resources and work together to collect information essential to compiling an effective response to the investigation. In certain cases, a combined strategy protected by a joint defense agreement is possible and appropriate.[10] Ideally, all counsel under a joint defense agreement will independently develop and maintain good working relationships with the prosecutor.

VI. Early Analysis by Counsel

It is usually possible, early on during the course of an internal investigation, to get a sense of whether there was any wrongdoing, even if substantial detail still needs to be filled in. As soon as possible in the process, it is critical that the company and counsel consider best and worst case scenarios and make a judgment of what they can live with and what they cannot. This is one of counsel's most important functions. Assuming there is something more than *de minimis* criminal conduct, and the company lacks a compliance program, it is very likely the government will seek some sort of criminal conviction. What the penalty will be, in the event of a conviction or other disposition, is one of the most critical issues in the case. From the standpoint of a corporate executive, incarceration is typically the worst punishment. From the company's perspective, the worst thing that can happen is to be put out of business. Thus, counsel should analyze early on, to the extent possible, what the company's exposure could be. The conclusions reached from that analysis will often determine the course the company decides to navigate.

---

9   *See* Chapter 6 on Parallel Proceedings.

10   *See* Chapter 7 on Multiple Representation.

In addition to criminal issues, there are issues of civil proceedings to consider and, for companies that are government contractors, possible debarment issues. If the company needs the government to survive, debarment can be a death penalty for a company. Investigations that involve parallel proceedings are dangerous for any business, particularly those that are contractors with the federal government. A government contractor can be suspended or debarred for a conviction or a civil judgment for many different things including lack of business honesty that affects the present responsibility of a government contractor.[11] But a government contractor can also be suspended from its contract with the federal government even without a conviction or civil judgment. There is substantial discretion for the government to suspend contracts pending the conclusion of an investigation or trial.[12]

Depending on the circumstances, counsel may advise the company that the most effective strategy is to cooperate with investigators. Providing investigators the information they need to reach an investigative conclusion may be the most effective means of terminating the investigation before it has a devastating effect on resources and reputation. The longer an investigation proceeds, the less inclined prosecutors are to be lenient, because of all the work they have already put into the investigation. Cooperation may include making employees, including corporate officers, available for interview, and producing documents without requirement of a subpoena. It can also include a "voluntary" disclosure by providing investigators with the report written by counsel regarding the subject under investigation.

Of course, cooperation often is not the best legal strategy. A target of a criminal investigation, with no likely prospect of an acceptable disposition, might conclude that it is not in its interest to offer assistance to investigators. Under such circumstances, counsel should consider advising his or her client to decline to participate in voluntary interviews or to produce documents not covered by subpoena. There is usually little to be gained, and potentially much to lose, for the subject or target of a criminal investigation who agrees to sit down with investigators to "set the record straight."

Although cooperation, including "voluntary" disclosure, may pose certain hazards for the subject of an investigation, many companies may not have the option of *not* cooperating. A "non-cooperative" strategy can get complicated quickly in the context of parallel proceedings. A health care company may have no choice but to cooperate with administrative regulators if it desires to maintain its license or ability to participate in the Medicare program. The corporate defendant in a *qui tam* case may suffer a default if it refuses to answer discovery.

While non-cooperation brings with it the likelihood of adverse administrative and civil consequences, the risks of cooperation can be even greater. Sworn deposition

---

11   *See* 48 CFR § 9-406-2.

12   *See* 48 CFR § 9.407-1

testimony or documents in the civil case, otherwise not available to criminal prosecutors due to the protections offered by the Fifth Amendment, may turn out to be just the evidence the government needs to prove its criminal case. Moreover, a judicial decision in one proceeding can affect the company's ability to defend itself in a parallel case.[13] Counsel must walk the company through all these issues in determining investigative strategy. [14]

VII. Press Coverage

Press coverage can be harmful depending on how the press reports news of the investigation and how the company reacts. It is wise for the company to retain an experienced public relations advisor to counsel it on how to deal with the press, but it is critical that nothing be released to the press without counsel's approval. In the event of a criminal investigation, the spokesman for the company, if anything is to be said, should be counsel. In any event, there should be only one person speaking for the company.

Before making any public statements, the company should consider the effect on the governmental agency or prosecutor who is conducting the investigation. The press can react very quickly to the news of an investigation of a company. Corporations frequently feel a need to respond to press inquiries at the start of an investigation, before counsel has a grasp of the facts. A complete denial of wrongdoing made prior to knowing all the facts can later redound negatively to the company when dealing with the prosecutor. It can also affect how the public views the company if the statement has to be retracted or changed as additional facts emerge.

VIII. Statements that may Affect Stock Price

Once an investigation commences, any number of events and decisions related to the investigation may affect the company's stock price, including whether or not to announce the fact of the investigation. What the company says, or does not say, can lead to shareholder suits and a possible investigation by the Securities and Exchange Commission or other agency.[15] It is critical that advice from qualified securities counsel be sought if there is any chance this will be an issue. No statements about future earnings should be made until such discussions have taken place. In

---

13   A criminal conviction of the defendant in a parallel proceeding may be *res judicata* in a concurrent civil suit thereby depriving the party of defending that case. However, due to differences in standards in proof, the converse is not true. A favorable disposition in the criminal case will not necessarily end a civil suit for damages or an administrative investigation of non-criminal charges. *See, One Lot Emerald Cut Stones v. United States*, 409 U.S. 232 (1972).

14   The existence of parallel proceedings complicates all but a complete "non-cooperation" strategy, since it may be impossible to keep information provided in one proceeding from being introduced in another.

15   Depending on the nature and extent of the problem, the corporation may have a duty to disclose facts material to its business under the securities laws if the information, if disclosed, may be material to investors. *TSC Industries, Inc. v. Northway, Inc.*, 426 U.S. 438, 449 (1976).

addition, the company should advise employees with knowledge of the investigation not to trade company stock based on that knowledge.

IX. Get Control of the Documents and Computer Files

The fact that the company is under governmental investigation will likely quickly spread throughout the company or, at a minimum, those parts of the company that are affected. It may well become public knowledge. If wrongdoing that is the subject of the investigation exists, it is not uncommon to have employees responsible for the wrongful conduct attempt to destroy evidence of their involvement. That can include destruction or alteration of documents, deletion of computer files and intimidation of employees. It is critical that the company do everything possible to prevent such activity because such actions will make the company's internal investigation much more difficult and potentially cause the government to take a much harsher stance against the company.

As a first step, counsel should designate an employee, working under the direction of counsel, to locate the most critical documents, to be placed under counsel's control. If the documents are needed for company business, copies should be made or the originals should be made available under controlled circumstances. While segregating these documents may inconvenience some company personnel, doing so may ultimately prove to be one of the wisest moves the company can make.[16]

Computer files must be immediately safeguarded. Many companies do regular backups but access to the backups is often not secure. Backup files often can be checked out by many employees in the company. If computers require employees to sign-on, employees under suspicion should be shut out of the system or what they can do on the system should be limited. Virus programs should be up to date as an increasing problem in such cases is virus sabotage.

X. Notices to Employees

Employees should be instructed that they are not to produce corporate documents to any third party, including the government, and that any request for corporate documents should be brought to the attention of counsel. Employees should also be advised to inform counsel if they are contacted by the government for an interview. They should be further advised that they should not create new documentation discussing the allegations under investigation; that work should be left to counsel, who can protect the product he or she creates.

XI. Product or Brand Name Harm

Depending on the nature of the company's business, company officials and counsel should also consider the potential for damage to the company's business that may result from the investigation. For a consumer-oriented business, there may be a

---

16   *See* Chapter 5.

danger of damage to the reputation of a brand name product. More frequently, in all types of business, there may be reason for concern about the possible effects on customer loyalty. If, for example, an engine parts manufacturer were being investigated for allegedly supplying defective parts under a government sub-contract, some or all of the company's customers might reconsider using the company as their supplier, once news of the investigation was made public. Where such potential dangers exist, the company must decide ahead of time on a strategy for dealing with them. The company may decide to notify some or all customers that an investigation is underway, before news of it becomes public, so that the company can get its side of the story out first. If such a strategy is chosen, however, it is important that whatever the company may say is not something that could be detrimental to the company later.

XII. Plan in Advance

These are some of the myriad issues that may arise when a company comes under government investigation. Rather than consider them under pressure, a better policy is to have advance plans on how to handle certain situations that may arise.

Instituting a compliance program should be one part of such a planning process.[17] But there are many other considerations that go into managing a crisis arising as result of a governmental investigation. One such step is to educate management about the realities of having the government look into corporate affairs. Management should be aware that corporate officers and employees may be prosecuted for corporate wrongdoing; that the company can be held responsible for any act by an employee if within that employee's authority and if the acts were done to benefit the company, even if contrary to company policy. When these principles are taught to employees and management, it is more likely that criminal conduct will be discovered early or potentially be avoided altogether.

---

17   *See* Chapter 8.

CHAPTER 5:
CONDUCTING THE
INVESTIGATION

There are many subjects that must be considered under the rubric "Conducting the Investigation." In the course of conducting an internal investigation generated as a result of a governmental inquiry or investigation, counsel for the company will almost always need to (a) interview employees, (b) review documents, (c) report the facts and render legal advice to their client; and (d) deal with the prosecutor(s). It is those subjects that are covered in this chapter.

I. Interviewing Employees

When a company comes under criminal investigation, the company itself faces potential criminal liability, but the illegal activity was actually the result of specific actions by one or more of the company's employees.[1] At the same time, it is usually these same employees who have the requisite knowledge to allow the company to learn the facts necessary to defend itself.

In most of these situations, there will be no attorney-client privilege between the company's counsel and the individual employees involved (although, as discussed below, counsel's communications with those employees may, in most situations, be protected from disclosure by the attorney-client privilege belonging to the company or by the work product doctrine). Moreover, voluntary disclosure programs (for example, with the Department of Justice or the Department of Defense) may require the company to disclose to the government information that has been provided by employees and that may lead to potential charges against those employees. Of course, the company may, in any case, decide to do this of its own accord for strategic reasons, even without the requirements of a disclosure program.

This raises serious questions which must be confronted by counsel very early in the investigation. Should employees be advised to obtain separate legal counsel? Should the company provide such counsel? What are the company's obligations to employees? What are the company's options if employees refuse to cooperate?

---

1   The term "employees," as used here, includes officers and directors of the company.

II. Preparing for Employee Interviews

As a general rule, before interviewing critical employees, it is useful for counsel to become familiar with the facts by interviewing less critical employees and by reviewing documents. Referring to relevant documents can help employees to remember events and can help counsel determine whether the employees are telling the truth.

When the company is conducting an internal investigation without the pressure of a governmental investigation, it can set its own agenda of how the investigation should proceed. Counsel will usually begin by interviewing more tangentially involved employees, who can provide background and help build a case against the employees who may have been more directly involved in the wrongdoing.

With the pressure of a government investigation, however, counsel will normally not have that luxury. The order in which employees are interviewed in any particular case is often determined by the nature of the investigation and by the actions of the government investigators, who may interview specific employees or place them before a grand jury.

When the government is conducting an investigation, counsel must go directly and immediately to the employees with the most knowledge, and may need to interview employees who are suspected of being involved in the wrongdoing before interviewing employees who played a lesser role or who have only second-hand knowledge. The most involved employees will normally be the ones who have the greatest ability to convey relevant facts and, in such circumstances, it is critical for counsel to learn as much as possible as quickly as possible. Counsel should also interview quickly all employees who have been subpoenaed or who the company believes will be subpoenaed. Any employee who has already been interviewed by the government should also be promptly interviewed by counsel to try to learn the direction of the government's investigation. Those employees should be asked whether they know of others who have been interviewed by the government and what documents were of particular interest to the government during their interview.

In all cases, the effectiveness of an interview depends on the complexity of the investigation, the background knowledge obtained by counsel prior to the interview and, most importantly, whether counsel have had a prior opportunity to review documents. But it is often not possible to do a thorough document review and analysis prior to employee interviews, both because of the pressure of the government investigation and because the documents may be voluminous, complicated, or not immediately available. Under such circumstances, it is rare that all pertinent information will be obtained in the first interview.

In planning employee interviews, it is also important to consider the circumstances of the interview. Whether or not the government is involved in the investigation, most employees will not be happy about being interviewed and many will evidence concern, particularly at the thought of implicating themselves or a co-worker. Even those willing to cooperate will not want the fact that they are cooperating widely known. It is, therefore, very important for counsel to consider, prior to setting up the interview, where it will take place and how the employee will be notified of the interview. Counsel will want to insure, with all the pressures already built into the situation, that the employee is not worried about his or her co-workers knowing of the interview.

III. Conducting the Interviews

It is helpful to have non-contentious interviews to the extent possible. Background and open-ended questions should be used at the beginning of the interview, together with a non-confrontational review of documents. More contentious questions and a cross-examination style, if necessary, should be held off for later. Counsel should never inject their own personal opinions into the interview or suggest a theory or set of facts to an employee, either to help the employee recollect events or for any other reason. Apart from concerns about avoiding possible charges of obstruction of justice, in cases where the government may also be involved (as discussed below), planting suggestions in an employee's mind may interfere with counsel's ability to discover what really happened.

IV. Ethical Concerns

In conducting interviews, it is also important that the employees feel confident that their comments will remain confidential. However, this is often something that the interviewer cannot realistically promise. Clearly, the information will normally be passed on to the company, or at least those persons in the company in charge of the investigation. Depending on whether the company decides to cooperate with government investigators, the information may also be disclosed to the government. If the employees incriminate themselves in the course of an interview, they may, by cooperating, talk themselves out of a job or into jail.

Because of these issues, there is a potential conflict of interest between the company and its employees, and this raises serious ethical concerns for counsel conducting such an interview. Counsel for the company must balance competing factors early in the investigation. Counsel's first and primary job is to gather facts so as to be able to give their client legal advice. To do that, counsel must interview employees effectively, but avoid conflict of interest situations while doing so. Counsel must maintain the company's attorney-client privilege and avoid inadvertent disclosure of confidential information, but still retain the ability to cooperate with the government if it is deemed necessary.

One helpful step in reducing the risk of later accusations of conflict of interest is the use of a written script, described later in this chapter. The advice and warnings given in this script will, among other things, clarify for the employee the purpose of the interview, the employee's rights and options, and the nature and extent of the confidentiality and privileged status that will attach to whatever is said in the interview to come. It will make clear to the employee that he or she is not personally represented by company counsel and that the attorney-client privilege belongs to the company and not the employee. Counsel may in fact have an ethical obligation to do that.[2]

V. Retaining Separate Counsel for Employees

The clearest example of a situation where a conflict of interest between the company and its employees may arise is where an employee has committed a criminal act that could be imputed to the company under the theory of vicarious liability. In such a case, the company may well have to consider whether separate counsel should be obtained for employees and whether each employee with potential liability needs a separate counsel or whether they can be represented together as a group, or possibly in sub-groups. Other issues which must be considered, if separate counsel are to be retained, include the selection and payment of employees' counsel as well as joint privileges and joint defense agreements.[3]

Unfortunately, due to the nature of how investigations proceed, conflicts of interest may not become apparent until the employee is actually being interviewed. The fact that there is a potential conflict does not necessarily mean that the employee must obtain his or her own counsel. It is important, however, for the company's counsel to advise the employee at the start that they represent the company and not the employee.

It is frequently asked whether, even in the absence of a clear conflict of interest, employees should also be advised of their right to have their own counsel. In most instances, absent state law, state bar requirement, company or union policy, or a provision in the company's by-laws, employees have no right to have their own counsel present while being interviewed by the company's counsel. The company does not stand in the shoes of the government and, since the company is a private entity, the employee has no constitutionally protected rights in an internal investigation conducted by the company.

Offering to provide separate counsel for employees may, in fact, make the investigation more difficult. Employees who are concerned by the investigation are likely to accept such an offer, if it is made. That will almost inevitably slow down the investigative process, since each employee will want time to consult with his or her counsel and the employee's counsel may then advise their client not to speak to the company's counsel at all.

On the other hand, there are advantages to obtaining separate counsel, if it is done for potentially culpable employees, in that the company can thereby separate itself from the employees who committed the wrongdoing. Also, to the extent the company is paying for an employee's counsel, the employee is less likely to become

---

2   *See United States v. Inter. Brotherhood of Teamsters*, 119 F.3d 210, 217 (2d Cir. 1997).

3   Joint defense agreements are discussed in Chapter 7.

hostile or adverse to the company. Often, an effective middle ground is to only make an offer of separate counsel to those employees who are most likely to have criminal exposure.

If the company does obtain separate counsel for employees, it is preferable that the company itself select the lawyers who will act as employee counsel. But, if an employee does select his or her own lawyer, the company should not reject the lawyer merely for that reason. Whether or not the company should pay for an employee's counsel may depend on the company by-laws and state law. If, however, the company has agreed to pay for any employee's counsel, it should pay for all of them, regardless of how they are to be selected.

In selecting outside counsel to represent employees, it is critical that the company's counsel know the counsel selected for the employees so that they can be confident of being able to trust what each employee's counsel says and does. While the employees' counsel must be independent, in most cases company and employee counsel work together to maximize the result for both. If personal familiarity is not possible, the company's counsel need to at least know the employees' counsel well enough to be comfortable that they will not be kept in the dark or, even worse, misled. Moreover, the employee's counsel must be experienced at trial and respected by the prosecutors. If a prosecutor believes that he or she can "walk over" an employee's counsel, it is more likely that the employee will ultimately wind up becoming a government witness.

VI. Termination of Non-Cooperative and Culpable Employees

A. Non-Cooperative Employees

If an employee refuses to submit to an interview, the company should consider terminating that employee's employment. Virtually all states have statutes or court decisions that define an employee's duty to cooperate. This duty includes cooperating with an employer in an internal investigation and answering the employer's questions. *See, e.g., United States v. Sawyer,*[4] (observing that as an employee of Hancock, Sawyer had an obligation to aid Hancock's in-house counsel with their internal investigation).[5] While employees have a Fifth Amendment right under the U.S. Constitution not to make self-incriminating statements to the government, they have no equivalent right to refuse to make a statement to their employer, and certainly no constitutional right to keep a job with the company after refusing to talk with company representatives.[6]

---

4   878 F. Supp. 295, 296 (D. Mass. 1995)

5   *See* John T. Savarese and Carol Miller, *Protecting Privilege and Dealing Fairly with Employees While Conducting an Internal Investigation,*, 1121 PLI/Corp. 525, 560 (1999).

6   *See generally,* Savarese, *supra,* at 560 (recognizing that whether a corporation can fire an employee who refuses to be interviewed depends on only the particular state law involved, the employee's contractual rights, and the specific facts of each case); *see also Flesner v. Technical Communications Corp.*, 575 N.E.d 1107, 1115 (Mass. 1991) (noting there is no constitutional right to maintain at-will employment).

However, as in the case of any employee termination related to the investigation, the company should determine, prior to terminating an employee for failure to cooperate, whether such an action could adversely affect its own interests (as discussed below).

B. Placing the Blame on Employees

It is often beneficial for a company to try to put the blame on "rogue" employees. By terminating "guilty" employees, the company can try to send the government a message that it will not tolerate wrongdoing. Likewise, it may help the company to get a reduced penalty (or even avoid prosecution entirely) to voluntarily give government investigators statements by these employees, even though those statements may not be subject to compelled production by subpoena on account of attorney-client or work product privilege. There are obvious ancillary benefits to cooperating with the government, even if obtained at the expense of employees.

Before proceeding down this path, however, the company should try to ascertain the likely effect of such actions on the government's investigation, as well as the impact on its workforce. If the conduct is not egregious, terminating guilty employees and turning over their statements to the government may well backfire in several ways.

First, other employees may publicly or privately rebel. It is one thing to turn against employees whose conduct is beyond the pale, or egregious, or in violation of public safety. It is quite another to place the blame on employees for conduct that has been tolerated by the company over a period of time, has been done for the company's benefit, or is widespread. Other employees may be unwilling to cooperate after they learn that the company is firing employees and/or turning over their statements to the government.

From the government's perspective, the termination may be viewed as simply a strategic sacrifice of a minor player by the company, instead of a sign that the company is serious about getting to the root of the wrongdoing. And there is always the risk that, having turned over certain information on a particular employee to the government, the company will have waived attorney-client privilege and may have to turn over other witness interviews and information.[7]

Moreover, at the very least, an employee cannot realistically be expected to cooperate with the company after being terminated. Ultimately, the government's case may well be made by obtaining testimony from employees. And, while some of those employees may be subjects of the company investigation, and may even be the source of the problem being investigated, the importance of retaining their cooperation in conducting the investigation may outweigh the potential benefits of

---

7   *See* Chapter 3, on attorney-client privilege.

terminating them. Also, a terminated employee may well walk into the government camp, or may turn out to be dangerous to the company in other ways: for example, by publicly exposing other wrongdoing by the company's employees or by testifying in civil suits.

In addition, government contractor employers risk being named as defendants in "*qui tam*" actions brought by disgruntled former employees under the federal False Claims Act, 31 U.S.C. §§ 3729 *et seq.* The False Claims Act permits private citizens, often former employees with "inside knowledge" (and sometimes an ax to grind), to bring civil lawsuits on behalf of the federal government for fraud in connection with the performance of government contracts. The financial incentive for terminated employees to bring such suits is great: they may be entitled to anywhere from 15 to 25 % of any settlement or judgment on behalf of the Government.

C. Precautions in Terminating Guilty or Non-Cooperative Employees

A terminated employee may also respond to termination with a wrongful termination suit or other similar litigation. Although not protected from corporate action by the Fifth Amendment or other rights under the U.S. Constitution, employees do have other specific rights which may be determined by union or employee contracts, collective bargaining agreements, policies provided in employment manuals, state constitutions, common law or statutes. Any or all of these may give the employee protection against being fired and may subject the company to penalties or damages for wrongful termination. Counsel must ensure that the investigation does not violate these rights, or else they risk having the company face litigation for any of a variety of torts, including wrongful termination or defamation.

In any given situation, the company may well be fully within its rights in terminating or otherwise disciplining an employee who was involved in the wrongdoing or refuses to cooperate. However, there are too many different potential factual issues, as well as legal principles, state laws and regulations, varying by jurisdiction, to allow anything but general guidelines to be given here. For example, in some states employees are deemed to be "at will", which effectively means they can be terminated for any reason or no reason at all. But the company may have altered that relationship through employee contracts, union collective bargaining agreements, or even statements in employee handbooks. An employee may also have a union right not to have discipline imposed unless a union representative is present when the employee is interviewed.[8]

Before terminating an employee who has disclosed—or even admitted to involvement in—illegal activity within the company, an employer should also consider the impact of any applicable "whistleblower" protection. There are numerous federal and state statutes, as well as state common law doctrines, which protect

---

8   *See NLRB v. Weingarten, Inc.*, 420 U.S. 251 (1975).

employees from discharge in retaliation for the disclosure, or threatened disclosure, of illegal employer conduct.[9] An employer should carefully consider the implications of any applicable whistleblower laws, for example, before terminating a lower-level employee who admits to having played a role in illegal activity on instructions from a supervisor. An unfortunate consequence of terminating such an employee could be that while the company escapes significant liability for the supervisor's underlying wrongdoing, it may nonetheless find itself liable to the low-level employee who disclosed the conduct to the company.

Prior to the company terminating any employee, counsel with specific expertise in these areas of employment law should be involved in the decision-making process to advise the company's counsel. An employee who refuses to cooperate, or was involved in company wrongdoing, should not be disciplined before first ascertaining whether he or she has some legal protection, whether as a "whistleblower" or otherwise.

VII. Preparation of Employees and Other Witnesses for Interviews by Government Agents or Grand Jury Appearances

As pointed out above, when the company's counsel conducts an internal investigation, information is typically learned through a review of company documents and interviewing employees. It is through the knowledge thereby gained that counsel will best be able to advise the company on its options, both with regard to government investigations, criminal and administrative, and with regard to civil litigation.

Not surprisingly, however, government investigators and prosecutors build their cases the same way. Controlling the information the government obtains, within the bounds of the law and while avoiding any appearance of obstruction of justice, is therefore part of the job of counsel for the company.

Employees who are to testify or be interviewed by the government will do better if the company's counsel have conducted an investigation and are themselves better prepared to assist the employees. The same principle applies if the company's counsel must brief lawyers retained by the company to represent its employees.

Employee witnesses generally have no idea of how a government interview or grand jury process works and are often intimidated by these procedures. Lack of knowledge, or nervousness about the situation, may lead an employee to provide answers that unnecessarily give the appearance of wrongdoing by the employee, or by others in the company, when in fact there has been none. This is particularly true where government agents ask questions in a leading manner in an effort to obtain confirmation of their pre-conceived view of the case. Employees may

---

9   *See, e.g.,* 15 U.S.C. § 1674 (Consumer Protection Act); 15 U.S.C. § 2622 (Toxic Substances Control Act); 29 U.S.C. § 660 (Occupational Safety and Health Act); 33 U.S.C. § 1367 (Longshoreman's and Harborworker's Act); 42 U.S.C. § 7622 (Air Pollution and Control Act); 45 U.S.C. § 441 (Railroad Safety Act), N.Y. Labor Law § 740(1)-(7).

inadvertently expose themselves to obstruction of justice charges or perjury simply because they are nervous or uneducated about the process.

From the government's perspective, the best place to interview an employee is at the employee's home, away from company management and lawyers. Employees will be more relaxed at home, more likely to talk, and less likely to consider seeking advice from counsel. The government agents may even suggest that the employee does not need to consult counsel or to talk to company representatives.

In fact, of course, employees have no obligation to talk to the government, other than pursuant to subpoena. But most employees, like most citizens generally, are unaware of this fact and, unless the company explicitly advises its employees of their rights in advance, they will almost certainly talk with government investigators voluntarily. This is likely to be detrimental to the company and possibly to the employee as well. Employees need to be advised that they have the right to consult with counsel before talking with government investigators, that it is in their own interest to do so and that, assuming the company has so decided (which is likely), the company will pay for the cost of that representation.

It is perfectly appropriate for the company to advise employees of their rights and duties with regard to talking to government investigators. Obviously, the company should never instruct an employee not to talk to the government. But there is nothing inappropriate about a company advising employees that they may be contacted by government investigators or a prosecutor, that they have a right not to be interviewed absent a subpoena, that it is advisable for them to have counsel present, and that the company will provide and pay for them to be represented by counsel. It is often wise to give employees this advice as part of a written script (as discussed later in this chapter).

Employees must be prepared for questions designed to trick them or lead them into providing the government with answers that the government wants, even if those answers are not accurate. Employees need to understand that they can have counsel if desired, regardless of intimations by a government agent that an attorney is not needed, and that they need not consent to on-the-spot interviews or interviews at their homes.

As when preparing a witness for deposition or trial, counsel should instruct the employee, when responding to government questions, not to speculate and to listen carefully to each question. The employee should be instructed to avoid volunteering information that is not directly in response to the question.

When preparing an employee (or any other witness), or showing them documents to refresh recollection, it is critical that counsel not try to influence the employee with their own opinions or views. Counsel should not selectively show documents that only support the company's side of the case. Counsel clearly should not use the recollections of other employees to try to influence the employee's own recollection. In addition to protecting the company's interests, counsel needs to ensure that

70 Corporate Fraud Investigations & Compliance Programs

the prosecutor can never allege witness tampering or obstruction of justice, since this could be harmful both to counsel and to the company itself.

VIII. Obstruction of Justice

The potential for an obstruction of justice charge against the company, and possibly even its counsel, is something that should be of concern to all counsel conducting internal investigations. The principal obstruction of justice statutes, along with the relevant case law considerations, are as follows:

A. The Statutes

There are three main obstruction of justice statutes.[10] These are: 18 U.S.C. § 1503—Obstruction of Judicial Proceedings; 18 U.S.C. § 1505—Obstruction of Proceedings Before Governmental Departments, Agencies and Committees; and 18 U.S.C. § 1512—Tampering with a Witness, Victim or an Informant. In general, each of these statutes protects federal proceedings from the use of force, intimidation, misleading conduct, harassment, or corrupt means to influence or impede the proceedings.[11] Although all three statutes deal with obstruction of justice, there are significant differences between them.

1. Section 1503

18 U.S.C. § 1503 contains two different prohibitions. First, it criminalizes specific forms of obstruction such as efforts to interfere with or retaliate against jurors or federal judicial officers. Numerous forms of interference or retaliation have been successfully prosecuted under the section, including efforts to kill a juror or officer;[12] forcing a juror out of business;[13] and offering bribes.[14]

Second, section 1503 contains an "omnibus" clause that prohibits attempting to influence, obstruct or impede the due administration of justice through corrupt means, by threat of force, or by threatening communication. The omnibus clause has been successfully applied to a wide range of conduct, including obtaining

---

10 Counsel should also be aware that other statutes also apply to specific industries or types of investigations. For example, 18 U.S.C § 1516 prohibits obstruction of federal audits; 18 U.S.C. § 1517 precludes obstruction of examinations of financial institutions; and 18 U.S.C. § 1518 proscribes obstruction of criminal investigations of health care offenses.

11 Sections 1503 and 1505 apply to attempts to obstruct justice directed toward jurors and officers of the court. Both sections also formerly applied to attempts to obstruct justice directed toward witnesses. The omnibus clauses in both sections were also traditionally used to prosecute witness tampering.

12 *United States v. Chandler*, 604 F.2d 972 (5th Cir. 1979).

13 *United States v. Campanale*, 518 F.2d 352 (9th Cir. 1975).

14 *United States v. Russell*, 255 U.S. 138 (1921).

grand jury transcripts;[15] bribing a judge to disclose grand jury testimony;[16] and attempting to learn a juror's views before a verdict is reached.[17]

A prosecution under section 1503 requires proof that: (1) a judicial or a quasi-judicial proceeding is pending;[18] (2) the defendant knows that the judicial proceeding is pending, and that the person toward whom the interference is directed is an actual or potential juror or court officer;[19] and (3) the defendant acted corruptly with the specific intent to obstruct justice or interfere with the proceeding or due administration of justice.[20] Actual obstruction of justice is not a required element of proof; only an endeavor to obstruct is needed.[21] Even the fact that actual obstruction may have been an impossibility does not constitute a defense.[22] And, for conviction, there is no need to show that the defendant knew the proceeding was a "federal" one.[23]

A great deal of the section 1503 case law concerns whether a "judicial proceeding" was "pending." In general, a grand jury investigation constitutes a judicial proceeding for purposes of section 1503.[24] However, the use of a grand jury subpoena to assist an administrative agency's investigation does not constitute a judicial proceeding under section 1503.[25] Rather, the grand jury's proceedings must be intended to "result in indictment or conviction" in order to constitute a judicial proceeding under Section 1503.[26] As neither the FBI nor the IRS perform judicial functions, investigations by these agencies are not "judicial proceedings" under section 1503.[27] In the civil arena, the filing of a complaint indicates that a proceeding is "pending."[28]

2. Section 1505

Section 1505 parallels section 1503, but applies to pending administrative proceedings rather than judicial ones. The statute reaches both investigative and

---

15 *United States v. Jeter*, 775 F.2d 670 (6th Cir. 1985).

16 *United States v. Howard*, 569 F.2d 1331 (5th Cir. 1978).

17 *Caldwell v. United States*, 218 F.2d 370 (D.C. Cir. 1954).

18 *United States v. Reed*, 773 F.2d 477 (2d Cir. 1985).

19 *See Pettibone v. United States*, 148 U.S. 197 (1893).

20 *United States v. Collis*, 128 F.3d 313 (6th Cir. 1997).

21 *Osborn v. United States*, 385 U.S. 323 (1966); *United States v. Russell*, 255 U.S. 138 (1921).

22 *United States v. Brimberry*, 744 F.2d 580 (7th Cir. 1984).

23 *Pollina v. United States*, 475 U.S. 1141 (1986).

24 *United States v. Mullins*, 22 F.3d 1365 (6th Cir. 1994).

25 *United States v. Ryan*, 455 F.2d 728 (9th Cir. 1971).

26 *United States v. Brown*, 673 F.2d 278 (9th Cir. 1982).

27 *United States v. Scoratow*, 137 F. Supp. 620 (W.D. Pa. 1956); *United States v. Ryan*, 455 F.2d 728 (9th Cir. 1971).

28 *United States v. Metcalf*, 435 F.2d 754 (9th Cir. 1970).

72   Corporate Fraud Investigations & Compliance Programs

adjudicative functions of a federal agency.[29] Like section 1503, section 1505 applies to a wide variety of conduct that may constitute obstruction, including advising a witness to give inaccurate and incomplete answers to questions.[30] Similarly, alteration, destruction and concealment of documents all violate section 1505,[31] and it is not necessary for a subpoena to have already been issued for the documents at the time of the alteration, destruction or concealment.[32]

3. Section 1512

18 U.S.C. § 1512 was enacted as part of the Victim and Witness Protection Act of 1982. It enlarges the kinds of prohibited conduct subject to prosecution by expressly including misleading conduct and harassment, which are not specifically covered by sections 1503 or 1505.[33] In order to obtain a conviction, the government must show that the defendant (1) knowingly (2) engaged in intimidation, physical force, threats, misleading conduct, or corrupt persuasion (3) with the intent to influence, delay, or prevent testimony or cause any person to withhold a record, object, or document (4) from an official proceeding.[34]

Various actions designed to intimidate a witness or present false testimony constitute violations of section 1512.[35] And, like the omnibus clause witness tampering prosecutions under sections 1503 and 1505, section 1512 does not require that the witness be under subpoena or that the defendant know the person will be called as a witness.[36]

---

29   *United States v. Vixie*, 532 F.2d 1277 (9th Cir. 1976). As the FBI does not possess adjudicative or rulemaking authority, section 1505 does not apply to its proceedings. *United States v. Higgins*, 511 F. Supp 453 (W.D. Ky. 1981).

30   *United States v. Bowling*, 630 F.2d 694 (10th Cir. 1980) (questions by the Customs Service); *United States v. Cohn*, 452 F.2d 881 (2d Cir. 1971) ("false and evasive" testimony before the grand jury).

31   *United States v. Sutton*, 732 F.2d 1483 (10th Cir. 1984) (directing destruction of documents requested by Department of Energy); *United States v. Vixie*, 532 F.2d 1277 (9th Cir. 1976) (submitting false documents to IRS).

32   *United States v. Kelley*, 36 F.3d 1118 (D.C. Cir. 1994).

33   In enacting section 18 U.S.C. § 1512, Congress deleted the references to protecting witnesses in sections 1503 and 1505 in favor of section 1512's more specific and expansive prohibitions. As a result, courts are divided as to whether the omnibus clauses in section 1503 and 1505 continue to apply to witness tampering. *Compare United States v. Masterpol*, 940 F.2d 760 (2d Cir. 1991) and *United States v. Aguilar*, 994 F.2d 609 (9th Cir. 1993) (holding that section 1503 no longer applies to witness tampering) with *United States v. Kenny*, 973 F.2d 339 (4th Cir. 1992) and *United States v. Moody*, 977 F.2d 1420 (11th Cir. 1992) (holding that section 1503 continues to permit prosecutions for witness tampering).

34   18 U.S.C. § 1512(b).

35   *United States v. Maggitt*, 784 F.2d 590 (5th Cir. 1986)(threatening to kill witness); *United States v. Rodolitz*, 786 F.2d 77 (2d Cir. 1986)(lying to witness to coerce false testimony before grand jury.)

36   *Stein v. United States*, 337 F.2d 14 (9th Cir. 1964).

There are at least two significant distinctions between 18 U.S.C. § 1512 and sections 1503 and 1505. Under section 1512, there is no requirement of "corrupt" intent,[37] and the proceeding interfered with does not have to be pending.[38] Thus, section 1512 potentially reaches significantly more kinds of conduct that do either sections 1503 or 1505.

B. Application of Obstruction of Justice Statutes to Attorneys

With the increase in the statutory and regulatory requirements imposed on companies, the number of investigations and prosecutions, as well as civil suits for alleged violations of these schemes, has also risen. Concomitantly, the potential for obstruction of justice charges based on actions taken when investigating the alleged violations has also increased.

Traditional prosecutions of witness tampering demonstrate that sections 1503, 1505 and 1512 can be applied to attorneys who engage in certain improper conduct.[39] For example, successful prosecutions have been brought for persuading a witness to avoid service of process,[40] encouraging the giving of false testimony,[41] and convincing a witness to forget events.[42] Efforts to make a witness "unavailable" for trial also violate the obstruction of justice sections.[43] Similarly, compromising documentary evidence clearly violates the obstruction of justice statutes.[44] These precedents can clearly be applied to attorneys in other similar factual settings. "Zealous representation" by defense counsel is generally not recognized as a defense to obstruction charges in these situations.[45]

The more subtle questions of applying the obstruction of justice statutes to attorneys arise when an attorney is conducting an internal investigation and therefore has contact with potential witnesses concerning the facts of the case. The

---

37   18 U.S.C. § 1512. It remains to be seen whether the courts will interpret the statute as requiring more than a general intent *mens rea*.

38   18 U.S.C. § 1512(e)(1).

39   The government can also prosecute an attorney under 18 U.S.C. § 1622 for subornation of perjury. An obstruction of justice charge is much more likely to be brought than a subornation charge, however, because the subornation charge requires the government to prove not only an effort to obstruct justice by attempting to procure perjury, but also to prove that perjury actually occurred. *Catrino v. United States*, 176 F.2d 884 (9th Cir. 1949).

40   *United States v. Bittinger*, 24 F. Cas. 1149 (W.D. Mo. 1876).

41   *United States v. Brown*, 948 F.2d 1076 (8th Cir. 1991).

42   *United States v. McComb*, 744 F.2d 555 (7th Cir. 1984).

43   *See, e.g.*, such extreme measures as inducing a witness to undergo surgery or falsely creating a heart attack. *United States v. Minkoff*, 137 F.2d 402 (2d Cir. 1943); *United States v. Ardito*, 782 F.2d 358 (2d Cir. 1985).

44   *United States v. Ruggiero*, 934 F.2d 440 (2d Cir. 1991). It is not necessary that a subpoena have been issued in order for the destruction or alteration to constitute obstruction, *id.* at 450, nor is it necessary that the documents in fact have investigative worth. *Id.* at 445-46.

45   *See United States v. Cintolo*, 818 F.2d 980 (1st Cir. 1987); *United States v. Cioffi*, 493 F.2d 1111 (2d Cir. 1973).

obstruction of justice considerations arise in three contexts: interviewing witnesses, preparing clients and witnesses for interviews by the government or court testimony, and interacting with government agents.

C. Obstruction Concerns When Interviewing Witnesses[46]

While all good lawyers try to conduct impartial and objective interviews, that is sometimes difficult in practice under the stress of a pending government investigation and with a client who is both nervous and demanding. Since there may be no attorney-client privilege with a particular witness, especially a non-employee witness, it is critical that the company's counsel, when interviewing a witness, recognize that the same witness may shortly thereafter be interviewed by the government and that the government may well ask about the substance of the witness's conversation with counsel.

For counsel, the most problematic of all three obstruction statutes may well be section 1512, because of its inclusion of "misleading conduct" as a proscribed activity. 18 U.S.C. § 1515(a)(3)(B) defines "misleading conduct" (for purposes of section 1512) to include "intentionally omitting information from a statement and thereby causing a portion of such statement to be misleading, or intentionally concealing a material fact, and thereby creating a false impression by such statement." As this definition includes omitting a material fact or making a false statement, counsel should be very careful when presenting documents or facts to potential witnesses without including all relevant information.

Section 1512's breadth can potentially interfere with the role of counsel in questioning witnesses. For example, in attempting to discover the true nature of the facts supporting the government's case, as well as any potential defenses to the allegations, counsel may well prefer to omit certain facts or inferences when dealing with some witnesses, much as investigating authorities regularly do, in order to discover whether the witnesses are independently knowledgeable of important information. Counsel may suspect that certain witnesses are adverse to the company's position and, therefore, may not wish to disclose to those witnesses any information that tends to reveal the company's defensive posture or strategy. Counsel often will not want to reveal too much information to a witness during an interview, because doing so may defeat the fact-finding function of the internal investigation by causing the witness to incorrectly assume that counsel are already in possession of the "true facts" and that the witness's role is merely to corroborate these facts. In these such situations, seemingly routine interviewing strategies of counsel based on legitimate concerns can easily and inadvertently lend themselves to being portrayed as "misleading conduct."

---

46   While the rest of this chapter has discussed interviews primarily in the context of "employees", the present discussion of obstruction of justice issues has been framed more broadly and "witnesses" is accordingly used in lieu of "employees." The principles discussed here apply equally to counsel's conduct towards third-party witnesses who are not employees of the company.

Apparently in an effort to accommodate the necessary functions of counsel, section 1512 contains an affirmative defense that actions that are "solely of lawful conduct" and for which "the defendant's sole intention was to encourage, induce, or cause the other person to testify truthfully" do not violate the statute's general prohibition.[47] Since this is an affirmative defense under the statute, however, the attorney will bear the burden of demonstrating the legitimate nature of the questionable conduct. It is thus a prudent measure, if possible, to have another attorney or supporting personnel present for the interviews to act as a later witness to the nature of the conversation.

The potential for obstruction charges accordingly argues in favor of carefully advising every witness that the company's counsel are not acting as the witness's personal attorney, so that the witness clearly understands his or her relationship to counsel and the fact-finding nature of the interview. In this regard, counsel should always be cognizant that they may be interviewing an employee who is already a *qui tam* "relator" under the False Claims Act or who is otherwise already cooperating with the government's investigation. And, of course, the possibility always exists that an employee, although not a cooperating government witness at present, may later become one.

None of these safeguards or cautions is meant to suggest that counsel should refrain from conducting whatever interviews are considered appropriate. But it is critical that counsel not inject a personal or "company" view of events into a witness's head, either in an effort to help the witness recall facts or for any other reason. An aggressive U.S. Attorney may well seek to investigate the actions of counsel conducting interviews in this way. Such an investigation, even if without merit, may well disqualify counsel from further representation of the client. *See, e.g., United States v. Castellano,*[48] in which the United States moved to disqualify counsel on grounds, among others, that counsel had urged a witness not to cooperate with law enforcement authorities. The trial court ruled that such conduct may give rise to a genuine fear of prosecution for obstruction of justice on the part of defense counsel, thereby rendering his representation ineffective, but that insufficient facts had been presented to warrant disqualification at that time.[49]

D. Preparing Witnesses

Counsel should also be careful when preparing witnesses for testimony. As a routine matter, lawyers generally instruct their witnesses concerning the process of testifying. However, some of these instructions may be perceived as improper "persuasion" under section 1512 in the later light of the witness's actual testimony. For example, many lawyers routinely advise clients and witnesses that they should feel free to respond to questions with the disclaimer "I don't recall"—especially as

---

47   18 U.S.C. § 1512(d).

48   610 F. Supp. 1137 (1985).

49   *Id.* at 1146.

many witnesses will otherwise tend to voluntarily speculate or testify as to what "usually" happens, instead of testifying as to their actual, specific recollections. However, feigning the inability to recall actual knowledge that the witness does in fact possess can constitute obstruction of justice.[50] "The blatantly evasive witness" engages in obstruction of justice just "as surely by erecting a screen of feigned forgetfulness as one who burns files or induces a potential witness to absent himself."[51] Thus, counsel should be careful to inform witnesses that the response, "I don't know," is not to be used as a device to avoid answering uncomfortable questions, but merely as a legitimate response to questions calling for information genuinely outside a witness's recall.

Similarly, advising a witness to invoke the privilege against self-incrimination, in order to improperly prevent the witness from testifying, can constitute obstruction of justice.[52] Thus, any witnesses for whom the Fifth Amendment privilege is a real issue should be carefully advised as to the nature and scope of their privilege and the proper method of invoking it.

E. Federal Agents

As a general rule, interacting with federal agents will not subject counsel to the possibility of obstruction of justice charges. As the precedents cited above indicate, neither section 1503 nor section 1505 applies to FBI or IRS investigations. Most other federal investigative agencies will similarly not be included under the purview of these statutes. At present, however, it is unclear whether the more expansive prohibitions in section 1512 will be interpreted to apply to investigations by the FBI and other investigative agencies, in light of that section's more general language regarding "official proceedings" (as opposed to the references to pending "judicial" or "administrative" proceedings in sections 1503 and 1505 respectively). There are apparently no cases to date addressing this specific question.

Moreover, there is at least one kind of situation in which counsel may well be placed in jeopardy of obstruction charges under section 1503 through comments made to investigating officials. In *United States v. Wood*,[53] the government charged Wood, a defense counsel, with a violation of section 1503 for statements that he made to FBI agents. Wood had spoken to the FBI agents concerning actions taken by his client, the former chairman of the Navajo Nation, whom the government was investigating for potential corruption charges. Although the appellate court's opinion does not detail the statements, they apparently concerned Wood's efforts to convince the FBI agents that his own actions and those of his client concerning the conveyance of an automobile were not illegal. The government alleged that Wood

---

50 *United States v. Williams*, 874 F.2d 968 (5th Cir. 1989).

51 *United States v. Cohn*, 452 F 2d. 881 (2d Cir. 1971).

52 *United States v. Cintolo*, 818 F.2d 980 (1st Cir. 1987); *United States v. Capo*, 791 F.2d 1054 (2d Cir. 1986); *United States v. Cioffi*, 493 F.2d 1111 (2d Cir. 1973).

53 958 F.2d 963 (10th Cir. 1992).

knew the statements he made to the agents would be repeated by the agents as part of their testimony before the grand jury. The indictment claimed that Wood made "false, fictitious and fraudulent statements and representations to [FBI agents], knowing that those special agents interviewed him in furtherance of an investigation by the United States Grand Jury ... in order to prevent that Grand Jury from learning the true facts and purpose concerning [the automobile conveyance]."[54]

Wood had successfully moved to dismiss the section 1503 count in the indictment, arguing that the indictment did not specify what statements he had allegedly made to the agents that violated the statute. The appeals court rejected this argument and remanded the case for retrial on the obstruction count. The Court, however, "express[ed] no opinion on whether the conduct charged—*i.e.*, making unsworn false statements to FBI agents who were investigating on behalf of a sitting grand jury—is proscribed by 18 U.S.C. § 1503."[55]

Clearly, counsel in the *Wood* case was doing far more than merely "spinning" the client's version of the facts to the investigating agents in an effort to prevent his client's possible indictment. However, the prosecution in *Wood* raises the possibility that counsel could be charged with obstruction for making those kinds of statements to FBI agents under some circumstances. In this regard, *United States v. Aguilar*,[56] indicates, without so holding, that statements to an FBI agent may be within the ambit of section 1503 if the defendant knew that the statements made to the agent would be presented to the grand jury. And, *United States v. Fayer*,[57] while stressing that, to be violative of section 1503, "corrupt" advice given to a witness must be related to the grand jury's investigation, and not merely the FBI's investigation, nevertheless seems to assume that, if the advice is related to a grand jury investigation, such a prosecution is possible.

IX. Preparation of a Script

In order to minimize any later suggestion of obstruction of justice on the part of counsel, as well as to help avoid potential conflict of interest issues and to prepare employees for possible contact by the government, it is important that employees be advised of certain very specific things, preferably in the form of a script. This script should be maintained by the company as evidence of what it did. While the

---

54   *Wood*, 958 F.2d at 975.

55   *Wood*, 958 F.2d at 975 n.19. The court also noted that to the extent the agents were acting on behalf of the grand jury, there was some question as to whether Wood was properly charged in count one of the indictment under 18 U.S.C. § 1001, relying on Tenth Circuit precedent that false affidavits given in compliance with a grand jury subpoena were not within the jurisdiction of the Department of Justice, but rather the jurisdiction of the grand jury, to which section 1001 did not apply. Interestingly, the court thus also pointed out that there was a potential question as to whether the two counts were therefore "mutually exclusive."

56   21 F.3d 1475 (9th Cir. 1994). *Aguilar* was subsequently affirmed in part and reversed in part, on other grounds. *See* 515 U.S. 593 (1995).

57   573 F.2d 741 (2d Cir. 1978).

warnings and advice contained in the script can be given orally, which may tend to put the employees more at ease, a written script may be particularly helpful to the company in situations where the government appears or is likely to be hostile. A written script is useful to an employee because the employee can maintain and refer to if confronted by a government (or other third party) investigator.

At a minimum, in the script, counsel should advise the employee of the following (to the extent they apply):

- that the government is conducting an investigation of specific company conduct;
- that the company has asked counsel to investigate this conduct and that employees are being asked to cooperate;
- that the purpose of the interview is to allow counsel to gather facts to assist counsel in giving legal advice to the company;
- that the attorney(s) conducting the interview represent the company and not the employee;[58]
- that the attorney-client privilege protects the interview, but that the privilege belongs to the company, not to the employee;
- that the employee should not advise other employees or third persons of what was discussed in the interview, because the attorney-client privilege may thereby be jeopardized;
- that the company intends to keep the interview confidential, but that it is possible the company may later make the employee's statements available to the government (or some other party) to the extent necessary to protect the company's interests;
- that the company will retain other counsel for the employee to talk to, if the employee needs separate counsel, and that the company will pay for such representation;
- that it is possible government investigators may seek to interview the employee, even at the employee's home;
- that, in the event this happens, the employee has the right to either talk to the government or refuse to do so, and that this decision is up to the employee, not the company and not the government;
- that, before making this decision, the employee has the option of talking to counsel hired by the company and/or to an attorney hired for the purpose of advising employees of their rights and duties and paid for by the company;

---

58   In commercial litigation, it is not uncommon for the company's counsel to also represent witnesses and employees, including former employees. This is much less likely to work effectively in criminal investigations, as there is a much greater probability of a conflict of interest. *See* Chapter 7.

- that the company recommends that the employee talk to counsel obtained for this purpose, but that the employee is free to talk to any attorney he or she wants, or to no counsel at all;
- that the employee should advise the company if the government seeks an interview with the employee; and
- that the employee should be truthful at all times.

Besides being for the benefit of the employee and helping to avoid any subsequent charge of obstruction of justice against counsel, these warnings, once they are given, will make it difficult for an employee to later claim the existence of an individual attorney-client privilege with the company's counsel and to try, on that basis, to prevent the company from disclosing his statements to the government or third party.

X. Creating a Record

The reasons for writing down what employees tell counsel are too obvious to belabor. Less obvious, however, are the risks involved in doing so. The principal risk is discoverability. The notes of the interview can be subpoenaed or otherwise obtainable by third parties in any number of ways. These include a civil or administrative discovery request, a grand jury subpoena, or even a subpoena of the employee's previous statements by a defendant in a criminal trial where that employee is subsequently called by the government as a witness against the defendant.

Whether a record of the interview can later be obtained by the government or third parties is often determined by the contents of the interview. If the notes are a substantially verbatim record of what the witness said, the notes may have to produced (at least to the witness himself, and therefore, effectively, to any third party with which the witness may then be cooperating).[59] On the other hand, under the work product doctrine, if the notes contain counsel's thoughts and impressions about the witness and how the statement fits in with other parts of the investigation, they will likely not have to be produced.[60] In short, the less the notes directly quote what the witness said, and the more they combine the attorney's own thoughts with what the witness said, the more protection a report of the interview will have.[61]

While substance is usually more important than form, this is one area in which form is important. To better protect the written report of an interview under both the attorney-client and work product doctrine, the document should expressly state that it is being prepared in anticipation of litigation and in connection with legal advice being given to the client. Since there is always the possibility of later

---

59   *See* Rule 26(b)(3) of the Federal Rules of Civil Procedure.

60   *See, In re Sealed Case*, 856 F.2d 267, 273 (D.C. Cir. 1988).

61   *See* Chapter 3.

XI. Documents

A. The Importance of Document Gathering and Production

Documents often form the foundation of the investigation. It is frequently a review of documents that most educates counsel or that turns up information that helps unravel the wrongdoing. Vital information can be found in a wide variety of document types, including internal memos, transactional documents, calendars, financial records, travel records and phone logs. Documents often contain the most detail about the events under investigation and can be used to help employees refresh their recollection.

Despite this fact, most clients tend to view document production, even to the government pursuant to a subpoena, as a burdensome and expensive irritant, and often give it less than their full attention. Because of this, it is critical that counsel advise the company of the importance of the document gathering and production process and stress the potentially very harmful consequences of not taking it seriously.

Documents often provide the best record of the conduct under investigation. Motive and intent can often be established through documents and, in white-collar criminal prosecutions, documents can play a large role in determining intent. Prosecutors are very interested in determining "intent" and their decision concerning the company's intent may be the decisive issue whether the company will face a criminal charge. The government is fully aware of this and, as a consequence, document subpoenas are often broad and sweeping. Inadequate preparation for compiling and organizing the relevant documents can lead to a whole range of disasters, from simple failure of counsel to adequately learn the facts of the case, to waiver of attorney-client privilege because of inadvertent production of privileged documents. Moreover, if the government concludes that documents are being withheld, destroyed or altered, obstruction of justice charges may enter the picture.

For this reason, even before the process of reviewing documents begins, counsel must take action to prevent potential irreparable harm. First, counsel must ensure that relevant documents are not altered, lost or destroyed. Counsel must further ensure that all company personnel with a need to know are advised that documents should not be moved, altered or destroyed. This can be done by a memo sent by counsel to all relevant employees. However, if there is a concern that such a memo might cause a particular employee to alter or destroy documents, that situation must be dealt with separately, as discussed below.

Counsel should also immediately focus on the company's document destruction policy, to ensure that no documents are destroyed pursuant to the policy during the pendency of the investigation. It would not present a serious concern if documents relevant to a government investigation were destroyed, pursuant to a legitimate policy, prior to the investigation. It would be a serious concern, however, if such documents were destroyed, for whatever reason (even pursuant to a legitimate policy), once the company had been placed on notice of an investigation, even if no subpoena had yet been received.[62]

It would not be easy for a lawyer to convince an angry and skeptical prosecutor that his or her client did not intend to obstruct justice when it destroyed a year's worth of documents after an investigation had already commenced. Even if the prosecutor takes no action as a result of the destruction, it will place a strain on relations at the start of an investigation that may be difficult to overcome. And there may also be a final irony, in that the destroyed documents may well have been ones that would have been helpful to the company.

B. Finding and Reviewing the Documents

As a preliminary matter, counsel should identify an employee with knowledge of the company's files, who will be in charge of retrieving documents for the company, and that person should be supervised by a lawyer. Counsel should make it clear to this employee, and to his or her supervisors, that this is an important job. If possible, a single lawyer should supervise the entire document production, even if documents are being produced from multiple locations.

A system must be put in place which will ensure that all documents are located, including copies of the same document in different hands. This is important, because some copies may have handwritten notes written by the employees who received them. It is a virtual certainty that many documents will turn out not to have been maintained by the company in the manner and locations that management expects. While the company may have central files, department files, and even individual files, management rarely is aware of all the locations in which documents are located. Counsel should insist upon obtaining detailed records of where each document was actually located as well as where searches for documents were conducted.

The files of potential wrongdoers should be reviewed and all documents appropriate to a particular case should be examined, including such items as calendars, correspondence, telephone calling records, expense reports, and telephone message slips. If there is a concern that an employee may try to hide or destroy files, counsel should consider obtaining them without first requesting them from the employee, and perhaps without the employee's knowledge at all.

Prior to undertaking such an action, however, counsel should ascertain the state of the law in the relevant jurisdiction for possible torts that may impose liability under the rubric of "invasion of privacy." The key issue in reviewing an employee's files, without the employee's consent, is usually whether the employee

---

62 The same concern would arise in a civil case, if relevant documents were destroyed after the company was on reasonable notice of pending (or even anticipated) litigation, even though no discovery requests had yet been made.

had a "reasonable expectation of privacy" under the circumstances.[63] To assist the company avoid these and similar problems, employment manuals should contain provisions that prohibit all illegal conduct and the manual should state that there is no expectation of privacy in mail, electronic mail or the contents of an employee's desk, and that all private property should be maintained off-site. Even with such precautions, however, counsel should be careful about searching private property located in the company offices, particularly belongings that are clearly personal, such as purses and wallets.[64]

C. Organization of Documents

When handling a document production, counsel must ensure the integrity of the original documents, while at the same time producing a minimum of disruption to the company's business. Counsel must ensure that an appropriate system is put in place to organize, maintain, number, secure and copy the documents, and to prepare for producing them to the government (or to the opposing party in a civil litigation). The documents should be listed in an index, so that they can be found when needed. The index should indicate where each document was obtained and who produced it. Most lawyers have their own method of organizing documents and it is not discussed further herein. Typically, depending on the size of the case and the number of documents, as well as the budget allotted, counsel can decide to organize documents manually, index them on computer, or scan them full text by electronic imaging. Whatever system is selected, it is critical that counsel be able to locate promptly whatever documents they may need.

A detailed privilege log should be created as the documents are gathered and privileged documents should be retained separately from other documents to help avoid inadvertent disclosure. In addition, a list of "bad" documents, those potentially harmful to the company's position, should be compiled in one place. This will aid counsel in evaluating the potential problems in the case.

XII. Report of the Investigation

To many lawyers, the logical conclusion to a comprehensive internal investigation is to write a report. A written report can provide detailed facts and legal advice and is proof positive that an investigation was undertaken. This may assist the company in dealing with the government, either before an investigation commences or

---

63   *See generally, e.g., Sheppard v. Beerman*, 18 F.3d 147, 152 (2d Cir.), *cert. denied*, 513 U.S. 816 (1994); *Ali v. Douglas Casle Communications*, 929 F. Supp. 1362, 1381-83 (D. KS 1996); *O'Bryan v. KTIV Television*, 868 F. Supp. 1146, 1159 (N.D. Iowa 1994), *aff'd and rev'd in part on other grounds*, 64 F.3d 1188 (8th Cir. 1995); *Maws v. Marriott Corp.*, 830 F. Supp. 274, 283 (D. Md. 1992); *Simmons v. Southwestern Bell Tel. Co.*, 452 F. Supp. 392, 394 (W.D. Okla. 1978), *aff'd*, 611 F.2d 342 (10th Cir. 1979); *Sanders v. American Broadcasting Cos., Inc., 978 P.2d 67 (Cal. 1999) (citation omitted).*

64   *See, K-Mart Store No. 441 v. Trotti*, 677 S.W. 2d 632 (Tex. App. 1984).

in settlement discussions with the government. It is easier to understand a complex report when it is in written form and it can be reviewed more than once and by persons who could not be present for an oral report.

However, it should not automatically be concluded that the report should be in written form. A written report, if it falls into the hands of the government or a private litigant, can be devastating. For example, there may be smoking gun evidence in the report and it may contain statements about "wrongdoers", which may cause those persons to sue for defamation or other torts (as discussed later in this chapter).

Conversely, an oral report, while not as comprehensive, provides some clear advantages. The report will be given from counsel's notes, which will contain not only facts, but counsel's intermingled opinions, thoughts and legal advice. As opinion work product, the report will thus be virtually assured of protection from disclosure to third parties,[65] and will have a strong supplemental level of immunity in addition to the attorney-client privilege which will normally also attach to it.

Some factors counsel should consider in deciding whether the report of the investigation should be written or oral include:

1. whether there is any obligation that the report be disclosed to a government agency;

2. the likelihood of the report being obtained by a civil litigant or by the government in a criminal case;

3. the potential culpability of the company as set forth in the report; and

4. whether a report needs to be written to document the efforts ordered by the board of directors and to evidence its fulfilling its fiduciary duty to the company.

If the decision is made to prepare a written final report, it should be drafted to maximize the likelihood that the attorney-client privilege and work-product doctrine will attach, and be preserved. The more the report contains opinion work product, the more likely it will not be discoverable. Further, the report should state and evidence that it is delivering legal advice to the client, and not business advice. It should not merely report facts and findings, but should analyze those facts and findings in support of the rendition of counsel's legal advice.

A. Content of the Report

Whether the report is in oral or written form, a statement should be made, in the report itself, that the report is part of an investigation ordered by the board of directors in order to obtain legal advice from counsel, and that it is a confidential

---

65   *See* Chapter 3.

communication covered by both attorney-client privilege and the work product doctrine. The report should indicate:

- why the investigation was conducted, including why the company sought to obtain legal advice through the investigation;
- the investigative steps counsel took during the course of the investigation;
- the facts that were uncovered during the investigation, including a summary of critical documents;
- a description of the participants involved in the activities under investigation and their potential culpability, if any; and
- the legal authority which counsel believes governs or covers the issues.

In addition, it is useful to include recommendations regarding corrective measures in the event the report ever gets into the hands of a prosecutor. However, doing this can turn out to be a problem if the report is subsequently obtained by civil litigants, who may try to use such statements as admissions against interest.

B. Dissemination of a Written Report

A lot of time and effort will have been expended in efforts to protect the report from disclosure, and counsel should stress to management the importance of not inadvertently waiving the attorney-client privilege through dissemination of the report to persons who should not receive it. Every page of the report should contain a statement that it is confidential and subject to the attorney-client privilege and work-product doctrine.

Copies of the reports should be numbered and a list of persons who are given copies to read should be maintained. After a set period of time, all copies should be returned. Persons obtaining the report should be instructed not to make notes on their copies. All copies should be maintained in a file separate and apart from regular company files in a further effort to maintain the highest level of protection.

C. Oral Report

An oral report will generally have substantially less detail than a written report. However, that does not mean that the oral report should be given to a wider group of participants than would receive the written report. The minutes of meetings of the board of directors should note that a report was given to the board and should identify any other persons who heard it. The minutes should further state that the report was a privileged communication between counsel and the company and that legal advice was given to the company in connection with the report.

D. Protecting the Company from Suits Arising from the Report

In a comprehensive report, counsel will usually identify the employees responsible for the wrongdoing and detail their wrongful conduct. In essence, the report will typically indicate that certain named employees of the company may have committed a crime or been dishonest. While the company has an interest in getting to the bottom of wrongdoing or criminal conduct, these employees may believe that their reputations have been harmed and decide to bring suit against the company, or even against the attorney(s) who wrote the report.[66] Suits for infliction of emotional distress and defamation are among the most common causes of action used as a basis for litigation in such cases.

Defamation is defined as a false statement that is published to third parties and is unprivileged.[67] One defense to defamation is, accordingly, that the statements are truthful.[68] Counsel should therefore be particularly careful to be completely accurate when assigning blame to individuals in a report. If there is a conflict in the evidence, counsel are better off saying so, rather than putting their credibility on the line behind one view of the facts or the other. This does not preclude counsel from making recommendations.[69]

In order to further protect against such suits, the report should not be disseminated more widely than is absolutely necessary. Counsel should emphasize that their statements about wrongdoing are opinions, not statements of fact, because statements of opinion have protection under the law that statements of fact do not.[70]

In addition to the defense of truth, there is an even more broad defense to a charge of defamation, called "qualified privilege." This allows an employer to make statements about employees to persons having a need or duty to know.[71] If statements are kept within those parameters, this can provide an effective defense to defamation or to other potential claims.

E. Maintaining Confidentiality after Disclosure of the Report (Waiver)

Most courts have ruled that the voluntary disclosure of a report of investigation constitutes an absolute waiver of both the attorney-client privilege and work product doctrine protections: in essence a total waiver. This means that any third party

---

66 Former United States Attorney General Griffin Bell, while in private practice, was sued by an employee identified in a report as having committed criminal acts. *See Pearce v. E.F. Hutton Group*, 664 F. Supp. 1490 (D.D.C. 1987).

67 *See Restatement (Second) Of Torts* § 558 (1977).

68 *See, e.g., Cox Broadcasting Corp. v. Cohn*, 420 U.S. 469, 489-90 (1975); *Thomas v. Pearl*, 998 F.2d 447, 452 (7th Cir.), *cert. denied*, 510 U.S. 1043 (1994); *Gilbert v. Ben-Asher*, 900 F.2d 1407, 1411 (9th Cir.), *cert. denied*, 498 U.S. 865 (1990); *see also Restatement (Second) Of Torts*, § 581A (1977).

69 *See Restatement (Second) Of Torts* § 595 (1977).

70 *See, e.g., Gertz v. Robert Welch, Inc.*, 418 U.S. 323, 340 (1974) (*dictum*); *Gross v. New York Times Co.*, 82 N.Y.2d 146, 153-54, 623 N.E.2d 1163, 1168 (1993); *Restatement (Second) Of Torts* § 595 (1977). However there are limits to this principle, and a statement that clearly implies it is based upon unstated facts that may be false cannot be protected merely by prefacing it with the words: "in my opinion." *Milkovich v. Lorain Journal Co.*, 497 U.S. 1, 18-19 (1990).

71 *See, e.g., ContiCommodity Services, Inc. v. Ragan*, 63 F.3d 438, 442 (5th Cir. 1995), *cert. denied*, 517 U.S. 1104 (1996).

can successfully subpoena the report. The reasoning behind the ruling is that a client should not be permitted to selectively waive the privilege in order to gain a benefit in one situation and then later, with different parties, to act as if there had been no waiver. In essence, once confidentiality is gone at all, it is gone forever.[72]

In *Westinghouse Electric Company v. Republic of the Philippines*,[73] the Republic of the Philippines sought discovery of an internal report conducted by Westinghouse's outside counsel concerning a prime contract to construct the first Philippine nuclear power plant. Westinghouse had disclosed its internal report to the Securities & Exchange Commission (SEC) and to the Justice Department as part of its cooperation with a Department of Justice investigation. In the subsequent "parallel" civil litigation, the Republic of the Philippines sought access to the internal report and Westinghouse resisted. Upon consideration of the matter, the Third Circuit held that a party disclosing privileged information to the government, for the purpose of cooperating in the government investigation, thereby waives the privilege completely and exposes documents to civil discovery in litigation between the discloser and a third party.[74] In rejecting the "selective waiver rule" urged by Westinghouse, the court held that the agreements by the SEC and the Department of Justice to maintain the confidentiality of the information did not preserve the privilege with respect to litigation against a third party in an unrelated civil proceeding.[75]

The Third Circuit's decision in *Westinghouse* is consistent with the Fourth Circuit's ruling in *In Re Martin Marietta*.[76] In that case, Martin Marietta submitted findings from its internal report to the government as part of its effort to resolve a criminal investigation. The Fourth Circuit determined that, by its submission to the government, the company had waived any attorney-client privilege attaching to the disclosed report, as well as any attaching to the underlying details of the internal report upon which it was based, holding that any disclosure of a confidential communication outside a privileged relationship will waive the privilege as to all information related to the same subject matter.[77]

A similar rule to the one recognized in *Westinghouse* and *Martin Marietta* for waiver of attorney-client privilege has also been applied to the work-product doctrine. In *In Re Steinhardt Partners* LLP,[78] the Second Circuit determined that a

---

72 See *In re Subpoenas Duces Tecum (Fulbright and Jaworski)*, 738 F.2d 1367 (D.C. Cir. 1984). Some courts have ruled that there is no general waiver when disclosure is made to an agency pursuant to subpoena. *See, e.g., Diversified Industries, Inc. v. Meredith*, 572 F.2d 597, 610 (8th Cir. 1978) (*en banc*). This is a minority view and not widely held.

73 951 F.2d 1414 (3d Cir. 1991).

74 *Id*. at 1417-18.

75 *Id*. at 1427.

76 856 F.2d 619 (4th Cir. 1988).

77 856 F.2d at 622.

78 9 F.3d 230, 234 (2d Cir. 1993).

treasury note trader's voluntary submission of a legal memorandum to the SEC during the course of an SEC investigation, waived the protections of the work-product doctrine as to subsequent civil litigants seeking to obtain the memorandum. The court rejected the trader's assertion that he was presented with a Hobson's choice between waiving work-product protection through the cooperation with investigative authorities or not cooperating with the authorities.

> Whether characterized as forcing a party in between a Scylla and Charybdis, a rock and a hard place, or some other tired but equally evocative metaphoric cliché, the "Hobson's choice" argument is unpersuasive given the facts of this case. An allegation that a party facing a federal investigation and the prospect of a civil fraud suit must make difficult choices is insufficient justification for carving a substantial exception to the waiver doctrine.[79]

If counsel believe that a report must be disclosed for the benefit of the company, then efforts should be undertaken to show that the company still intends to preserve the report's confidentiality despite the disclosure. This at least preserves the argument, accepted by a few courts, which seem to have looked at the realities faced by a company having to deal with the government, and have accordingly ruled that, where disclosure is made under a confidentiality agreement, there is no waiver.[80] Counsel should try to obtain an agreement with the government attorneys stating:

- that the report is being requested by the government;
- that it is the intent of the government that the report will be kept confidential and not disclosed to third parties; and
- that, by submitting the report, the company is not waiving the attorney-client privilege or the work product doctrine.

Thus, a decision to make a voluntary disclosure to the government of an internal report prepared by outside counsel must factor in the possibility that such a disclosure may be held to constitute a waiver of privilege in all parallel proceedings. Although it may be possible to preserve the privilege by entering into a confidentiality agreement with the government, the success of such an approach cannot be guaranteed.[81] At a minimum, counsel must advise the company about the risks involved in making disclosures in one forum when the potential for concurrent proceedings exists.

XIII. Guidelines for Protecting Investigative Materials from Disclosure

The company should make every effort to ensure that reports of the investigation can be kept confidential and that the government cannot compel their disclosure.

---

79   9 F.3d at 236.

80   While not commonly accepted or widely used, counsel should also consider the issue of the self-evaluative privilege. *See* Chapter 3.

81   *In re Steinhart Partners*, 9 F.3d at 233.

88   Corporate Fraud Investigations & Compliance Programs

This is not meant to suggest that, for strategic reasons, the company may not ultimately decide to voluntarily disclose some or all of the report. But disclosure should always, to the extent possible, be kept as an option to be freely chosen by the company.

In order to achieve this goal, there are specific steps that can and should be taken by counsel in order to help preserve the attorney-client and work-product doctrine while conducting an internal investigation.[82]

1. Counsel should request formal company authorization to conduct the internal investigation. Such authorization should be granted, if possible, by the board of directors or the audit committee. When an investigation is begun because of a governmental investigation, the grant of authority should state that the investigation is being ordered so the company can obtain legal advice and that confidential communications between the attorney and the company's employees will be necessary, in order for the attorney to provide that legal advice;

2. By the same token, in order to establish the predicate for the work-product doctrine to attach to the investigative report, and to all documents and other materials obtained and prepared during the conduct of the investigation, the board resolution and engagement letter should clearly recite and describe that the investigation is being conducted because of the imminence, or at least the foreseeability, of litigation, or in response to a government investigation or inquiry directly affecting the company.[83] It should also state, with as much detail as possible, all the potential civil and criminal litigation that counsel can reasonably anticipate arising, as well as any detail available about the

---

82   Portions of this chapter are duplicative of material found elsewhere in this book. This was done specifically to emphasize the importance of undertaking efforts to protect the report of investigation.

83   Whether the work-product doctrine applies at all to an internal corporate investigation may depend upon whether the investigation was conducted in response to a government investigation or inquiry, or the threat of a private civil suit. An investigative report prepared in response to a government investigation or inquiry is likely to be considered as having been prepared because litigation was foreseeable. If, however, an internal investigation is undertaken proactively, with no reasonable prospect of litigation, it may be difficult to support the application of the work-product doctrine to the investigative report. A purely proactive investigation may be considered to have been conducted for primarily business or fact-finding purposes, and not to have been primarily motivated by the prospect of litigation, much less by the imminence of litigation. *See, e.g., In re Leslie Fay Cos.*, 161 F.R.D. 274, 280-82 (S.D.N.Y. 1995) [the corporate investigative report was not work-product, even though the company forsaw securities fraud litigation and the SEC had initiated its own prior investigation. The investigation was conducted primarily for business reasons where it and the subsequent report was used to make decisions on terminating responsible personnel; to determine the magnitude of the fraud and implement corrective measures; and to reassure creditors and future lenders]. *See also* Richard S. Pabst, *The Corporate Dilemma: Is It Possible To Preserve A Privilege For Environmental Audits?*, 41 La. B. J. 110, 112 (1993), observing that since most environmental audits are performed routinely, and not as a result of litigation, the claim of attorney work-product in connection therewith will probably fail.

governmental investigation.[84] To best protect the work-product doctrine, a wide scope to the authorization is preferred;

3. When outside counsel is retained, a written retainer agreement should be executed which tracks the language of the formal authorization. This agreement should focus on the need for confidentiality and the maintenance of the attorney-client privilege and work-product doctrine;[85]

4. The investigation should be conducted by attorneys, and all persons working on the investigation, including consultants and accountants, should be hired by the attorneys, and not the company itself, and should report to the attorneys;

5. Senior management should instruct all employees to cooperate with investigating counsel, and to communicate with counsel about matters within the scope of their duties in strict confidence;

6. All documents generated during the course of the investigation should be stamped "Privileged and Confidential: Attorney-Client Privilege and/or Attorney's Work-Product", and should be so marked at the time they are created. This is helpful to demonstrate that there was an expectation of confidentiality;

7. Files generated by the investigation should be maintained separately from other records, and access to these files should be limited to counsel and persons in the company working with counsel on the investigation;

8. Interviews should be conducted in private, and only counsel or their agents should take notes. Counsel should ensure that no verbatim statements are taken from witnesses and that all notes and reports of witness interviews contain attorneys' impressions, conclusions, legal theories or other views.[86] No interviews should be recorded. If verbatim or substantially verbatim statements are taken, counsel's notes made during the investigation may be obtained in discovery or

---

84 The language used in the authorization, however, should also clearly recognize the potential for other litigation not presently foreseen, and should indicate that the potential anticipated litigation "includes but is not limited to" the specific possibilities described.

85 "When a party or the party's attorney has an agent do work for it in anticipation of litigation, one way to ensure that such work will be protected under the work product doctrine is to provide "[c]larity of purpose in the engagement letter...." *McEwen v. Digitran Sys., Inc.*, 155 F.R.D. 678, 683 (D.Utah 1994). Otherwise stated, " '[c]learly the most effective way to guard against inadvertent loss of the protection offered by the work product doctrine is to ensure that management's written authorization to proceed with the investigation identifies, as specifically as possible, the nature of the litigation that is anticipated.' " *Id.* at 683 n. 6 (citing Richard H. Porter, *Voluntary Disclosures to Federal Agencies: Their Impact on the Ability of Corporations to Protect From Discovery Materials Developed During the Course of Internal Investigations*, 39 Cath.U.L.Rev. 1007, 1016 (1990)). An affidavit from counsel indicating that such work was done at his direction in anticipation of specified litigation will also help a party meet its burden under Rule 26(b)(3) of establishing that the work was done in anticipation of litigation. *See Martin v. Monfort, Inc.*, 150 F.R.D. 172, 173 (D.Colo.1993)."

86 *See generally* ABA Seminar on White Collar Crime, *Preserving the Attorney-Client and Work-Product Privileges While Conducting Internal Corporate Investigations* (1989).

by subpoena, or as "Reverse Jencks" material in a criminal trial. (*See* Fed. Rules Crim. P. 26.2); and

9. Any report written by counsel should reference the company's initial request and authorization for the investigation or audit and the need for confidentiality. It should clearly indicate that it is being written by counsel to give legal advice to company management. Legal advice and analysis should be included throughout the report. The document should specifically refer to potential litigation risks and should prominently include counsel's thought processes.[87]

XIV. Other Steps to Establish and Preserve Attorney-Client Privilege and the Work-Product Doctrine in the Context of an Internal Company Investigation

Consideration should also be given to the type of management directive described in *Upjohn*. There, the company's chairman provided a memorandum to all company officials expected to be interviewed, instructing them to communicate directly with outside counsel only, and to treat the matters discussed with counsel as highly confidential. The Supreme Court held that this type of management directive established a clear company intent that communications would remain confidential,[88] a useful predicate in preserving the company attorney-client privilege.

All communications between counsel and company management should be considered and treated as confidential and privileged. Not only should counsel discuss privileged matters only with company officials who have a "need to know," but company officials should not have such discussions with other officials, except on a need-to-know basis.

Counsel conducting the investigation should ensure that, except where joint representation is intended or desirable, an attorney-client relationship is not formed between counsel and company employees.[89] Otherwise, there is a danger that the company employee could waive the privilege when the company wishes its preservation, or attempt to block waiver where the company believes waiver to be in its best interest.[90] Unless joint representation is to be undertaken, part of the process of guarding against the formation of an attorney-client relationship between company counsel and a company employee is for counsel to make it clear to the

---

87 *See The Legal Audit, supra; see also*, Murphy, *Conducting the Compliance Audit: 18 Hints for Survival*, 1 CCQ 4 (Summer 1991).

88 449 U.S. at 387.

89 Considerations of such joint representation, and the potential formation of a common interest or joint defense agreement, are discussed in Chapter 7.

90 Ordinarily, the privilege covering communications between corporate employees and corporate counsel belongs to the company, and not to individual employees, who may not block the company from waiving the privilege. However, under certain circumstances an individual employee may assert attorney-client privilege, notwithstanding the corporate employer's waiver of its privilege. *See United States v. Inter. Brotherhood of Teamsters*, 119 F.3d 210, 215 (2d Cir. 1997).

employee that he or she represents only the company, and not the employee. To preserve the work-product doctrine, recognized in *Hickman* as applying to counsel's interview notes,[91] counsel should strive to include therein his or her legal theories, opinions and mental impressions, so that the notes will qualify as opinion work-product, practically invulnerable to discovery.[92]

Preexisting company documents, unless previously constituting attorney-client communications or attorney work-product, will ordinarily not be privileged or protectable.[93] There will, however, be documents prepared in connection with an internal investigation. Those which constitute attorney-client and work-product should be appropriately labeled, numbered, segregated, and access thereto controlled. Where counsel does not personally prepare such documents they may, nevertheless, be protected if prepared for and under the direction and control of counsel. The latter should contain a specific caption that they have been so prepared, in order to assist counsel in providing the company with legal advice.

It is also necessary to guard against potential waiver in any consultation with outside experts. Such experts should be retained directly by counsel conducting the investigation, specifically for the purpose of assisting counsel in providing legal advice to the company. Retainer agreements between counsel and experts should reflect this purpose, and the experts should be under counsel's supervision and control.

XV. Additional Protection

With regard to the report of the investigation, if the primary consideration is the preservation of the attorney-client privilege and the work-product doctrine, an oral report is preferable. Any corporate minutes reflecting such oral report should not state the content of the report, but merely that the report was given, contained legal advice to the company, and was confidential and privileged, being delivered solely to company officials with a need to know and who had retained counsel to conduct the investigation.

---

91   329 U.S. 495, 510 (1947).

92   *See, e.g.*, Duplan Corp. v. Moulinage et Retorderie de Chavanoz, 509 F.2d 739, 734 (4th Cir. 1974), *cert. denied*, 420 U.S. 997 (1975). *But see Westinghouse*, 951 F.2d at 1431 n.17. However, if the company intends to voluntarily release the final investigative report to the government, there is a real prospect that counsel's notes will be discoverable by a future litigation opponent. That may temper the degree to which those notes should reflect counsel's opinion work-product.

93   *See Gould, Inc. v. Mitsui Mining & Smelting Co.*, 825 F.2d 676, 679-80 (2d Cir. 1987). Preexisting privileged documents should, of course, continue to be handled in a manner to preserve the privilege, as should documents constituting trade secrets or containing other proprietary information. The application of the work-product doctrine to otherwise non-privileged documents which are specifically selected or organized by counsel and are, therefore, reflective of counsel's mental processes, is beyond the scope of this discussion.

Once rendered, the final report should be safeguarded against the kind of disclosure which could effect a waiver of the attorney-client privilege or work-product doctrine. The contents of either an oral or written report should not be discussed or shared with anyone without a need to know, or otherwise beyond the company managers who hold the attorney-client privilege. Similar care should be taken to ensure that the contents of the report are not disclosed under circumstances which either results in their being revealed to an adversary, or increases the likelihood thereof. Care should also be take to properly address, label, store and safeguard any written final report. The report itself should be marked as "Confidential-Protected Attorney-Client Information and Work-Product Matter," or similar labeling. The report should be specifically addressed to the company official(s) or body which retained counsel and ordered the investigation. Copies of the report should be limited, and numbered. The original and all copies of the report should be retained in a secure and limited-access repository, separate from normal company documents. A distribution log should be kept, and all company officials receiving the report of any copy thereof should be required to return it to counsel.

The investigative report and underlying documents must be treated as confidential materials. The company attorney-client privilege may be lost if the results of the investigation are disseminated beyond those company officials who have a need to know the contents.[94]

Under certain circumstances, the company may wish to issue a press release upon the completion of an internal investigation. If the release is carefully drafted, it may not constitute a waiver of the attorney-client privilege or the work-product doctrine, provided the press release merely states a conclusion, *e.g.*, that certain previously reported allegations were found to be "entirely unsubstantiated," without disclosing any of the facts leading to this conclusion, or the substance of the internal investigative report.[95]

XVI. Dealing with the Prosecutor

Ultimately, counsel's most important task is to keep the company from being indicted. Counsel should contact the prosecutors as early as possible in the investigation. Counsel should advise the prosecutors that they have been retained to represent the company, and should offer to accept service of subpoenas on behalf of the company. Counsel should also offer to assist in arranging for service of subpoenas on employees of the company, regardless of whether or not those employees will also be represented by counsel. Cooperation in these areas will promote a good working relationship with the prosecutor, while at the same time

---

94   *See Diversified Industries, Inc. v. Meredith*, 572 F.2d 596, 609-11 (8th Cir. 1978).

95   *See In re Dayco Corp. Derivative Sec. Lit.*, 99 F.R.D. 616, 619 (S.D. Ohio 1983). *But see In re Leslie Fay Companies, Inc. Securities Litigation*, 161 F.R.D. 274, 277 (S.D.N.Y. 1995) [where the investigation and its results were made public to relieve the concerns of creditors, customers and shareholders, there was a waiver].

serving to limit the number of direct contacts between investigators and the company and its employees.

Early on, it is critical to learn from the prosecutors whether the company is a target or subject of the investigation. A negative answer is not necessarily good news; the investigation may still be in its early stages. A positive answer, however, may help the company in deciding how to proceed. Identification of the company as a target may severely limit the advisability of voluntary cooperation. On the other hand, depending upon the facts and evidence available to the prosecutors, cooperation may be the best practical option even if the company receives notice that it is a target. There is no simple formula for deciding whether cooperation is in the best interests of the company. It is ultimately a judgment call based on the individual facts of each investigation.

It is usually possible, early on during the course of an internal investigation, to get a sense of whether there was any wrongdoing, even if substantial detail needs to be filled in. As soon as possible in the process, it is critical that the corporation and counsel consider best and worst case scenarios and make a judgment of what they can live with and what they cannot. Assuming there is something more than *de minimis* criminal conduct, and the company lacks a compliance program, it is very likely the government will seek some sort of penalty if there is a conviction. What the penalty is, of course, will be one of the most critical issues in the case.

From the standpoint of a corporate executive, incarceration is typically the worst punishment. From the company's position, the worst thing that can happen is to be put out of business. If the company needs the government to survive, debarment can be a death penalty for it. Thus, investigations that involve parallel proceedings, for companies that are contractors with the federal government, can be hazardous indeed. A government contractor can be suspended or debarred for a conviction or a civil judgment for many different things including lack of business honesty that affects the present responsibility of a government contractor.[96] But a government contractor can also be suspended from its contract with the federal government, even without a conviction or civil judgment. There is substantial discretion for the government to suspend contracts pending the conclusion of an investigation or trial.[97] Debarment or suspension are often termed the "corporate death penalty".

Regardless of the situation, counsel should make every effort to stay on good terms with the prosecutors. It is important that counsel be viewed as honest and credible by the prosecutors. If counsel are successful in establishing a good relationship with the prosecutors, they may obtain sufficient information, even on an informal basis, to help the company develop a much clearer picture of the direction of the investigation. At a minimum, a good working relationship with the prosecutors will assist counsel to conduct an effective parallel internal

---

96   *See* 48 CFR 9-406-2.

97   *See* 48 CFR 9.407-1.

investigation and thereby position the company to more effectively respond to investigative inquiries.

It is important for counsel to try to learn what the facts are as the prosecutors see them. There are several reasons for this. First, the prosecutors may be wrong about some of the facts, and this may have a significant impact on their ultimate decision whether or not to bring criminal charges. Second, the prosecutors may well know facts that counsel are unaware of, and this will result in an untenable situation for counsel if not remedied. If counsel argue their case to the prosecutors without knowing the correct facts, they will quickly lose credibility. Moreover, the easiest way to be embarrassed—and to forfeit any prospect of shaping the investigation—is to discover that the government knows some critical facts while counsel are unaware of them.

In some cases, when done very carefully, counsel can engage in voluntary exchanges of information with the prosecutors in an effort to convince them that, because of the information being provided, they should not seek an indictment. However, it is critical that counsel have an agreement with the prosecutors, prior to any such voluntary disclosures of information, that the prosecutor will not later claim waiver of attorney-client privilege or the work-product doctrine.[98]

Counsel and client should keep in mind, however, that voluntary disclosures of information can instead have the unintended effect of confirming the prosecutors' suspicions about the merits of the investigation. The prosecutors can be given an unintended psychological boost if they come away from the voluntary exchange with a sense that the investigation is indeed worth the investment of time and resources. On the other hand, if counsel can demonstrate that a critical element of the case will be extremely difficult to prove, it is that much more likely that the prosecutors will choose to spend their time on other matters. For this reason, it is important to consider making a presentation to the prosecutors before they and their agents become personally "invested" in the case. An investigation which drags on for many months tends to take on a life of its own and becomes ever more difficult to terminate as expended investigative hours and resources pile up.

Counsel's job, in addition to finding out the government's case and theories, is to convince the prosecutors that the prosecutors may not win their case. Losing a case, particularly one that has taken substantial governmental resources to investigate, is a prosecutor's worst fear and counsel must subtly play on that. Counsel should make clear to the prosecutor that the company will mount a vigorous defense in the event of indictment. The prosecutors must decide not only whether a crime was committed but whether they will win a trial, and counsel must work on both these fronts when trying to persuade the prosecutors not to indict the company.

---

98   *See* Chapter 3.

Unfortunately, a criminal indictment, by itself, can cause major harm to a company, particularly to a government contractor, which can be suspended from government contracting simply on the basis of an outstanding indictment. An important strategy in dealing with the prosecutor is trying to agree on a compromise. One major fruitful area for compromise is often the possibility of negotiating a civil disposition of the case. The parameters of what that might entail should be discussed with management prior to raising such an issue with the prosecutor. In addition, it is helpful to have such discussions with the prosecutors after disclosing some evidence to them that is not favorable to the proposed government case. In short, it is helpful if counsel can give the prosecutors an incentive to negotiate. This can only be accomplished, however, if counsel have acquired a solid command of the facts, and this can only come about through conducting a thorough investigation.

In order to avoid indictment, the company may find it necessary to make a presentation to the government. As a general rule, this should only be undertaken if the company's counsel believe the prosecutors have an open mind about the case. It is helpful if counsel can discover the specific concerns that the prosecutors have, and then address those concerns specifically, rather than making a general presentation. First, dealing only with the prosecutors' concerns will allow the company to target them and make a more persuasive case. Prosecutors will be less likely to want to proceed with a criminal case, with its heavy burden of proof, if the company's counsel have good answers to the prosecutors' concerns. Moreover, counsel may have discovered potential problems or illegal conduct of which the government is as yet unaware. A general presentation, covering everything that counsel have found out, may inadvertently give the government new information that could harm the company.

Prior to meeting with the prosecutors, counsel should have reached a conclusion about the conduct of the employees whose conduct caused the problem. If counsel concludes that there was no criminal conduct, or only technical violations of law, or even that there were violations but they were not intended, the company may decide to support its employees and not sacrifice them to protect the company. In other cases, again depending on the conduct of the employees in question, counsel may decide that there is no reason to protect the employees and may defend against the company's potential vicarious liability by placing sole blame on the employees. This strategy must be discussed with appropriate company officials who understand the risks associated with the strategy.[99]

When considering whether to bring charges against a company, prosecutors will look at many factors, including: whether the company has a prior criminal history; whether it has cooperated with the investigation; whether there are civil remedies available which can serve as punishment; whether the criminal conduct was committed for profit at the expense of another; and whether deterrence to others is

---

99   *See* Chapter 5.

needed or will be served by a prosecution. If the company can show that it had programs in place to try to prevent such conduct, even if not formal compliance programs, the likelihood of discussions with the prosecutors being successful increases. Clearly, if a company has an effective compliance program, that fact should be communicated, because it may help in convincing the prosecutors either not to indict or proceed against the company at all or else to accept a civil disposition of the case, with a fine and an enhanced compliance program taking the place of an indictment.

Convincing a prosecutor not to proceed with criminal charges is never an easy task. The most powerful strategy in counsel's arsenal is to play to the major fear of a prosecutor: that he or she will lose. This fear may exist because the case is not attractive to a jury, because the client is sympathetic, or because the evidence will not justify a verdict beyond a reasonable doubt. Depending on the type of case, counsel may be able to argue that the violation was a technical violation of the statute not a substantive one, or one that was not intended. Counsel can try to place the blame on one or more employees. Whether or not this will be effective may depend, at least in part, on whether the company has a compliance program in place, whether the conduct in question was affirmatively prohibited by the company, and whether it has remedied the harm and taken steps to prevent future reoccurences (including terminating the employees involved or otherwise disciplining them). If the company has not been in trouble before, that fact will also be important.

Of the various possible strategies open to counsel, possibly the most useful, since the prosecutor "needs" to walk away with something, lies with the option of finding a civil or administrative penalty that is appropriate.

In the end, however, assuming the case is not open and shut or egregious, the decision to prosecute will most often be determined by what the prosecutors believe was the intent of the company when it undertook the action in question. Counsel can make a strong case if there was no quest for illegal gain, or harm to the government, or if counsel can argue that regulations were complicated and subject to misinterpretation. In most company investigations, the conduct of just a few employees may determine whether the company did anything illegal. In such cases, counsel can make a good argument for exercising prosecutorial discretion not to prosecute. And a good relationship with the prosecutors only enhances the possibility of such an argument succeeding.

Ultimately, there is only so much counsel can do to move the prosecutors to a decision about what to do with the case. While this may be frustrating for the company, delay of a decision to prosecute almost always works in the company's favor in the long run, particularly if it has used the time to prepare its defense.

The entire chapter, to this point, has been premised on the assumption that a government criminal investigation is underway. There will be times, however, when counsel will be asked to give advice to the company on whether the company should voluntarily report to the government evidence it has discovered that the company has violated the law, when there is no government investigation pending.

Voluntary self-reporting is a two-edged sword. The Federal Sentencing Guidelines push hard in this area by applying a significant five-point reduction for self-reporting (the largest mitigating factor available), when combined with acceptance of responsibility.[100] This mirrors a trend across federal agencies to deal more leniently with self-reporting companies, in both criminal and civil contexts. For example, the Department of Justice has specific voluntary disclosure guidelines that offer amnesty or immunity to corporations that report criminal antitrust or environmental violations.[101] The benefits that accrue to self-reporting companies include a tendency not to prosecute such companies criminally, a reduction in fines and other penalties, and a lower risk of auditing and inspection.

On the other hand, notwithstanding the general movement towards a corporate duty of investigation and compliance, no general principle of law requires a company to "turn itself in" for every conceivable violation that comes to its attention.[102] Executives and company counsel need to carefully consider the potential consequences of raising a red flag with authorities. Statements to authorities could be deemed admissions, or a waiver of the attorney-client privilege, and there is always the danger that the government will broaden an investigation to encompass far more than the isolated instance (or instances) that triggered the self-reporting. Further complicating the analysis is the issue of whether illegal or questionable activity might be deemed "material" to investors, thus requiring disclosure under the securities laws.[103] The issues that arise in situations where there is no investigation are sometimes more difficult strategically than decisions faced in the course of a government investigation.

---

100 By itself, an effective compliance program qualifies for a three point reduction in culpability. *See* Sentencing Guidelines § 8C2.5(f), (g) (1998). This is discussed in detail in Chapter 8.

101 *See*, Black, *Corporate Internal Investigations*, Vol. C5, Business Law Monographs (1998) at § 3.02[3][c].

102 *See* Black, *Corporate Internal Investigations*, Vol. C5, Business Law Monographs (1998) at § 3.02[3][a] ("[a] corporation and its directors generally have no affirmative duty to report or disclose evidence of criminal conduct or the results of internal investigations to law enforcement authorities").

103 *See generally id. at* § 3.02[3][b].

CHAPTER 6:
PARALLEL CIVIL, CRIMINAL & ADMINISTRATIVE PROCEEDINGS

I. The Significance of Parallel Proceedings

Counsel who are dealing with an allegation of corporate misconduct must be alert to the possibility of, and the risks posed by, "parallel" criminal, civil or administrative actions. The term "parallel" proceedings refers to simultaneous or successive investigations or litigation arising from a common set of facts. A company may face parallel proceedings initiated by the Department of Justice and other government agencies, or by a government agency and a private party (*e.g.*, a "whistleblower"). For example, an alleged corporate fraud might result in a *criminal* investigation or prosecution of the company or company employees, a *civil* action against the company under the False Claims Act[1] ("FCA") or other federal statute,[2] and *administrative* claims by one or more government agencies for regulatory sanctions or debarment.

In today's legal environment, corporate counsel must always bear in mind the threat of parallel proceedings with respect to a matter. Sometimes the threat is obvious because the multiple proceedings all are out in the open. Frequently, however, a matter first arises in a single arena—as a criminal investigation, a civil suit, or an administrative action or investigation—and only later does the parallel proceeding commence or surface. It cannot safely be assumed that the immediate problem confronting the company is the only one that will have to be dealt with before the matter is over. To the contrary, it may be only the tip of the legal iceberg[3]—other and possibly worse problems may loom ahead just beneath the surface.

---

1   31 USC §§ 3729, *et seq.*

2   White collar criminal statutes may contain provisions for civil penalties, *see, e.g.*, RICO (18 USC § 1964 and the Securities Act of 1933 (15 USC § 77t); or corresponding statutes may authorize civil suits. *See, e.g.*, the Internal Revenue Code (26 USC § 7402) and the Sherman Act (15 USC § 15).

3   For example, an administrative subpoena issued to a company by an agency Inspector General's office may signal trouble on several fronts, criminal as well as administrative.

This risk of parallel proceedings must be assessed at the outset of any internal investigation, and thereafter on an ongoing basis, and factored into the company's strategy for responding to the immediate problem. Counsel must be aware that decisions made responding to one proceeding can have substantial consequences elsewhere. For example, the response to a notice for the civil deposition of a company officer may have a profound effect on a subsequent criminal investigation just over the horizon.

The basic concern, of course, is how each of the various parallel proceedings may impact upon the others. Essentially, there are two principal issues to be considered. The first is whether the outcome of one proceeding may have some preclusive effect upon another by virtue of the doctrines of *res judicata* or collateral estoppel. The second is whether the litigation of one proceeding may result in either obtaining or disclosing evidence that could be helpful or harmful in another proceeding; that is, what might be termed the "discovery issue."

II. The Preclusive Impact of One Proceeding upon a Parallel Proceeding

A criminal conviction will bind a company in subsequent civil and administrative proceedings with respect to issues resolved as part of the criminal prosecution.[4] Further, because of the doctrine of respondeat superior, a criminal conviction of an individual officer or employee of a business may bind the business in subsequent civil or administrative proceedings.[5] However, because of the difference in the applicable standards of proof, an acquittal in a criminal case ordinarily cannot be used to bar the government from pursuing civil or administrative proceedings.[6] For the same reason, an adverse judgment in a civil or administrative proceeding will not be binding against the defendant in a criminal prosecution.[7]

Administrative adjudications can have preclusive effect in parallel civil or administrative proceedings, provided that the party against whom preclusion is invoked had a full and fair opportunity to litigate the relevant claim or issue in the original proceeding.[8] For example, it has been held that a debarment proceeding is sufficiently adjudicatory and final to give rise to claim preclusion in other proceedings.[9]

---

4   *See, e.g., Gelb v. Royal Globe Ins. Co.*, 798 F.2d 38, 43 (2d Cir. 1986), *cert. denied*, 479 U.S. 1081 (1987); *Chisholm v. Defense Logistics Agency*, 656 F.2d 42 (3d Cir. 1981).

5   *United States v. DiBona*, 614 F. Supp. 40 (E.D. Pa. 1984).

6   *One Lot Emerald Cut Stones v. United States*, 409 U.S. 232, 235 (1972); *United States v. JT Construction Co.*, 668 F. Supp. 592 (W.D. Tex. 1987).

7   *United States v. General Dynamics Corp.*, 828 F.2d 1356, 1361 n.5 (9th Cir. 1987).

8   *See Jorden v. National Guard Bureau*, 877 F.2d 245, 249-50 (3d Cir. 1989); *Nasem v. Brown*, 595 F.2d 801, 805 (D.C. Cir. 1979).

9   *U.S. v. Peppertree Apartments*, 942 F.2d 1555, 1558-60 (11th Cir. 1991) (HUD debarment collaterally estopped respondent from contesting double damages civil action brought by government); *Facchiano v. Dept. of Labor*, 859 F.2d 1163, 1167 (3d Cir. 1988).

Another issue that has arisen is whether the Double Jeopardy Clause of the Fifth Amendment can be invoked to preclude a criminal prosecution after the imposition of a punitive sanction (*e.g.*, civil money penalties) in a civil or administrative proceeding based on the same set of facts, or conversely, whether a prior criminal prosecution might bar a subsequent civil or administrative action seeking money penalties. The Supreme Court's decision in *United States v. Halper,* 490 U.S. 435 (1989), provided a glimmer of hope that the Double Jeopardy Clause might be applied in the context of parallel proceedings. In *Halper,* the Court found the imposition of civil money penalties totaling $130,000 for a loss to the government of $600 was punitive and violated the double jeopardy prohibition because the defendant previously had been convicted criminally based on the same underlying facts.[10]

In 1997, however, the Supreme Court revisited the issue in *Hudson v. United States,* 522 U.S. 93 (1997). In that case, the Office of the Comptroller of the Currency had assessed penalties against three individuals who were also precluded from participating in the affairs of any banking institution. Subsequently, the individuals were indicted on a number of criminal charges involving the same set of facts which gave rise to the civil penalties. Relying on the *Halper* decision, the lower courts dismissed the indictments. The Supreme Court reversed and reinstated the indictments, stating "[t]he Clause protects only against the imposition of multiple *criminal* punishments for the same offense."[11] The Court repudiated its previous decision in *Halper,* stating that it had failed to determine as a preliminary matter that the sanction in that case was "criminal in nature."[12] The *Halper* decision, the Court concluded, "was ill considered" and "proved unworkable."[13] Thus, after *Hudson,* the double jeopardy bar has no application, absent multiple criminal punishments or civil sanctions that are "so punitive in form and effect as to render them criminal despite Congress' intent to the contrary."[14]

III. The Discovery Issue

Turning to the discovery issue, the paramount concern is that the defense of a civil action or administrative proceeding may prejudice the company with respect to a parallel criminal proceeding. In many criminal cases, the safest course for a corporate defendant may be to play its cards close to the vest and disclose as little as possible about the facts of the case or the potential defenses.[15] The need to defend

---

10   490 U.S. at 438-39.

11   522 U.S. 93, 118 S.Ct. 488, 493 (emphasis in the original) citing *Helvering v. Mitchell*, 303 U.S. 391, 399 (1935).

12   522 U.S. at ___, 118 S.Ct. at 494.

13   *Id.*

14   522 U.S. at ___, 118 S.Ct. at 495, citing *United States v. Ursery,* 518 U.S. 267, 289 (1996).

15   Of course, a corporation has no Fifth Amendment privilege that it may invoke to stay silent, as an individual could. *See United States v. Kordel*, 397 U.S. 1, 8 & n.9 (1970). Nonetheless, as a practical matter, corporations usually can utilize essentially the same strategy of silence in the

against a parallel civil action or administrative proceeding may cause a company (or its employees) to forego such a strategy and make statements that later can be used against them in the criminal case.[16] Similarly, in the course of defending a civil or administrative matter, a company may make revealing disclosures or even effectuate a waiver of the attorney-client and attorney work product privileges with respect to the criminal case.[17]

Civil discovery rules allow for extremely broad discovery and can provide the government access to evidence not normally available in a criminal investigation.[18] A company's refusal to submit to civil discovery to prevent the disclosure of prejudicial information can result in a default and entry of judgment against the corporation. Furthermore, in criminal cases, the Fifth Amendment prohibits any adverse inference being drawn against a company or its employees because the employees assert their privilege against self-incrimination. In civil cases, however, it is permissible to draw an adverse inference based on an assertion of the privilege.[19] These considerations frequently lead companies and their employees to provide information or testimony in defense of a civil or administrative matter. But testimony in a civil deposition, for example, may come back to haunt a defendant in a parallel criminal investigation. There is nothing so convincing in a criminal case as the admission of a key fact by the defendant (or an employee by whose testimony the corporate defendant is bound).

Likewise, the defense of a criminal investigation may prejudice the defense of a parallel civil or administrative action. As noted above, a refusal to provide information or testimony may trigger an adverse inference or even a default judgment. Conversely, in order to defend against criminal charges, a company sometimes may make voluntary disclosures to the government which could be used against it in a parallel civil or administrative action. For example, the company may decide to waive its attorney-client and work product privileges and disclose the results of an internal investigation in an effort to persuade the government that there was no criminal misconduct, although the company may have been negligent or innocently violated applicable legal requirements. Such admissions could be devastating in a parallel proceeding where a lesser standard of liability applies.

On the other hand, the defense of a civil or administrative matter sometimes may provide an opportunity for discovery that the company otherwise could not obtain,

---

face of a criminal investigation by relying on a combination of their employees' Fifth Amendment rights and their own attorney-client and attorney work product privileges.

16   *See Mainelli v. United States*, 611 F. Supp. 606, 615 (D. R.I. 1985).

17   There is a split among the federal circuits as to the scope of the waiver effected by a disclosure of privileged information to a government agency, but the great majority hold that such a disclosure effects a complete waiver of the privilege. *See United States v. Massachusetts Institute of Technology*, 129 F.3d 681, 685 (1st Cir. 1997)(collecting cases).

18   *See* Fed.R.Civ.P. 26.

19   *See Baxter v. Palmigiano*, 425 U.S. 308, 318 (1976).

of at least some of the government's evidence and theories with respect to a parallel criminal case. The government might attempt to block such discovery by asserting the law enforcement investigatory privilege as a basis for withholding evidence.[20] This privilege, however, is not absolute, and the government often fails to invoke it correctly.[21]

IV. The Government's Use of Parallel Proceedings as an Enforcement Tool

Parallel proceedings have become a key tool in the government's white collar enforcement effort. It is increasingly common in complex cases for the government to pursue the full range of criminal, civil and administrative remedies and sanctions at its disposal—all at the same time. From the government's perspective, this "new litigation environment" presents a challenge requiring "greater cooperation, communication and teamwork between the criminal and civil prosecutors who are often conducting parallel investigations of the same offenders and matters."[22] In order to facilitate such cooperation and maximize the efficient use of resources, government attorneys have been directed to consider investigative steps common to civil and criminal prosecutions, and to agency actions, so that strategies can be jointly coordinated in appropriate cases. Justice Department procedures encourage parallel proceedings by requiring government attorneys to perform:

- timely assessment of the civil and administrative potential in all criminal case referrals, indictments and declarations;

- timely assessment of the criminal potential in all civil case referrals and complaints;

- effective and timely communication with cognizant agency officials, including suspension and debarment authorities, to enable agencies to pursue available remedies;

- early and regular communication between civil and criminal attorneys regarding *qui tam* cases [*i.e.*, False Claims Act cases initiated by private parties] and other

---

20 *See Dellwood Farms, Inc. v. Cargill, Inc.*, 128 F.3d 1122 (7th Cir. 1997); *In re Sealed Case*, 856 F.2d 268, 271 (D. C. Cir. 1988); *Friedman v. Bache Halsey Stuart Shields, Inc.*, 738 F.2d 1336, 1341-42 (D.C. Cir. 1984); *Black v. Sheraton Corp. of America*, 564 F.2d 531, 544 (D.C. Cir. 1977).

21 When an agency moves to suspend a contractor—a temporary exclusion imposed upon a suspected wrongdoer pending the outcome of an investigation and any ensuing judicial proceedings—the applicable regulations specifically provide for limiting disclosure of the government's evidence where it is determined that a substantial interest of the government in parallel proceedings would be prejudiced. Nevertheless, the courts have opined that agencies must still work to "carve out" as much evidence as is reasonable for release to the respondent to assist in defending itself. *ATL, Inc. v. United States*, 736 F.2d 677, 685 (Fed. Cir. 1984). There generally is no comparable regulatory limit on discovery where a debarment —which is an exclusion for a fixed period, usually some number of years—is concerned.

22 *See*, Memorandum from the Attorney General to DOJ Attorneys dated July 28, 1997, at Appendix 1.

civil referrals, especially when the civil case is developed ahead of the criminal prosecution; and

- coordination, when appropriate, with state and local authorities.[23]

V. The Government's Right to Proceed on Multiple Fronts

From the perspective of an embattled company, the government's pursuit of simultaneous civil and criminal proceedings raises questions about fundamental fairness. The company is confronted with a dilemma—does it aggressively defend itself in the civil action and run the risk of prejudicing its position in the parallel criminal investigation? Or does it gear its strategy to defending the criminal matter and thereby risk prejudicing its defense of the civil action? Nevertheless, the right of the government to proceed on multiple fronts was settled almost thirty years ago in favor of allowing such proceedings. Under most circumstances, the government may choose to proceed civilly, administratively and criminally against a single defendant or investigative subject at the same time.

In *United States v. Kordel*, 397 U.S. 1 (1970) the Supreme Court rejected constitutional challenges to parallel civil and criminal proceedings based on the Fifth Amendment privilege against compulsory self-incrimination and on due process grounds. In *Kordel*, the government instituted a civil *in rem* action against two food products on the grounds that the company distributed them in violation of the Food, Drug, and Cosmetic Act.[24] The government served upon the company, its president and vice-president, extensive interrogatories calling for detailed information about the company's products. After the government notified the company that it was also considering a criminal prosecution for violations based on the same facts as those in the civil case, the company moved for a stay of further proceedings in the civil case, or to extend the time for responding to the interrogatories until after resolution of the anticipated criminal proceedings. The district court denied the motion and ordered the company to answer the interrogatories, which it did through its president. The civil case eventually was settled, but the government filed criminal charges against the company's president and vice-president. The interrogatory answers helped the government secure the criminal convictions of those two executive officers.

On appeal, the Sixth Circuit reversed the convictions on the basis that the defendants had been compelled to incriminate themselves in the civil suit under threat of serious penalty to the company if they refused. The Supreme Court rejected that conclusion and reinstated the convictions. It ruled that there had been no Fifth Amendment violation. "[The company's president] need not have answered the interrogatories. Without question, he could have invoked his Fifth Amendment privilege against compulsory self-incrimination. Surely, [he] was not barred from

---

23 *Id.*, Memorandum at 2.

24 21 U.S.C. §§ 301 *et seq.*

asserting his privilege simply because the corporation had no privilege of its own, or because the proceeding in which the government sought information was civil rather than criminal in character."[25]

Turning to the due process challenge, the Supreme Court did not rule out the possibility of a due process violation if the circumstances of parallel proceedings offend concepts of fundamental fairness, but it found no such defect in *Kordel*. It noted that the facts before it did not involve circumstances in which "the Government has brought a civil action solely to obtain evidence for its criminal prosecution or has failed to advise the defendant in its civil proceeding that it contemplates his criminal prosecution; nor with a case where the defendant is without counsel or reasonably fears prejudice from adverse pretrial publicity or other unfair injury; nor with any other special circumstances that might justify that unconstitutionality or even the impropriety of this criminal prosecution."[26] The Court implied that had it found such "special circumstances" to exist, the parallel proceedings would have been constitutionally impermissible.

What limitations do exist on the government's ability to use parallel proceedings against a defendant? In *United States v. LaSalle National Bank*, 437 U.S. 298 (1978), a case involving parallel civil and criminal IRS investigations, the Supreme Court indicated that the government may not abuse the civil discovery process by using it for the sole purpose of obtaining evidence for a parallel criminal investigation. The Court recognized that the "improper purpose doctrine" would limit the government's right to pursue parallel proceedings if the government failed to act in good faith.[27] At the same time, however, the Court stated that there was no impropriety if an agency uses discovery with mixed motives, to seek evidence that could support both civil and criminal proceedings. Thus, the burden of showing that the government manipulated the parallel proceedings in bad faith is a difficult one.[28]

Although some courts have suggested that *LaSalle* may be limited to parallel IRS proceedings,[29] others have applied it to non-IRS proceedings.[30] Still other courts, without citing *LaSalle*, have indicated that Fifth Amendment and ethical concerns are implicated when the government directly or indirectly sponsors a civil lawsuit to aid a criminal investigation.[31] In practice, however, courts are reluctant to find a

---

25 *Id.*, 397 U.S. at 7-8.

26 *Id.* at 11-12.

27 437 U.S. at 314.

28 *Id.* at 316.

29 See *United States v. Educational Development Network Corp.*, 884 F.2d 737, 742 (3d Cir. 1989).

30 See *United States v. Cahill*, 920 F.2d 421, 428 (7th Cir. 1990).

31 See, e.g., *In re Grand Jury Subpoena*, 836 F.2d 1468, 1472 n.6 (4th Cir. 1988).

due process violation when the government proceeds against a company on multiple fronts. The motivations for the government's actions, whether civil or criminal, are rarely simple or easy to discern, and the government normally enjoys a presumption that it acts in good faith. Courts are hesitant to intervene absent a showing of bad faith by the government,[32] and usually it is difficult to make such a showing.

The law is clear, however, that the government cannot use the grand jury process for the purpose of eliciting evidence for use in a parallel civil case.[33] By law, matters occurring before the grand jury are secret.[34] Grand jury testimony and exhibits are available to Justice Department prosecutors for use in a criminal investigation or prosecution. However, such materials may not be disclosed to other government attorneys for use in preparing a civil suit except by court order based upon a showing of particularized need.[35] Agency attorneys or employees may be specially deputized to assist Justice Department prosecutors in their criminal enforcement efforts and then be granted access to grand jury materials, but solely for that purpose. The law is violated if the deputized attorney simultaneously acts as an agency lawyer with respect to the same matter or if he transmits grand jury materials to the agency for use in a parallel proceeding.[36]

Given that a company cannot, except in rare circumstances, prevent the government from pursuing parallel proceedings against it, what steps may it take to ameliorate the dilemma of simultaneously defending itself on two different fronts and the attendant risks of prejudicing its position on one or both fronts? There are two possibilities—securing a protective order with respect to testimony adduced in the civil or administrative proceeding, or securing a stay of the civil/administrative proceeding. As will be discussed below, a protective order is ineffective in many jurisdictions and a stay, although efficacious, is often difficult to obtain.

VI. The Use of Protective Orders to Resolve Parallel Proceedings Issues

The problem with using protective orders in an effort to resolve parallel proceedings issues is illustrated by *In re Grand Jury Subpoena*, 836 F.2d 1468 (4th Cir.

---

32   *See SEC v. Dresser Industries, Inc.*, 628 F.2d 1368, 1375-76 (D.C. Cir.)(*en banc*), *cert. denied*, 449 U.S. 993 (1980).

33   *United States v. Sells Engineering, Inc.*, 463 U.S. 418, 432 (1983); *United States v. Proctor & Gamble Co.*, 356 U.S. 677, 683-84 (1958).

34   Fed.R.Crim.P. 6(e).

35   *United States v. Sells Engineering, Inc.*, 463 U.S. 418 (1983).

36   *See United States v. Gold*, 470 F. Supp. 1336 (N.D. Ill. 1979).; *General Motors Corp. v. United States*, 573 F.2d 936 (6th Cir.), *appeal dism. en banc*, 584 F.2d 1336 (6th Cir. 1978), *cert. denied*, 440 U.S. 934 (1979); *but see United States v. John Doe, Inc., I*, 481 U.S. 102, 108-09 (1987)(Rule 6(e) is not violated when a government attorney who legitimately utilized grand jury materials in the course of a criminal investigation later reviews those same materials while preparing to represent the government in related civil proceedings).

1988). In that case, former officers and directors of a parent company whose subsidiary was under investigation by a Maryland federal grand jury, received notice that their deposition testimony was being sought in a civil action pending in federal district court in Virginia. The Virginia litigation involved issues concerning the activities of the subsidiary and its parent, but the deponents were not parties to the case. The deponents moved for a stay of civil discovery pending completion of the Maryland grand jury investigation. After conducting a hearing on the matter, the Virginia district court denied the motion for a stay but, with the consent of all parties and the deponents, instead issued a protective order sealing the deposition transcripts and limiting access to the transcripts to the parties in the civil action. The protective order entered by the Virginia court specifically provided that the sealed depositions and information contained therein "shall not be made available to any state or federal investigating agency or authority."[37]

Shortly after the depositions were given, the Maryland grand jury issued a subpoena duces tecum for the production of the deposition transcripts of two of the officers. In a hearing on a motion to quash this subpoena, the Virginia judge explained that the protective order was entered to bar access to the transcripts by the Maryland grand jury and that the deponents were entitled to rely on the order to protect their Fifth Amendment rights. The Maryland district court was of a different view and denied a corresponding motion to quash after concluding that a civil protective order cannot be used to shield discovery matters from a subpoena issued by a grand jury.

Upon appeal, the Fourth Circuit refused to uphold the validity of the protective order. It framed the issues as involving the intersection of the three interests: (1) the authority of a grand jury to gather evidence in a criminal investigation; (2) the deponents' right against self-incrimination; and (3) the goals of the liberal discovery and efficient dispute resolution in civil proceedings.[38] The Fourth Circuit acknowledged that the grand jury subpoena sought discovery materials which were produced in reliance on the Virginia district court's protective order. Nevertheless, the court ruled that the officers were not entitled to rely upon the shield of a civil protective order to prevent disclosure of their depositions to the parallel grand jury proceeding in Maryland.

> A grand jury, subject only to the limitations of the fifth amendment, has the right to all relevant evidence. A protective order, while a significant impediment to a grand jury investigation, cannot effectively deal in all instances with the problems posed by civil litigants and witnesses who plead the fifth amendment during pretrial discovery. It is not therefore a substitute for invocation to privilege, and should not be afforded that status.[39]

---

37   *Id.* at 1469.

38   *Id.* at 1471.

39   *Id.* at 1474-75.

At least two other circuits agree with the Fourth Circuit's adoption of a per se rule preferring grand jury subpoenas over civil protective orders.[40] The Second Circuit disagrees and has refused to enforce a grand jury subpoena to require the disclosure of information subject to a valid protective order absent a showing that the protective order should not have been entered or the existence of some other extraordinary circumstance or compelling need.[41] The First Circuit declines to follow either approach, opting instead for a modified per se rule that a grand jury subpoena trumps a protective order unless the person seeking to avoid the subpoena can demonstrate the existence of exceptional circumstances clearly favoring subordinating the subpoena to the protective order.[42] Thus, in many jurisdictions, a company under investigation cannot rely on a protective order to safeguard it or its employees against "leakage" of information disclosed in one parallel proceeding. As a general rule, companies are wise to assume that any information or testimony provided in a civil or administrative proceeding eventually may find its way into a parallel criminal proceeding involving the same or similar matters.

VII. The Use of Stays to Resolve Parallel Proceedings Issues

A stay of the civil (or administrative) proceeding pending the outcome of the criminal proceeding is an effective way to resolve the parallel proceedings dilemma. However, a stay is often difficult to obtain. As discussed above, courts start from the proposition that "[i]n the absence of substantial prejudice to the rights of the parties involved, parallel proceedings are unobjectionable. . . ."[43] Thus, the party requesting the stay "must make out a clear case of hardship or inequity in being required to go forward."[44]

Generally, the courts have great discretion in deciding whether to grant a stay, and must balance the competing concerns of the (private or government) plaintiff with the harm to the defendant by letting both proceedings go forward at once.[45] Many courts follow a five-part test when reviewing the competing interests of the parties and determining whether to grant a stay: (1) the interest of the plaintiff in proceeding expeditiously with the civil action and the prejudice to the plaintiff of a delay; (2) the burden on the defendant; (3) the convenience of the courts; (4) the interests of persons not parties to the civil litigation; and (5) the public interest.[46]

---

40   *See In Re Grand Jury Subpoena*, 62 F.3d 1222, 1224 (9th Cir. 1995); and *In Re Grand Jury Proceedings*, 995 F.2d 1013, 1020 (11th Cir. 1993).

41   *See In Re Grand Jury Subpoena Duces Tecum*, 945 F.2d 1221, 1224-25 (2d Cir. 1991); *see also General Dynamics Corp. v. Selb Mfg. Co.*, 481 F.2d *cert. denied*, 414 U.S. 1162 (1974).

42   *See In Re Grand Jury Subpoena*, 138 F.3d 442, 445 (1st Cir. 1998).

43   *SEC v. Dresser Industries, Inc.*, 628 F.2d 1368, 1375 (D.C. Cir.)(*en banc*), *cert. denied*, 449 U.S. 993 (1980).

44   *Landis v. North American Co.*, 299 U.S. 248 (1936).

45   Milton Pollack, *Parallel Civil and Criminal Proceedings*, 129 F.R.D. 201, 203 (1989).

46   *Keating v. OTS*, 45 F.3d 322, 324-25 (9th Cir. 1995); *Arden Way Ass'n v. Boesky*, 660 F. Supp. 1494, 1496-97 (S.D.N.Y. 1987); *In re Mid-Atlantic Toyota Antitrust Litigation*, 92 F.R.D. 358,

The threshold issue in determining whether a stay is warranted is the degree to which the civil issues overlap with the criminal issues.[47] The court must be persuaded that there is a significant overlap of issues and that the defendant faces a real danger of prejudice if required to litigate both proceedings at the same time. Otherwise, there is no reason for the court even to consider granting a stay.

Next, the countervailing interest of the plaintiff in proceeding expeditiously must be weighed. One court has succinctly summarized this issue as follows: "[w]itnesses relocate, memories fade, and persons allegedly aggrieved are unable to seek vindication or redress for indefinite periods of time on end."[48] The defendant may be able to mitigate the court's concerns about delay causing deterioration of the evidence by agreeing that as much discovery as possible—*i.e.* document production and depositions of witnesses who do not have Fifth Amendment privilege issues—shall be completed before the stay of proceedings is imposed.

In most cases, the decision whether to grant a stay will turn on the court's evaluation of the competing interests of the plaintiff and the defendant. The remaining factors—the convenience of the courts, the interests of persons not parties to the civil litigation, and the public interest—usually will not weigh heavily either for or against a stay. In certain cases, however, one or more of these factors may tip the balance and become decisive.[49]

The stage of the parallel criminal proceeding may also substantially affect the determination of whether a stay should be granted:

> The strongest case for a stay of discovery in the civil case occurs during a criminal prosecution after an indictment is returned. The potential for self-incrimination is greatest during this stage, and the potential harm to civil litigants arising from delaying them is reduced due to the promise of a fairly quick resolution of the criminal case under the Speedy Trial Act.[50]

In contrast, pre-indictment requests for a stay are far more difficult to obtain because the risk of self-incrimination often is more speculative at that juncture and the prospective delay of the civil case is longer.[51] Sometimes, it is possible to procure a stay if the government is conducting an active parallel criminal

---

359 (D. Md. 1981); *Golden Quality Ice Cream Co. v. Deerfield Specialty Papers, Inc.*, 87 F.R.D. 53, 56-58 (E.D. Pa. 1980).

47   *Parallel Proceedings*, 129 F.R.D. at 203.

48   *In re Mid-Atlantic Toyota Antitrust Litigation*, 92 F.R.D. at 359; *see also Fidelity Nat. Title Ins. Co. v. National Title Resources Corp.*, 980 F. Supp. 1022, 1024 (D. Minn. 1997).

49   *See Walsh Securities, Inc. v. Cristo Property Mgmt., Ltd.*, 7 F. Supp. 2d 523, 528-29 (D.N.J. 1998).

50   *Id.* at 527, *quoting Parallel Proceedings*, 129 F.R.D. at 204.

51   *See Trustees of Plumbers and Pipefitters Nat. Pension Fund v. Transworld Mechanical, Inc.*, 886 F. Supp. 1134, 1139-40 (S.D.N.Y. 1995).

investigation.[52] If, however, no known investigation is underway, the chances of obtaining a stay are slim.[53]

It has been suggested that corporate defendants facing parallel proceedings are less likely candidates for a stay because they do not have a privilege against self-incrimination that would be adversely affected by the denial of a stay.[54] This contention, however, largely ignores reality. Although the corporate defendant, itself, does not have a Fifth Amendment privilege, in most instances key officers or employees will have legitimate self-incrimination concerns. Their desire to protect themselves from self-incrimination will hobble the corporation's ability to defend itself with respect to the civil proceeding. Moreover, frequently these individuals will be co-defendants of the corporation in the civil proceeding. In such cases, judicial efficiency is promoted by extending any stay granted to the individual defendants to the corporation as well.[55] Thus, in most cases, the analysis of whether a stay is warranted should not be altered simply because the defendant is a corporation rather than an individual.

In summary, corporations facing a criminal prosecution or investigation must develop and present a strong case in order to obtain a stay of a parallel civil proceeding. They must be able to articulate clearly and persuasively the harm that will be suffered if the stay is not granted, and to explain why that harm outweighs any countervailing interests that may exist.

VIII. A Balancing Act

Given the present state of the law on parallel proceedings, counsel must take many considerations into account when advising a corporate client how to proceed with an issue involving alleged misconduct. How many different proceedings does the company face, either now or in the foreseeable future? What are the implications of the company's response to investigative requests or discovery demands? What should company employees be told about the risk in submitting to interviews or depositions? If the company chooses not to cooperate with investigators, what will be the likely effect on the company, its employees, its licenses and its ability to continue conducting business with the government? What are the implications for the company and its employees of a decision to voluntarily disclose the results of an internal review to one set of government attorneys?

The starting point for resolving the complex issues presented by parallel proceedings is to understand the relative importance of the stakes involved in the different arenas insofar as the client is concerned. For individuals, including corporate

---

52   *See, e.g., Walsh Securities*, 7 F. Supp. 2d at 527; *Parallel Proceedings*, 129 F.R.D. at 204.

53   *Id.*

54   *In re Mid-Atlantic Toyota Antitrust Litigation*, 92 F.R.D. at 360.

55   *See Trustees of Plumbers and Pipefitters Nat. Pension Fund v. Transworld Mechanical, Inc.*, 886 F. Supp. at 1141.

directors and officers, the danger of a criminal conviction and possible incarceration usually will outweigh the consequences of a civil or administrative proceeding. But the company often has a different set of priorities. For example, if the company is a government contractor or does business in a highly regulated industry, the consequences of a criminal conviction usually are less severe than the economic "death penalty" that could result from a debarment or exclusion from program participation. For a company whose government business is not significant, the predominant concern may be the outcome of civil litigation, where the possible damages may exceed any likely criminal penalty. Once the priorities are correctly identified, it is possible to begin formulating a strategy for the client. The components of that strategy, however, can only be determined on a case-by-case basis.

CHAPTER 7:
MULTIPLE REPRESENTATION

I. Introduction

"Multiple representation" is the representation of more than one client by the same counsel in the same legal matter. Multiple representation issues arise early in just about every internal investigation case. The company acts through its employees;[1] but the company's interests may diverge from the interests of its employees and, where this is the case, continued multiple representation of those employees by the company's counsel would be improper. Applying the ethical rules regarding conflict of interest in the context of an internal investigation can be difficult, especially since, at the time a decision must first be made, the internal or government investigation will have normally just begun and counsel will have very little information available to them to judge the likelihood of a conflict. In addition, the very persons responsible for the decision to hire counsel[2] may themselves be surprised to learn that they need to have separate counsel. The main risk faced in embarking on a course of multiple representation that may later develop into a full-fledged conflict of interest is the risk of subsequent disqualification of company counsel.[3] This chapter is devoted to an analysis of multiple representation questions confronted during an internal investigation and the resulting implications for civil and criminal litigation that can develop.

II. Conflicts and Disqualification

Both the Model Rules of Professional Conduct and the Code of Professional Responsibility contain several provisions with regard to the conflicts of interest that can arise in the context of any multiple representation. Conflicts that are identified can be classified into two categories, waivable and nonwaivable. Even with full disclosure and client consent, conflicts that present interests that are directly ad-

---

1   The use of the term employees also includes officers of the company.

2   References to counsel herein refer to outside counsel hired to conduct an investigation on behalf of the company as distinguished from general counsel employed directly by the company.

3   *See United States v. Izydore*, 167 F.3rd 213, 220 (5th Cir. 1999); citing *Strickland v. Washington*, 466 U.S. 668, 689 (1984); *Wheat v. United States*. 486 U.S. 153 (1988).

verse cannot be waived.[4] In the context of internal and government investigations, the issues that have become the focus of published court decisions fall into three basic categories: the lawyer's duty to zealously advocate his or her client's interests,[5] the lawyer's obligation to protect the confidences of his or her client,[6] and the lawyer's duty to avoid even the appearance of impropriety in connection with the multiple representation.[7] In each of these areas, the issue of whether counsel had a conflict has been litigated in the context of a prosecutor's subsequent attempt to have counsel disqualified.

The legal standard for the disqualification of counsel is generally difficult to meet. Courts are loath to grant this type of relief and usually give broad deference to any individual with respect to his or her choice of counsel. Additionally, courts are sensitive to the tactical nature of such motions when brought by a prosecutor.[8] Nevertheless, the Sixth Amendment right to effective counsel does not provide a criminal defendant with an untrammeled right to choose counsel.[9] Where a conflict exists and is likely to affect counsel's ability to act on behalf of one of his or her clients, courts have not hesitated to curtail this freedom and to grant motions to disqualify on any of the three most common grounds (a threat to confidentiality, a threat to zealous representation, or the desire to avoid even the appearance of impropriety).

It is this heightened risk of a conflict of interest that is reflected in the requirement set forth in the Federal Rules of Criminal Procedure 44(c), which places a duty on the court to satisfy itself that there is no conflict when an indictment is returned and counsel from the same firm enter their appearance for more than one defendant.[10] Orders of the court to either permit the representation or to disqualify

---

4   *Wheat v. United States*, 486 U.S. at 158.

5   *See United States v. Freshour* 64 F.3d 664, (Unpublished Disposition) 1995 WL 496662 (6th Cir.) citing *Ford v. Ford*, 749 F.2d 681 (11th Cir. 1985) *cert. denied* 474 U.S. 909 (1985).

6   *United States v. Edwards*, 39 F. Supp. 2d 716 (M.D. La., 1999).

7   *Essex Chemical Corp. v Hartford Accident and Indemnity Co.*, 993 F. Supp. 241 (D.N.J. 1998). In *Essex*, the district court overruled the magistrate's order disqualifying company counsel under the appearance of impropriety doctrine without holding an evidentiary hearing on the disqualification motion.

8   *Morris v. Slappy*, 461 U.S. 1, 75 L.Ed. 2d 140, 108 S.Ct. 1692 (1988). Concomitant with a defendant's Sixth Amendment right to counsel is a defendant's right to hire the counsel of his choice. *Evans v. Artek Systems Corp.*, 715 F.2d 788, 791 (2nd Cir., 1983); *Government of India v. Cook Industries, Inc.*, 569 F.2d 737,739 (2nd Cir. 1978); *A.I Credit Corp. v. Washington Providence Insurance Co., Inc.* 1997 WL 231127 (S.D.N.Y.).

9   *Wheat*, 486 U.S. at 159.

10   The rule provides in part:

      Whenever two or more defendants have been jointly charged pursuant to Rule 8(b) or have been joined for trial pursuant to Rule 13, and are represented by the same retained or assigned counsel or by retained or assigned counsel who are associated in the practice of law, the court shall promptly inquire with respect to such representation and shall person-

counsel from representing one or both defendants are not interlocutory orders that can be immediately appealed.[11] Appellate courts reviewing trial court records on this issue have established a two-prong test for overturning a subsequent conviction where there was no order of disqualification: there must be an actual conflict; and the conflict must have actually prejudiced the defense.[12] However, the trial court making the determination in the first instance under a Rule 44(c) motion does not use this appellate review standard, requiring actual prejudice created by an actual conflict of interest, but rather weighs the likelihood that an actual conflict will emerge at trial. The trial court's decision is based on its view of the multiple representation, the particular facts presented, and the government's representations about how it intends to present its case. On appeal, an order disqualifying counsel is reviewed for abuse of discretion.[13] It follows necessarily that there will be instances where the court errs on the side of avoiding a conflict of interest, thereby disallowing the representation, knowing that, in the event of a conviction, there will likely be a claim of ineffective assistance of counsel.

On a Rule 44(c) motion, counsel's decisions regarding multiple representations and potential conflicts will be judicially evaluated after counsel have already committed themselves to the multiple representation. While the text of Rule 44(c) appears to restrict the court's obligation to conduct such an inquiry until after an indictment has been returned, it is also well settled that the court has an obligation to regulate the conduct of the grand jury. As a result, courts have entertained motions for a determination of conflict at the earlier grand jury stage of proceedings.[14] In this way, the prosecutor does not have to betray too much of his or her case in an effort to substantiate what he or she believes to be a conflict of interest relating to the multiple representation. Instead, the government can make its

---

ally advise each defendant of the right to the effective assistance of trial, including separate representation. Unless it appears that there is good cause to believe no conflict of interest is likely to arise, the court shall take such measures as may be appropriate to protect each defendant's right to counsel.

11 *Flanagan v. United States*, 465 U.S. 259, 270 (1984); *Richardson-Merrell, Inc. v. Kopller*, 472 U.S. 424, 430 (1985); *Firestone Tire and Rubber Co. v. Risjord*, 449 U.S. 368, 375 (1981).

12 Under *Strickland v. Washington*, 466 U.S. 668, 694 (1984), in order for the conviction to be overturned the court must determine: first, that there was an actual conflict, and not just a potential one; and, second, that the conflict actually prejudiced the defense, that is, that there is a reasonable probability that but for counsel's unprofessional errors, the result of the proceeding would have been different. *See also, United States v. Morelli*; 169 F.3rd 798 (3rd Cir., 1999).

13 *Wheat,* 486 U.S. at 164. Where the government planned to call one of the codefendants as a witness at another's trial, it was within the court's discretion to not allow the multiple representation and this did not violate the petitioner's Sixth Amendment rights.

14 Unfortunately these court rulings do not often result in published decisions, because they do not qualify for interlocutory treatment by the appellate courts. *In re Grand Jury Investigation No. 99-15125,* (9th Cir. 1999). The general unappealability of disqualification of counsel orders in civil and criminal proceedings is extended to the grand jury context. *In re Schmidt*, 775 F.2d 822, 823 (7th Cir. 1985).

motion based on little more than the existence of multiple grand jury targets with common representation and transfer the burden to the court, which must then hold ex parte in camera hearings to satisfy itself either that there is no potential for a conflict or that the potential conflicts can and have been knowingly and intelligently waived.

Counsel for the company need to be particularly careful not to create the impression that, through the multiple representation, they are preventing an individual officer from cooperating with government, or allowing a represented officer to serve as the scapegoat for the company's conduct.[15] The first of these could result in an obstruction of justice claim; the second an ethical violation on the part of counsel through a breach of his or her duty of loyalty to one of the clients.

III. Permissible Multiple Representation

The counsel who are conducting an internal investigation for the company are the logical choices to call upon to defend the company in criminal or civil cases growing out of the same issues that have been examined in that investigation. However, the very officer that made the decision to hire outside counsel may well expect that that counsel will also represent him or her in connection with a subpoena that he or she has been served with in his or her personal capacity.

Notwithstanding the many pitfalls that need to be avoided in a multiple representation situation, in some circumstances it is entirely appropriate for counsel conducting an internal corporate investigation to represent corporate officers and employees in the context of a grand jury investigation.[16] There is no ethical bar or constitutional proscription against multiple representation and, in fact, in many circumstances there are several advantages to engaging in such a practice. The attorney who has conducted the investigation is going to be much more intimately familiar with the facts and, through close and privileged communications with various officers, can put himself or herself in a position to know more than the government about the conduct being examined. There are also the obvious cost savings in legal fees to the company if it can avoid the need to hire separate and additional counsel for various officers and employees. There are other benefits to

---

15 *United States v. Allen,* 831 F.2d 1487, 1497 (9th Cir. 1987). *See also, Wood v. Georgia,* 450 U.S. 261, 268-69 (1981) ("Courts and commentators have recognized the inherent dangers that arise when a criminal defendant is represented by a lawyer hired and paid by a third party, particularly when the third party is the operator of the alleged criminal enterprise.")

16 *Wheat,* 486 U.S. at 159; *See also A.I. Credit Corp. v. Providence Washington Insurance Co.,* 1997 WL 231127 (S.D.N.Y.) The court allowed counsel for the defendant company to substitute for and replace the separate counsel that the codefendant company officer had originally retained over the plaintiff's objection. Applying principals of traditional agency law to the facts and allegations of the complaint the court found that the interests of the company and the officer were inextricably tied together and, in the absence of any right of indemnification, there was no conflict between them.

be gained as well. The fewer lawyers' schedules that have to be coordinated, the faster an internal investigation can progress. In addition, a reduction in the number of persons who have access to information related to the investigation will allow the company to maintain better control of that information and, with the judicious use of various privileges, leave the company in a better position to limit the government's access to the information.

However, these benefits will be more than outweighed if counsel undertakes a representation that ultimately leads to a conflict. It is important to accurately assess the likelihood of conflicts of interest developing between the company and any of its employees and to identify the need to obtain (and in some cases to pay for) separate counsel for those officers, as well as to take sufficient steps to protect the privileged status of communications and documents. Paying attention to these considerations in the earliest stages of the investigation protects the integrity of the investigation itself, as well as the company's choice of counsel. If counsel fails to pay attention to these issues at the beginning of an investigation, it is at his or her own peril, as well as that of the company.

The bottom line to all of this is that counsel needs to obtain informed consent from the company and from the individual officer(s) or employee(s) prior to undertaking any multiple representation. If there is any question, caution and common sense mandate the use of separate counsel for the particular officer(s) and employee(s) in question.

IV. Preventing Unintended Formations of Attorney-Client Relationships

Counsel for the company should be careful to avoid inadvertently establishing attorney-client relationships with individual officers and employees until counsel can determine whether potential conflicts of interest exist and whether multiple representation of these individuals is desirable. In the context of multiple representations or joint defense agreements, a failure by counsel to carefully define who their client(s) are can lead to a loss of key evidence that may harm the company and, in extreme cases, cause the outright disqualification of counsel.

The use of an initial script when conducting employee and officer interviews is discussed in Chapter 5. One of the purposes of this script is to prevent counsel from inadvertently creating an attorney-client relationship with officers and employees when interviewing them on behalf of the company in the early stages of an investigation. If the explicit warnings contained within the suggested script are followed and documented, this will also protect the company, and its choice of counsel, from a potential situation where an employee, who has become a grand jury target or a civil defendant with interests adverse to the company, attempts to prevent the use of information provided by the employee in the investigation, claiming that it was divulged in the context of an attorney-client relationship.

The existence of such a relationship is determined on the basis of what was reasonably believed by the prospective client at the time of the communication, and not necessarily what the lawyer intended. However, if the script is assiduously used at each interview throughout the investigation, the officer or employee being interviewed will be unable later to establish a reasonable belief in the existence of an attorney-client relationship.[17] Properly documenting this procedure at the interviews with a signed notice gives counsel a useful exhibit to attach to his or her opposition to any subsequent attempt to disqualify on these grounds. The issue of whether or not a conflict exists or is likely to exist can then be resolved on a case-by-case basis for each employee or officer, without the problem of counsel having already received information in a privileged attorney-client context.

One remaining problem, which counsel must bear in mind, is that, in the absence of an attorney-client relationship between the employee and counsel (or a joint defense agreement, discussed *infra*) at the time of the interview, the officer or employee can be asked questions about the nature and content of the interview in civil depositions, and by the grand jury.

V. Identifying Conflicts

The problem of identifying employees whose interests do conflict with those of the company becomes more difficult when counsel first becomes involved after a grand jury investigation has already begun. At that point, counsel must decide whether or not a conflict of interest exists, or is likely to arise, on the basis of much less information and without the benefit of his or her own internal investigation. Again, use of the script in connection with interviews and a clear statement of the scope of the representation set forth in the engagement letter go a long way towards protecting counsel's continuing ability to represent the company.

In situations where the company is the victim of fraud, any employee suspected of wrongdoing or criminal conduct will clearly have interests adverse to the company client. As the investigation proceeds and the roles of various employees are examined, new information may provide evidence that implicates additional or different personnel than those originally suspected of wrongdoing. Where these conflicts of interest were not readily apparent at the outset of the case, counsel will need to make certain that they have not compromised themselves with respect to continued representation of the company.

---

17   *See* Chapter 3; *see also Sackley v. Southeast Energy Group, Ltd.*, 1987 WL 12959 (N.D. Ill. 1987). Factors examined when making this determination are whether the attorney's services were billed to and paid by the company, whether the attorney ever represented the sole shareholder in individual matters, whether the shareholders treat the company as a corporation or partnership, and whether the shareholder could reasonably have believed that the attorney was acting as his individual attorney rather than as the company's attorney.

Where the company is itself the target of a criminal investigation, and the conduct of some of the management employees provides the basis of potential corporate liability, the company's defense may include claims that the act(s) of the employee(s) were beyond the scope of employment, or in violation of corporate policy. In these situations, separate counsel for the individual employees is clearly called for, because the company's counsel cannot both represent the employee and make these defenses on behalf of the company.

On the other hand, where the acts or omissions of senior management form the basis for the potential corporate liability, and where for whatever reasons there can be no "beyond the scope of employment" or "violation of corporate policy" defenses separating the interests of the company and the officers in question, the company and its senior officers may have a sufficient unity of interest that their defenses are virtually identical and there is no conflict. In these situations the company and its officers can be jointly represented.

Where there is a government investigation relating to the company, there will be several potential permutations of targets that can arise depending upon what direction the government is leading the grand jury. The company may not be a target at all, in which case the targeted employees generally should not be represented by counsel for the company. Alternatively, the government may have targeted only the company. In that instance, multiple representation of the company and employees can be made to appear as an attempt to control or silence potential employee witnesses. Similarly, there are those situations where the government is not in a position, or simply refuses, to indicate whom its ultimate targets are.

In all of these situations, counsel must make a careful assessment of the various employees' ability to implicate each other and the company, since this can give rise to potential conflicts in their respective defenses, and must be sure to obtain the informed consent of all the proposed clients. A thorough investigation into the facts, as well as a careful disclosure of the risks and benefits of the proposed joint representation and consent obtained from all clients, must be accomplished before the representation can be undertaken. In the context of obtaining the company's consent, care should be taken to insure that this decision is made on behalf of the company by an individual or a committee of the board that has sufficient authority and will not benefit personally from the proposed multiple representation. Only after determining that there is little or no likelihood of a conflict, and obtaining the required consents, should such a multiple representation be undertaken.

If separate counsel for the employees has already been obtained, the issue of conflicts caused by multiple representation can always be revisited as new information is developed. If it is later determined that separate counsel for the employees is not necessary, and that there is no conflict, nor likelihood of a conflict nor appearance of impropriety, counsel can, at that point undertake the representation of the officers in question. Conversely, if it later becomes apparent that there is a conflict or that a conflict is likely to arise between the company and a specific employee, the decision to obtain separate counsel for the particular employee can be made without prejudice to counsel's continued representation of the company. Where separate counsel has already been obtained, counsel can consider coordinating its defense efforts through a joint defense agreement, in situations where there is sufficient unity of interest to warrant it. Information and documents created in this fashion will normally be protected from direct discovery through the attorney-client privilege and/or the attorney work product doctrine.

VI. Indemnification

In situations where it has become apparent that separate counsel for particular employees or groups of employees is necessary, and depending on the status of the employee and the nature of the conduct in question, the company may have an obligation to indemnify that individual for his or her legal costs.[18] Because of the increased costs involved in hiring separate counsel, and a desire to remain loyal to its employees, the company may pressure company counsel to also represent that employee, especially where an alternative theory of the case provides a non-conflicting defense to the company and the employee.

As discussed above, there are several advantages to permitting multiple representations, including the obvious financial benefit to the company if counsel retained for the investigation can also provide services for individual employees, and this is especially true if the company has an obligation to pay those employees' legal costs. However, the advantages will be more than outweighed if counsel find themselves disqualified. In addition to the obvious loss of work for the attorneys, the hardship on the corporate client can be profound, depending on how far into the case counsel have proceeded before being disqualified.

It is important to realize that, even though the officer and the company (through someone with authority in the corporate organization other than the targeted employee) may consent to the multiple representation after full disclosure, the existence of a defensive position for either a particular employee or the company that is adverse to the interests of the other may be sufficient to establish an impermissible division of loyalty for counsel. In these situations it is best to retain separate counsel for the employee, not only to protect the company's right to assert all of its defenses but, as is mentioned above, to prevent the disqualification of counsel. The concern is not so much that counsel may commit some improper act, but rather that, as a result of the conflict, counsel might refrain from doing things they might otherwise have done but for the multiple representation. This is even more of a concern where the company is publicly held, and the possibility of shareholder derivative liability looms on the horizon.

---

18   *See* Model Business Corporation Act § 8.52. *See* Chapter 5.

VII. Joint Defense Agreements

"Joint defense agreements" refer to those situations where several defendants, having a common defensive interest, agree to share information. This can be done through a single attorney representing several defendants or, as is more typically the case in a corporate environment, with several defendants, each with separate counsel, all entering into an arrangement whereby they share information. Under such an arrangement, these communications, which would normally constitute a waiver of the attorney-client privilege, retain their privileged status. The doctrine, also known as the "common interest rule", permits these exchanges of information without waiver of the attorney-client privilege, since the defendants and their counsel all share a common interest.[19]

In addition to the pooling of information, the parties to the agreement can also better ascertain the direction and content of the government's investigation, as well as save funds, by eliminating duplication of effort by their respective counsel.

In spite of the substantial benefits to such an arrangement, there are also numerous risks that should be weighed at the outset. Despite any protestations to the contrary, there is no guarantee that one or more of the other parties to the agreement will not simply obtain information from others and then decide not to cooperate with the joint effort. There is also the possibility that one of the parties to the agreement will have a change of heart or succumb to government "requests" for cooperation and decide to testify for the government in exchange for a favorable plea arrangement. These arrangements can be made prior to indictment, at a time when counsel may believe that they are quietly conducting an internal investigation, without the company being a government target.

The implications of this scenario for the joint defense arrangement are potentially disastrous. It will be difficult to establish for the court what information the cooperating government witness knew on his or her own (where the right to waive the privileged nature of the witness's own communications with counsel belongs to the witness), and what information the witness has obtained solely through the association of the joint defense agreement (where the privilege inures to the benefit of the other defendants, and cannot be waived by the witness).

These issues are further compounded in those situations where the government is making use of a confidential informant. Counsel participating in a joint defense arrangement run the risk of having an enemy in their camp. While the ethical

---

19   *United States v. Schwimmer*, 892 F.2d 237 (2nd Cir. 1989). *Schimmer's* appeal of his conviction to the Second Circuit was remanded to the district court for a hearing to determine whether the government improperly invaded privileged information in the hands of an accountant hired by a party to a joint defense agreement. The documents obtained were not introduced at trial. However, a further hearing was necessary to determine if derivative use had been made of the information contained therein.

prosecutor may be careful not to question the informant about joint defense discussions, he or she may also be reluctant to direct the informant to withdraw from the joint defense arrangement, for fear that this will "tip off" the remaining members to the agreement as to the identity of the informant. The end result can be the disclosure, either intentionally or inadvertently, of privileged information to the government, through a cooperating participant to a joint defense agreement. On a subsequent motion to suppress or limit the government's evidence, counsel will have to establish (through disclosure in camera and under seal) the joint defense origin of evidence the government seeks to present. The government will then have the burden of establishing a source independent of the privileged communications for the evidence that it seeks to introduce.[20]

As a practical matter, however, if a co-defendant is cooperating with the government, anything that he or she learned about his or her codefendants in the context of a joint defense agreement will likely become known to the prosecutor, even if the prosecutor does not make direct use of the information, or the information is later deemed to be inadmissible.

In order to offset these risks, there are several steps that counsel for the company can take to protect the company, as well as the other members of the joint defense team. First, when the need for separate counsel for various employees is established, counsel for the company will be in a unique position to recommend counsel with the requisite white collar criminal background to represent some or all of the officers. Typically, these individuals will be known and trusted by the company's counsel and, being aware of the implications of a joint defense agreement from the beginning, will agree to the creation of a detailed joint defense agreement with a carefully worded and explicit withdrawal provision, prohibiting any further participation in the joint defense arrangements once discussions with the government have begun. Thus, prior to divulging any information to the government, the witness seeking to cooperate must make an affirmative withdrawal from the joint defense arrangement, returning any documents. Second, counsel for the company can limit the scope of the joint defense effort to areas where there is specific common ground, and not simply give all of its information to all joint counsel. In this way if there is a defection from the joint defense team, the amount of the damage

---

20   *United States v. Weissman,* 1996 WL 751386 (S.D.N.Y.,1996). In *Weissman,* the court noted the similar policy concerns that motivate a *Kastigar* hearing (*Kastigar v. United States,* 406 U.S. 441 (1972)), which imposes on the government the obligation to demonstrate that all of the evidence that it intends to put forth comes from a source other than the testimony compelled under a grant of use immunity. Thus, in the context of information that was the proper subject of a joint defense agreement (in this instance a memorandum describing client admissions to his counsel), the government was forced to show that it had an independent source for all of the information contained in the memorandum in order to sustain the use of it at trial. On the facts in *Weissman,* the government succeeded in meeting this burden for all parts of the memorandum in question.

to the company can be contained to those areas. Serious thought must be given to determining the proper scope, as well as the costs and benefits, of a joint defense effort before embarking on this path.

As discussed *supra,* the government can move to disqualify counsel, but also has the right to move for a "determination of conflict" under Federal Rule of Criminal Procedure 44(c). Rather than attempt to set forth a basis for disqualification, and meet the fairly heavy burden of showing that a conflict which cannot be waived exists, the prosecutor can shift this responsibility to the court with such a motion. Rule 44(c) then requires the court to make inquiry, holding hearings if necessary, to determine if such conflicts exist, in order to protect the subsequent proceedings from collateral attack based on claims of ineffective assistance of counsel. The court can hold individual ex parte in camera hearings, to determine whether the perceived conflict is one that can be waived, and if so, whether an informed waiver has been made.[21]

In the context of a joint defense agreement, where a joint participant in such an arrangement later cooperates with the government, the prosecutor may be able to prevail on such a motion by arguing that counsel, if not disqualified, will be tempted to use information gleaned from the witness under the former agreement against that witness during cross-examination on behalf of the company or other parties.

Counsel must also be sensitive to the nature of the communications that they permit under a joint defense agreement. The crime fraud exception to attorney-client communications applies with equal force to communications in a joint defense environment, and statements about future criminal conduct are not privileged, whether they are made by counsel's own client or by another attorney's client at a joint defense meeting. If such a statement is made, it creates an obligation on the part of all counsel present to notify the government of the planned criminal act.[22] It is for this reason that counsel, having entered into a joint defense agreement, may want to consider carefully whether any clients should attend joint defense meetings. While issues and facts can be more quickly exchanged in order to prepare a coordinated defense, the risk of disclosing matters beyond the scope of the agreement, or worse, having clients make statements indicating an intent to commit a future criminal act, could defeat the purpose of the joint defense agreement. If such statements are not properly treated by all counsel present, counsel teeter on the edge of giving credence to a government claim of obstruction of justice.

---

21   *United States v. Anderson et al*, 1998 WL 13934 (D.Kan., 1998).

22   *See, United States v. Thomson*, 50 F.3d 18, 1995 WL 107300 (9th Cir. 1995). In an unpublished decision, the court held that defendant's statements threatening the life and family of the judge in connection with the sentence that the judge imposed upon his codefendant spouse, were not protected under the joint defense doctrine, and were admissible in his subsequent trial.

There is also the risk that information collected and shared under the joint defense agreement may form the basis of civil liability between some of the parties to the agreement. In *Hu Friedy MFG Co., Inc. v. General Electric Company*,[23] the defendants moved for a protective order enforcing a joint defense agreement, to block the use of information that had been shared in a joint defense agreement in a prior civil litigation from being used by the same counsel for a different plaintiff in a subsequent suit. The defendants had marketed a product which included material supplied by plaintiff. A product liability action had been defended through the use of a joint defense agreement, where the information was shared. In the subsequent civil case, plaintiff suppliers were using information, previously obtained during the course of the joint defense, to prosecute their civil claim against the manufacturing defendant. In denying the motion, the court observed that the shared information referred to would be otherwise discoverable in the context of the subsequent civil proceeding and that, in the court's view, the defendant's objection amounted to little more than an objection to that particular counsel representing any plaintiff adverse to the defendant with respect to claims relating to the same subject matter. Noting the ethical proscription against agreements that make a restriction on a lawyer's right to practice a part of the settlement of any controversy, the court did not bar the use of the information.[24]

In order for the joint defense privilege to be recognized, courts have imposed varying degrees of scrutiny to the formation and content of these agreements. There is no requirement of a written agreement, but proving the existence and scope of such an agreement may be difficult if there is no writing.[25] The burden is on the proponent of the privilege to establish that there was a joint defense agreement in place, that the documents and communications in question furthered the "putative joint defense strategy", and that the privilege has not been waived.[26]

In *United States v. Weissman*,[27] discussed *supra*, the CFO was unable to establish that a joint defense privilege attached to statements he had made at a meeting

---

23   *Hu-Friedy MFG Co., Inc v General Electric Company*, 1999 WL 528545 (N.D. Ill., 1999)

24   *See Also Tribune Company, et al. V. Purcigliotti*, 1997 WL 540810 (S.D.N.Y.) The joint defense agreement itself was ordered produced, since it contained information about potential claims between the parties to it. Since these were antagonistic interests being discussed, and there was no articulated ground of privilege, the joint defense privilege could not therefore attach to the agreement itself.

25   *In re Grand Jury Proceedings*, 156 F.3d 1038; 41 Fed R. Serv.3d 851 (10th Cir. 1998) (motion to quash grand jury subpoena on joint defense grounds denied due to a lack of evidence of the existence of such an agreement and the failure to make a showing that the statement in question furthered a joint defensive strategy).

26   *In re Sealed Case No. 94-3019*, 29 F. 3rd 715, 720 (D.C. Cir. 1994); *In re Bevill, Bresler & Shulman Asset Management Corp.*, 805 F.2d 120, 126 (3rd Cir. 1986). *See Also United States v. Weissman* 22 F.Supp.2d 187, (S.D.N.Y 1998).

27   *United States v. Weissman*, 1996 WL 751386 (S.D.N.Y.,1996).

with the company's outside counsel and his counsel. At an evidentiary hearing on the issue, the defendant and his counsel testified that, prior to Weissman making any statements at the meeting, his counsel made an express reference to a joint defense privilege, indicating that the privilege would apply to all of their statements at the meeting. This testimony was not corroborated by that of another officer of the company, the company's general counsel, or the company's outside counsel, all of whom were present at the meeting. As a result, the privilege was deemed waived with respect to what transpired at the meeting since the defendant could not meet his burden of proving the existence of an agreement by the preponderance of the evidence.[28]

In the context of an internal investigation, where counsel for the company has identified enough of a potential conflict of interest to warrant obtaining separate counsel for some of the officers and/or employees of the company, counsel needs to pause prior to entering into a joint defense agreement. Counsel should consider the extent to which the officers so represented can implicate the company with their testimony, and should decide what subjects and types of information will be shared under the proposed joint defense agreement, or whether it is even advisable to go forward with such an agreement. If counsel decide that it is appropriate to enter into a joint defense arrangement, they must take steps to preserve the privilege of the company with respect to documents and information. Counsel should also make sure that the joint defense agreement itself is carefully memorialized in a written agreement with an explicit withdrawal provision which preserves and protects attorney-client communications from deliberate or inadvertent government discovery. Finally, the agreement should also contain an affirmative obligation to notify all other parties and withdraw from the agreement, returning all joint defense materials to the other parties, prior to any party to the agreement entering into discussions with the government.

---

28   *United States v. Weissman*, 1996 WL 751386 (S.D.N.Y.,1996).

CHAPTER 8:
CORPORATE SENTENCING GUIDELINES AND COMPLIANCE PROGRAMS

I. The Sentencing Guidelines

Since November 1, 1991, the sentencing of corporations convicted of criminal offenses in federal courts has been governed by the Sentencing Guidelines for Organizational Defendants.[1] These Guidelines are designed to "provide just punishment, adequate deterrence, and incentives for organizations to maintain internal mechanisms for preventing, detecting, and reporting criminal conduct."[2]

The Guidelines have effected radical changes in the sentencing of business entities (including corporations, partnerships, unincorporated organizations, and non-profit organizations). First, the Guidelines prescribe far stiffer fines than the norms previously imposed. Second, they create a novel carrot-and-stick mechanism which can substantially increase or decrease the penalty depending on the organization's "culpability score". Third, they mandate, in many cases, that the organization be placed on probation and receive ongoing supervision by the court, in addition to being fined.

The Guidelines are complex and are the subject of treatises devoted exclusively to them.[3] The discussion presented in this chapter is not intended to be comprehensive or exhaustive. Rather, it presents an overview of the Guidelines, and some of the principal aspects thereof which are most likely to be of interest to corporate counsel.

---

1   There is a limited exception to the coverage of the Guidelines. The fines to be imposed for certain special categories of offenses—notably, environmental, export control, and food and drug offenses—is not yet governed by the Guidelines although the other aspects of the sentences for such offenses is controlled by the Guidelines.

2   USSG Ch.8, intro. comment.

3   *E.g.*, Jed S. Rakoff, Linda R. Blumkin, and Richard A. Sauber, *Corporate Sentencing Guidelines: Compliance and Mitigation* (1998).

A. Remedying Harm from Criminal Conduct

In sentencing a corporate defendant, the Guidelines mandate that the first step for the court, before determining punishment, is to require the convicted business to take all appropriate steps to compensate the victims and otherwise remedy the harm caused or threatened by the offense.[4] Most commonly, this would take the form of restitution. Where appropriate, a court may also issue a remedial order such as a product recall for a food and drug violation or a clean-up order for an environmental violation. In addition, the business may be ordered to perform community service, particularly where it possesses knowledge, facilities or skills that uniquely qualify it to repair damage caused by the offense.[5]

B. Imposing a Fine as Punishment

The principal sanction imposed upon a convicted corporate defendant is a fine. If the court determines that the business is a "criminal purpose organization"—one operated primarily for a criminal purpose or primarily by criminal means—then the Guidelines require it to impose a confiscatory fine sufficient to divest the business of all its net assets.[6]

The fine for legitimate businesses convicted of a crime is determined by a complicated formula based on the gravity of the offense and the company's culpability as an organization.

1. The "Base Fine"

Initially, a "base fine" is derived which supposedly reflects the seriousness of the offense. The base fine equals the greatest of (1) the pecuniary gain from the offense; (2) the pecuniary loss caused by the offense (if the loss was caused intentionally, knowingly, or recklessly); or (3) the designated fine from an "offense level" table which arrays offenses in 32 gradations, according to their seriousness, with corresponding fines ranging from $5,000 to $72.5 million.[7]

2. The "Culpability Score"

Next, the company's "culpability score" is determined. This score, in turn, yields a "minimum multiplier" and a "maximum multiplier" that are applied to the base fine to calculate a "fine range," from which the court then selects the actual fine to be imposed upon the defendant. Every company starts with a "culpability score" of 5 points. This score, if unchanged, would translate into a minimum multiplier of

---

4   USSG §§ 8B1.1, 8B1.2.

5   USSG § 8B1.3.

6   USSG § 8C1.1.

7   USSG § 8C2.4.

1.00 and a maximum multiplier of 2.00, meaning that the actual fine range would extend from 100% to 200% of the "base fine".[8]

However, the "culpability score"—and the resulting fine range—can change dramatically as adjustments are made to factor in the role of management in the wrongdoing, the company's history of violations, the steps previously taken by the company to prevent and detect criminal conduct, and the company's cooperation with federal investigators after the offense occurs. These factors can increase a company's "culpability score" up to a maximum of 10 or more points, which would result in a fine range of from 200% to 400% of the "base fine". Conversely, the "culpability score" can be decreased to zero or below, which would result in a fine range of only 5% to 20% of the "base fine".[9]

3. Increasing the "Culpability Score"

The company's "culpability score" is increased if the company has a prior history of wrongdoing (criminal, civil or administrative adjudications based on similar misconduct), if senior personnel were involved in or tolerated the offense, or if the crime violates a court order or a condition of probation.[10] One or two points are added to the culpability score, depending on the circumstances, for a prior history of wrongdoing or for violation of a court order or probation condition.

Even more important than the company's prior record is the level and extent of involvement in, or tolerance of, the offense by senior personnel. Up to five points can be added if "high-level personnel" participated in, condoned, or were willfully ignorant of the offense. "High-level personnel" include directors, executive officers, an individual in charge of a major business or functional unit of the company, and an individual with a substantial ownership interest. Alternatively, a comparable increase in the company's culpability score is made if there was pervasive tolerance of the offense by "substantial authority personnel" throughout the organization, or within the relevant business unit. "Substantial authority personnel" include not only "high-level personnel," but also individuals who exercise substantial supervisory authority (*e.g.*, a plant manager, a sales manager), and any other individuals who, even if not a part of management, nevertheless exercise substantial discretion when acting within the scope of their authority (*e.g.*, an individual who negotiates or sets price levels, or who negotiates or approves significant contracts).[11]

---

8   USSG §§ 8C2.5, 8C2.6, 8C2.7, 8C2.8.

9   USSG §§ 8C2.5, 8C2.6.

10   USSG §§ 8C2.5(b), 8C2.5(c), 8C2.5(d), 8C2.6.

11   USSG § 8C2.5(b); *see also* § 8A1.2, comment. (n.3(b),(c),(e), and (j).

4. Decreasing the "Culpability Score"

Conversely, a company's "culpability score" is reduced if, prior to the offense, it had an effective compliance program to prevent violations of law, or if, after the offense, it cooperates with federal investigators and prosecutors.

Three points are subtracted from the company's "culpability score" if the offense occurred despite an effective program to prevent and detect violations of law—*i.e.,* a compliance program. (The elements of such a program will be discussed in a separate section, below). However, this reduction does not apply if any "high-level personnel," or persons responsible for administering the compliance program, participated in, condoned, or were willfully ignorant of the offense. In addition, there is a rebuttable presumption that the compliance program was not effective—and hence does not merit any credit—if any "substantial authority personnel" participated in the offense.[12]

Moreover, a prerequisite to the credit for having an effective compliance program is that the company make a prompt disclosure of any offense of which it learns. No reduction will be given if the company, after learning of the offense, "unreasonably" delays reporting it to appropriate authorities.[13] The Guidelines provide that a company is allowed a reasonable period of time to conduct an internal investigation before reporting an offense, and that no report is required if the company reasonably concludes, based on the information then available, that no offense had been committed.[14]

Regardless of whether the company had an effective compliance program before the fact, it may earn credits after the offense by cooperating with federal investigators and prosecutors. Five points are subtracted from the company's culpability score if it makes a prompt, voluntary disclosure of the offense after learning of it, cooperates fully in the investigation, and pleads guilty. Two points are subtracted for full cooperation and a timely plea in situations where the government's investigation was not instigated by the company, itself. One point is subtracted for "affirmative acceptance of responsibility"—that is, a guilty plea—without full cooperation in the investigation.[15]

To qualify for a reduction, the company's cooperation must be both timely and thorough. To be timely, the company's cooperation must begin essentially at the same time as it is officially notified of a criminal investigation. To be thorough, the company's cooperation must include the disclosure of all pertinent information known by the company.[16]

---

12 USSG § 8C2.5(f).

13 USSG § 8C2.5(f).

14 USSG § 8C2.5, comment. (n.10).

15 USSG § 8C2.5(g).

16 USSG § 8C2.5, comment. (n.12).

C. Probation

The Guidelines embrace, over objections by the corporate community, wide use of the probation sanction.[17] Probation is mandated in a broad range of cases, including those where it is necessary to secure payment of restitution or a fine; enforce a remedial order or community service; if, at the time of *sentencing*, the company lacks an effective compliance program; if either the company or "high-level personnel" who participated in the offense has a prior conviction for similar misconduct within five years; or if probation is deemed necessary to ensure that changes are made within the organization to reduce the likelihood of future criminal conduct.[18]

As conditions of probation, the company may be required to (1) make periodic reports to the court or a probation officer; (2) submit to regular or unannounced examinations of it books and records, and to interviews of its officers and employees regarding the affairs of the company; (3) disclose any criminal prosecution, civil litigation, administrative proceeding, or government investigation that has been instituted against it; and (4) advise the court of any material adverse change in its business or financial condition or prospects (if the probation is to ensure payment of restitution or a fine).[19] Furthermore, if the company does not already have a compliance program, or if the program it has is deemed ineffective, the company may be required to develop and submit to the court a (new) compliance program and a schedule for its implementation.[20]

II. Compliance Programs

The most obvious practical implication of the Sentencing Guidelines is the need for all businesses to institute effective compliance programs that, hopefully, will prevent criminal conduct in the first instance and, if not, at least will qualify the company for sentencing credit under the Guidelines. Indeed, the Delaware Chancery Court has held that, in light of the Guidelines, corporate management now has a duty to ensure that a company has an adequate system to internally detect illegal activity in a timely manner.[21]

---

17   Leonard Roland, *Corporate Punishment by the U.S. Sentencing Commission*, 4 FEDERAL SENTENCING REPORTER 50 (1991).

18   USSG § 8D1.1.

19   USSG § 8D1.4(b),(c).

20   USSG § 8D1.4(c)(1).

21   *In re Caremark Int'l Inc. Derivative Lit.*, 698 A.2d 959, 970 (Del. Ch. 1996).

A. An Effective Compliance Program

1. The Sentencing Guidelines

What constitutes an effective compliance program that will pass muster under the Sentencing Guidelines? The Commentary to the Guidelines outlines the elements of an "effective program to prevent and detect violations of law".[22] It states that failure to prevent or detect an offense does not necessarily mean that a program was ineffective and, thus, inadequate to reduce the company's culpability score. Instead, the "hallmark" of an effective program is that the company exercised "due diligence" in seeking to prevent and detect criminal conduct by its employees and other agents.

At a minimum, the company must take the following steps in order to demonstrate due diligence with respect to its compliance program:

(1) Establish compliance standards and procedures for its employees and other agents that are "reasonably capable" of reducing the prospect of criminal conduct;

(2) Assign specific senior manager(s) overall responsibility to oversee compliance;

(3) Use due care not to delegate substantial discretionary authority to individuals whom the company knows, or should know, are likely to engage in illegal activities;

(4) Communicate its standards and procedures effectively to all employees and agents, through training programs or practical written guides;

(5) Monitor compliance with its standards, both through audit-type procedures and by instituting and publicizing a reporting system (a "hotline," etc.) through which employees can report misconduct without fear of retribution;

(6) Enforce the standards through appropriate disciplinary mechanisms; and

(7) Respond appropriately to any offense that is detected, and take steps to prevent recurrences.[23]

In formulating a compliance program, each company must examine the nature of its business and its own prior history to determine what sorts of offenses pose the greatest risk, and then take steps designed to prevent and detect such offenses.

> For example, if an organization handles toxic substances, it must have established standards and procedures designed to ensure that those substances are properly handled at all times. If an organization employs sales personnel who have flexibility in setting prices, it must have established standards and procedures designed to prevent and detect price-fixing. If an organization employs sales personnel who have flexibil-

---

22   USSG § 8A1.2, comment. (n.3(k)).

23   *Id.*

ity to represent the material characteristics of a product, it must have established standards and procedures designed to prevent fraud.[24]

Not surprisingly, a company's failure to incorporate and follow applicable industry practice or to comply with applicable government regulations will weigh against a finding that the compliance program is an effective one.[25]

Another relevant factor in structuring a compliance program is the size of the organization. The Guidelines note that, the larger the organization, the more formal the program typically should be. Generally, a larger organization should have established written policies defining the standards and procedures to be followed by its employees and other agents.[26]

Thus, there is no "one size fits all" compliance program that is suitable for all companies, regardless of their business, their size, or their organizational structure. The Guidelines do not attempt to spell out the particulars of an actual compliance program but only to identify some of the basic elements that should be common to all such programs.

2. The Defense Industry Initiative

In 1986, several years before the advent of the Corporate Sentencing Guidelines, representatives of 18 major defense contractors drafted a set of principles of business ethics and conduct that established a framework for compliance programs in their industry. These principles became known as the Defense Industry Initiative on Business Ethics and Conduct. Part of the Initiative consisted of a questionnaire that addressed some of the nuts and bolts of a good compliance program. Because it provides useful practical guidance about structuring a compliance program, that questionnaire is set forth below. These questions are geared to defense contractors, and so some modifications will be appropriate for companies that are engaged in other industries. In addition, some companies may choose not to adopt all of the components of the compliance program designed by the Defense Industry Initiative.

Questionnaire

1. Does the company have a written code of business ethics and conduct?

2. Is the code distributed to all employees principally involved in defense work?

3. Are new employees provided any orientation to the code?

4. Does the code assign responsibility to operating management and others for compliance with the code?

---

24   *Id.*

25   *Id.*

26   *Id.*

5. Does the company conduct employee training programs regarding the code?

6. Does the code address standards that govern the conduct of employees in their dealings with suppliers, consultants, and customers?

7. Is there a corporate review board, ombudsman, corporate compliance, or ethics office or similar mechanism for employees to report suspected violations to someone other than their direct supervisor, if necessary?

8. Does the mechanism employed protect the confidentiality of employee reports?

9. Is there an appropriate mechanism to follow-up on reports of suspected violations to determine what occurred, who was responsible, and recommended corrective and other actions?

10. Is there an appropriate mechanism for letting employees know the result of any follow-up into their reported charges?

11. Is there an ongoing program of communication to employees spelling out and reemphasizing their obligations under the code of conduct?

12. What are the specifics of such a program?
   a. Written communication?
   b. One-on-one communication?
   c. Group meetings?
   d. Visual aids?
   e. Others?

13. Does the company have a procedure for voluntarily reporting violations of federal procurement laws to appropriate governmental agencies?

14. Is implementation of the code's provisions one of the standards by which all levels of supervision are expected to be measured in their performance?

15. Is there a program to monitor on a continuing basis adherence to the code of conduct and compliance with federal procurement laws?

16. Does the company participate in the industry's "Best Practices Forum"?

17. Are periodic reports on adherence to the principles made to the company's Board of Directors or to its audit or other appropriate committee?

18. Is there a report to the Board of Directors or a committee thereof on the efficacy of the company's internal procedures for implementing the company code of conduct?

19. Does the company have a code of conduct provision or associated policy addressing marketing activities?

20. Does the company have a code of conduct provision or associated policy requiring that consultants are governed by, and oriented regarding, the company's code of conduct and relevant associated policies?

3. Identifying Compliance Risk Issues

The first step in designing a good compliance program is to identify the risks of misconduct that must be safeguarded against. Although the primary purpose of a compliance program is to prevent employee misconduct that may render the company liable to others, another important purpose is to protect the company from misconduct that may victimize it alone. The Guidelines recognize that compliance programs must be individualized to take into account the particular company involved, the nature of its business, and its own prior history. Some of the most common risk areas include the following.[27]

a. Bribes, kickbacks and other improper payments or inappropriate gifts

Improper payments to government officials can result in criminal and civil liability.[28] Likewise, bribery of foreign government officials is prohibited by the Foreign Corrupt Practices Act.[29] Payments to non-government officials also can create criminal liability in certain circumstances. For example, federal statutes prohibit payments to personnel of financial institutions in connection with business transactions,[30] or corrupt payments to officials of public or private entities who receive federal funds,[31] or bribes to influence the operations of employee benefit plans.[32] In addition, a number of states have criminal commercial bribery statutes that prohibit payments to influence the conduct of an agent or employee with respect to the affairs of the agent's principal/employer.[33] And kickbacks are explicitly prohibited, both at the prime contractor and subcontractor levels, in connection with any federal government contract.[34]

b. Accounting practices

Every company must protect against the risk that an officer or employee may "cook the books" or alter certain figures in order to boost performance or hide problems. Congress has mandated that public companies maintain accurate books, records, and accounts, and develop systems of internal controls that will ensure

---

27 *See generally* Jed S. Rakoff, Linda R. Blumkin, and Richard A. Sauber, *Corporate Sentencing Guidelines: Compliance and Mitigation* § 5.08 (1998); Jeffrey M. Kaplan, Joseph E. Murphy, and Winthrop M. Swenson, *Compliance Programs and the Corporate Sentencing Guidelines*, Chap. 7 (1995).

28 *See* 18 U.S.C. § 201 (prohibiting bribery and illegal gratuities).

29 15 U.S.C. §§ 78a, 78m, 78dd-1, 78dd-2, 78ff.

30 18 U.S.C. § 215.

31 18 U.S.C. § 666.

32 18 U.S.C. § 1954.

33 *See United States v. Parise*, 159 F.3d 790, 804 & n.1 (3d Cir. 1998)(Garth, J., dissenting)(collecting state commercial bribery statutes); *see also* American Law Institute Model Penal Code § 224.8 (1962).

34 41 U.S.C. § 51 *et seq.*

that corporate assets can only be accessed in accordance with corporate policies.[35] Any intentional misstatement of a public company's finances or operating results will constitute a violation of the securities laws and will subject the company to significant criminal[36] and civil liability.[37]

c. Conflicts of interest

This is another fundamental issue for every company. Common breeding grounds for conflict issues involving company employees include relationships with the company's suppliers and outside employment. In many instances, such conflicts will work to the disadvantage of the company if the employee ends up placing a competing (personal) interest ahead of the company's interest. It is certainly possible, however, for the converse situation to occur and for an employee's conflict of interest to create liability for the company if it somehow profits from the situation. Another sensitive conflicts area, and one which normally involves senior management, is service on another corporation's board of directors. Such service may expose the manager to confidential information which, if imparted to the company, may limit the company's freedom to pursue certain transactions or else render it liable if it does pursue them.

d. Confidential information and trade secrets

In order to protect their own proprietary data and trade secrets, companies should remind employees of their duty to safeguard such information, both during the course of their employment and after they depart. At the same time, employees should be warned against acquiring a competitor's confidential or trade secret information—and against bringing such information with them from a prior employer when they join the company. Civil litigation over alleged thefts of trade secrets and proprietary data is increasingly common, and recent legislation makes theft of trade secrets potentially a federal criminal offense.[38]

e. Insider trading

Another risk for publicly held companies is that the directors, officers, or employees may engage in insider trading in the company's shares. The company's senior management often will have access to non-public information which will affect the value of the company's stock. More junior employees may possess such information as well, from time to time. Care must be taken to ensure that, whenever such situations occur, the "insiders" do not trade in the company's stock until the

---

35 15 U.S.C. §§ 78m(b)(2)(A)-(B).

36 15 U.S.C. § 78ff.

37 Investors sued 235 corporations for securities fraud in 1998—a record number—according to the Stanford Securities Class Action Clearing House at Stanford Law School.

38 18 U.S.C. §§ 1831, 1832.

information is publicly disclosed. In addition (although a far less common problem for most companies), there is also the risk that employees will trade on sensitive information acquired about other public companies.[39]

f. Product safety

If the company manufactures or processes tangible products, especially consumer goods, then product safety may well be a key risk area. Indeed, in highly regulated industries which implicate public health and safety, such as food and drugs, product safety is likely to be the single most important risk issue. In most instances, the business risk presented by defective or unsafe products will be civil liability rather than criminal prosecution. Where public health and safety is implicated, however, defective products may trigger strict criminal liability for both the company and its senior managers.[40]

g. Workplace safety

In industries such as manufacturing, construction, or extraction of natural resources, workplace safety may be a significant issue. Violations of legal standards regarding occupational safety may result in significant civil penalties or even, in some instances, criminal prosecution.[41]

h. Environmental issues

For many businesses, compliance with environmental laws will be a significant concern. Some environmental statutes are drafted in such sweeping terms as to create something approaching strict criminal liability in the event of a violation.[42] Environmental offenses are excluded from the "fines" section of the Corporate Sentencing Guidelines, although the "restitution" and "probation" provisions do apply.[43] Accordingly, the Guidelines provisions reducing the sanctions for companies that have an effective compliance program do not come into play directly insofar as environmental offenses are concerned. However, both the EPA and the Justice Department have adopted policies that are akin to the Guidelines in potentially reducing the penalties imposed on companies that uncover their own

---

39 *See United States v. O'Hagan*, 521 U.S. 642 (1997).

40 *See United States v. Park*, 421 U.S. 658 (1975); *United States v. Dotterweich*, 320 U.S. 277 (1943); *United States v. Cattle King Packing Co.*, 793 F.2d 232, 240 (10th Cir.), *cert. denied*, 479 U.S. 985 (1986).

41 29 U.S.C. § 666 (Occupational Safety and Health Act of 1970); 30 U.S.C. § 820 (Federal Mine Safety and Health Act of 1977).

42 *See, e.g., United States v. Weitzenhoff*, 1 F.3d 1523, 1529 (9th Cir.), *reh'g denied and amended*, 35 F.3d 1275 (9th Cir. 1993)(construing criminal provision of the Clean Water Act). *See* Chapter 11.

43 *See* USSG § 8A1.1 comment. (n.2).

violations through a compliance program, and then promptly disclose and correct those violations.[44]

i. Antitrust issues

Antitrust issues such as price fixing, collusive bidding, and market allocation are a concern in many industries. In recent years, the Antitrust Division of the Justice Department has obtained record amounts of fines through its prosecutions, including some $1.4 billion in 1998 alone.[45] Lately the Antitrust Division has made the prosecution of international cartels one of its highest priorities. The Division has uncovered and prosecuted international cartels in a variety of industries, including food and feed additives, chemicals, vitamins, graphite electrodes (used in making steel), and marine construction and transportation services. As a result, the Division obtained nearly $440 million in fines in its international cartel prosecutions in 1997 and 1998—an amount roughly equivalent to the total fines imposed in all of the Division's prosecutions (domestic and international) over the previous 20 years.[46]

It should be noted that corporations convicted of antitrust offenses are subject to some special, harsher rules under the Sentencing Guidelines.[47] First, in determining the base fine to be imposed on the offending company, 20 percent of the volume of affected commerce is used instead of the pecuniary loss. Second, and perhaps more significantly, the minimum and maximum multipliers that are applied to the base fine cannot be less than 0.75. This severely limits the benefit that a company can achieve by lowering its culpability score through such measures as an effective program to prevent and detect violations of law. In comparison, for other offenses, a company might be able to reduce its minimum multiplier to as low as 0.05 and its maximum multiplier to as low as 0.20 if its culpability score was low enough.[48]

j. Government contracts issues

Companies engaged in contracting with the federal government are especially vulnerable to civil or criminal liability for misconduct. There are a number of statutes

---

44 *See* EPA Final Policy Statement, "Incentives for Self-Policing: Discovery, Disclosure, Correction and Prevention of Violations," 60 Fed. Reg. 66706 (Dec. 22, 1995); Department of Justice Guidance Document, "Factors in Decisions on Criminal Prosecutions for Environmental Violations in the Context of Significant Voluntary Compliance or Disclosure Efforts by the Violator" (July 1, 1991).

45 Ronald G. Shafer, *Washington Wire*, The Wall Street Journal, October 15, 1999, at A1.

46 "International Cartel Prosecutions: Antitrust Division Policies Relating to Plea Agreements in International Cases," remarks of Gary R. Spratling, Deputy Assistant Attorney General, Antitrust Division, before the 13th Annual National Institute on White Collar Crime at 1 (March 4, 1999), available at http://www.usdoj.gov/atr/public/speeches/2275.htm.

47 USSG § 2R1.1(d).

48 USSG § 8C2.6.

which impose civil liability upon government contractors for engaging in fraudulent conduct or failing to comply with applicable contracting rules.[49] The government employs a number of auditors and investigators to audit and review the performance of government contractors. Furthermore, the government has enlisted the assistance of "whistleblowers" (frequently, these are disgruntled current or former employees) to expose fraud by offering them a share of any recovery obtained from the errant contractor.[50] An equally daunting array of criminal statutes may be applied to government contractors who engage in misconduct.[51] And federal prosecutors usually are even more likely to pursue alleged fraud against the government than misconduct involving only private parties.

The most common types of fraud encountered in government contracting include defective pricing, cost mischarging, product substitution, progress payment fraud, antitrust violations, kickbacks, bribery, gratuities, and conflicts of interest.[52]

k. Employee relations

Discrimination and harassment issues are a concern for virtually all employers. Federal statutes and regulations forbid discrimination in the workplace based on race, color, sex, religion, national origin, marital status, age, or disability.[53] Discrimination or harassment can subject a company to civil liability for compensatory damages and, in cases involving malice or reckless indifference, to punitive damages as well.[54] However, employers may be able to insulate themselves from liability for punitive damages by implementing good-faith efforts to prevent discrimination in the workplace.[55]

l. Other issues

While the foregoing compliance issues are common to many businesses, they are by no means a comprehensive listing. There are a number of additional issues that are less common but very significant to particular businesses or industries. Certain highly regulated industries, such as banking and health care, face numerous compliance risks that derive from the specialized laws and regulations which govern

---

49 *E.g.*, the False Claims Act, 31 U.S.C. § 3729, the claim forfeiture statute, 28 U.S.C. § 2514, the Contract Disputes Act, 41 U.S.C. § 601 *et seq.*, and the Truth in Negotiations Act 10 U.S.C. § 2306a.

50 31 U.S.C. § 3730 (*qui tam* provision of the False Claims Act).

51 *E.g.*, 18 U.S.C. § 1001 (false statements); 18 U.S.C. § 287 (false claims); 18 U.S.C. § 371 (conspiracy to defraud the United States).

52 *See* "Handbook on Fraud Indicators for Contract Auditors," IGDH 7600.3 (March 31, 1993); Inspector General, Department of Defense Pub. No. IG/DOD 4075.1-H (1987).

53 *See* Title VII of the Civil Rights Act of 1964, 42 U.S.C. § 2000e; Americans with Disabilities Act of 1990, 42 U.S.C. §§ 12101-12213 (Supp. III 1991).

54 Civil Rights Act of 1991, 42 U.S.C. § 1981.

55 *See Kolstad v. American Dental Ass'n*, 119 S. Ct. 2118, 2129 (1999).

their conduct. Their compliance programs must be customized accordingly.[56] Other businesses, although not highly regulated, may have particular attributes that create significant compliance risks. For example, marketing organizations are vulnerable to charges of fraudulent sales techniques. Once again, their compliance programs must be designed to combat these risks.

In summary, as the Sentencing Guidelines note, any compliance program must be individualized for the particular company. Identifying the relevant compliance risk issues is an important task that will require input from counsel and senior management (including, in all likelihood, the accounting or audit department and human resources). The effectiveness of the compliance program is likely to be directly proportional to the time and effort invested in constructing it.

4. Codes of Conduct

Codes of conduct usually are a centerpiece of a compliance program. Even before the advent of the Corporate Sentencing Guidelines, the Defense Industry Initiative recommended such codes as a principal tool for achieving compliance. And the Sentencing Guidelines now make such a code virtually mandatory. As discussed above, the commentary to the Guidelines sets forth seven essential elements of an "effective program to prevent and detect violations of law." The first is that the company have "established compliance standards and procedures."[57] The fourth is that it have taken "steps to communicate effectively its standards and procedures to all employees and other agents, *e.g.*, by requiring participation in training programs or by disseminating publications that explain in a practical manner what is required."[58] It would be difficult, if not impossible, for a company to achieve these goals without utilizing a code of conduct.

A corporate code of conduct should accomplish several distinct, but related, objectives. First and foremost, it should address, in a straightforward, practical manner, the compliance risk issues that are relevant to the particular company. The code should alert employees to the risks and spell out their duty to avoid them.

Second, the code should identify the personnel involved in the administration of the company's compliance program, from the senior executive(s) in charge of the program down through any lower-level contact personnel.[59] In addition, the code should outline the system for reporting suspected misconduct. The Sentencing

---

56 The office of Inspector General ("OIG") of the Department of Health and Human Services has developed and issued compliance program guidelines for various sectors of the health care industry. Copies of these guidelines can be found on the OIG website at http://hhs.gov/oig.

57 USSG § 8A1.2, comment. (n.3(k)(1)).

58 USSG § 8A1.2, comment. (n.3(k)(4)).

59 The Sentencing Guidelines require that "[s]pecific individual(s) within high-level personnel of the organization must have been assigned overall responsibility to oversee compliance with [the company's] standards and procedures." USSG § 8A1.2, comment. (n.3(k)(2)).

Guidelines mandate that a company "hav[e] in place and publiciz[e] a reporting system whereby employees and other agents [can] report criminal conduct by others within the organization without fear of retribution."[60] Thus, the code should state unequivocally that any employee may approach the compliance administrator or his/her subordinates to discuss potential violations of the code without fear of retribution. Indeed, the code should encourage employees to contact compliance personnel whenever an ethical issue arises and they are uncertain about whether or how the code applies.

Third, the code should announce that employees who violate code provisions will be sanctioned for their misconduct, and it should indicate the range of sanctions that may be applied. The sanctions may range from a reprimand for minor or unintentional violations up to termination for cause for serious violations. The Sentencing Guidelines recognize that "the form of discipline that will be appropriate will be case specific.[61] If the company is serious about its code of conduct, then it must be prepared to enforce it and to impose serious sanctions for significant misconduct. Furthermore, the Guidelines note that disciplinary actions sometimes may need to be taken not only against the offender but also against individuals responsible for the failure to detect an offense.[62]

The code of conduct should be distributed to all company employees and agents. (Some companies restrict distribution to managers, but this limitation is inadvisable in light of the Sentencing Guidelines and the fact that even low level employees can trigger significant liability for the company if they engage in misconduct). Many companies require that employees certify that they have received and read the code of conduct. Indeed, some companies make this an annual ritual. Such certifications can provide useful evidence of the company's effort to "communicate effectively its standards and procedures," as the Guidelines require. However, the certifications can end up undercutting the company's position if they reveal serious lapses in the distribution process. Thus, a company must be diligent about keeping its code distribution and certifications complete and up to date if it decides to utilize certifications.

5. Administration and Enforcement of the Compliance Program

It is not sufficient for a company simply to promulgate a good code of conduct and to establish and publicize a system for reporting violations. The corporation must follow up promptly on any reports of suspected misconduct that it receives, by investigating them and taking corrective action if appropriate. The company also should provide feedback to the employees who made the reports so that they know that their allegations were taken seriously and that an appropriate resolution was reached. Employees who believe that their complaints have been ignored by the

---

60   USSG § 8A1.2, comment. (n.3(k)(5)).

61   USSG § 8A1.2, comment. (n.3(k)(6)).

62   *Id.*

corporation are far more likely to become "whistleblowers" who initiate litigation against the company than employees who believe that their complaints have been considered and responded to.

In addition, the corporation must engage in proactive enforcement efforts, "by utilizing monitoring and auditing systems reasonably designed to detect criminal conduct."[63] Many companies already have such systems in place with respect to accounting issues, employing an internal audit program and/or audits by independent accountants to detect any errors or improprieties in their books. Comparable audit or monitoring systems need to be established with respect to the other compliance risk issues that the company has identified.

Given the wide variety of issues that will be components of most corporate compliance programs, it is readily apparent that there are several different departments within the company that may have significant roles to play. These include the inside audit or accounting department, the security department, human resources, and the legal department. Indeed, it is likely that certain of these departments already operate some sort of compliance program with respect to particular issues in their bailiwicks. For example, accounting already may perform an internal audit function; human resources may have a program to detect and remedy issues relating to discrimination and harassment; and the security department may investigate reports of illegal activities. Nonetheless, the Sentencing Guidelines require that these various compliance efforts be coordinated as part of a single program (at least insofar as compliance with criminal laws is concerned) and that one or more high-level executives be assigned overall responsibility—and accountability—for overseeing the company's compliance efforts.[64]

Which senior executive(s) should be placed in charge of the compliance program? There is no single correct answer. Many companies, especially smaller ones, will designate one compliance officer. Larger organizations often designate individual compliance officers by substantive areas, and may utilize a compliance committee in lieu of a single compliance officer, or a combination of an individual compliance officer who is supported by a committee from different areas. In decentralized organizations it may be desirable to delegate most compliance efforts to executives of the subsidiaries or business units, although there remains a clear need for coordination of the programs of the various subsidiaries or units. However, increasing the number of compliance officers presents problems of communications, possible inconsistency, and lack of accountability. Further, the more compliance officers an organization has, the higher the risk that one will be found to have condoned questionable conduct, thereby enhancing the company's culpability score under the Sentencing Guidelines.[65]

---

63   USSG § 8A1.2, comment. (n.3(k)(5)).

64   USSG § 8A1.2, comment. (n.3(k)(2)).

65   *See* Jeffrey M. Kaplan, Joseph E. Murphy, and Winthrop M. Swenson, *Compliance Programs and the Corporate Sentencing Guidelines*, § 8.11 (1995).

In any event, the corporate compliance officer needs the following basic conditions for credibility and effectiveness within a corporation:

(1) Should have sufficient stature (rank) within the organization and personal credibility;

(2) Should have unrestricted access to the CEO and the board, or a designated board committee;

(3) Should have a high degree of trust and respect among the senior management team;

(4) Should have sufficient authority to assemble resources for causing internal procedural change and carrying out investigations;

(5) Should have access to information and support mechanisms that will provide monitoring, measuring, early warning and detection;

(6) Should be evaluated and rewarded for his effectiveness in proactively carrying out the compliance role; and

(7) Should have the skills to operate effectively with the press, public forums and the legal process.[66]

Most of the foregoing conditions are relatively self-explanatory. However, it is useful to underscore the need for the compliance officer to have direct access to the CEO and the board or a board committee on an as-needed and confidential basis. This is essential because the compliance officer must be able to deal effectively with alleged senior management wrongdoing, including potentially questionable conduct by the CEO. Moreover, as a practical matter, regular reports to the board or a designated board committee should enhance the authority and independence of the compliance officer.[67]

In structuring a compliance program, company management must be mindful of one significant potential problem posed by such programs—they can end up providing a roadmap of corporate misconduct to adverse parties such as the government, civil litigants, or disaffected shareholders. It is increasingly common for such parties to seek the results of internal audits or investigations from the company in connection with a government investigation or litigation. Accordingly, the compliance program must be structured and operated in such a manner as to minimize this risk.

There is no blanket shield that a corporation can draw over the workings of its compliance program. A corporation has no Fifth Amendment privilege against self-incrimination. The potential shields that are available to the company consist

---

66   *Id.* § 8.01.

67   *Id.* § 8.12.

of the attorney-client privilege, the attorney work-product doctrine and, in some instances, the self-evaluative privilege.[68]

Accordingly, a company must rely on the attorney-client privilege and the attorney work-product doctrine in order to protect the confidentiality of various aspects of its compliance program, such as investigative materials and results. This means that counsel—be it inside counsel or outside counsel—must play a key role in the compliance program and, in particular, must be in charge of any sensitive internal investigations undertaken as part of that program. To the extent that the compliance program, or aspects thereof, is administered by non-legal personnel, such as the audit department, human resources, etc., it is likely that the results of their work will be discoverable in subsequent proceedings.[69]

Note that the inherent limitations of the attorney-client privilege and the work-product doctrine probably will prevent them from shielding the compliance program *in toto*, including all of its workings. For example, if the compliance program calls for employees to report suspected misconduct to non-legal personnel, it is unlikely that this initial report will be deemed privileged although an ensuing investigation of the complaint would be privileged if conducted by counsel. A different result may obtain if all reports of misconduct are funneled through counsel in the first instance, but this often will be impracticable in many companies and, moreover, many of the reports generated by a compliance system may be routine complaints of the sort that do not require the involvement of counsel. These competing considerations must be taken into account in structuring the compliance system in order to balance the need for confidentiality with the practical requirements of operating the program.

B. Responding to Suspected Offenses

The Sentencing Guidelines are designed to couple corporate self-policing (through a compliance program) with self-reporting of any company offenses that do occur. As discussed above, in order to gain credit for having an effective compliance program, the company must make a prompt disclosure of any offense of which it learns. No reduction will be given if the company, after learning of the offense, "unreasonably" delays reporting it to appropriate authorities.[70]

---

68 The attorney-client privilege, the work product doctrine and the self-evaluative privilege and their role in internal investigations are discussed in Chapter 3.

69 Employee communications with an agent of counsel, such as an accountant or investigator, can be covered by the attorney-client privilege but only if counsel is using the agent to facilitate the rendering of legal advice and the agent is working under counsel's direct supervision. *See United States v. Schwimmer*, 892 F.2d 237, 244 (2d Cir. 1989); *United States v. McPartlin*, 595 F.2d 1321, 1337 (7th Cir.), *cert. denied*, 444 U.S. 833 (1979).

70 USSG § 8C2.5(f). The Guidelines provide that a company is allowed a reasonable period of time to conduct an internal investigation before reporting an offense, and that no report is required if the company reasonably concludes, based on the information then available, that no offense had been committed. USSG § 8C2.5, comment. (n.10).

In fact, under the Guidelines, self-reporting of corporate offenses is deemed more important than operating an effective compliance program. Regardless of whether the company had an effective compliance program in place, it may reduce its culpability score after an offense occurs by cooperating with federal investigators and prosecutors. Five points are subtracted from the company's culpability score if it makes a prompt, voluntary disclosure of the offense after learning of it, cooperates fully in the investigation, and pleads guilty.[71] Note that the magnitude of this credit significantly exceeds the additional three-point credit that a company can obtain for having an effective compliance program.

To qualify for a reduction in its culpability score, the company's cooperation with the government must be both timely and thorough.[72] If no government investigation is pending, the company may conduct an internal investigation for a reasonable period of time before deciding what action, if any, to take.[73] However, if the company is officially notified of a criminal investigation, then it must begin cooperating almost immediately in order to receive credit for timely cooperation.[74] To be considered thorough, the company's cooperation must include the disclosure of all pertinent information known by the company.[75]

Although the Guidelines are designed to create a substantial incentive for companies to report their own criminal violations and to cooperate with government investigations of potential violations, there are some significant countervailing concerns. For example, the Guidelines create a dilemma with respect to conducting an effective internal investigation. It is difficult, if not impossible, for internal investigations to secure candid and complete responses from company employees with knowledge of wrongdoing if the employees believe that any admissions of culpability will be turned over to the government.[76] Similarly, disclosure of privileged investigative reports to government prosecutors likely will effect a complete waiver of the company's privilege, thereby exposing it to having its own investigation used against it in related civil litigation.[77]

On a more fundamental level, it is not clear that the Guidelines, as currently structured, create an environment where it is always in a company's best interest to report on itself. A company's "reward" for turning itself in is to be prosecuted and receive a reduced sentence when, absent its confession, it might have escaped

---

71   USSG § 8C2.5(g). Two points are subtracted for full cooperation and a timely plea in situations where the government's investigation was not instigated by the company, itself. *Id.*

72   USSG § 8C2.5, comment. (n.12).

73   USSG § 8C2.5, comment. (n.10).

74   USSG § 8C2.5, comment. (n.12).

75   *Id.*

76   Leonard Orland, *Corporate Punishment by the U.S. Sentencing Commission,* 4 Federal Sentencing Reporter 50, 52 (1991).

77   *See United States v. Massachusetts Institute of Technology,* 129 F.3d 681, 685 (1st Cir. 1997) (and cases therein cited). See Chapters 3 and 5.

prosecution altogether. In certain cases a prosecutor may be dissuaded from charging a confessing company if it can sufficiently demonstrate its corporate good citizenship. However, a company has absolutely no assurance that it will receive such a favorable outcome in return for its disclosure of wrongdoing.

By comparison, the Department of Defense has an established voluntary disclosure program for government contractors which offers greater incentives to participants—generally, volunteers have not been prosecuted on the basis of their disclosures and have avoided suspension or debarment from government contracting as well. Yet, there are still some real disincentives to disclosure even under that program that, at least in some instances, may outweigh the advantages.[78] The balance is likely to be far closer—and to tip more often against disclosure or cooperation—in cases under the Guidelines, since there is no promise of immunity from prosecution and since, unless the company is a government contractor, there is no risk of suspension/debarment absent cooperation.

The upshot is that the Guidelines make it vital for companies to consult immediately with counsel whenever they are confronted with an apparent offense or a government investigation, so that an informed decision can be made about the course to be followed. The stakes are too great for an organization to attempt to muddle through on its own, even for a brief period.

---

78   See Benjamin B. Klubes, *The Department of Defense Voluntary Disclosure Program*, 19 Public Contract Law Journal 505, 519-55 (1990).

CHAPTER 9:
CONDUCTING AN INTERNAL INVESTIGATION OVERSEAS

I. Background

For several different reasons, there is an increasing need for American corporations to conduct internal investigations outside the United States. While it is estimated that U.S. industry loses about $400 billion a year to criminal and fraudulent behavior,[1] such behavior is much more pervasive in many other countries. It is not surprising, therefore, that many American corporations which generate substantial amounts of revenue from overseas operations increasingly find it necessary to conduct internal fraud investigations overseas. Also, with the growing number of global acquisitions and mergers, American companies are also finding it necessary to conduct internal investigations to assure compliance with the Foreign Corrupt Practices Act.[2]

Additionally, overseas companies themselves are now beginning to recognize the destructive impact that fraudulent and corrupt behavior can have on the integrity and future of a business, in spite of some historical commonly accepted business practices to the contrary in many parts of the world. In today's competitive global economy, companies need to protect themselves from the potentially devastating effects of fraud and corruption.[3] When some or all of an investigation must be conducted overseas, there is a whole panoply of additional issues facing lawyers who must conduct such investigations.

Investigations overseas can arise in a number of different ways. The government of the country in which the company is doing business may commence an investigation. It is more likely that the United States government will commence an investigation of an American company, which will require that an internal investigation

---

1   *See* "For Any Lawyer Trying to Help Keep an Honest Company Straight," 85 A.B.A.J. 64, June 1999 (quoting loss estimate by The Association of Certified Fraud Examiners).

2   15 U.S.C. § 78

3   David Adams noted in the *St. Petersburg Times* that "[p]residents, and their friends and associates, have been named in one scandal after another, from bribery in Buenos Aires and embezzlement in Ecuador to money laundering in Mexico and drug-tainted campaign contributions in Columbia.", *The St. Petersburg Times, January 1, 1996, Page 1A.*

be conducted overseas. More recently, foreign governments have conducted investigations of foreign companies operating in their jurisdiction relating to fraud, bribery, embezzlement and other acts of corruption.[4] In the past, this type of investigation was unheard of in many countries. In many instances, the corporation will itself want to conduct an overseas investigation to help defend itself from a governmental investigation. Other reasons to conduct an investigation include that the corporation is concerned that it has been defrauded or because of concerns regarding its operations or relationships with third parties.

When a U.S. corporation begins an investigation in a foreign country, whether of its own operations or of third parties, the lawyer conducting the investigation must be prepared to deal with many factors that would not arise if conducted within the United States. The lawyer must, therefore, plan the investigation accordingly, before it begins.

Investigatory tactics that are common in the U.S. are often difficult or impossible in foreign countries. For example, most information in the U.S., such as bank and corporate information, can be obtained, even if only by subpoena. In many foreign countries it is illegal to obtain bank information. In some countries, actual corporate identities and corporate owners are protected even from that country's law enforcement agencies, or held by nominees in bearer form. Therefore, typical methods of obtaining information are often not fruitful and, even if the information can be obtained, the investigator must be concerned whether the information/evidence can be used in a U.S. or foreign court.[5] It is common, even for entities that were created for honest reasons and that conduct business honestly, to be under secret or veiled ownership. In many cases, even the nominee owners or firms that engage in business solely to incorporate entities or open bank accounts may not know who are the true owners and beneficiaries.

Corruption can be a serious problem when conducting foreign investigations. Government officials may have been compromised and many are just not interested, whether for personal or political reasons. It is often critical to a foreign investigation to have and be able to count on known and reliable local contacts. Those local contacts are often critical resources before the investigation begins, or during the commencement of an investigation, in order to have sufficient background to understand local relationships and customs. In some countries, long standing family or political relationships will create walls of opposition, often invisible to the outsider. It is not uncommon for people who appear to be on opposite sides of a position to, in reality, be allies. Many government officials frequently don't

---

4   For example, "IBM Argentina's once-stellar reputation has been soiled amid a court investigation of several executives accused of paying $37 million in bribes to high-level officials to clinch a $250 million computer modernization contract with state-owned Banco Nacion." *The Washington Times, Page A17, December 4, 1996.*

5   In some countries, it is not uncommon for unethical and corrupt investigators to claim to be able to search for and get "secret" information. Often, they simply take money for the search, do nothing and announce that their sources found no information.

themselves understand how to conduct a fraud investigation, or fear it is against their own self interest or not an important issue to their country; many simply do not care to help a "rich" American corporation. Dealing with foreign government officials is often best accomplished by working through the appropriate levels of the United States embassy.

Every effective fraud investigation is largely dependent on the "paper trail"—the documentary investigation and resulting documentary evidence. However, in many countries it is rare for records of almost any kind to be centralized. Therefore, any files that are available may not be immediately evident; an effort to search and locate files that are geographically dispersed is critical, and multiple, yet different, sets of transaction records are not uncommon. Any important records should be immediately copied, cataloged and safely stored in order to protect against destruction or outright disappearance. In many countries, government files are not computerized and you can not rely on help from the local officials who maintain the records. In those countries where records are computerized, the extent of computerization varies greatly and the age and sophistication of the systems may be very different than more modernized U.S. standards.

While electronic surveillance in the U.S. is typically prohibited, or at best rare in general business settings, in many foreign countries it is common. Any sensitive investigation within a foreign jurisdiction should be preceded with a sweep for electronic surveillance devices and continued at regular intervals throughout. In addition, documents, equipment and files, whether originals or copies, should be secured appropriately. It is not uncommon for such material to be compromised in order for the target to gather intelligence on the investigation, or worse, destroyed as a means to scuttle the investigation.

Counsel must become familiar with local custom as well as local law. In cases with potential political impact, counsel must prepare for possible government interference and even intimidation. In some countries the office of the attorney general, or some equivalent, may attempt to obstruct an investigation simply for political gain, or possibly even personal gain. The same can sometime be said of congressional involvement.

Practices that in the U.S. are illegal or unethical may not be in the foreign country or may simply not be enforced. Accounting standards may be different than in the U.S. and major accounting firms in the U.S. may find that their opinions on accounting issues differ from those of their partners in different countries.

In many countries, the targets of an investigation may have significant contacts with the media. Individual targets, or companies potentially affected by the investigation, may have the ability to turn the press against the investigation for strategic gain. In fact, it is not unheard of that religious leaders are brought in to sway public opinion against an investigation. In some Latin American countries, for example, churches act to sway public opinion on issues of the day, often very effectively.

Justice systems and the effectiveness of the courts outside of the United States can be very different. Reliance on the courts and justice system overseas should not be taken for granted. Counsel should investigate in advance the integrity, or lack of integrity, of the local court system and whether judges are corrupt or can be bought. In addition to obtaining that information from local practitioners, the World Bank and the State Department have information on court systems of foreign countries which can be very useful. If litigation is a possibility, the integrity of the justice system must be determined before the time and expense of litigation is expended. In addition, counsel should determine whether there are existing agreements between countries for honoring judgments as well as requests for information.

II. The Foreign Corrupt Practices Act

The Foreign Corrupt Practices Act[6] (FCPA) makes illegal "corrupt" payments to foreign government and political officials. This prohibition is very important to any American company doing business in a foreign jurisdiction or about to do business with or acquire any foreign business.[7] The law prohibits any issuer of U.S. securities, domestic concerns or their officers, directors, employees, and certain other specified persons[8] from making payments to foreign political officials.[9] The acts prohibited by the FCPA must be for the purpose of obtaining or retaining business, or directing business to any person.[10] However, the business does not need to be with the foreign government, only that the payment be made to a prohibited government party.[11]

A second and equally important requirement of the FCPA mandates certain rules relating to corporate recordkeeping.[12] In addition to making certain that American companies are not infected with payments or acts that violate the statute, it is critical to ascertain that the accounting controls and records of the company comply as well. This is particularly important when acquiring foreign companies whose accounting practices may be vastly different and not historically in conformity with

---

6   15 U.S.C. § 78.

7   The FCPA is no longer just a U.S. law. The 29 member nations of the Organization for Economic Cooperation and Development and five non-member nations have adopted a "Convention on Combating Bribery of Foreign Public Officials in International Business Transactions." *See, Business Crimes Bulletin*, Vol. 5, No. 1, February 1998 "Major Victory for U.S. as Foreign Corrupt Practices Act Goes Global" by Gregory J. Wallace.

8   15 U.S.C. §§ 78dd-1(a) as to "issuers" and 15 U.S.C. §§ 78dd-2(a) as to "domestic concerns."

9   The statute not only prohibits actual payments, but also acts that are in "furtherance of any offer, payment, promise to pay or authorization of the payment of any money, gift, promise to give or authorization of anything of value." *See* 15 U.S.C. §§ 78dd-1(a) and 2(a).

10   *Id.*

11   There are certain affirmative defenses that were created in the statute that the lawyer and forensic accountant should be familiar with but are beyond the scope of this material. *See* 15 U.S.C. §§ 78dd-1(b), 1(c), 2(b) and 2(c).

12   15 U.S.C. § 78m(b).

U.S. GAAP rules.[13] The purpose of the FCPA's recordkeeping requirements is to prevent off book transactions that are, in essence, slush funds that cannot later be traced, or transactions that are falsely classified in the books and records of the company. The statute requires that "issuers" of securities make and keep books, records and accounts, which, in reasonable detail, accurately and fairly reflect the transactions and dispositions of the assets of the issuer.[14] Specifically, issuers' accounting systems must be such that "transactions are executed in accordance with management's general or specific authorization",[15] "transactions are recorded in such a way as to allow preparation of a report that is in conformity with generally accepted accounting principles,"[16] access to assets is permitted only in accordance with management's general or specific authorization,"[17] and "the recorded accountability for assets is compared with the existing assets at reasonable intervals and appropriate action is taken with respect to any differences."[18] In order to assure the continuing proper accounting by an acquisition target or foreign subsidiary, it is necessary to first confirm that adequate internal controls and compliance policies are in place and complied with. Violations of the FCPA can be serious and sanctions can be serious as well.

In sum, depending on the type of investigation, the country where it is ongoing and the notoriety of the matter, counsel may face difficulties and impediments to conducting an investigation that he has not previously encountered. While at least some of these can be planned for in advance, there can be many that come up unexpectedly. When this occurs, counsel would be wise to obtain as much input as possible from persons with expertise in the local area, as prior investigative experience in the United States is not always the best source of answers in such situations.

---

13 Generally Accepted Accounting Principles.
14 15 U.S.C. § 78m(b)(2)(A).
15 15 U.S.C. § 78m(b)(2)(B)(i).
16 15 U.S.C. § 78m(b)(2)(B)(ii).
17 15 U.S.C. § 78m(b)(2)(B)(iii).
18 15 U.S.C. § 78m(b)(2)(B)(iv).

Chapter 10:
Investigations in the Health Care Industry

Introduction

"Let the message be very, very clear. We have made health care fraud a priority and we will pursue it as vigorously as we can." With these words in 1993, U.S. Attorney General Janet Reno announced that the Department of Justice had designated health care fraud as the number two federal law enforcement priority after violent crime. During the following years, the Department of Justice, joined by other federal and state enforcement and regulatory authorities, private health insurers, and plaintiffs lawyers across the United States, has instituted an unprecedented program that has had a tremendous impact on the financial health and welfare of the entire health care industry. Consider the following:

- A health care fraud specialist has been established in every local United States Attorney's Office across the country.

- In 1997 alone, 167 new federal jobs were added to the health care fraud fighting force, along with an additional 77 FBI agents dedicated to health care issues. These include dedicated health care fraud prosecutors and auditors assigned to local U.S. Attorney's Offices.

- The Department of Health and Human Services ("HHS") Office of Inspector General ("OIG") is implementing a seven-year plan to hire 243 new investigators and to staff Medicare fraud field offices in every state.

- HHS OIG claims to have saved $17 billion through its anti-fraud efforts since its funding was increased in 1997. "Results like this give it a lifetime that goes on for many, many years. . . . The credenzas of our attorneys are still stacked with very good cases." McCarty Thornton, Senior Counsel to HHS OIG at a health care fraud and abuse conference in June of 1999.[1]

- Medicare and Medicaid enforcement funding will increase from $100 million in 1999 to more than $160 million over the next three years.[2]

---

1   *Compliance Hotline*, "OIG Outlines Coming Attack on Health Care Fraud," June 28, 1999 at 1.

2   *Id.* at 3.

- Civil fraud matters have increased from 270 in fiscal year 1992 to more than 4000 in fiscal year 1997.

- Whistleblower suits alleging health care fraud under the *qui tam* provisions of the False Claims Act have increased from 17 in 1992 to almost 300 in 1998.[3] Some estimates are that there may be as many as 2,000 additional whistleblower suits in the pipeline.

- State Medicaid Fraud Control Units are active in nearly every state and are increasingly coordinating activities with federal authorities.

- Statutory changes in 1996 and 1997 have increased the criminal, civil and administrative penalties to which health care providers are subject and have vastly increased the resources available to enforcement authorities.

The combination of all of these factors and events have created increased risk of financial penalties to all health care providers and organizations, from the smallest physician practice to regional and national hospital, nursing home, integrated systems and multi-national pharmaceutical companies. In addition, statutes mandating exclusion from participation in the Medicare and Medicaid programs, combined with the potential for huge civil and criminal penalties, have induced large health care providers to enter into civil settlements in amounts that were unheard of only a few years ago. For example, in 1994, National Medical Enterprises paid $379 million to settle civil and criminal charges related to allegations of false billing and kickbacks for patient referrals to psychiatric hospitals. Recently, national laboratory companies settled charges related to billings for certain laboratory tests for Medicare beneficiaries as follows: Damon Clinical Laboratories—$119 million; Laboratory Corporation of America—$187 million; and SmithKline Beecham Clinical Laboratories—$325 million. In 1996, Caremark Corporation entered into a $161 million settlement related to alleged kickbacks to physicians for ordering synthetic human growth hormone products. These settlements and many others like them have encouraged government authorities and private plaintiffs to devote more and more resources to health care fraud investigations and cases.

In the face of this array of potential problems, what can organizations involved in the health care industry do? Establishing an effective compliance program to prevent and detect potential wrongdoing is probably the most useful and cost-effective action a health care organization can take. The benefits of a corporate compliance program and what is involved in establishing one is the subject of another chapter of this book.[4] For publicly traded companies in the health care industry, whether or not to have a compliance program is no longer an option. As summarized later in this chapter, and described in more detail in the chapter on compliance programs, recent caselaw has held that the failure of a health care

---

3   *Id.*

4   See Chapter 8.

organization to have a compliance program may be a breach of fiduciary duty on the part of the board of directors and management of the company.

More directly related to this book's focus on investigations, there are myriad situations in which a health care organization might need to conduct an internal investigation. For example, the compliance program may identify potential billing problems. It becomes incumbent on the organization at that time to investigate whether incorrect billings have, in fact, been submitted; whether the billing errors were the result of intentional behavior or an accident or misunderstanding; whether overpayments were received from government or private insurance payors; and whether some form of voluntary self-reporting is appropriate or required. Besides the compliance program, information about potential problems can come to a provider's attention in many ways. A former employee may raise claims of billing fraud in wrongful termination lawsuits or in exit interviews. Government agents may come to employees' homes to interview them. Competitors may think it is in their business interest to bring potential fraud and abuse to the attention of authorities. Providers may receive administrative or grand jury subpoenas from a variety of government regulatory agencies or prosecutors. Issues may arise in surveys or other state or federal inspections. Worst of all, a team of heavily armed federal and/or state agents may arrive at a health care facility or office to execute a search warrant, seize records and, possibly, attempt to interview employees. How the organization responds to each of these situations may have a significant impact on the ultimate outcome of whether criminal or civil fraud charges will be brought; whether regulatory agencies will seek to impose crippling monetary penalties or exclude the provider from participation in government health care programs; or whether the government can be convinced that any mistakes were the result of honest error or conflicting regulatory advice.

In the following sections, we will outline the civil, criminal and administrative statutes and regulations most often involved in health care fraud investigations and related claims. This discussion will include descriptions of how the government uses these statutes and regulations in pursuing claims against health care providers, as well as summaries of some of the key investigations undertaken during the past few years. Next, we will discuss the unique aspects of and special considerations involved in conducting internal investigations for health care organizations. Finally, we will discuss how corporate compliance programs have become a requirement for the prudent conduct of business in the health care industry and how compliance programs relate to and affect internal investigations.

The Primary Weapons of the Government in Health Care Fraud Investigations

I. Federal False Claims Statutes

The civil and criminal False Claims Acts are currently among the favorite tools of federal health care fraud investigators and prosecutors. Under these statutes, virtually identical behavior could result in claims under either the civil False Claims Act or its criminal counterpart. This can have severe ramifications for health care providers who find themselves the subject of an investigation. False Claims Act investigations often proceed on parallel criminal and civil tracks, with the ultimate decision on which track to choose deferred until the end of the investigation. To make matters more difficult, the decisions on whether to proceed under civil or criminal statutes, or not at all, are based on highly subjective factors, such as intent. Many investigators come into cases with a bias toward believing that incorrect billings are intentional rather than resulting from confusion, negligence or inadvertent error. Government lawyers can and do use the possibility of a criminal prosecution as leverage to extract higher civil settlements from their targets. In addition to the pressure of parallel civil and criminal proceedings,[5] the sometimes staggering potential fines and penalties make many providers reluctant to take on the risk of losing at trial. Finally, a conviction of a single count of a criminal False Claims Act indictment can result in mandatory exclusion from participation in federal health care programs for a minimum of five years. If found liable of filing a civil false claim, a provider may be excluded under the discretionary permissive exclusion authority of the HHS OIG.[6] Thus, in the health care arena, parallel proceedings can have three or more tracks; civil, criminal and administrative. In addition, there may be simultaneous or follow-on investigations or inquiries from state Medicaid authorities or private payors. These multi-level investigations have become the rule rather than the exception in recent years. This adds further complexity to the problems of dealing with potential False Claims Act investigations.

A. Civil False Claims Act

1. Background

The civil False Claims Act (the "FCA" or "Act")[7] has a long history in attacking fraud by government contractors. It was originally signed into law by President Lincoln during the Civil War to curtail what was perceived as rampant fraud by defense contractors.

> The original Statute was enacted by the Congress of the United States in March, 1863, several months before the Battle of Gettysburg. There is historical evidence that a critical position known as Little Roundtop was almost overrun by Confederate troops because of a lack of Union rifles and ammunition. Armament which had been purchased from private suppliers arrived in boxes that contained only sawdust.

U.S. v. General Electric, 808 F. Supp. 580, 581 (S.D. Ohio 1992) (*citing* Coddington, The Gettysburg Campaign).

---

5   The complexities of responding to parallel proceedings are discussed in detail in Chapter 6.

6   The exclusion authority of the HHS Inspector General is discussed in this Chapter in § VIII.

7   The FCA, 31 U.S.C. §§ 3729-3733, is presented in its entirety in Appendix 3 hereto.

Over a century later, principles underlying the original FCA began to appear in federal health care legislation. When Congress enacted the Medicare and Medicaid programs in 1965 by amending the Social Security Act, it included a provision prohibiting false statements made for the purpose of obtaining program benefits. In the 1980s, Congress authorized the Secretary of HHS to impose civil money penalties on providers who submitted false or fraudulent Medicare or Medicaid claims. During the same period, Congress increased the potential monetary rewards to individuals who filed *qui tam* (or "whistleblower") lawsuits to enforce the Act and clarified that no proof of specific intent was required for liability. More recently, Congress passed the Health Insurance Portability and Accountability Act of 1996 (Pub.L. No. 104-191) ("HIPAA"), which added new criminal sanctions for false claims violations, created a perpetual source of funding for government enforcement efforts, and required that the Department of Justice ("DOJ") and HHS collaborate and share resources with other federal, state, local, and private forces to investigate and prosecute waste, fraud, and abuse in federal health care programs.

2. Elements of the Civil FCA

In its current form, the FCA imposes civil liability after the government proves by a preponderance of the evidence that the defendant submitted or caused to be submitted a "claim for payment" to the federal government, that the claim was "false or fraudulent," and that the defendant acted "knowingly."[8] "Knowingly" means that a person has "actual knowledge" or acts in "deliberate ignorance" or "reckless disregard"[9] of the truth or falsity of the information.[10] *No proof of specific intent to defraud is required* for liability.[11] Health care providers have an affirmative duty to insure that claims are accurate before submitting them to the government.[12]

---

8   31 U.S.C. § 3729(a)(1).

9   Courts have generally recognized that "deliberate ignorance" or "reckless disregard" equates to gross negligence. *See, e.g., U.S. v. Krizek*, 111 F.3d 934, 942 (D.C. Cir. 1997)("[T]he best reading of the [False Claims] Act defines reckless disregard as an extension of gross negligence."); *U.S. v. Entin*, 750 F. Supp. 512, 518 (S.D. Fla. 1990)("The scienter standard was eased in order to preclude 'ostrich' type situations, where an individual has 'buried his head in the sand' and failed to make any inquiry which would have revealed the false claim. (citations omitted) One congressional sponsor of the amended Act explained the new scienter standard: 'While the Act was not intended to apply to mere negligence, it is intended to apply in situations that could be considered gross negligence where the submitted claims to the government are prepared in such a sloppy or unsupervised fashion that resulted in overcharges to the government. The Act is also intended not to permit artful defense counsel to require some proof of intent as an essential ingredient of proof. . . .' (citation omitted). Thus actual knowledge is not a prerequisite to liability—constructive knowledge will suffice.").

10   31 U.S.C. § 3729(b).

11   *Id.*

12   Certifications in Medicare claim forms impose "a duty to investigate the truth, accuracy, and completeness of claims before they are submitted." OIG Compliance Guidance for Home

Damages for FCA violations can be as high as three times the amount of the false or fraudulent claim, plus civil monetary penalties of "not less than $5,000 and not more than $10,000" per claim.[13] Every bill submitted to Medicare or Medicaid can constitute a "claim" for purposes of the FCA. A provider can limit its damages to double the amount of the false claim by disclosing the fraud to the government within 30 days of discovery and by cooperating with the government's investigation. However, this option is only available if no civil, criminal, or administrative action has been initiated by the government and the provider did not have knowledge of existence of any investigation at the time it made the disclosure.[14]

The FCA presents advantages to government prosecution not available under other health care fraud statutes. The government must prove its case only by the lower "preponderance of the evidence" standard applied in civil cases, rather than the more stringent "beyond a reasonable doubt" standard in criminal cases. Moreover, the large size of the mandatory minimum civil money penalties serves as a deterrent to litigation and encourages settlement. In addition, although the United States Supreme Court has not yet taken up the question, lower courts have recently held that the government is not required to prove that it suffered actual damages to trigger FCA protections.[15]

Government lawyers have attempted to increase their advantages in FCA matters by taking the position that each incorrect or inaccurate line item or code on a Medicare or Medicaid bill constitutes a separate false claim. At least one defendant has successfully challenged this interpretation, contending that the entire claim form constitutes the "claim" for FCA analysis and not the individual line items.[16] Although the District of Columbia Circuit has held against the government on this

---

Health Agencies, 63 Fed. Reg. 42410, 42417 (1998). Providers have "a legal duty to ensure that [they are]not submitting false or inaccurate claim to government and private payors . . . ." *See, e.g., id.* at 42411.

13   31 U.S.C. § 3729(a).

14   31 U.S.C. § 3729(a)(7).

15   *U.S. ex rel. Thompson v. Columbia/HCA*, 20 F. Supp.2d 1017, 1047 (S.D. Tex. 1998) ("[A] pecuniary injury to the public fisc is no longer required for an actionable claim under the FCA.")(*citing Rex Trailer Co., Inc. v. U.S.*, 350 U.S. 148 (1956) and *U. S. v. Ridglea State Bank*, 357 F.2d 495 (5th Cir. 1966)); *see also id.*, at 1033 (citing *U.S. ex rel. Schwedt v. Planning Research Corp.*, 59 F.3d 196, 198 (D.D.C. 1995); *U.S. ex rel. Hagood v. Sonoma Co. Water Agency*, 929 F.2d 1416, 1421 (9th Cir. 1991); *U.S. v. Rohleder*, 157 F.2d 126 (3d Cir. 1946); *U.S. ex rel. Pogue v. American Healthcorp, Inc.*, 914 F. Supp. 1507, 1508-09 (M.D. Tenn. 1996); *U.S. v. Kensington Hosp.*, 760 F. Supp. 1120, 1126 (E.D. Pa. 1991); *U.S. ex rel. Walle v. Martin Marietta Corp.*, 1997 U.S. Dist. LEXIS 138, No. 92-3677, 1997 WL 4566 at *1 (E.D. La. 1997)).

16   *U.S. v. Krizek*, 111 F.3d at 940 ("Moreover, even if we considered fairness to be a relevant consideration in statutory construction, we would note that the government's definition of claim [that each of multiple CPT codes entered on a form HCFA 1500 was one claim, rather than the form HCFA 1500 itself] permitted it to seek an astronomical $81 million worth of damages for alleged actual damages of $245,392.")

issue, government lawyers in other jurisdictions continue to argue that each line item constitutes a separate false claim.

Even if the courts ultimately and uniformly reject the argument that individual codes or line items on Medicare bills are separate claims, potential claims or penalties under the FCA can be enormous. The complexities and frequently confusing guidance from the Medicare and Medicaid programs often result in inadvertent billing errors and honest mistakes. When a provider, such as a hospital, may see thousands of patients in a year, a billing error can occur over and over before it is finally caught and corrected. Each time a bill containing the error is submitted to a federal health care program, it may trigger damages and penalties under the FCA even if the government ultimately concludes that the error was not intended specifically to increase the provider's reimbursement improperly. Treble damages and civil money penalties may result from "deliberate ignorance" and "reckless disregard," as noted above.

3. *Qui Tam* Actions

The FCA also provides that a private citizen may bring a civil action for violations of the Act on behalf of both himself and the federal government.[17] These civil actions are referred to as "*qui tam*"[18] or "whistleblower" lawsuits, and the plaintiff is referred to as the "relator." Relators filed approximately 840 *qui tam* lawsuits in the first eight years following the 1986 FCA amendments, with about 190 cases involving fraud claims in HHS programs such as Medicare or Medicaid. In the last three years, relators have filed more than 1,300 *qui tam* cases, with approximately 750 alleging health care fraud.[19] Health care fraud judgments or settlements totaled approximately $1.4 billion during the same three year period, with *qui tam* cases accounting for $935 million of that amount.[20]

---

17 31 U.S.C. § 3730(b). After the initial draft of this chapter was prepared, the U.S. Supreme Court on its own initiative requested briefing and heard oral arguments on whether a private citizen has standing under Article III of the Constitution to litigate claims of fraud upon the government. *Vermont Agency of Natural Resources v. U.S. ex rel. Stevens*, No. 98-1828. Additionally, a panel of the Fifth Circuit Court of Appeals recently held that the provision of the FCA that permits a *qui tam* relator to proceed with a lawsuit after the government declines to intervene is unconstitutional, violating the "Take Care Clause" in Article II of the Constitution and the separation of powers doctrine. *Riley v. St. Luke's Episcopal Hosp.*, 196 F.3d 514 (5th Cir.), *reh'g en banc granted*, 196 F.3d 561 (5th Cir. 1999).

18 "'*Qui Tam*' is abbreviation of Latin phrase '*qui tam pro domino rege quam pro si ipso in hac parte sequitur*' meaning 'Who sues on behalf of the King as well as for himself.' It is an action brought by an informer, under a Statute which establishes a penalty for the commission or omission of a certain act, and provides that the same shall be recoverable in a civil action, part of the penalty to go to any person who will bring such action and the remainder to the state or some other institution. It is called a '*qui tam* action' because the plaintiff states that he sues *as well for the state as for himself*. (citations omitted)." Black's Law Dictionary (6th ed. 1990).

19 "Department of Justice, Health Care Fraud Report - Fiscal Year 1998," p.12/32.

20 *Id.*

The FCA establishes two jurisdictional bars to *qui tam* suits. First, the relator must be the "first to file." *Qui tam* actions are barred if the transactions at issue are or have been the subject of either a civil suit filed by another person[21] or of civil or administrative civil money penalty proceedings in which the government is a party.[22] Additionally, an individual may not bring a *qui tam* suit if there has previously been a "public disclosure" of the allegation through criminal, civil, or administrative hearings, government reports, or the news media, unless the relator is an "original source" of the disclosed information. 31 U.S.C. § 3730(e)(4).

Qui tam lawsuits are filed under seal with the court, and the complaint and statement of material evidence is served only on the U.S. Attorney General and the relevant U.S. Attorney. The government has 60 days to review the plaintiff's submission and determine whether it wishes to join the lawsuit. During this period, the lawsuit is reviewed by DOJ, HHS, and OIG to determine whether there is an existing investigation of the subject matter of the lawsuit. At the end of the review period,[23] the government decides whether to join the lawsuit or to decline participation. The relationships between *qui tam* relators and DOJ attorneys can be uneasy, particularly when the amount of the relator's award is calculated.[24]

Monetary rewards to *qui tam* relators can be significant.[25] If the government intervenes and prosecutes the case, the relator receives at least 15 percent but not more than 25 percent of the proceeds or settlement, depending upon his or her contribution to the prosecution.[26] If the government elects not to proceed, the relator may

---

21   *See U.S. ex rel. Lacorte v. SmithKline Beecham*, 149 F.2d 227, 230 (3d. Cir. 1998)(31 U.S.C. § 3730(b)(5) intended to prevent duplicative lawsuits).

22   31 U.S.C. §§ 3730(b)(5), (e)(3).

23   Courts regularly extend this period to allow the government to conduct further factual investigation.

24   *U.S. v. General Electric*, 808 F. Supp. at 584 ("This is not the first case where this Court has noted the antagonism of the Justice Department to a whistleblower. The reason continues to be unknown, but the attitude is clear."); BNA Health Care Fraud Report (4/22/98), p283 ("While [in the court's determination of relator percentage award,] DOJ was quick to dispute all of the relators' contribution to the case, the local government agents involved in the case rushed to the support of Merena and the other two whistleblowers.")

25   The size of recent *qui tam* awards appears to have fueled the sharp increase in FCA actions filed. BNA Health Care Fraud Report (4/22/98), p283, *citing U.S. ex rel. Merena v. SmithKline Beecham Corp.*, 52 F. Supp.2d 420 (E.D. Pa. 1998)($325 million settlement, relators awarded $52 million); Government Contract Litigation Reporter (8/26/99), p10, *citing U.S. ex rel. McLendon v. Columbia/HCA Healthcare Corp., et al.*, No. 97-CV-0890 (N.D. Ga., settlement entered July 19, 1999)($61 million settlement, relator awarded $9.82 million); Mealey's Litigation Report: Insurance Fraud (5/25/99), citing $16.5 million settlement for *qui tam* cases against dialysis service providers, relators awarded $3.3 million); BNA Health Care Fraud Report (9/9/98), p668, *citing U.S. ex rel. Kneepkens v. Dialysis Holdings, Inc.*, D. Mass., Civil Action No. 97-10400-GAO, filed 8/17/98 (total settlement $15 million, relator awarded $1.5 million).

26   31 U.S.C. § 3730(d)(1).

prosecute the case at his or her own expense.[27] If successful, the relator receives at least 25 percent but not more than 30 percent of the judgment or settlement collected.[28] Whether the government intervenes, or the relator proceeds alone, the successful relator is entitled to have its reasonable expenses, attorneys' fees, and costs paid by the defendant.[29]

The FCA protects employees who bring *qui tam* actions (*i.e.*, whistleblowers) from retaliatory discharge or other employment discrimination.[30] Employees who are discharged for whistleblowing are entitled to reinstatement, double back pay, special damages, costs, and attorneys' fees.[31] Even employees who initiate or participate in creating the false or fraudulent claim may bring *qui tam* actions, and collect a reduced share of the proceeds, unless they are convicted of criminal conduct arising from their role in the civil false claim.[32]

B. Criminal False Claim Statutes

Prosecutors rely on a number of criminal statutes to investigate and prosecute fraud in the health care industry, but two statutes most squarely address false billing claims. First, the Social Security Act prohibits false statements or representations in applications for payment or benefits under Federal health care programs, designating them as felony offenses punishable by a $25,000 fine and imprisonment for up to five years.[33] In addition, the knowing presentation of a false, fictitious, or fraudulent claim to any agency or department of the United States has long been subject to fine and imprisonment to a maximum of five years.[34]

---

27   See footnote 15, *supra*, on whether *qui tam* relators have standing to prosecute FCA lawsuits after the government does not intervene.

28   31 U.S.C. § 3730(d)(2).

29   31 U.S.C. § 3730(g).

30   31 U.S.C. § 3730(h).

31   *Id.*

32   31 U.S.C. § 3730(d)(3).

33   42 U.S.C. § 1320a-7b(a)(1). The false statements statute also imposes an affirmative duty on providers to return payments that a provider later learns resulted from improper billings. "(a) Whoever . . . (3) having knowledge of the occurrence of any event affecting (A) his initial or continued right to any such benefit or payment, or (B) the initial or continued right to any such benefit or payment of any other individual in whose behalf he has applied for or is receiving such benefit or payment, conceals or fails to disclose such event with an intent fraudulently to secure such benefit or payment either in a greater amount or quantity than is due or when no such benefit or payments is authorized," shall be guilty of a criminal violation. 42 U.S.C. § 1320a-7b(a)(3). In addition to being subject to prison and monetary penalties, providers who are convicted of program-related crimes or felonies must be excluded from participating in the Medicare and Medicaid programs for a period of five years. *See* 42 U.S.C. § 1320a-7(c)(3)(B).

34   *See* 18 U.S.C. § 287; *see also* 18 U.S.C. § 24(a)(2). In 1996, HIPAA also created new offenses and expanded existing criminal statutes in the health care field. *See* 18 U.S.C. § 24(a), relating to theft or embezzlement in connection with health care (18 U.S.C. § 669); false statements relating to health care matters (18 U.S.C. §1035); health care fraud (18 U.S.C. §1347); and

The relationship between *qui tam* lawsuits and criminal prosecutions can be a close one. On July 2, 1999, a Florida jury convicted two Columbia/HCA Healthcare Corporation mid-level managers on six counts involving fraud in federal health care programs.[35] The criminal charges arose out of a *qui tam* lawsuit filed by John Schilling, a company reimbursement manager at Fawcett Memorial Hospital in Port Charlotte, Florida.[36] Schilling alleged that Columbia knowingly filed cost reports containing false statements, which created approximately $3.5 million in improper reimbursements. As a component of the *qui tam* filing, Schilling turned over evidence for investigation that, in turn, led to criminal charges against and convictions of the two Columbia managers.[37]

II. Application of Civil False Claims Act in the Health Care Industry

The civil and criminal False Claims Acts and related provisions have been used to investigate and prosecute a wide variety of practices in the health care industry, including the following: "billing for services not rendered, billing for services not medically necessary, double billing for services provided, upcoding (*e.g.*, billing for a more highly reimbursed service or product than the one provided), unbundling (*e.g.*, billing separately for groups of laboratory tests performed together in order to get a higher reimbursement), fraudulent cost reporting by institutional providers."[38] The following cases illustrate the application of the FCA to specific health care reimbursement practices.

A. Physician Billings—"Upcoding"

On January 11, 1993, the United States filed suit against George O. Krizek, M.D., a Washington, D.C. psychiatrist. The five count complaint included claims for "(1) 'Knowingly Presenting a False or Fraudulent Claim', 31 U.S.C. § 3729(a)(1); (2) 'Knowingly Presenting a False or Fraudulent Record', 31 U.S.C. § 3729 (a)(2); (3) 'Conspiracy to Defraud the Government,' (4) 'Payment under Mistake of Fact'

---

obstruction of criminal investigations of health care offenses (18 U.S.C. §1518); *see also* 18 U.S.C. §24(b), which expanded the following pre-existing criminal Statutes to cover "health care benefit programs": false, fictitious, or fraudulent claims (18 U.S.C. §287); conspiracy to commit offense or defraud United States (18 U.S.C. § 371); theft or embezzlement from employee benefit plan (18 U.S.C. § 664); theft or bribery concerning programs receiving Federal funds (18 U.S.C. § 666); false or fraudulent statements or schemes, generally (18 U.S.C. §1001); false statements and concealment in relation to documents required by ERISA (18 U.S.C. § 1027); frauds and swindles (18 U.S.C. §1341); fraud by wire, radio, or television (18 U.S.C. § 1343); offer, acceptance, or solicitation of remuneration to influence operation of employee benefit plan (18 U.S.C. §1954). For a more detailed discussion of the changes brought about by HIPAA, see *infra* at VI(B)(8).

35 BNA Health Law Reporter (7/8/99), p1100 (citing *U.S. v. Jarrell*, M.D. Fla., No. 97-52-CR-FTM-24 (D), *jury verdict* 7/02/99).

36 *See* discussion in Section II.B., *infra*.

37 *Id.*

38 "Department of Justice Health Care Fraud Report, Fiscal Year 1998," at 4/32.

and (5) 'Unjust Enrichment'."[39] At trial, the government sought reimbursement for three times actual damages of $245,392 and a $10,000 civil penalty for each of 8,002 claims submitted over a six year period,. The government asserted a total claim in excess of $81 million.[40]

The extraordinary amount of the recovery sought reflects the detail involved in physician billing for Medicare services. Physicians submit claims for Medicare reimbursement on forms known as the Health Care Financing Administration ("HCFA") 1500.[41] The HCFA 1500, when completed, contains information identifying the patient and physician and describing the services rendered.[42] The services rendered are identified by a five-digit code number provided in the American Medical Association's "Current Procedural Terminology" ("CPT") manual, which details terminology and numerical identifying codes for physician services.[43] Dr. Krizek's services were primarily billed under two CPT codes: 90843 for psychiatric sessions of approximately 20 to 30 minutes and 90844 for sessions lasting approximately 45 to 50 minutes.[44]

The practice of submitting bills coded for a service at a higher level of reimbursement than was actually provided is referred to as "upcoding."[45] The government argued that Dr. Krizek billed using the higher code, even though "the reimbursable service [that he] provided was not as extensive as that which was billed for."[46] However, Dr. Krizek maintained that he had provided other reimbursable services, including consultations with other professionals and prescription management that added time spent with each patient. The Court determined that the CPT manual was ambiguous on what specific services were required for billing the higher code and rejected the government's argument that Dr. Krizek billed for services not provided.

> The Court will not impose False Claims Act liability based on such a strained interpretation of the CPT codes. The government's theory of liability is plainly unfair and unjustified. Medical doctors should be appropriately reimbursed for services legitimately provided. They should be given clear guidance as to what services are reimbursable. The system should be fair. The system cannot be so arbitrary, so perverse, as to subject a doctor whose annual income during the relevant period averaged between $100,000 and $120,000 dollars, to potential liability in excess of 80 million dollars [footnote omitted] because telephone calls were made in one room rather than another. . . . The Court finds that Doctor Krizek did not submit false claims when he

---

39   *U.S. v. Krizek*, 859 F. Supp. 5, 7 (D.D.C. 1994).

40   *Id.*

41   *Id.*

42   *Id.*

43   *Id.*

44   *Id.* at 10.

45   *Id.* at 7.

46   *Id.* at 9.

submitted a bill under CPT Code 90844 after spending 45-50 minutes working on a patient's case, even though not all of that time was spent in direct face-to-face contact with the patient.[47]

While the Court did not impose liability for Dr. Krizek's interpretation of the higher code, it did recognize that his failure to exercise oversight and care for other bills submitted under his name rose to the level of a "knowing" violation of the FCA. Dr. Krizek had essentially delegated all responsibility for billing to his wife or a particular employee. Their billing method generally "assumed" that any patient that Dr. Krizek saw received the longer psychiatric session, even though they rarely sought clarification or input from Dr. Krizek on the actual services provided.[48] As a result, on some days, Dr. Krizek billed Medicare or Medicaid for more than twenty hours of services.[49]

Both Dr. and Mrs. Krizek maintained that this method constituted, at most, simple negligence and did not rise to the level of a knowing violation of the FCA.[50] The Court agreed that the FCA is not triggered by "mere negligence," but did apply in "situations that could be considered gross negligence where the submitted claims to the government are prepared in such a sloppy or unsupervised fashion that [it] resulted in overcharges to the government."[51] The Court noted that Mrs. Krizek had made "no effort" to determine how long Dr. Krizek had spent with any particular patient, that she "presumed" the longer session, and that Dr. Krizek himself had "failed utterly in supervising these agents in their submission of claims on his behalf."[52] The Court held that these facts met the standard of gross negligence. "While we are in an age of computers, this does not mean that we can blindly allow coding systems to determine the amount of reimbursement without the physician being accountable for honestly and correctly submitted proper information, whether by code or otherwise."[53] However, on remand from the government's appeal, the trial court summarized the view of many in the health care industry that government prosecutors blindly and doggedly pursue real fraud and innocent mistakes with the same fervor.

> The Government insists on pursuing a case that should long have been over. If the Court acceded to all of the Government's requests, this litigation would proceed well into the next century. The Government has won its case and gained a substantial recovery. Dr. Krizek is now retired and is no longer practicing psychiatry. Although apparently a fine physician, he is now a broken man. Not only is he out of the medical profession, but also he is suffering from the advanced stages of cancer. The Government refuses to let go of this case. When it began its case, the Government was seek-

---

47   *Id.* at 10-11.

48   *Id.* at 11.

49   *Id.* at 12.

50   *Id.* at 12-13.

51   *Id.* at 13.

52   *Id.*

53   *Id.* at 14.

ing over $80 million worth of damages, a figure that the Court of Appeals declared was 'astronomical.' *Krizek III*, 111 F. F.3d at 940. Despite the fact that Dr. Krizek is incapable of paying such a sum, the Government continues to relentlessly pursue Dr. Krizek, who is at this point a broken and sick man. The Government's pursuit of Dr. Krizek is reminiscent of Inspector Javert's quest to capture Jean Valjean in Victor Hugo's Les Miserables. While the Government's vigor in pursuing violators of the law is to be commended, there comes a point when a civilized society must say enough is enough. That point has been reached in this case.[54]

B. Hospital Cost Reimbursement—Cost Report Fraud

While the FCA is regularly applied against single practitioners, small practice groups, or smaller corporate entities in the health care field, it is also the weapon of choice in claims against large corporate providers, in part due to the large recoveries accompanying the higher volume and complexity of claims submitted. The civil, criminal, and *qui tam* provisions of the FCA came together in the current litigation confronting the Columbia/HCA corporation, one of the nation's largest corporate health care providers. Unlike physicians, who are reimbursed by Medicare on a "fee-for-service" basis, hospitals are reimbursed, in part, based on certain costs incurred in the provision of patient care. Alleged fraud in the reporting of these costs lies at the heart of Columbia's difficulties.

The Columbia case began as a *qui tam* lawsuit filed by relator James Alderson, a former hospital financial officer for a Columbia subsidiary in Whitefish, Montana. Alderson maintains that he was instructed to prepare two sets of cost reports, in accordance with company policy, but to submit to Medicare only the one showing higher reimbursable costs. Alderson states that he was terminated after protesting this method of accounting and, as a consequence, he filed a *qui tam* suit. Since the suit alleged that this accounting practice was national in scope, Alderson's counsel was able to transfer the case to federal court in Florida.[55]

As required by the *qui tam* provision in the FCA, the government performed its investigation of the *qui tam* filing and elected to join the lawsuit on February 2, 1999. The Plaintiff United States' Complaint ("Complaint") alleges eight causes of action: (1) False Claims Act: Presentation of False Claims (31 U.S.C. § 3729(a)(1)); (2) False Claims Act: Making or Using False Record or Statement (31 U.S.C. § 3729 (a)(2)); (3) False Claims Act: Reverse False Claims (31 U.S.C. § 3729(a)(7)); (4) Unjust Enrichment; (5) Payment by Mistake; (6) Disgorgement of Illegal Profits; (7) Common Law Fraud; and (8) Common Law Recoupment.[56]

---

54   *U.S. v. Krizek*, 7 F. Supp.2d 56, 60 (D.D.C. 1998).

55   *U.S. ex rel. Alderson v. Columbia/HCA, et al.*, M.D. Fla., No. 97-2035-CIV-T-23E. Columbia/HCA is currently the focus of at least 25 *qui tam* lawsuits. Millin's Health Fraud Monitor (10/4/99), at 3.

56   Complaint, ¶¶ 355-380.

166 Corporate Fraud Investigations & Compliance Programs

Generally, the Complaint alleges that Columbia/HCA (with its predecessor entities, affiliates, and subsidiaries, herein "Columbia") submitted claims for reimbursement on cost reports although knowing that the claims were fraudulent, and maintained accounting records known as "reserve" cost reports that demonstrated such knowledge. The Complaint sets forth particularly damaging facts, including that Columbia had written company policies which required that its accounting components interpret Medicare reimbursement law "aggressively" and requiring the creation of cash reserves for claims on cost reports that would "probably" be disallowed if audited by Medicare. Work papers for the reserve cost reports were inartfully stamped "CONFIDENTIAL. Do not Discuss or Release to Medicare Auditors."[57]

The Complaint also alleges that Columbia made false statements, certifications, and claims on cost reports on the following matters: (1) capital-related costs (*e.g.*, lease payments and home office costs); (2) interest expenses (*e.g.*, bond discounts, debt cancellation costs, expenses incurred in issuing bonds, and bond trustee operating fees); and (3) depreciation and non-allowable costs (*e.g.*, personal comfort items, physician recruitment and dues, advertising and marketing expenses, and property, franchise, and other taxes). The Complaint finally alleges that Columbia sought to increase reimbursement improperly by allocating costs covered within the hospital's prospective payment system payments ("PPS")[58] to outpatient hospital areas and cost-based home health agency subsidiaries which could be reimbursed a second time through Medicare Part B, a different component of the Medicare reimbursement system.

The government cites specific business practices of Columbia that violated Medicare statutes, regulations, and program instructions. These program violations, under the government's theory, create false claims or statements resulting in FCA liability. As an example, certain paragraphs allege that failure to follow provisions in Medicare manuals alone creates a violation of the FCA, as follows:

> Medicare providers also may declare debts uncollectible by determining that the patient is indigent or medically indigent, but are required to document that determination. This documentation should include the method used to make such determination and the information used to substantiate it. [Provider Reimbursement Manual] § 312.

Complaint, ¶ 293.

> On a reserve workpaper . . . however, [Columbia created a cash reserve] for 80% of the $305,434 claimed for bad debts. The [Columbia] consultant determined that the

---

57   *See* Complaint, ¶¶ 215, 216.

58   The PPS system for hospital reimbursement provides for payments for hospital services to Medicare beneficiaries according to set amounts established for specific diagnoses with modifiers based on geographic location. Under PPS, hospitals are no longer reimbursed exclusively based on their costs, and only certain costs may be included on hospital cost reports.

cost report included claims for debts due to patients' indigency, despite a lack of the requisite documentation.

Id. at ¶ 296.

If a provider has properly identified and accounted for a cost center, that cost center must be reported separately on the cost report. . . . If a department meets the definition of a cost center as set out in the regulations, and the provider has done the necessary record keeping, the cost center must be reported separately.

Id. at ¶ 328.

Upon information and belief, all defendants' reserve analyses indicated that they had the data available to treat departments separately, as the [Provider Reimbursement Manual] requires.

Id. at ¶ 330.

[Columbia] knew when it prepared the cost report that the hospital had not maintained adequate records to support the separation of the cardiac cost center into three cost centers. . . .

Id. at ¶ 337.

The Complaint also alleges FCA liability for false certifications. The government alleged that the improper practices cited in the Complaint violated the omnibus provider certification at the end of the cost report, which reads, in part, as follows:

[T]o the best of my knowledge and belief, it [the Hospital Cost Report] is a true, correct and complete statement prepared from the books and records of the provider in accordance with applicable instructions, except as noted. . . . I further certify that I am familiar with the laws and regulations regarding the provision of health care services, and that the services identified in this cost report were provided in compliance with such laws and regulations.

Complaint, ¶¶ 55, 57.

A *qui tam* lawsuit has also been filed against the accounting firm that assisted Columbia in preparing financial records. A former Columbia executive filed a *qui tam* lawsuit against KPMG LLP, alleging that its accounting practices for Columbia resulted in the submission of false claims to the Medicare program.[59] Tracking the claims made in the *Alderson* lawsuit, the *Schilling* complaint generally alleges that KPMG and Columbia "systematically defrauded" the government by making exaggerated reimbursement claims, creating "reserve cost reports" and "reserve papers" that "explicitly identified many (but not all) of the exaggerated and unallowable claims," and violating various auditing standards.[60]

---

59   BNA Health Care Fraud Report (6/2/99), at 462, *citing U.S. ex rel. Schilling v. KPMG Peat Marwick LLP*, M.D. Fla., No. 98-901-CIV-T-17F, unsealed 5/28/99. *See also* discussion at Section I.B., *supra.*

60   As of the date of this writing, the government's claims against Columbia are still pending. Unofficial reports have been circulating, however, regarding serious settlement discussions and a potential settlement in the neighborhood of $1 billion.

C. Skilled Nursing Facilities—Quality of Care

Although considerable debate surrounds the application of fraud theories in this context, the government has also extended the reach of the FCA to address quality of care concerns for nursing home residents and other Medicare or Medicaid beneficiaries. The Department of Justice has proceeded on the theory that when a nursing home provider bills the Medicare or Medicaid programs, it represents that it has provided necessary and sufficient care to residents in exchange for Medicare and Medicaid payment. If the requisite level and quality of care is not provided, the government's theory asserts that the provider has submitted a false claim, and a cause of action lies under the FCA.

The U.S. Attorney for the Eastern District of Pennsylvania brought an action under the FCA against Tucker House II, Inc. ("Tucker House"), a Philadelphia nursing home, and its managing entity, GMS Management-Tucker, Inc. ("GMS"), a subsidiary of Geriatric & Medical Companies, Inc. ("Geri-Med"). The government claimed that Tucker House and GMS repeatedly submitted false or fraudulent claims to Medicare and Medicaid for nursing services and nutrition that were not adequate for three residents of the facility. Those residents were alleged to be severely undernourished and suffering from deep pressure ulcers, or bedsores. The government sought FCA damages in an amount to be proven at trial, with a $10,000 penalty per false claim, three times actual damages, and costs of bringing the lawsuit.

Tucker House and GMS entered into consent orders with the government to settle the case. Tucker House acknowledged that GMS had failed to provide the services required under their management agreements and admitted that as a consequence, claims were submitted with deliberate ignorance or reckless disregard for the truth. In addition to paying a $25,000 penalty, Tucker House agreed to implement specific clinical practices to insure quality of care, including the development and implementation of a nutritional monitoring program, the initiation of treatment protocols for pressure ulcers as set forth in industry standards, and monthly reporting to the U.S. Attorney and HCFA on nutrition for at-risk residents. Tucker House also agreed to cooperate with and pay for an independent party who would inspect the facility not less than quarterly for compliance with the consent order. GMS entered into a consent order, but denied wrongdoing. Geri-Med also entered into a similar consent order, paid a $575,000 fine, and agreed to implement a corporate compliance program that would emphasize protocols for meeting patients' nutritional needs.

Building on the Tucker House action, on September 14, 1998, the U.S. Attorney for the District of Maryland filed a civil action under the FCA requesting injunctive relief and damages during a federal investigation into substandard care of residents at the Greenbelt Nursing & Rehabilitation Center, in Greenbelt, Maryland. The lawsuit alleged that the facility systematically provided substandard care and submitted claims for payment that falsely represented that the services were rendered in compliance with applicable laws. The injunctive relief called for the immediate implementation of specific practices to protect residents.

The Greenbelt situation arose after the facility had been cited for various deficiencies by the state surveying agency. The facility subsequently certified to HCFA that it had corrected the cited deficiencies and was in substantial compliance with program requirements. Nonetheless, the U.S. Attorney and agents from the HHS OIG and the Federal Bureau of Investigation ("FBI") continued to investigate the facility after it made this certification of compliance to HCFA. Upon finding continued substandard care at the facility, the U.S. Attorney and the facility operator agreed to the procedures and treatments set forth in the 24-page motion for preliminary injunction. However, despite the facility's consent order with the U.S. Attorney, HCFA elected to terminate the facility's participation in the Medicare program. Greenbelt was consequently closed and the residents transferred to other facilities.

Debate has been extensive and sharp on the application of the FCA to quality of care cases. Unquestionably, such cases represent a significant expansion of the reach and potential liability under the FCA. Several concerns become immediately apparent. First, the FCA prohibits the knowing submission of a "false or fraudulent" claim for payment to the government. Applying the FCA to quality of care matters suggests that "inadequate" or negligent care is equivalent to providing no care at all. Quality of care issues have traditionally been dealt with through negligence claims by private plaintiffs or through the administrative oversight process by government regulators, not by government prosecutors, and the FCA provides no guidance as to what level of care is "adequate." While government attorneys say that they will only use the FCA when quality breakdowns are egregious, that is a vague standard.

Moreover, nursing home facilities are already subject to significant money sanctions for failure to comply with quality of care standards. Costs associated with defending or settling a FCA action could drain funds from activities associated with direct patient care, such as nursing, recreational, or dietary services. Finally, government application of the FCA to enforce standards of care in long-term care facilities could precipitate *qui tam* lawsuits by nursing home staff, residents, or their family members who may disagree with the nursing home operator as to what quality of care a resident requires.

III. Enforcement Initiatives—Results and Outlook

A. Legislative Reform of the FCA

As the *Krizek, Columbia, Tucker House*, and *Greenbelt* cases indicate, the health care industry has come under increasing pressure through application of the FCA by a phalanx of private individuals and federal and state administrative, investigative, and prosecutorial entities.[61] To rein in the increasingly broad application of the Act, providers sought legislative relief in the 105th Congress through federal legislation introduced in the House of Representatives on March 19, 1998, and in the Senate on April 29, 1998.[62] The DOJ and HHS opposed passage, and on June 3, 1998, HHS Inspector General June Gibbs Brown and DOJ Deputy Attorney General Eric H. Holder, Jr. issued separate memoranda to their respective departments providing guidance on use of the FCA in civil health care matters. At that time, Deputy Attorney General Holder wrote: "This guidance is being issued to emphasize the importance of pursuing civil False Claims Act cases against health care providers in a fair and even-handed manner, and to implement new procedures with respect to the development and implementation of national initiatives."[63] After the guidance memoranda was issued, the 105th Congress permitted the proposed federal legislation to die without action.

Six months later, Deputy Attorney General Holder reviewed the initial DOJ guidance and concluded that "the Guidance Memorandum—and the policies and procedures contained therein—has been extremely effective and that major revisions are not necessary at this time."[64] Holder also pointed out that DOJ must continue to conduct thorough investigations before alleging FCA violations.[65] However, on August 5, 1999, the General Accounting Office ("GAO") reported that "DOJ's process for assessing the U.S. Attorneys' Offices compliance [with the guidance] may be superficial."[66] GAO stated that provider associations continue to request

---

61 The governmental units that conduct most health care investigations include: U.S. Department of Justice and Offices of U.S. Attorneys; Office of Inspector General of the Department of Health and Human Services; Federal Bureau of Investigation; Internal Revenue Service; U.S. Postal Inspectors; State Medicaid Fraud Control Units; Medicare contractors (intermediaries and carriers); and state boards that oversee medical professionals.

62 H.R. 3523 and S. 2007.

63 Memorandum, "Guidance on the Use of the False Claims Act in Civil Health Care Matters," dated June 3, 1998, from Eric H. Holder, Jr., Deputy Attorney General, to All United States Attorneys, All First Assistant United States Attorneys, All Civil Health Care Fraud Coordinators in the Office of United States Attorneys, and All Trial Attorneys in the Civil Division, Commercial Litigation, at 1.

64 Memorandum, "Review of June 3, 1998, Guidance on the Use of the False Claims Act in Civil Health Care Fraud Matters," dated February 3, 1999, from Eric H. Holder, Jr., to All United States Attorneys, All First Assistant United States Attorneys, All Civil Health Care Fraud Coordinators in the Offices of United States Attorneys, and All Civil Division Fraud Attorneys.

65 *Id.* at 2; BNA Health Care Fraud Report (11/18/98), pp 868-9 (DOJ health care fraud attorney Shelly Slade states, "Nothing in the guidance is intended to bar a [DOJ] attorney from using a subpoena, a civil investigative demand, or other [legal tools] to obtain evidence from a provider before contact is made in an effort to resolve the case.' By contrast, Slade, said, 'The guidance really encourages that sort of investigation . . . before allegations [of False Claims violations] are made.'" As cases cited in this chapter indicate, some pre-charge investigations can last for years; thus, the Guidance could be seen as leaving providers with less relief than may have been achieved through legislative changes.

66 "DOJ's Implementation of False Claims Act Guidance in National Initiatives Varies," GA/HEHS-99-170, August, 1999, at 4.

that a minimum threshold of alleged overpayments be established before False Claims Act investigations are initiated, while one provider criticized the DOJ guidance as "vague enough to allow DOJ to characterize intimidating and unfair use of the act as compliance with the guidance."[67]

B. HHS—Comprehensive Strategy on Waste, Fraud, and Abuse

Despite the continued debate on the proper reach and application of the FCA, government reports suggest that fraud and abuse control efforts have returned prodigious results.[68] In February 1999, HHS reported that "improper Medicare payments" to providers declined over 45 percent between fiscal years 1996 and 1998[69] and that "more than $1.2 billion in fines and restitution have been returned to the Medicare Trust Fund during fiscal years 1997 and 1998."[70] The department has used the exclusion remedy created by HIPAA to banish more than 5,700 entities and individuals from participating in federal health care programs, more than double the amount from two years before.[71] Criminal convictions increased by 20 percent in 1997 and another 16 percent in 1998.[72] HHS concludes that "[s]ince 1993, actions affecting HHS health care programs have saved taxpayors more than $38 billion, and have increased convictions and other successful legal actions by more than 240 percent,"[73] and reports the following accomplishments:

1. Improper Payments Reduced by 50%

The Government Management Reform Act of 1994 mandated an annual audit of government programs using private sector accounting methodology. Since then, HHS has performed annual audits of HCFA to determine whether HCFA has paid Medicare claims in compliance with program requirements. HHS states that "according to the Inspector General, the Medicare error rate has declined by almost one half, from 14 percent in 1996 to 7.1 percent in Fiscal Year 1998." The Inspector General attributes this result to fraud and abuse control efforts by HCFA and HHS.[74]

2. Operation Restore Trust

In 1995, HHS, HCFA, and the Administration on Aging initiated a two-year major anti-fraud initiative called "Operation Restore Trust" in five key states. The

---

67   *Id.* at 16.

68   Department of Health and Human Services Fact Sheet, "A Comprehensive Strategy to Fight Health Care Waste, Fraud and Abuse," (February 10, 1999).

69   *Id.* at 1.

70   *Id.*

71   *Id.*

72   *Id.*

73   *Id.*

74   *Id.* at 2.

government identified "$23 in overpayments for every $1 spent" after auditing various health care providers and suppliers, including home health care, skilled nursing facilities, and durable medical equipment. As a result of the pilot program, HHS announced in 1997 that it would expand the program nationwide.[75]

3. Increased Enforcement Funding Through HIPAA

The 1996 passage of HIPAA included a mechanism for the continued and increased funding of health care fraud control. HIPAA created the "Health Care Fraud and Abuse Control Account," which is funded in part by the Medicare Trust Fund "to help finance expanded fraud and abuse control activities." According to HHS "additional funding began with $104 million in FY 1997, and will total $137.5 million in FY 1999, divided between HHS and the Department of Justice." This funding is specifically intended to "coordinate federal, state and local health care law enforcement programs, conduct investigations, provide guidance of the health care industry on fraudulent health care practices, and establish a national data bank to receive and report final adverse actions against unscrupulous health care providers and suppliers."[76]

4. OIG Presence in New States

The Health Care Fraud and Abuse Control Account has also provided funding to the OIG to move into an additional 12 states, "increasing from 26 to 38 the number of states in which the OIG is present."[77]

5. Beneficiary Rewards for Fraud and Abuse Reporting

HIPAA also created "The Incentive Program for Fraud and Abuse Information" ("TIPS"), implemented in July 1998. Medicare beneficiaries, their family members, and other individuals who report instances of fraudulent or abusive practice in the health care industry are eligible to receive 10% of any monies recovered, up to a maximum of $1,000. Information on the TIPS program has been distributed to Medicare beneficiaries through the government and associations for senior citizens.[78]

6. "Fraud Buster" Initiatives

The Administration on Aging has trained paid and volunteer long-term care ombudsman, insurance counselors, and other service providers to the elderly to recognize and report instances of fraud and abuse in skilled nursing facilities and other health care providers. The AOA has also awarded over $2 million in grants to

---

75 *Id.*

76 *Id.* at 2.

77 *Id.* at 2-3.

78 *Id.* at 3.

states to train retired professional to serve as "fraud busters," who will review explanations of benefits with program beneficiaries in order to detect instances of fraud and abuse.[79]

C. HCFA—Comprehensive Plan for Program Integrity

HCFA's "Comprehensive Plan for Program Integrity" ("Plan") details some areas in which providers can expect continued scrutiny and action. The Plan announces three broad goals for HCFA: (1) Reduce the error rate for all Medicare fee-for-service payments to 5% by FY 2002; (2) Conduct medical review on an additional 10% of the baseline number of 91 million claims that would have been reviewed in FY 2000; and (3) Reduce the percentage of home health services provided for which improper payments is made from 35% to 10% in California, Illinois, New York and Texas.[80] The Plan also indicates that HCFA will continue and likely increase its focus in the areas of inpatient hospital care, congregate care, managed care, community mental health centers care, and nursing homes.[81]

1. Inpatient Hospital Services

"Inpatient hospital claims comprised about 20 percent of the errors identified [by HHS OIG] in the FY 1996 and FY 1997 audits or $4-5 billion in trust fund losses each year."[82] This loss is attributed by the OIG to the provision of medically unnecessary services, failure to document services rendered, and incorrect coding of hospital claims.[83] HCFA intends to "reduce the overall rate of erroneous payments from 11 to 5 percent of total dollars by the year 2002."[84] One announced strategy is to identify payment errors by reviewing claims submitted for "changes in patterns of DRG coding, the prevalence of readmissions of the same patient to the same facility on the same day, and changes in patterns of very short stay admission."[85]

2. Congregate Care

Congregate care refers to "groups of beneficiaries, regardless of their health status, [who] congregate in one location (skilled nursing facility, custodial care, adult day care, etc.)".[86] HCFA highlights two practices for increased scrutiny: "gang visits" and duplicate payments.[87] Gang visits occur in two different ways: when

---

79 *Id.* at 5-6.

80 Executive Summary, "Comprehensive Plan for Program Integrity," at 1/16. http://www.hcfa.gov/medicare/fraud/part1.htm, (last updated March 4, 1999).

81 *Id.* at 3-4/16.

82 "Addressing Service Specific Vulnerabilities; Inpatient Hospital Care," http://www.hcfa.gov/medicare/fraud/part1.htm (last updated March 4, 1999).

83 *Id.*

84 *Id.*

85 *Id.*

86 "Addressing Service Specific Vulnerabilities: Congregate Care," *Id.*

87 *Id.*

"[s]ervices and supplies are provided to most or all of a group of congregated beneficiaries, whether or not the service or supplies were medically necessary" and when "[p]roviders and suppliers bill for services and supplies not furnished and can do so easily because the congregate nature of the beneficiaries gives easy access to Medicare and Medicaid numbers."[88] Duplicate payments occur when Medicare pays for custodial care services also covered by Medicaid or private payors.[89] HCFA intends to address the congregate care issues through greater study of HCFA data and systems, support of state investigations to gather further information, scrutiny of fraud and abuse potential with the implementation of prospective payment system for congregate care providers, and increased education of providers, beneficiaries and their families, and the public.[90]

3. Managed Care Plans

Managed care plans received more than $35 billion for services rendered in 1998.[91] HCFA intends to identify whether managed care providers have engaged in providing inadequate amounts of services to their members. It will also determine whether managed care organizations have engaged in improper marketing or enrollment practices. As HCFA continues to collect data, it will add a "Payment Safeguard Contractor" to assist in traditional Medicare regulatory compliance monitoring and will enhance and increase the existing Medicare managed plan monitoring program.[92]

4. Community Mental Health Centers

A community mental health center is defined by the Social Security Act as "an entity that provides those services outlined in the Public Health Service Act. . . ."[93] The services include: outpatient services for children, the elderly, individuals with serious mental illness, and those area residents recently discharged from inpatient treatment from a mental health facility; twenty-four hour emergency care; day treatment, partial hospitalization services, or rehabilitation services; and screening services prior to inpatient admission to mental health facilities.[94] HCFA notes rapid growth in payments to such centers, along with evidence of centers not providing required services or providing services to ineligible individuals, as well as engaging in cost-reporting fraud.[95] To remedy these violations, HCFA proposes to begin immediately terminating providers engaged in egregious violations of

---

88   *Id.*

89   *Id.*

90   *Id.*

91   "Addressing Service Specific Vulnerabilities: Managed Care," *Id.* at 17/25.

92   *Id.* at 17-18/25.

93   "Addressing Service Specific Vulnerabilities: Community Mental Health Center Care," *Id.* at 19/25.

94   *Id.*

95   *Id.*

program requirements; advise federal and state oversight agencies of the applicable standards; increase on-site inspections and verification of enrollment information; and increase medical review by fiscal intermediaries and review of cost reports.[96]

5. Skilled Nursing Facilities

Providers of skilled nursing services will find that they remain under heightened scrutiny. HCFA notes that 1.6 million citizens currently reside in approximately 16,800 nursing homes across the country.[97] Although HCFA acknowledges favorable results of the recent enforcement efforts, it also points out the following problem areas: state inspection surveys are too predictable; inconsistent assessments of substandard care among states; substandard care on clinical issues, including pressure or bed sores and malnutrition and dehydration; and continuing physical and verbal abuse and neglect of residents, as well as theft of their property.[98] HCFA proposes extensive inspection and enforcement efforts in the nursing home industry, including: prompt termination of nursing home providers who fail to immediately correct deficiencies that put residents in immediate jeopardy; imposition of civil money penalties for each instance of serious or chronic noncompliance, rather than for each day that a facility fails to correct noncompliance; staggered facility inspections, including weekends and evenings; increased federal oversight of state inspections; and increased education and development of "best practice guidelines" regarding resident weight loss and dehydration.[99]

IV. The Federal Anti-Kickback Statute

A. The Statute

One of the more potent weapons in the anti-fraud arsenal of the DOJ and HHS is Section 1128B(b) of the Social Security Act, referred to herein as the "Anti-Kickback Statute". Many of the enforcement activities of DOJ and the HHS OIG are focused on potential violations of the Anti-Kickback Statute. Because of the complexities of the statute and because activities which are common and appropriate in other industries are criminal violations in the health care industry, providers and their counsel must be thoroughly familiar with its requirements.

The Anti-Kickback Statute broadly prohibits (1) the solicitation or receipt of any remuneration, including a kickback, bribe, or rebate, in return for Medicare or Medicaid patient referrals, as well as (2) the offer or payment for such kickback, bribe, or rebate to "induce" such referrals. Thus, the Statute prohibits

---

96   *Id.* at 20-21/25.

97   "Addressing Service Specific Vulnerabilities: Nursing Home Enforcement," *Id.* at 21-24/25.

98   *Id.* at 22/25.

99   *Id.* at 22-24/25.

both the offering and the receiving of any type of remuneration in exchange for patient referrals.

The Statute declares in relevant part:

> Whoever knowingly and willfully solicits or receives any remuneration (including any kickback, bribe, or rebate) directly or indirectly, overtly or covertly, in cash or in kind
>
> (A) in return for referring an individual to a person for the furnishing or arranging for the furnishing of any item or service for which payment may be made in whole or in part [under Medicare or a state health care program, including Medicaid], or
>
> (B) in return for purchasing, leasing, ordering or arranging for or recommending purchasing, leasing, or ordering any good, facility, service, or item for which payment may be made in whole or in part [under Medicare or a state health care program, including Medicaid], shall be guilty of a felony and upon conviction thereof, shall be fined not more than $25,000 or imprisoned for not more than five years, or both. 42 U.S.C. § 1320a-7b(b)(1).

A virtually identical provision is directed at any person who knowingly and willfully "offers or pays any remuneration" to induce referrals of Medicare or Medicaid patients. 42 U.S.C. § 1320a-7b(b)(2).

The regulations and interpretive case law have construed "remuneration" in the widest possible sense as encompassing anything of value. Thus, suspect incentive arrangements between hospitals and physicians have included the following:

- payment of incentives for each referral;
- free or significantly discounted office space or equipment;
- free or significantly discounted billing, nursing, or other staff services;
- free training for physician's office staff;
- compensation guarantees;
- low interest or interest free loans which may be forgiven based upon referrals;
- payment of physician's travel and other expenses for conferences;
- coverage on hospital's insurance plans at inappropriately low cost; and
- payment for services in an amount which exceeds fair market value.[100]

---

100 These and other suspect arrangements are set forth in a May 7, 1992 Special Fraud Alert entitled "Hospital Incentives to Physicians" issued by the HHS OIG. In the Alert, the OIG expressed concern about a number of hospital incentive programs used to compensate physicians (directly or indirectly) for referring patients to the hospital, noting that these arrangements implicated the Anti-Kickback Statute. The Alert stated that financial incentive packages that incorporate these or similar features may be subject to prosecution under the Anti-Kickback Statute, if one of the purposes of the incentive is to influence the physician's medical decision as to where to refer his or her patients for treatment. *See generally Feldstein v. Nash Community Health Serv. Inc.*, 51 F. Supp.2d 673, 682 (E.D.N.C. 1999).

The Anti-Kickback Statute contains very severe penalties. The $25,000 fine and five years' imprisonment limitation pertains to each separate act of solicitation, payment or receipt of payment—no matter how large or small the amount. Thus, in the typical situation involving multiple or routine payments, the total fines and jail time can quickly escalate.[101]

Another significant penalty is exclusion from the Medicare or Medicaid program.[102] Fear of this potentially devastating penalty is a likely factor behind recent large settlements in Anti-Kickback and False Claims Act cases brought by the federal government.[103] For example, in June of 1995, Caremark, Inc. (a home health care company) paid the federal government $161 million in fines, restitution and penalties to settle allegations of a systematic kickback scheme.[104] Moreover, although the caselaw is not conclusive, an increasing number of courts have held that a kickback violation can, by itself, support a criminal False Claims Act prosecution.[105] If that trend becomes the norm, it could sharply increase the already high criminal and civil exposure of healthcare providers for potential kickback violations.

The Anti-Kickback Statute does not require any proof of monetary damage to the Government. Damages instead are based on the amount of kickbacks received by the defendant.[106]

---

101 In *U.S. v. Davis*, 117 F.3d 459, 461 (11th Cir. 1997) the defendants (a doctor and two healthcare company officers) were convicted and individually fined between $8.1 to $ 9.1 *million* dollars for a scheme to violate the Anti-Kickback Statute and submitting related false claims.

102 Pursuant to 42 U.S.C. § 1320a-7(b)(7), the Secretary of HHS has the discretion to exclude from Medicare and Medicaid "any individual or entity" that has engaged in "fraud, kickbacks and other prohibited activities," as discussed more fully in Section VI, *infra*.

103 *See* "On the Ropes: Beefed-Up Anti-Kickback Laws, Growing Cohort of Whistleblowers Pound Away at Healthcare Fraud," *Modern Healthcare*, June 28, 1999 (noting that "the ultimate weapon wielded against accused providers is the threat of exclusion from Medicare and Medicaid").

104 *See U.S. v. Brown*, 108 F.3d 863, 865 (8th Cir. 1997).

105 *See U.S. v. Lewis*, 1998 U.S. Dist. LEXIS 20647 at *30-*31 (N. D. Ill. Dec. 29, 1998) (*citing* cases); *U.S. v. American Healthcorp, Inc.*, 977 F. Supp. 1329, 1338 (M.D. Tenn. 1997); *U.S. v. Columbia/HCA Healthcare Corp.*, 938 F. Supp. 399, 404-05 (S.D. Tex. 1996) (noting a "rash of district court decisions outside the Fifth Circuit" that allow kickbacks to serve as the basis for false claim prosecutions), *aff'd in part and rev'd in part*, 125 F.3d 899 (5th Cir. 1997). By contrast, the Fifth Circuit has held that violations of the Anti-Kickback Statute do not, in themselves, constitute actionable false claims. *See U.S. v. Columbia/HCA Healthcare Corp.*, 125 F.3d 899, 902 (5th Cir. 1997). This makes sense, because kickbacks often involve services that (in contrast to false claims) were medically necessary and actually provided at a fair cost. In these circumstances, it is difficult to see how the government has been defrauded.

106 For example, in *United States v. Adam*, 70 F.3d 776 (4th Cir. 1995), a physician was convicted of receiving "lease" kickback payments from another physician, and was fined $40,000 and sentenced to 18 months in prison. The Court held that the sentence should be enhanced because the defendant received substantial kickbacks (more than $50,000) and abused a position of trust. 70 F.3d at 781-82.

B. History of the Statute

The antifraud and abuse provisions were originally added to the Social Security Act in 1972. In 1977, Congress amended the Statute to impose criminal penalties against individuals or entities participating in the Medicare or Medicaid program that offer, pay, solicit, or receive "remuneration" (including any "kickback, bribe, or rebate") for referral of Medicare or Medicaid beneficiaries. In 1980, Congress added a requirement that, for criminal penalties to be imposed, the individual or entity charged with a violation must have "knowingly and willfully" violated the Statute. The Statute took its current form upon adoption of the Medicare and Medicaid Patient and Program Protection Act of 1987, which toughened the penalties by raising the offense level to a felony (from misdemeanor) and authorizing the Secretary of HHS to exclude a person or entity from participation in the Medicare or Medicaid program for violating the Statute.

In the 1970's and 1980's, violations of the Anti-Kickback Statute were not prosecuted with vigor. The government's attention was simply not as focused on healthcare fraud, and the high hurdle of proving actual intent to defraud was a further disincentive to prosecution. However, the 1987 amendments, subsequent caselaw, and—most importantly—the Government's recent decision to make healthcare fraud a top federal law enforcement priority, all have combined to make the Anti-Kickback Statute a powerful and highly visible enforcement vehicle for the federal authorities.

Consequently, in the 1990's the pace of criminal prosecutions and multi-million dollar settlements under the Anti-Kickback Statute has been growing steadily, with no end in sight.[107] Federal prosecutors and law enforcement authorities have made it clear that they intend to set "examples" for the medical community. Scores of doctors, clinicians, and hospital executives are being indicted, arrested, and convicted for Anti-Kickback Statute violations.[108] These defendants are frequently

---

107 *See* "On the Ropes: Beefed-Up Anti-Kickback Laws, Growing Cohort of Whistleblowers Pound Away at Healthcare Fraud," *Modern Healthcare*, June 28, 1999 (describing the "mushrooming number of kickback cases" fueled in part by whistleblower (qui tam) lawsuits and False Claim Act prosecutions).

108 *See, e.g.*, "Clinics Inquiry Reveals Web of Medicare Fraud," *St. Petersburg Times*, Sept. 26, 1999, at 4-B (noting 34 arrests resulting from "Operation Takeback", which uncovered a "pervasive" kickback scheme among Florida sonogram operators); "Fraud Conviction Offers Lessons for Health Care Providers and Counsel," *Legal Backgrounder*, Sept. 3, 1999 (noting the well-publicized 1999 convictions of two hospital executives and two physicians in Kansas City for kickback violations); "Man Gets Probation for Taking Kickbacks," *St. Petersburg Times*, Aug. 17, 1999 at 3-B (noting more than 30 indictments in a five-year federal investigation into kickback scheme); "Eight Facing Medicare Kickback Charges," *St. Petersburg Times*, June 24, 1999 at 1 (describing a 68-count indictment that "links five physicians and three lab officials to payments for patient referrals and defrauding Medicare").

Investigations in the Health Care Industry 179

being sentenced to substantial jail terms and ordered to pay substantial fines.[109] The Medicare and Medicaid programs are making huge recoveries from fines, penalties and settlements being extracted in Anti-Kickback (and related False Claims Act) prosecutions.[110] These recoveries have not gone unnoticed by state authorities, who in some instances have passed or are considering local versions of the Anti-Kickback Statute and False Claims Act.[111]

C. Intent Requirement

Cases interpreting the Anti-Kickback Statute have delineated a two step process in proving the requisite intent. First, the defendant, through the business arrangement, must have the intent or purpose to induce referrals. Second, conviction under the Statute requires that the defendant act "knowingly and willfully"—that is, with awareness of the unlawfulness of his or her conduct. In a situation involving incontrovertible evidence of "remuneration" tied to patient referrals, a defendant's best line of defense might be to argue that he or she did not have the requisite intent to either induce a referral or to violate the law. However, the recent trend (with the exception of the *Hanlester* case, discussed below) has been to interpret both intent requirements quite broadly.

---

109 *See U.S. v. Vaghela*, 169 F.3d 729, 732 (11th Cir. 1999) (medical center office manager sentenced to three concurrent 21 month terms of imprisonment and three years of probation); *U.S. v. Addis*, 1998 U.S. App. LEXIS 31072 at *4 (7th Cir. Dec. 8, 1998) (doctor sentenced to 37 months imprisonment and a $40,000 fine), *cert. denied*, __ U.S. ___, 119 S. Ct. 1483 (1999); *U.S. v. Starks*, 157 F.3d 833, 837 (11th Cir. 1998) (President and employee of drug rehabilitation companies sentenced to concurrent terms of 24 and 30 months); *U.S. v. Davis*, 117 F.3d 459, 461 (11th Cir. 1997) (doctor and two officers of nutritional therapy company sentenced to terms of 41 months and 46 months, and individual fines ranging from $8.1 to $ 9.1 million dollars); "Eight Facing Medicare Kickback Charges," *St. Petersburg Times*, June 24, 1999 at 1 (describing how three physicians face maximum jail terms of 25 to 30 years and fines of $1.25 to $1.5 million dollars for alleged kickback and Medicare fraud violations). In Kansas City, a federal jury recently convicted both the CEO and the Senior Vice President of a hospital for kickback violations. *See* "Feds Close Criminal Portion of Medicare Probe," *Kansas City Business Journal*, Aug. 27, 1999 at 1.

110 *See, e.g.*, "Home Health Cos. Resolve Civil, Criminal Charges for $61 Million," *Health Law Litigation Reporter*, Sept. 1999 (noting $61 million settlement by Olsten Corporation and its subsidiary, Kimberly Home Health Care Inc., to settle a variety of kickback and Medicare fraud charges); "False Claims Suit Settled for $16.5 Million," *Modern Healthcare*, June 21, 1999 at 58 (describing $16.5 million settlement by international renal care company Fresenius Medical to settle kickback charges). Settlements with the government typically impose the additional burden of a strict government-supervised compliance program, as typified by the Olsten case. *See* "Home Health Cos. Resolve Civil, Criminal Charges for $61 Million," *Government Contract Litigation Reporter*, Aug. 26, 1999 at 10 (noting that Olsten agreed to enter into a "corporate integrity agreement" with HHS as part of its settlement).

111 *See* "Colo. Medicaid Theft Exceeds $20 Million," *Denver Rocky Mountain News*, Aug. 20, 1999 at 22-A.

1. Intent to Induce

The "intent to induce" component of the Anti-Kickback Statute has been interpreted very broadly by the leading cases. This requirement is satisfied if just "one purpose" of the prohibited payment is to induce referrals.[112] Thus, even payments made for otherwise valid Medicare or Medicaid expenses can be the subject of Anti-Kickback prosecution, if part of an overall scheme to induce additional patient referrals.

At its heart, the inducement requirement involves a *quid pro quo*: the conveyance of compensation or some other benefit in exchange for patient referrals (or the prospect of future referrals). Since defendants are unlikely to admit to having such intent, and documentation evidencing such intent might be scarce or non-existent, much of the inquiry focuses on the circumstances surrounding the business arrangement. The following circumstances have been held to be indicative of an intent to induce:

- one of the parties would be a source of referral business;
- other forms of remuneration were being offered or paid to the potential referral source;
- the referral source was being offered or paid something not otherwise available to the general public;
- the parties have taken some steps to correlate the payments to the referrals;

---

112 In *United States v. Greber*, 760 F.2d 68 (3d Cir. 1985), *cert. denied*, 474 U.S. 988 (1985), the Third Circuit addressed whether payments made to a physician for professional services in connection with tests performed by a laboratory could be the basis for Medicare fraud. A laboratory provided physicians with diagnostic services, billed the Medicare program for the services, and when payment was received, forwarded a portion to the referring physician. The defendant (an osteopathic physician who owned the diagnostic laboratory) contended that the laboratory merely paid the referring physicians "interpretation fees" for their initial consultation services as well as for explaining test results to patients. The amount paid to the referring physician was more than Medicare allowed for such services. The court stressed that the Statute "is aimed at the inducement factor" and held that "if one purpose of the payment was to induce future referrals, the medicare Statute has been violated." 760 F.2d at 69, 71. Elaborating, the court stated, "If the payments were intended to induce the physician to use [the laboratory's] services, the Statute was violated, even if the payments were also intended to compensate for professional services." *Id.* at 72.

In *United States v. Kats*, 871 F.2d 105 (9th Cir. 1989), the Ninth Circuit Court of Appeals followed the *Greber* ruling. In *Kats*, the owner of a diagnostic laboratory agreed to kick back 50% of Medicare payments received by the laboratory as a consequence of referrals from a medical services company. The court held that the trial court's instruction that the jury could convict the defendant unless it found the payment "wholly and not incidentally attributable to the delivery of goods or services" accurately stated the law. *Id.* at 108. The court quoted with favor the "one purpose" test stated in *Greber* and stated that *Greber's* interpretation "is consistent with the legislative history." *Id.* And in *United States v. Bay State Ambulance and Hospital Rental Service, Inc.*, 874 F.2d 20 (1st Cir. 1989), the First Circuit adopted a somewhat less expansive definition of intent, holding that the Anti-Kickback Statute required proof that the "payments were made primarily as inducements." *Id.* at 30.

Investigations in the Health Care Industry 181

- there was an increase in patient referrals once payments, or offers of payments, were made; and

- there was an attempt to disguise the payment as being for some other non-existent or minimal service.[113]

2. "Knowingly and Willfully"

In *Hanlester Network v. Shalala*,[114] the Ninth Circuit set forth a high standard of proof for the Statute's specific intent component:

> We construe "knowingly and willfully" in § 1128B(b)(2) of the Anti-Kickback Statute as requiring appellants to (1) know that § 1128B prohibits offering or paying remuneration to induce referrals, and (2) engage in prohibited conduct with the specific intent to disobey the law.

Under *Hanlester*, the government would need to prove that a defendant specifically intended to violate not just the law in general, but to violate the Anti-Kickback Statute in particular—a tough standard, and an exception to the general rule that ignorance of the law is no excuse. *Hanlester* would allow defendants to assert that they were not aware of (or did not intend to violate) the Statute, and therefore cannot be guilty of acting with the requisite specific intent.

Recent cases, however, have almost uniformly rejected the *Hanlester* approach, holding that the government need only prove general unlawful intent, without specific knowledge of (or intent to violate) the Anti-Kickback Statute.[115] Unlawful intent can be inferred from some of the same circumstances that would establish intent to induce (*e.g.*, hidden payments in the form of fake "consulting" fees, below-market rents, free equipment, or other indirect forms of compensation).[116]

---

113 *See United States v. Greber*, 760 F.2d 68, 70 (3d Cir. 1985); *Hanlester Network v. Shalala*, 51 F.3d 1390, 1399 (9th Cir. 1995).

114 51 F.3d 1390, 1400 (9th Cir. 1995).

115 *See U.S. v. Starks*, 157 F.3d 833, 837-39 (11th Cir. 1998) (affirming trial court instruction that "willfully" only requires "the specific intent to do something the law forbids, that is with a bad purpose, either to disobey or disregard the law"; ignorance of the law is no excuse because "the giving or taking of kickbacks for medical referrals is hardly the sort of activity a person might expect to be legal"); *U.S. v. Davis*, 132 F.3d 1092, 1094 (5th Cir. 1998) (the Anti-Kickback Statute requires "knowledge only that the conduct in question was unlawful, and not necessarily knowledge of which particular Statute makes the conduct unlawful"); *U.S. v. Jain*, 93 F.3d 436, 440-41 (8th Cir. 1996) (conviction for kickbacks only requires proof that defendant "knew that his conduct was wrongful, rather than proof that he knew it violated a 'known legal duty'"); *U.S. v. Anderson*, 1999 U.S. Dist. LEXIS 12229 at *37-*38 (D. Kan. July 26, 1999) (defendant must "specifically intend to do something the law forbids"); *U.S. v. Neufeld*, 908 F. Supp. 491, 497 (S.D. Ohio 1995) ("willful" requirement satisfied by "the purpose to commit a wrongful act"). One state court has even concluded that "willful" under the Statute simply imposes no *mens rea* requirement at all. *Medical Dev. Network, Inc. v. Professional Resp. Care*, 673 So.2d 565, 567 (Fla. DCA 1996).

116 Conversely, the fact that payments were made in the open, and not hidden from HHS or the DOJ, might help demonstrate a lack of specific intent to violate the Anti-Kickback Statute. *Cf.*

Thus, the recent majority view on unlawful intent would allow for much broader prosecution than under the restrictive *Hanlester* test.

D. Safe Harbor Regulations

In recognition of the extreme breadth of the Anti-Kickback Statute, the 1987 amendments required the Secretary of HHS to promulgate regulations (herein, "Safe Harbor Regulations") specifying payment practices that would *not* be subject to criminal prosecution or exclusion from Medicare or Medicaid. HHS published initial Safe Harbor Regulations on July 29, 1991, and additional safe harbor proposals in 1993 and 1998.[117]

The regulations carve out certain types of transactions that the HHS OIG considers legitimate and beneficial and which (if all conditions are satisfied) will not subject the healthcare provider to criminal or civil prosecution, or exclusion from the Medicare and Medicaid programs. Safe harbors are affirmative defenses, and defendants therefore have the burden of proving that they fall within the exception. The Safe Harbors established by the OIG include the following:

- salary payments to *bona fide* employees (any amount paid by an employer to a physician who has a bona fide employment relationship with the employer for the provision of services);[118]

- discounts or reductions in price if they are properly disclosed and appropriately reflected in costs claimed or charged;

U.S. v. Butcher, 1998 U.S. Dist. LEXIS 22137 at *11, *29 (N.D. Fla. Dec. 7, 1998) (finding no Medicare fraud where defendants "made no attempt to conceal their actions, but acted openly in accordance with their interpretation of the Medicare regulations").

117 On November 19, 1999, the HHS OIG promulgated new final regulations which added eight new safe harbor provisions. See "Clarification of the Initial OIG Safe Harbor Provisions and Establishment of Additional Safe Harbor Provisions Under the Anti-Kickback Statute," 64 Fed. Reg. 63518 (1999).

118 This is a broad exception from the Anti-Kickback Statute and generally permits an employer to pay an employee in whatever manner he or she chooses for providing covered items or services. To satisfy this exception, the employee must be a bona fide employee, based on the definition of "employee" that the Internal Revenue Service uses. Generally, this requires that the employee be subject to the control and direction of the employer, not only as to the results to be accomplished by the employee's work, but also as to the details and means by which the results are accomplished. Also, the remuneration must constitute compensation for the employee's services as an employee. In addition, some government enforcement authorities further believe that the employee safe harbor only applies to employees engaged in the "provision of covered items or services." In their view, therefore, the safe harbor would not apply to employees engaged only in marketing or other activities not directly related to patient care. This interpretation has not been accepted by any court as of the date of this writing.

For hospital and hospital-based physicians, it is recommended that all contracts between the physician and the hospital be (1) based on their fair market value of services, (2) unrelated to physician income or billings, and (3) limited to goods and services necessary for the provision of medical services by the hospital-based physician and typical of what hospitals provide hospital-based physicians.

- group purchasing organizations in which (1) there is a written contract specifying the amounts paid to the purchasing agent, (2) compensation is set at either a fixed amount or a fixed percentage, and (3) the purchasing agent discloses to the contracting provider the amounts received from the vendors with respect to purchases made on behalf of the provider;

- certain space and equipment leases;

- the sale of physician practices; and

- investment interests (including certain joint ventures).[119]

It is important to note that a business arrangement must comply with every condition to a safe harbor in order to be immune from prosecution. However, even if technically illegal, certain business arrangements that are similar to established safe harbors might fall within a "grey" area that the HHS OIG may choose not to prosecute, given its finite resources.[120] Since 1998, healthcare providers concerned about the legality of a proposed arrangement can seek advisory opinions from the Secretary of HHS.[121] Such opinions are binding on HHS and the parties making the request and, while technically not binding on other agencies, would be entitled to great deference.[122]

---

119 The regulations governing physician ownership of hospitals, clinics and other healthcare entities are highly complex, with the threat of criminal sanctions overlaying what used to be normal business arrangements. Recently, Columbia/HCA Healthcare Corp. stopped providing doctors with ownership shares in hospitals out of concern for potential anti-kickback violations. *See* "Columbia/HCA Quietly Cutting Physician Roster," *The Tennessean*, Aug. 27, 1999 at 1-E.

120 Concurrent with issuing the original Safe Harbors in 1991, the OIG noted the following concerning potentially "grey" arrangements:

> [T]he arrangement may violate the Statute in a less serious manner, although not be in compliance with a safe harbor provision. Here there is no way to predict the degree of risk. Rather, the degree of the risk depends on an evaluation of the many factors which are part of the decision-making process regarding case selection for investigation and prosecution. Certainly, in many (but not necessarily all) instances, prosecutorial discretion would be exercised not to pursue cases where the participants appear to have acted in a genuine good-faith attempt to comply with the terms of a safe harbor, but for reasons beyond their control are not in compliance with the terms of that safe harbor. In other instances, there may not even be an applicable safe harbor, but the arrangement may appear innocuous. But in other instances, we will want to take appropriate action.

See 56 *Fed. Reg.* 35952 (July 29, 1991). Given the recent, highly aggressive federal campaign of Anti-Kickback prosecutions, the varying judicial interpretations of the intent required for conviction, and the prospect of varying state anti-kickback laws, reliance on potential "grey" area classification could entail substantial risks.

121 *See* 42 U.S.C. § 1320a-7d(b). The Secretary of HHS is authorized to issue advisory opinions on such key issues as whether a payment is an illegal "remuneration" under the Anti-Kickback Statute, and whether any actual or proposed activity could result in sanctions or exclusion from Medicare or Medicaid. *See* 42 U.S.C. § 1320a-7d(b)(2).

122 *See* 42 U.S.C. § 1320a-7d(b)(4)(A); *Zimmer, Inc. v. Nu Tech Medical, Inc.*, 1999 U.S. Dist. LEXIS 9870 at *16 (N.D. Ind. March 31, 1999). As an illustration, the OIG recently issued Advisory Opinion No. 99-8 (posted July 13, 1999) that permits podiatrists to be present at a shoe retailer's stores, while noting that similar arrangements in nursing homes (or that involved

The Safe Harbor Regulations have no effect on state anti-fraud and anti-kickback laws. Nor do the Regulations have any effect on the so-called Stark legislation, which independently prohibits certain referrals by physicians to an entity in which the physician has an economic interest. An arrangement that complies with a safe harbor conceivably could violate a state law or the Stark legislation and, therefore, be illegal.[123] Compliance with all applicable laws should be determined on a case-by-case basis.

E. Scope of Enforcement

The Anti-Kickback Statute is extremely broad, and criminalizes many healthcare industry arrangements that in other industries are common, beneficial or innocuous.[124] At its worst, the Statute epitomizes what can go wrong when the heavy hand of government intrudes into ordinary market-based relationships.[125] The recent, vigorous enforcement of the Statute by federal authorities has forced doctors and hospitals to abandon a number of fee and cost-sharing arrangements that were adopted in response to the equally vigorous governmental pressure to reduce healthcare costs. Hospitals have been forced to seek regulatory and legal guidance on such mundane issues as restocking ambulances and providing doctors with free parking—activities that literally could be construed as illegal "kickbacks".[126] The kickback statute even extends into the emerging field of e-commerce, with questions about the legality of pharmacy sites receiving service fees for referral of prescription drug customers.[127]

The Federal Anti-Kickback Statute has the potential for over-broad enforcement, given its criminalization of what some argue to be free-market forces. As noted,

---

doctors and pharmacies) would be considered suspect. *See* "In-Store Podiatrist Plan Gets OIG Nod," *Health Care Fraud Litigation Reporter*, July 1999 at 4.

123 For further discussion of the Stark legislation, *see infra* at Section V.

124 *See Feldstein v. Nash Community Health Serv. Inc.*, 51 F. Supp.2d 673, 688 (E.D.N.C. 1999) (noting that "the language of the anti-kickback law is extremely broad and could be read to prohibit many otherwise legitimate business arrangements between hospitals and physicians") (*quoting* Janos & Niewenhous, 40 Boston Bar J. at *8); "Fraud Conviction Offers Lessons for Health Care Providers and Counsel," *Legal Backgrounder*, Sept. 3, 1999 (noting the "fine line to be drawn between attempting to induce referrals and hoping that referrals may result from a hospital-physician relationship").

125 Indeed, in an early draft of its Safe Harbor Regulations, HHS suggested that the Statute could be interpreted, literally, to prohibit a physician from receiving a dividend from a large publicly traded pharmaceutical company if he or she prescribed one of the company's products for a Medicaid patient, knowing that ordering that product could eventually increase dividends.

126 *See* "Agency to Rewrite Rules on Kickbacks; Hospital-Ambulance Arrangements," *Dayton Daily News*, Aug. 3, 1999 at 4-B (HHS "has begun writing a new regulation intended to clarify when hospitals can give free supplies to ambulance crews and when such help is an illegal kickback").

127 *See* "U.S. Govt and Industry Consider Regulation of On-Line Pharmacy," *Marketletter*, June 28, 1999.

the leading interpretative cases have found violations of the Statute as long as "one purpose" of the payment is to induce referrals. Thus, even if a physician or laboratory provides medical services (1) that are indisputably needed; (2) competently performed; and (3) billed at market rates, that provider can be *criminally* responsible if *part* of its motivation was to "induce" future Medicare or Medicaid patient referrals.[128]

The potential breadth of the Anti-Kickback Statute, its severe penalties, and its vigorous use in the front line of recent federal criminal enforcement efforts, all underscore the need for healthcare providers to be fully familiar with the Statute, HHS regulations and OIG Safe Harbors. A detailed, pro-active compliance program to prevent "suspect" financial arrangements, and to educate employees about the many nuances of the Statute, is perhaps the best way to minimize the threat of criminal prosecution under the Act.

V. The Prohibitions Against Self-Referrals—The Stark Law

A. The Stark Law: Prohibition on Physician Self-Referrals

The Stark law[129] bars physicians from referring Medicare or Medicaid patients to an entity providing certain designated health services, in which the physician (or his family) has any financial relationship.[130] In essence, Stark bars physicians from entering into financially beneficial relationships with healthcare entities to which they refer business. Like the Anti-Kickback statute,[131] Stark is intended to avoid medical decisions being unduly influenced by monetary considerations.

---

128 On January 9, 1998, HHS issued proposed regulations that would create a "safe harbor" exception "to make clear that compensation arrangements are generally permissible as long as they are at fair market value, further a legitimate business purpose and are not tied to the volume or value of physician referrals." *See* Federal News Service, May 13, 1999 (prepared testimony of Kathy Buto, Deputy Director of HCFA's Center for Health Plans & Providers before the House Ways & Means Committee Health Subcommittee).

129 Social Security Act, 42 U.S.C. § 1395nn (1999). The statute's name derives from its author and chief sponsor in Congress, Representative Fortney "Pete" Stark (D-CA).

130 The statute provides in relevant part as follows:

[I]f a physician (or an immediate family member of such physician) has a financial relationship with an entity . . . then —

(a) the physician may not make a referral to the entity for the furnishing of designated health services for which [Medicare or Medicaid] payment otherwise may be made. . . and

(b) the entity may not present or cause to be presented a claim under this title or bill to any individual, third party payor, or other entity for designated health services furnished pursuant to a referral prohibited [herein].

42 USC § 1395nn(a)(1).

131 *See* discussion *supra.*

In contrast to the widely utilized Anti-Kickback statute, Stark has not been a part of the federal government's recent crackdown on healthcare fraud and abuse.[132] Nonetheless, given its potentially very broad applicability and stiff monetary penalties, physicians, hospitals, clinics and other healthcare providers are advised to learn about and act in conformity with the statute and its requirements.

In its original incarnation, the Physician Self-Referral Act of 1989 (known as Stark I) only barred self-interested physician referrals to clinical laboratories.[133] The motivation for the law was the belief, backed up by studies, that some physicians with ownership interests in clinical laboratories tended to make inappropriate and excessive patient referrals to those clinics, thereby driving up healthcare costs.[134]

The Omnibus Budget Reconciliation Act of 1993 included amendments to Stark I that greatly expanded the scope of the statute.[135] The amendments (known generally as Stark II) added 10 new categories of "designated health services" to the self-referral prohibition. Thus, in addition to clinical laboratory work, Stark II now encompasses physical therapy, occupational therapy, radiology services, radiation therapy, durable medical equipment and supplies, nutrients, prosthetics and orthotics, home health services, outpatient prescription drugs, and hospital services.[136]

As in the Anti-Kickback statute, the Stark law defines the term "financial relationship" extremely broadly. A financial relationship encompasses *any* direct or indirect ownership or investment interest, as well as any compensation arrangement.[137] For management services organizations ("MSOs") contracting with physicians,

---

132 Enforcement of Stark has lagged because final regulations have not yet been issued by HCFA. Moreover, as discussed below, the current proposed regulations are highly complex and controversial. *See, e.g.*, "Healthcare Struggles With Stark Reality," *Modern Healthcare*, July 5, 1999 at 30 (noting that "after all the time and effort that have been spent on the [Stark] laws, people are still struggling to interpret and apply them"). In the view of some commentators, the Stark laws "were designed to emphasize self-compliance and to work without government involvement", whereas the Anti-Kickback statute—which covers similar ground but with felony criminal penalties—has been the natural choice for federal prosecutors. *See id.*

133 A proposed regulation for Stark I was published on March 11, 1992, with the final regulation appearing on August 14, 1995. For a general legislative history of the statute, *see* "Strong Medicine Needed For Fighting Health-Care Fraud," *Chicago Daily Law Bulletin*, July 13, 1999 at 6.

134 *See* "Healthcare Struggles With Stark Reality," *Modern Healthcare*, July 5, 1999 at 30.

135 HCFA published proposed regulations for Stark II on January 9, 1998. To date, final regulations for Stark II have not been published. At a congressional hearing in May of 1999, HCFA stated that final Stark II regulations would be issued sometime in the year 2000. *See Modern Healthcare*, May 31, 1999 at 24.

136 *See* 42 USC § 1395nn(h)(6).

137 *See* 42 USC § 1395nn(a)(2). The statute allows physicians to own publicly traded investment securities (including stocks and bonds) in any company with a total equity of at least $75 million. 42 U.S.C. § 1395nn(c). This exception underscores the breadth of the statute's definition of "financial relationship".

the prohibited situation most likely to be encountered is an ownership or investment interest.

The Stark law does not require any specific intent. Thus, even if a physician was
unaware that a family member had an interest in the referral entity, the physician
could still be held liable. Consequently, compliance with the statute is extremely
important to avoid penalties.

Unlike the Anti-Kickback Statute, the Stark law does not have a criminal component and only assesses civil money penalties. Nonetheless, the civil penalties under Stark can be very significant. Medicare and Medicaid will not pay for any
service rendered in violation of Stark.[138] An entity that violates Stark must refund
all monies received for services rendered in violation of the law.[139] Even more importantly, violators of Stark can be excluded from the Medicare and Medicaid programs.[140] Finally, any person who bills for a service that they knew (or should
have known) violates Stark may be fined up to $15,000 per violation.[141]

The Stark law contains some important exceptions. To comply with the Stark
self-referral prohibition, every financial relationship between an entity providing
health services (such as a hospital) and a physician making referrals to that entity
must fall within a Stark exception. For example, any arrangement in which a physician provides services to a hospital as an independent contractor, or serves as the
hospital's medical director, must fall under a Stark exception. Further, where a
physician group has a relationship with a facility and a physician within that group
has a medical directorship with the facility, both relationships must fit within an
exception.

The Stark law's major exceptions to the ownership or investment
prohibition include:

- physician services "provided personally by (or under the personal supervision of) another physician in the same group practice . . . as the referring physician";[142]

- in-office "ancillary services" that are furnished "personally by the referring physician" or a physician in the same group practice (or by individuals directly under their supervision) and billed by such practice;[143]

---

138   42 U.S.C. § 1395nn(g)(1).

139   42 U.S.C. § 1395nn(g)(2).

140   *See* 42 U.S.C. § 1320a-7(b)(7).

141   42 U.S.C. § 1395nn(g)(3).

142   42 U.S.C. § 1395nn(b)(1).

143   42 U.S.C. § 1395nn(b)(2). This exception does not apply to "durable medical equipment. . . nutrients, equipment, and supplies", and is subject to additional restrictions depending on where
the treatment was administered. *Id.*

188 Corporate Fraud Investigations & Compliance Programs

- pre-paid plans (e.g., services provided by a qualified health maintenance organization to an individual enrolled with the organization);[144]

- designated health services "furnished in a rural area", provided that "substantially all" such services are furnished to local residents;[145] and

- hospital ownership, provided that the referring physician is authorized to perform services at the hospital, and has an ownership interest "in the hospital itself (and not merely in a subdivision of the hospital)."[146]

The Stark law also excludes the following as not being prohibited "compensation arrangements":

- *bona fide* leases of office space or rental equipment, and physicians' personal service contracts, that are (1) set forth in writing; (2) reflect fair market value; and (3) for a term of at least one year;[147]

- *bona fide* employment relationships—that is, any fair market salary "paid by an employer to a physician (or an immediate family member of such physician) who has a bona fide employment relationship with the employer";[148]

- remuneration by a hospital to a physician that either (1) "does not relate to the provision of designated health services" or (2) represents a recruiting incentive paid "to induce the physician to relocate to the geographic area served by the hospital";[149]

- isolated fair market value transactions (*e.g.*, a one time sale of property or a practice);[150]

- certain pre-existing group practice arrangements in which a hospital bills for services provided by the group, provided that the agreement is in writing, reflects fair market values, and is not otherwise tied to referrals;[151] and

- payments by a physician for items or services (*e.g.*, laboratory services) at fair market value.[152]

---

144 42 U.S.C. § 1395nn(b)(3).

145 42 U.S.C. § 1395nn(d)(2).

146 42 U.S.C. § 1395nn(d)(3).

147 42 U.S.C. §§ 1395nn(e)(1), 1395nn(e)(3).

148 42 U.S.C. § 1395nn(e)(2). The remuneration cannot in any way be tied to "the volume or value of any referrals by the referring physician." *Id.* The only exception is for qualified "physician incentive plans", which allow the volume or value of referrals to be taken into account under certain carefully prescribed conditions. *See* 42 USC § 1395nn(e)(3)(B).

149 42 U.S.C. §§ 1395nn(e)(4)-(5).

150 42 U.S.C. § 1395nn(e)(6).

151 42 U.S.C. § 1395nn(e)(7).

152 42 U.S.C. § 1395nn(e)(8).

exception most pertinent to independent contractor relationships (and medical directorships) is the exception for personal service arrangements, which is similar to the personal services "safe harbor" under the Anti-Kickback Statute.[153] The Stark exception, however, is more flexible in its application.[154]

The Stark II exceptions are often quite technical, and require analysis by experienced counsel. The proposed Stark II regulations have generated considerable controversy because of their length and complexity, with commentators deriding them as "murky"[155] and a "quagmire."[156] Recognizing this problem, Congress recently required HHS to issue written advisory opinions concerning whether a referral to a designated health service (other than a clinical laboratory) is barred under the statute.[157]

An area of particular controversy has been the Stark II prohibition on compensation arrangements.[158] Recently, Representative Bill Thomas (R-CA), the Chairman of the House Ways and Means Committee's Sub-Committee on Health, introduced legislation (H.R. 2651) that would effect a major change to the Stark law by eliminating restrictions based on compensation arrangements.[159] In a recent counter-proposal (H.R. 2650), Representative Pete Stark (the statute's namesake) proposed more modest changes, notably scrapping the convoluted Stark II

---

153 Note that an "exception" under Stark is a bright-line test, as opposed to the more nuanced "safe-harbor" approach under the Anti-Kickback statute. Compliance with a Stark exception is mandatory. Failure to fall within an exception triggers a "financial relationship" that violates the statute. By contrast, failure to fall within an Anti-Kickback safe harbor does not render a transaction illegal *per se*. The Stark exceptions were designed to deal only with physician self-referrals, not kickbacks. Given the similar purposes behind the statutes, however, it is possible that compliance with a Stark exception could insulate a transaction under the Anti-Kickback statute as well.

154 Stark (unlike the Anti-Kickback statute) does not require an exact schedule of services, or that the precise length of time and charge for each interval of service be set forth in advance in the agreement. Moreover, the Stark exception does not require that aggregate compensation be set forth in advance.

155 *See Modern Healthcare*, May 31, 1999 at 24.

156 *See* "Medicare Regulatory Fixes Proposed; AAFP Applauds Efforts," *U.S. Newswire*, July 28, 1999.

157 This advisory opinion procedure was enacted in Section 1877(g)(6) of the Balanced Budget Act of 1997.

158 As one report recently noted, "[f]ew physicians oppose the [Stark] restrictions based on ownership and investment, but the compensation element has received lots of objection—and ridicule—over the years." "Bill Thomas, the Anti-Stark," *Medical Economics*, September 20, 1999.

159 The Thomas proposal includes other features designed to streamline and simplify compliance with the Stark II regulations. *See* "Bill Thomas, the Anti-Stark," *Medical Economics*, September 20, 1999; "Physician Anti-Referral Legislation Revisited," *Medical Laboratory Observer*, September 1, 1999; "Providers Unite on Repeal of Compensation Ban," *Modern Healthcare*, August 2, 1999 at 12. Not surprisingly, healthcare providers have been enthusiastic proponents of these proposed changes to Stark. *See, e.g.*, "Medicare Regulatory Fixes Proposed," *U.S. Newswire*, July 28, 1999.

exceptions to the compensation ban in favor of a simpler, over-arching standard that would allow compensation based on a "fair-market value" standard.[160]

In sum, the Stark and Anti-Kickback statutes underscore the importance of clearly identifying and documenting fair-market value in proposed transactions between physicians and other healthcare providers.[161] Although the federal government is not actively enforcing Stark at the present, the statute's goals and implementation methods are similar to the widely enforced criminal Anti-Kickback Statute. Moreover, although the basis for doing so might be questionable, innovative *qui tam* whistleblowers might file False Claim Act lawsuits predicated on violations of Stark.[162] Consequently, healthcare providers should remain vigilant about complying with Stark, and scrutinize financial relationships with referral sources to make sure that they qualify for one of the Stark exceptions.

VI. The Health Insurance Portability and Accountability Act of 1996

In August 1996, the Health Insurance Portability and Accountability Act (PL104-191) ("HIPAA") was signed into law. HIPAA made significant changes to many aspects of our health care system. Those provisions which are relevant to fraud and abuse liability and to investigations of health care providers are discussed here.

A. Fraud and Abuse after HIPAA

Title II of HIPAA, entitled "Preventing Health Care Fraud and Abuse: Administrative Simplification: Medical Liability Reform," makes substantial changes to existing fraud and abuse laws as well as adding to the arsenal of weapons available to the government to combat fraud and abuse in the health care industry. The following list identifies some of the more significant fraud and abuse provisions contained in HIPAA (following that, we summarize its key provisions):

1. Establishes a coordinated fraud and abuse control program and provides a financing mechanism;

2. Establishes a Medicare Integrity Program providing for contracts with private entities with expertise to detect and expose health care fraud;

---

160 *See* "Providers Unite on Repeal of Compensation Ban," *Modern Healthcare*, August 2, 1999 at 12. Of course, problems could still arise even under a pure "fair-market value" standard. For example, if an MSO operates at a loss, the government could argue that the physician payments to the MSO were below fair market value, and thus not within a Stark exception.

161 The Stark statute defines fair-market value as "the value in arms length transactions, consistent with the general market value." 42 U.S.C. § 1395nn(h)(3). For rentals, the fair-market value is defined as "the value of rental property for general commercial purposes (not taking into account its intended use)"; leases of space cannot factor in any extra increment of value associated with proximity to a potential referral source. *Id.*

162 *See* "Healthcare Struggles With Stark Reality," *Modern Healthcare*, July 5, 1999 at 30.

3. Expands the Medicare and Medicaid Anti-Kickback Statute to other federal health care programs;

4. Provides for increases in civil money penalties;

5. Tightens the intent standard for the imposition of civil money penalties;

6. Creates a separate health care fraud criminal sanction;

7. Expands the list of sanctions applicable to health care fraud; and

8. Establishes a process for additional guidance regarding the application of health care fraud and abuse sanctions, including the mandatory issuance of advisory opinions under the Anti-Kickback Statute and the issuance of fraud alerts.

B. HIPAA Provisions

1. Section 201. Fraud and Abuse Control Program

Subtitle A of Title II of HIPAA, 42 U.S.C. § 1320a-7c, establishes a Fraud and Abuse Control Program. The Department of HHS, in conjunction with the OIG and the Attorney General, are charged with establishing a program to: (1) coordinate federal, state and local law enforcement programs to control fraud and abuse with respect to "health plans," including for the first time private health insurance, as well as the federal and state health care programs;[163] (2) conduct investigations, audits, evaluations and inspections; (3) facilitate the enforcement of criminal laws and civil money penalty sanctions; (4) provide for modification and establishment of safe harbors; (5) issue advisory opinions and Special Fraud Alerts; and (6) report final adverse actions taken against health care providers, suppliers and practitioners.

The creation of the Fraud and Abuse Control Program was intended to establish a program for bringing together in a coordinated fashion what had heretofore been disjointed and sometimes contradictory efforts by federal, state and private entities and to target fraud and abuse at every level of the health care system. This program is expected to result in a considerable increase in the sharing of information and in joint activities by the various enforcement authorities.

HIPAA also establishes a Health Care Fraud and Abuse Control Account in the Federal Hospital Insurance Trust Fund. 42 U.S.C. § 1395I(k). Besides an annual appropriation, the Trust Fund may accept money gifts and bequests. In addition, certain portions of criminal fines and civil monetary penalties will be transferred to the Trust Fund. The funds contained in the Trust are used to cover the

---

163   The Act defines "health plans" to include (1) a policy of health insurance, (2) a contract of a service benefit organization, or (3) a membership agreement with a HMO or other prepaid health plan.

cost of (1) investigations; (2) financial and performance audits of health care programs and operations; (3) provider and consumer education; (4) prosecuting health care matters; and (5) inspections and other evaluations of health care providers and practitioners. These funds are already being used to hire and train FBI agents, prosecutors and auditors to investigate and prosecute health care fraud matters.

2. Section 202. Medicare Integrity Program

HIPAA also establishes a "Medicare Integrity Program" intended to "promote the integrity of the Medicare program by entering into contracts" with outside entities. Pursuant to these contracts, private parties with specialized expertise will be retained by the government to detect and expose health care fraud and abuse. Activities to be conducted pursuant to the Medicare Integrity Program include: (1) "medical and utilization review and fraud review" of Medicare reimbursed providers; (2) "audits of cost reports"; (3) determination of "whether payment should not be, or should not have been made" and recovery of improper payments; and (4) education of providers of services, beneficiaries and others with respect to program integrity issues. This program is significant, in part, because it will create a cadre of government contractors with expertise in investigation of potential health care fraud. These contractors presumably will have an easier time analyzing claims for reimbursement in the context of a very complex regulatory scheme than most state and federal prosecutors and investigators, whose responsibilities encompass a much broader range of potential criminal activities than health care fraud. On May 19, 1999, HCFA announced that it had selected twelve private companies to perform fraud fighting activities under the Medicare Integrity Program.

3. Section 203. Beneficiary Incentive Programs

Among other things, Section 203 of HIPAA, 42 U.S.C. § 1395b-5, requires HCFA to establish a program of education and inducements to encourage Medicare beneficiaries to report potential fraud and abuse by their health care providers. This program includes the payment of bounties to persons who report potential fraud that "serves as the basis for the collection" by enforcement authorities of improper payments to providers.

4. Section 204. Application of Fraud and Abuse Penalties to All Federal Health Care Programs

HIPAA expands current fraud and abuse sanctions to include all "Federal Health Care Programs." 42 U.S.C. § 1320a-7b. HIPAA defines Federal Health Care Programs as "any plan or program which is funded directly, in whole or in part, by the United States Government." 42 U.S.C. § 1320a-7b(f). The former version of Section 1320a-7b applied only to the Medicare and Medicaid programs. This allowed health care providers to plead guilty to fraud against other federally funded health care programs such as the Federal Employees Health Benefits Program ("FEHBP") and CHAMPUS, the military civilian health benefits plan without incurring certain mandatory penalties which will be discussed later in this chapter.

Now, fraud committed against any federally funded health program is covered by the false statements and anti-kickback provisions of the Social Security Act.

5. Section 205. Guidance Regarding Application of Fraud and Abuse Sanctions

HIPAA requires the Secretary of HHS to publish an annual notice in the Federal Register soliciting proposals for (1) the modification of existing safe harbor provisions; (2) the creation of additional safe harbors; (3) advisory opinions on various health care fraud and abuse issues; and (4) Special Fraud Alerts. 42 U.S.C. § 1320a-7d. The safe harbor provisions in the Anti-Kickback Statute are binding on the government and if followed to the letter, provide some comfort that conduct that might otherwise be alleged to violate the Statute will not be prosecuted.

6. Revisions to Current Administrative Sanctions for Fraud and Abuse

HIPAA created the following revisions to the existing administrative sanctions program for fraud and abuse:

- **Section 211. Mandatory Exclusions**—HIPAA creates a mandatory exclusion from participation in all Federal health care programs following felony convictions relating to health care fraud and controlled substances. Conviction of a misdemeanor subjects the violator to permissive (not mandatory) sanctions. 42 U.S.C. § 1320a-7(a).

- **Section 212. Minimum Periods for Permissive Exclusions**—Convictions of misdemeanor criminal health care fraud offenses, criminal offenses relating to fraud in non-health care federal or state programs, convictions relating to obstruction of investigation and misdemeanor convictions relating to controlled substances would result in a minimum three-year exclusion. Exclusions resulting from activities concerning an individual's professional competence carry a minimum exclusion of one year. Further, permissive exclusions resulting from the revocation or suspension of an individual or entity's license would be not less than the period of suspension or revocation. 42 U.S.C. § 1320a-7(c)(3).

- **Section 213. Permissive Exclusions/Ownership Interest**—HIPAA authorizes the exclusion of individuals with a direct or indirect ownership or control in a sanctioned entity where the individual "knows or should have known" of the activity in question or is "an officer or managing employee of the entity." 42 U.S.C. §1320a-7(b)(15).

- **Section 214. Practitioner's Failure to Comply with Statutory Obligations**—HIPAA establishes a minimum period of exclusion for practitioners providing services or items which are not medically necessary for the patient or which fail to meet professionally recognized standards of care. Prior to HIPAA, the Secretary would have been required to establish that the individual was "unwilling or unable" to meet such obligations. 42 U.S.C. § 1320c-5(b)(1).

- **Section 216. Risk-Sharing Arrangements**—HIPAA creates an exception to the Anti-Kickback Statute which would apply to "any remuneration between an organization and an individual entity providing items or services, or a combination thereof, pursuant to a written agreement between the organization and the individual if: (1) the organization is a Medicare certified HMO; or (2) the written agreement contains a "risk-sharing arrangement," placing the individual or entity at substantial risk for the cost or utilization of services which the individual or entity is obligated to provide. This exception is designed to recognize alternative forms of delivery arrangements, such as incentive pools, which otherwise would have violated the Anti-Kickback Statute. 42 U.S.C. § 1320a-7b(b)(3).

7. Changes in Civil Monetary Penalties Under the Social Security Act

HIPAA also made revisions to the Social Security Act administrative civil monetary penalties applicable to health care providers for improper claims. 42 U.S.C. § 1320a-7a. These revisions apply to acts or omissions occurring on or after January 1, 1997. The most relevant revisions are listed below.

- Expands coverage of the civil money penalty provisions to all federal health care programs, not just Medicare and Medicaid;

- Increases the maximum civil money penalty amount from $2,000 to $10,000 and the maximum assessment amount from twice the amount claimed to three times the amount claimed;

- In addition to penalties for false claims and kickbacks, HIPAA authorizes civil money penalties for a pattern or practice of presenting a claim for items or services that is based on a code that the person "knows or should know will result in a greater payment to the person than the code the person knows or should know is applicable to the item or service actually provided;"

- Clarifies the intent standard under the civil money penalty provisions to require that improper claims be submitted "knowingly" and defines "should know" to mean that a person "acts in deliberate ignorance of the truth or falsity of the information . . .", or "acts in reckless disregard of the truth or falsity of the information." This provision further specifically states that the standard does not require proof of specific intent to defraud;

- Authorizes civil money penalties for knowingly presenting a bill for "a pattern of medical or other items or services that a person knows or should know are not medically necessary." The civil money penalties for providing medically unnecessary services and services that do not meet quality standards is increased from the actual or estimated cost to "up to "$10,000 for each instance;"

- Authorizes civil money penalties for offers of remuneration (including, under specified circumstances, waivers of copay requirements) to beneficiaries of federal or state health care programs that the "person knows or should know is likely to influence" the beneficiary in choosing to order an item or service.

8. Criminal Law Revisions

HIPAA makes a number of changes to the criminal law that provide new risks to health care companies. Among them are the creation of several new health care related crimes including: health care fraud; theft or embezzlement; false statements relating to health care matters; obstruction of criminal investigations of health care offenses; and money laundering. In addition to the creation of the new criminal offenses, HIPAA expands coverage of health care related crimes to include offenses against private insurers as well as publicly funded health insurance like Medicare and Medicaid.[164]

- **Section 242. Health Care Fraud**—HIPAA establishes a new criminal offense of "Health Care Fraud." It is defined as "knowingly and willfully" executing, or attempting to execute, a scheme or artifice: "(1) to defraud any health care benefit program; or (2) to obtain, by means of false or fraudulent pretenses, representations or promises, any of the money or property owned by, or under the custody or control of, any health care benefit program." Violations of this section may result in fines or imprisonment for not more than 10 years. If the violation results in serious bodily injury, the maximum period of imprisonment is 20 years. If a violation results in death, the maximum jail sentence is life imprisonment. 18 USC § 1347.

- **Section 243. Theft or Embezzlement**—HIPAA establishes a new criminal offense of Theft or Embezzlement in Connection with Health Care. A person can be convicted of this crime who "knowingly or willfully embezzles, steals, or otherwise without authority converts to the use of any person other than the rightful owner, or intentionally misapplies any of the moneys . . . property or assets of a health care benefit program . . ." The offense is a felony punishable by fine and imprisonment for up to ten years if the value of the property involved is greater than $100, and for up to one year if the property is worth $100 or less. 18 USC § 669.

- **Section 244. False Statements**—HIPAA creates a criminal offense of False Statements Relating to Health Care Matters for an individual or entity who "knowingly and willfully falsifies, conceals or covers up," or "makes any materially false, fictitious or fraudulent statements in connection with the delivery of, or payment for, health care benefits, items or services. Violations of this provision may result in fines or imprisonment for not more than five years or both. 18 U.S.C. § 1035.

- **Section 245. Obstruction of Criminal Investigations**—HIPAA creates a criminal offense of Obstruction of Criminal Investigations of Health Care Offenses for an individual who "willfully prevents, obstructs, misleads, delays or attempts to prevent, obstruct, mislead or delay the communication of information or records relating to a violation of a federal health care offense to a criminal investi-

---

164   18 USC § 24; *see also* discussion at §I.B., *supra*.

gator. . . ." Penalties include fines and/or imprisonment of not more than five years or both. 18 USC § 1518.

- **Section 246. Laundering of Monetary Instruments**—HIPAA also expands the federal money laundering Statute to include "any act or activity constituting an offense involving a Federal health care offense." 18 USC § 1956(c)(7).
- **Section 247. Injunctions Against Fraud**—HIPAA specifically grants to the government the authority to seek injunctions in federal court to enjoin those "violating or about to violate" federal health care laws. 18 USC § 1345(a)(1). It further provides authority for the government to freeze assets of persons allegedly involved in health care fraud. 18 USC § 1345(a)(2).
- **Section 248. Authorized Investigative Demand Procedures**—Another section of HIPAA grants the Department of Justice the authority to issue investigative subpoenas "[I]n any investigation relating to any act or activity involving a Federal health care offense. . . ." Such subpoenas can require "the production of any records . . . which may be relevant to an authorized law enforcement inquiry. . . ." 18 USC § 3486. This provision allows the government to obtain books and records related to an investigation without first convening a grand jury.
- **Section 249. Forfeitures for Federal Health Care Offenses**—Finally, HIPAA requires a court in imposing sentence on a person convicted of a federal health care offense to "order the person to forfeit property, real or personal that constitutes or is derived, directly or indirectly, from gross proceeds traceable to the commission of the offense." 18 USC § 982.

Together, the provisions of HIPAA added considerably to the methods and techniques available to health care enforcement authorities. They further complicated the already difficult circumstances of health care providers who are paid by federal or state health programs and by private health insurers.

VII. The Balanced Budget Act of 1997

In 1997, before the ink was dry on HIPAA, Congress again added new provisions relating to healthcare fraud and abuse. In August 1997, almost a year to the day after final passage of HIPAA, Congress enacted the Balanced Budget Act of 1997 (Pub. L. No. 105-33) (the "BBA"). The following is a summary of the new fraud and abuse provisions contained in the BBA.

A. Section 4301: Permanent Exclusion for Those Convicted of Three Healthcare Related Crimes

Section 4301 provides that with respect to convictions occurring on or after the date of enactment of the BBA, individuals convicted on one previous occasion of one or more offenses for which exclusion for participation in the Federal healthcare programs may be imposed, the period of exclusion must be for at least ten years. Where the individual has been convicted on two or more previous occasions, the period of exclusion "shall be permanent." 42 U.S.C. § 1320a-7(c)(3)(G).

B. Section 4302: Authority to Refuse to Enter into Medicare Agreements with Individuals or Entities Convicted of Felonies

Section 4302 of the BBA authorizes the Secretary of HHS to refuse to enter into Medicare Part A or Part B provider agreements with providers who have been convicted of a felony under Federal or state law. The Statute does not provide a list of applicable felonies, but instead provides HHS with discretion to determine whether the offense of which the applicant was convicted was "detrimental to the best interest of the program or program beneficiaries." This provision allows the Secretary to consider felonies which occurred prior to the enactment of the BBA. 42 U.S.C. §§ 1395cc(b)(2)(D); 1395u(h)(8).

C. Section 4303: Exclusion of Entity Controlled by a Family Member of a Sanctioned Individual

Section 4303 addresses the issue of transfers of ownership or controlling interest in an entity participating in a healthcare program in an attempt to avoid the mandatory exclusion provisions of existing law. It provides that an entity transferred to "an immediate family member . . . or a member of the household" of a sanctioned individual may be excluded by the Department. It is interesting to note that this section applies not only to transfers to immediate family members, *i.e.*, husbands, wives, children, siblings, etc., but also to "any individual sharing a common abode as part of a single family unit with the person, including domestic employees and others who live together as a family unit, but not including a roomer or boarder." 42 U.S.C. §§ 1320a-7(b)(8)(A)(iii), 1320a-7(j).

D. Section 4304: Imposition of Civil Money Penalties

The BBA adds two new situations in which civil money penalties may be imposed on healthcare providers. First, civil money penalties may be assessed against persons or entities which "arrange or contract (by employment or otherwise)" with an individual or entity that the person or entity "knows or should know" is excluded from a Federal healthcare program. The "knows or should know" standard included in this provision is defined under HIPAA as acting "in deliberate ignorance of the truth or falsity of the information, or acts in reckless disregard of the truth or falsity of the information." This provision is intended to prevent excluded individuals and entities from continuing to provide services and collect payment from Federal healthcare programs through contracts with non-excluded individuals and entities. Second, the BBA provides for what are called "intermediate sanctions" for violations of the anti-kickback provisions of the Medicare and Medicaid Statutes. Previously the Anti-Kickback Statute provided only for the imposition of criminal penalties or exclusion of individuals or entities committing violations. This provision provides for civil penalties short of requiring mandatory exclusion of the provider. Violations can result in civil money penalties of $50,000 plus damages of as much as three times the amount of remuneration involved in the prohibited activity. 42 U.S.C. §§ 1320a-7a(a)(6), (7).

An interesting distinction between the two new civil money penalties is that the imposition of civil money penalties for contracting with an excluded individual or entity can be based on the "knows or should know" intent standard, while the civil money penalties for violations of the Anti-Kickback Statute requires a "knowingly and willfully" intent.

E. Section 4311: Improving Information to Medicare Beneficiaries

Section 4311 of the Act is a continuation of the government's efforts to induce Medicare beneficiaries to report fraud and abuse by their healthcare providers. This section provides a requirement for a notice to all beneficiaries requesting that they carefully check any explanation of benefits ("EOB"), or itemized statement because errors do occur and because Medicare fraud, waste and abuse is a significant problem. In addition, a notice to beneficiaries must include: (1) a statement of the beneficiary's right to request an itemized statement of the Medicare items and services reimbursed by the program; (2) a description of the anti-fraud and abuse program established by HIPAA; and (3) a toll-free number available for the reporting of "complaints and information about fraud, waste and abuse." 42 U.S.C. § 1395b-2(c).

This provision requires the healthcare provider, not the Medicare program, to supply an itemized statement upon request. Failure to provide a requested itemized statement is punishable by a civil money penalty of not more than $100. In addition, an individual who receives such an itemized statement may submit it to HHS along with a written request for a review of the statement. The request for review should be accompanied by a list of the items or services that the individual believes were not provided or any other billing irregularity. 42 U.S.C. § 1395b-7(b).

F. Section 4312: Disclosure of Information and Surety Bonds

In order to address concerns that providers of services and supplies to Medicare and Medicaid patients are occasionally undercapitalized and, thus, unable to repay to the government any overpayments received either through inadvertence or as a result of fraudulent practices, Section 4312 provides that provider agreements for suppliers of durable medical equipment ("DME") may not be issued or renewed unless the supplier provides the following information:

1. Full and complete information as to the identity of each person with an ownership or control interest in the supplier or in any subcontractor in which the supplier directly or indirectly has a five percent or more ownership interest;

2. The name of any disclosing entity in which a person with an ownership or control interest in the supplier also has an ownership or control interest in the disclosing entity; and,

3. A surety bond in the amount of not less than $50,000. The Statute also provides for similar surety bonds by home health agencies. These provisions may be

waived if a comparable bond is required under state law. 42 U.S.C. §§ 1395m(a)(16), 1395x(o).

G. Section 4313: Provision of Certain Identification Numbers

Section 4313 of the BBA requires that Medicare providers supply both their employer identification numbers and social security account numbers, along with the identity of each person with an ownership or control interest in the entity, and the identity of any subcontractor in which the entity has a direct or indirect ownership of five percent or more. 42 U.S.C. §§ 1320a-3(a)(i), 1320a-3a(a)(3); 1320a-3a(a)(C)(j); 1320a-3a(C).

H. Section 4314: Advisory Opinions Regarding Certain Physician Self-Referral Matters

Section 4314 of the BBA requires HHS to issue written advisory opinions regarding "whether a referral relating to designated health services (other than clinical laboratory services) is prohibited." It is unclear why clinical laboratory services were excluded from this provision. It may, however, be related to the fact that HHS finally issued implementing regulations under the original Stark legislation on self-referrals which specifically address clinical laboratory services issues. 42 U.S.C. §1395nn(g)(6)

I. Section 4317: Requirement to Furnish Diagnostic Information

Numerous recent investigations by enforcement authorities have focused on an alleged lack of medical necessity for services provided to Federal health program beneficiaries. In light of the prominence of this issue, Section 4317 of the BBA requires that physicians or other practitioners "provide diagnostic or other medical information" when ordering items or services. The information must be provided to the party which will provide the services ordered and must be provided at the time the item or service is ordered. This section makes the provision of medical necessity documentation a condition of payment and failure to do so could be the basis for false claims liability. This requirement is intended to apply to diagnostic X-rays; diagnostic laboratory tests; other diagnostic tests; durable medical equipment; prosthetic devices; and braces and artificial arms, legs and eyes. 42 U.S.C. § 1395u(p)(4).

J. Section 4320: Definitions of Reasonable Costs

Section 4320 of the BBA is intended to clarify prior determinations that certain items and services do not qualify for the definition of "reasonable costs" and are, thus, not reimbursable by Medicare. The prohibited costs primarily come under the heading of common sense exclusions, but, in the past, some providers improperly sought reimbursement for them. The prohibited costs include: entertainment, including tickets to sporting and similar entertainment events; gifts or donations; personal use of motor vehicles; costs for fines or penalties arising from violations of federal, state or local laws; and educational expenses for spouses or dependents of providers, employees or contractors. 42 U.S.C. § 1395x(v)(8).

K. Section 4321: Nondiscrimination in Post Hospital Referral to Home Health Agencies and Other Entities

The Government has been concerned with the frequent practice of hospitals when referring patients who need post hospital services (most often home health services), to refer to home health agencies or other suppliers with which the hospital has an affiliation. Hospitals are required to employ a discharge planning process which includes an evaluation of the patient's need for post-hospitalization services and identifies available providers of those services. Section 4321 of the BBA requires that beneficiaries be notified of available home health services that "serve the area in which the patient resides and that request to be listed by the hospital as available." Beneficiaries must be provided with information regarding any "qualified provider" of home health services and must disclose its own financial interest in any home health provider. In order to monitor compliance with this provision, Section 4321 also requires that specific information be maintained by the hospital including: (1) the nature of its financial interest in the home health provider; (2) the number of individuals who are discharged from the hospital and who were identified as requiring home health services; and (3) the percentage of such individuals who receive home health services from a provider in which the hospital has a financial interest. 42 U.S.C. §§ 1395x(ee)(2), 1395cc(a)(1), 1320b-16.

VIII. Exclusion and Other Administrative Penalties Related to Federal Health Care Programs

A. Introduction

As part of the overall federal enforcement program, Congress has established a structure and criteria under which HHS can "exclude" individuals and entities from participation in Medicare and certain State health care programs.[165] In this context, exclusion means that services or items furnished by or at the direction of an excluded individual or entity are not eligible for reimbursement under "Medicare, Medicaid, and all other Federal health care programs. . . ."[166] The specter of exclusion not only deters misconduct, but also dramatically increases the Government's leverage in dealing with waste, fraud and abuse in the federally

---

165   42 U.S.C. 1320a-7.

166   42 C.F.R. §1001.1901(b)(1). "Federal health care program" is defined as "any plan or program that provides health benefits, whether directly, through insurance, or otherwise, which is funded directly, in whole or in part, by the United States [other than Federal Employee Health Benefit Program]" or under "any State Health care program." 42 U.S.C. §1320a-7b(f). The term is used most frequently in reference to Medicare, Medicaid, Tricare, and insurance programs for veterans. *See* "Publication of the OIG Special Advisory Bulletin on the Effect of Exclusion From Participation in Federal Health Care Programs," 64 *Fed. Reg.* 52791 (1999), n1.

funded health care programs.[167] The following is a brief discussion of the history of the exclusion sanction, as well as the process required for its imposition.

B. History of Exclusionary Authority

Congress first required the exclusion of "physicians and other practitioners convicted of program-related crimes from participation in Medicare and Medicaid" in 1977.[168] In 1981, Congress added CMPs as an additional sanction and extended the reach of exclusion and CMPs from physicians and practitioners to include individuals and entities who submitted false, fraudulent, "or otherwise improper claims" to Medicare or Medicaid.[169] In 1987, Congress distinguished conduct that would result in automatic exclusion from conduct that allowed HHS the discretion to exclude the offending parties.[170]

As discussed earlier in this chapter, HIPAA and the BBA broadened the scope of exclusion and CMPs, extending the sanctions from Medicare and Medicaid to all Federal and State health care programs.[171] The BBA explicitly provided that HHS could impose CMPs "against health care providers or entities that employ or enter into contracts with excluded individuals for the provision of goods and services or items to Federal program beneficiaries."[172] HHS can assess CMPs plus treble damages for each violation:

> [Penalties include] a civil money penalty of not more than $10,000 for *each item or service* [provided by an excluded entity or individual] . . . or in cases [involving kickbacks, bribes, or rebates] $50,000 for *each such act*. In addition, [the excluded party or provider employing or contracting with an excluded party] shall be subject to an assessment of not more than 3 times the amount claimed for each such item or service . . . (or, in cases [involving kickbacks, bribes, or rebates], damages of not more than 3 times the total amount of remuneration offered, paid, solicited, or received, without regard to whether a portion of such remuneration was offered, paid, solicited, or received for a lawful purpose).[173]

---

167   Approximately 17,000 individuals and entities have been excluded from participating in Federal health care programs to date. The HHS Office of Inspector General estimates that it will exclude about 3,000 more such parties during the fiscal year 1999. BNA Health Care Fraud Report, October 6, 1999, at 863.

168   "Publication of the OIG Special Advisory Bulletin on the Effect of Exclusion from Participation in Federal Health Care Programs" ("Special Advisory Bulletin"), 64 *Fed. Reg.* 52791, 52792 (1999) (*citing* the Medicare-Medicaid Anti-Fraud and Abuse Amendments, Public Law 95-142).

169   *Id.* (citing Civil Monetary Penalties Law, Public Law 97-35).

170   *Id.* (citing the Medicare and Medicaid Patient and Program Protection Act of 1987, Public Law 100-93).

171   *See* Section VI B.6, and Section VII, *supra*.

172   *Id.*; 42 U.S.C. §1320a-7a(a)(6).

173   42 U.S.C. §1320a-7a (emphasis supplied).

Imposing CMPs on providers who either directly or indirectly transact business or contract with excluded parties has the effect of shifting the program oversight burden from HHS to the health care community.[174] The HHS OIG recently acknowledged as much, offering its view on the relationship between exclusion and self-monitoring by the provider community.

> Exclusion is one of the most important tools we have to protect beneficiaries and stem fraud and abuse in federal health care programs. . . . To ensure that Medicare, Medicaid, and other federal health care programs are protected, we need the cooperation of the entire health care community to help make sure excluded individuals are not involved in any way in the care of federal program beneficiaries.[175]

The exclusion authority also prohibits federal reimbursement to individuals or entities that "know or should know" that services or products were supplied at the medical direction or prescription of an excluded physician.[176] Providers will find little or no relief in attempts to isolate excluded practitioners or employees from direct patient care by assigning them to administrative or other job duties, as the OIG defines reimbursement broadly.

> This payment ban applies to all methods of Federal program reimbursement, whether payment results from itemized claims, cost reports, fee schedules or a prospective payment system (PPS). . . . This prohibition applies even when the Federal payment itself is made to another provider, practitioner or supplier that is not excluded. The prohibition . . . also extends to payment for administrative and management services not directly related to patient care, but that are a necessary component of providing items and services to federal program beneficiaries. . . . In addition, no Federal program payment may be made to cover an excluded individual's salary, expenses or fringe benefits, regardless of whether they provide direct patient care.[177]

The OIG concedes the severity of exclusion as a remedy. "In many instances, the practical effect of an OIG exclusion is to preclude employment of an excluded individual *in any capacity* by a health care provider that receives reimbursement, indirectly or directly" from a government payor.[178] The OIG "urges" that the provider community "check the OIG List of Excluded Individuals/Entities on the OIG website (www.hhs.gov/oig) prior to hiring or contracting with individuals or entities," as well as conduct periodic checks of its current staff and contractors.[179]

---

174 *Id.*

175 Remarks of Inspector General June Gibbs Brown, News Release, Office of Inspector General—Office of Public Affairs, September 28, 1999. Industry associations argue that HHS-imposed self-policing places "a heavy administrative burden on direct providers, forcing them to track every product manufactured by an excluded company to make sure they are not using these products for Medicare/Medicaid patients." BNA Health Care Fraud Report, October 6, 1999, at 863.

176 Special Advisory Bulletin, 64 *Fed. Reg.* at 52792.

177 *Id.* at 52792-52793.

178 *Id.* at 52793 (emphasis supplied).

179 *Id.*

C. Grounds for Exclusion

The law enumerates situations in which persons and entities must be excluded from participation in Federal health care programs and when they may be excluded, subject to the exercise of discretion by HHS. The OIG bears the responsibility for overseeing the application of exclusion against individuals and entities in both mandatory and permissive circumstances.

1. Mandatory Exclusion

Exclusion from participation in Federal health care programs is mandatory when an individual or entity has been convicted of (a) "a criminal offense related to the delivery of an item or service under [the Social Security Act] or under any State health care program"; (b) a crime relating to neglect or abuse of patients; (c) any felony convictions related to "fraud, theft, embezzlement, breach of fiduciary responsibility, or other financial misconduct" within the health care industry; and (d) felony convictions related to the misuse of controlled substances.[180] No exclusion under this provision may be for a term of less than five years, except under extremely narrow circumstances.[181] Factors such as the degree of financial loss suffered by the government program, repeat offenses, impact on victims of the crime, the sentence imposed by the criminal court, prior criminal record, and degree of overpayment received by the offender, may be viewed as aggravating factors and used as a basis for lengthening the period of the exclusion beyond the minimum five-year period.[182] There are also mitigating factors for consideration when aggravating factors justify an exclusion longer than five years, but mitigating factors cannot reduce the length of the exclusion below five years.[183]

2. Permissive Exclusion

There are a broad range of circumstances that trigger HHS discretion to exclude an offender from Medicare programs for less than five years. As set forth at 42 U.S.C. § 1320a-7(b), the grounds for permissive exclusion are:

a. Convictions relating to misdemeanor or non-program fraud, in general;

b. Convictions relating to obstruction of any investigation of program-related crimes;

c. Misdemeanor convictions relating to controlled substances;

---

180   42 U.S.C. § 1320a-7(a); 42 C.F.R. § 1001.101. *See also Manocchio v. Kusserow,* 961 F.2d 1539 (11th Cir. 1992) (rejecting constitutional challenge to mandatory exclusion provision).

181   42 U.S.C. § 1320a-7(c)(3)(b); 42 C.F.R. § 1001.102(a).

182   42 C.F.R. § 1001.102(b).

183   The mitigating factors include: (1) whether the offender was convicted of three or fewer misdemeanors; (2) whether the amount of financial loss to government programs was under $1500; (3) conditions which served to reduce the offender's criminal culpability; and (4) the individual's cooperation with investigations that resulted in others being convicted or excluded from Medicare programs or other civil penalties. 42 C.F.R. § 1001.102(c).

204 Corporate Fraud Investigations & Compliance Programs

d. Revocation or suspension of license by State licensing authority, or surrender of the license during disciplinary proceedings;

e. Exclusion or suspension under Federal or State health care programs for reasons related to professional competence, performance, or integrity;

f. Claims for excessive charges or unnecessary services and failure of certain organizations (including health maintenance organizations) to furnish medically necessary services;

g. Fraud, kickbacks, and other prohibited activities;

h. Exclusion of entities directly or indirectly controlled by a sanctioned individual (including ownership or control of at least five percent of a health care organization);

i. Failure to disclose required information;

j. Failure to supply requested information on subcontractors and suppliers, including ownership or significant business transactions;

k. Failure to supply payment information requested or to permit examination of financial records by HHS;

l. Failure to grant immediate access as required by HHS or state agencies to determine compliance with program requirements or to review books and records;

m. Failure by a hospital to take corrective action as required by 42 U.S.C. § 1395ww(f)(2)(B);

n. Default on health education loans or scholarship obligations; and

o. Direct or indirect ownership or control, or an officer or manager position, held by an individual in a sanctioned entity when the individual knew or should have known of the basis for the entity's sanction.

Both the statutes and regulations provide additional guidance regarding the proper circumstances for exclusion and establish periods for permissive exclusion ranging from one to three years.[184] Aggravating and mitigating factors should be weighed in determining the length of exclusion for each offense.[185] Unlike mandatory exclusions, however, HHS has discretion to reduce the length of the exclusion below that suggested by the regulation, so long as appropriate mitigating circumstances exist.[186]

3. Permanent Exclusion for Three Program Convictions

The BBA establishes incremental sanctions for health care related offenses, culminating in the "three strikes and you're out" permanent exclusion of individuals

---

184   42 U.S.C. §1320a-7(c)(3)(D); 42 C.F.R. § 1001.201(b).

185   42 C.F.R. §1001.201(b).

186   42 C.F.R. §1001.201(b)(1).

convicted of three offenses that require mandatory exclusion.[187] Individuals convicted of a health care-related crime after August 5, 1997 will be excluded for a period of 10 years if they have been convicted "on one previous occasion of one or more offenses for which a [mandatory] exclusion may be effected."[188] The exclusion "shall be permanent" if the individual had been convicted "on 2 or more previous occasions of one or more offenses for which [mandatory] exclusion may be effected. . . ."[189]

4. Exclusion In Other Statutory Provisions

Two other permissive exclusions exist outside of 42 U.S.C. § 1320a-7. First, Congress established an elaborate system for imposing CMPs for improperly filed claims, including claims for items or service for which false or misleading information was given.[190] Under the regulations, HHS may also elect to exclude a program participant in lieu of or in addition to imposing a CMP or assessment.[191] The regulations also enumerate various factors that must be considered in assessing the amount of CMPs, such as the circumstances surrounding the violation and whether there is a history of prior offenses.[192] These factors must be considered in determining whether to exclude a person under the same regulatory provisions. Apart from establishing upper limits per violation and providing general references to obvious factors to be considered, the regulations provide wide latitude in determining penalties, assessments, and exclusions.[193]

Second, a practitioner may be excluded from participation in Medicare and other related programs if a peer-review organization (PRO) submits a report to HHS stating that the individual has failed to meet appropriate standards of care or has provided medically unnecessary services.[194] If HHS concurs in the findings of the PRO report and determines that the practitioner is unwilling or unable to comply, HHS may exclude the practitioner, either permanently or for any other period not less than one year, from eligibility to provide services on a reimbursable basis.[195] Regulations promulgated by HHS set out the procedures used in PRO review.[196]

---

187   42 U.S.C. §1320a-7(c)(3)(G).

188   42 U.S.C. §1320a-7(c)(3)(G)(i).

189   42 U.S.C. §1320-7(c)(3)(G)(ii).

190   42 U.S.C. § 1320-7a(a); 42 C.F.R. § 1003.102.

191   42 C.F.R. § 1003.105(a)(1).

192   42 C.F.R. § 1003.106(a).

193   *See* 42 C.F.R. Part 1003.

194   42 U.S.C. § 1320c-5(b).

195   *Id.*

196   *See* 42 C.F.R. Part 1004.

D. Due Process Protections in the Exclusion Process

Generally, if HHS proposes to exclude an individual or entity either on a mandatory or permissive basis, it must provide written notice of its intent, the basis for the exclusion, and the potential effect of an exclusion.[197] Within thirty days of receipt of notice (which will be deemed to be five days after the date on the notice) the individual or entity may submit documentary evidence and written argument and request oral argument concerning whether the exclusion is warranted and any related issue.[198] If HHS proposes to exclude an individual or entity for failure to grant immediate access to records, failure to take corrective action required by HCFA, or a default on health education loans or scholarship obligations, there is no requirement that thirty day notice be provided.[199]

The due process protections afforded individuals and entities proposed for exclusion differ depending on the nature of the alleged violation. The following discussion divides the various bases for program exclusion into categories according to the extent of due process protections under HHS procedures.

1. Mandatory Exclusion Requiring No Hearing

The basis for mandatory exclusion from participation in Federal health care programs is a criminal conviction for either program-related crimes or patient abuse.[200] An individual or entity is considered to have been "convicted" of a criminal offense where there has been:

a. Judgment of conviction entered by a Federal, State or local court, regardless of whether there is an appeal pending or whether the conviction or other record of criminal conduct has been expunged;

b. Finding of guilt against the individual or entity by a Federal, State or local court;

c. Plea of guilty or *nolo contendere* by the individual or entity accepted by a Federal, State or local court, or;

d. The individual or entity has entered into participation in a first offender, deferred adjudication, or other arrangement or program where judgment of conviction has been withheld.[201]

Where an exclusion is based on the existence of a conviction, a determination by another government agency, or similar prior determination, the individual or entity excluded may request a hearing before an administrative law judge (ALJ) only on

---

197   42 C.F.R. § 1001.2001(a).

198   *Id.*

199   42 C.F.R. §1001.2001(b).

200   42 U.S.C. § 1320a-7(a).

201   42 U.S.C. § 1320a-7(i); *Travers v. Shalala*, 20 F.3d 993, 996 (9th Cir. 1994) (first-offender program classified as a conviction under 42 U.S.C. § 1320a-7(i)(4)).

the issues of whether a basis for the imposition of the sanction exists and whether the length of the exclusion is unreasonable.[202] No hearing on the length of the exclusion can be requested when HHS imposes a mandatory exclusion for five years, since those circumstances permit no discretion over the terms of the exclusion and mitigating circumstances may not be considered.[203]

Courts have established that HHS reliance on past convictions as a basis for exclusion does not violate the double jeopardy or *ex post facto* clauses of the United States Constitution. These and other challenges to the constitutionality of the statute have been rejected.[204]

2. Permissive Exclusion by Judicial or Agency Determination

Five bases for permissive exclusion are derivative from determinations made by courts or other Federal or State agencies:

a. Conviction related to fraud;

b. Conviction related to obstruction of an investigation;

c. Misdemeanor conviction related to controlled substances;

d. License revocation or suspension, and

e. Suspension or exclusion under a Federal or State health care program.[205]

As in the case of mandatory exclusions, the regulations provide that where an exclusion is based on a prior conviction or determination by a government agency, the basis for the underlying determination is not reviewable, nor can it be collaterally attacked on substantive or procedural grounds.[206] The government will not re-examine determinations made during a separate hearing, at which time the petitioner or respondent presumably benefited from a hearing on the merits. Although there is no hearing on the merits, mitigating circumstances may be addressed by the sanctioned party to reduce the term of the exclusion.

---

202   42 C.F.R. § 1001.2007(a)(1).

203   42 C.F.R. § 1001.2007(a)(2); *Kahn v. Inspector General of the United States Department of Health and Human Services*, 848 F. Supp. 432, 436-7 (S.D.N.Y. 1992)("[T]he Secretary, once determining that [defendant] had been convicted of a program-related offense, had no discretion over [defendant's] exclusion.")

204   *See Manocchio v. Kusserow*, 961 F.2d 1539 (11th Cir. 1992); *Greene v. Sullivan*, 731 F. Supp. 838 (E.D. Tenn. 1990).

205   42 U.S.C. § 1320a-7(b)(1)-(5); 42 C.F.R. §§ 1001.201, 301, 401, 501, and 601.

206   42 C.F.R. § 1001.2007(d).

3. Allegations Requiring Hearing Before Exclusion

a. ALJ Hearing Required

Generally, a party may be excluded from participating in Medicare and other related programs while the appeal of its exclusion is pending before the ALJ.[207] However, there are exceptions to this rule, including when an individual or entity is excluded under 42 U.S.C. § 1320a-7(b)(7) (fraud, kickbacks), which entitles the sanctioned party to a hearing before an ALJ before any exclusion based on such determination can take effect.[208] However, if HHS determines that the health or safety of the individual receiving services warrants the exclusion taking effect immediately, a hearing may not be a prerequisite for the exclusion to begin.[209]

CMPs, however, may not be imposed prior to such time as a party has been given written notice and an opportunity for the determination to be made on the record after a hearing.[210] An exclusion thus may accompany a CMP only after a full hearing. However, a majority of cases under 42 U.S.C. § 1320a-7a result in negotiated settlements, thus reducing the frequency of hearings before an ALJ to resolve these matters.[211]

An exclusion issued under 42 U.S.C. § 1320c-5, which relates to exclusions based on PRO recommendations, may require a hearing prior to exclusion if the practitioner in question is located in a rural health professional shortage area or in a county with a population of less than 70,000 people.[212] This hearing is intended to address the risk inherent in allowing a practitioner to continue working in a community where there may be no alternative sources of medical services.[213] If the practitioner does not fall within this specific provision, the HHS notice of sanctions to the practitioner is effective fifteen days from the receipt of the notice.[214]

b. Hearing procedures

Under the regulations, the government has the burden of going forward and the burden of persuasion as to liability and aggravating circumstances.[215] The individual or entity subject to exclusion has the burden of proving mitigating circumstances.[216] Both sides may obtain document production, and the ALJ may consider

---

207   *Ram v. Heckler*, 792 F.2d 444, 447 (4th Cir. 1986).

208   42 U.S.C. §1320a-7(f)(2).

209   *Id.*

210   42 U.S.C. § 1320a-7a(c)(2).

211   *See* L. Foley and L. Morris, *Protecting Medicare and Medicaid: An Examination of the Powers of the Health and Human Services' Inspector General*, 40 Fed. B. News & J. 45 (1993).

212   42 U.S.C. §1320c-5(b)(5).

213   *Id.*

214   42 C.F.R. § 1004.110(b).

215   42 C.F.R. § 1005.15(b)(2).

216   42 C.F.R. § 1005.15(b)(1).

hearsay evidence.[217] The ALJ's decision, based on written findings of facts and conclusions of law, may affirm, increase, or decrease the penalty, assessment, or exclusion proposed by HHS.[218] The decision may be appealed by either side to the HHS Departmental Appeals Board.[219] Exclusion cases under 42 U.S.C. §§ 1320c-5 and 1320a-7 are reviewed by the district courts, while CMPs are reviewed in the courts of appeal.[220]

E. Reinstatement into Federal Health Care Programs

An individual or entity excluded from participation in Federal health care programs may apply for reinstatement at the end of the minimum period of exclusion.[221] HHS may at that time determine that there is no basis for further continuance of the exclusion, and that there are reasonable assurances that the types of actions which formed the basis for the original exclusion have not recurred and will not recur.[222] The exclusion will not be lifted unilaterally by HHS; an application by the excluded party is required.[223] Regulations setting out procedures to be used during the reinstatement process may be found at 42 C.F.R. § 1001.3001.

IX. Compliance Programs Are a Virtual Requirement in the Health Care Industry

The combination of civil, criminal and administrative penalties to which health care providers are subject, along with the tremendous increase in the federal, state and private resources now devoted to identifying and prosecuting fraud, waste and abuse in the health care industry, make the implementation of an effective compliance program mandatory for all but the most risk seeking providers of health care items and services.

In 1996, the Delaware Court of Chancery held that, at least in the health care industry, corporate directors and officers may be held personally liable for damages when they have failed to implement an effective program for monitoring and reporting on the corporation's compliance with applicable laws and regulations. This case, *In Re Caremark International, Inc. Derivative Litigation,*[224] represents a significant change from the previously accepted view that directors and officers were not required to implement compliance programs unless they had a reason to believe that unlawful activity was occurring. The case is discussed in more detail in

---

217   42 C.F.R. §§ 1005.7(a), 1005.7(c), 1005.17(b).

218   42 C.F.R. § 1005.20(b).

219   42 C.F.R. § 1005.21(a).

220   *See* 42 U.S.C. §§ 1320c-5(b)(4), 1320A-7(f), 1320a-7a(e), and 405(g).

221   42 U.S.C. § 1320a-7(g); 42 C.F.R. §§ 1001.3001-3005.

222   42 U.S.C. § 1320a-7(g)(2); 42 C.F.R. § 1001.3002(a)(1).

223   42 U.S.C. §1320a-7(g)(1); 42 C.F.R. § 1001.3001.

224   1996 Del. Ch. LEXIS 125 (September 25, 1996).

the chapter on the Corporation's Duty to Investigate.[225] It documents the judicial adoption of recent trends in the principles of corporate governance. These trends require a higher standard of oversight on the part of directors with respect to corporate activities.[226] For example, in 1994, the American Law Institute ("ALI") published its Principles of Corporate Governance, which stated that a failure of directors and officers to institute and periodically evaluate compliance systems in corporate organizations can form the basis for personal liability of the officers and directors.[227] In order to avoid liability, directors should implement compliance programs which, upon objective scrutiny, are effective in ensuring that the behavior of the company is in compliance with the law.[228] *Caremark* represents the first time that these principles were used to evaluate the actions of directors of a health care organization when considering issues of personal liability.

In *Caremark*, the court held that several factors had combined to impose greater responsibility on boards of directors in compliance matters. First was the "increasing tendency, especially under federal law, to employ the criminal law to assure corporate compliance with external legal requirements. . . ."[229] Second was the adoption in 1991 of the United States Sentencing Commission's Organizational Sentencing Guidelines.[230] These Guidelines provide for penalties that "often massively exceed those previously imposed on corporations."[231] In addition, the Guidelines "offer powerful incentives for corporations today to have in place compliance programs to detect violations of law, promptly to report violations to public officials when discovered, and to take prompt, voluntary remedial efforts."[232] These developments, in conjunction with the serious responsibilities of boards of directors and senior officers to make informed decisions, make it imperative for corporations to implement monitoring and reporting systems that are reasonably designed to provide accurate information regarding the corporation's compliance with legal requirements. The court held that this requirement would be imposed even in the absence of information that would give the directors and officers reason to suspect that wrongdoing was occurring.[233]

In addition to the obvious benefit of avoiding personal liability for directors and officers, an effective compliance program brings numerous other benefits to a health

---

225 *See* Chapter 2.

226 *See generally* Principles of Corporate Governance, American Law Institute, 1994.

227 *See also* Richard S. Gruner, *Personal Liability of Corporate Officers and Directors for Inadequate Law Compliance Systems*, C110 ALI-ABA 169 (1995).

228 *See* Richard S. Gruner, *Officer and Director Liability for Inadequate Legal Compliance Systems*, Preventative Law Reporter, Summer 1995.

229 *Caremark*, 1996 Del. Ch. LEXIS at *32.

230 For further information about the Sentencing Guidelines, see Chapter 8.

231 *Caremark, supra* at 180.

232 *Id* at *33.

233 *Id.* at *37-38.

care company. As discussed in detail in the chapter on compliance programs,[234] an effective compliance program can be the catalyst for: (1) avoiding criminal conduct by the company or its employees; (2) dissuading enforcement authorities from bringing criminal charges; (3) establishing a lack of criminal or fraudulent intent at trial; and (4) providing for a substantially reduced penalty in the event of a criminal conviction. In short, a compliance program provides the most cost-effective way to protect the company and the individuals involved in management from the potentially massive liabilities which could arise from a government or private fraud investigation.

In addition to the more general benefits of compliance programs outlined above, there is another that is quite specific to health care providers. If a company in the health care industry that does not have a compliance program is investigated and charged with civil, criminal or administrative violations, it is virtually certain that any subsequent resolution of the matter will involve the mandatory imposition of a compliance program. "The Office of Inspector General imposes corporate integrity obligations on health care providers as part of global settlements of governmental investigations arising under a variety of false claims statutes. A provider consents to these obligations in exchange for the Office of Inspector General's agreement not to exclude that health care provider from participation in Medicare, Medicaid and other Federal health care programs."[235] The compliance programs imposed by the government are typically much more onerous and expensive than any compliance program designed by the health care organization itself. Typical corporate integrity agreements entered into as settlements of health care fraud investigations remain in effect for five years.[236] The compliance programs they impose on settling organizations include at least the following requirements.

- Hire a compliance officer and appoint a compliance committee;
- Develop written standards and policies;
- Implement a comprehensive employee training program;
- Audit billings to Federal health care programs;
- Establish a confidential disclosure program;
- Restrict employment of ineligible persons; and
- Submit a variety of reports to the Office of Inspector General.[237]

All of these activities must be carried out at company expense. While most of the requirements are part of any effective compliance program, the reporting obligations can be very expensive and very intrusive. They typically require audits by

---

234 *See* Chapter 8.

235 Office of Inspector General Web Page: http://www.hhs.gov/progorg/oig/cia/index.htm, "Corporate Integrity Agreements."

236 *Id.*

237 *Id.*

outside firms and will not accept the work product of the company's own internal auditors. They frequently require company employees to submit to interviews by outside entities and require advance waivers of the attorney-client privilege. They also frequently impose personal liability upon officers and directors for violations of the corporate integrity agreement. Finally, they can result in bad publicity and damage to a company's reputation and standing in the community.

X. Special Considerations In Health Care Investigations

Health care investigations involve all of the issues and considerations that are the subjects of the other chapters in this book. There are a number of additional issues, however, that are unique to health care investigations.

A. Potential Duty to Self-Report

Most people clearly understand that it is illegal to submit false information to a government program in order to obtain benefits to which one is not entitled. Medicare and other health care fraud statutes clearly prohibit such behavior. There is an additional concern, however, of which all health care providers must be aware. Even if one obtains payments from Medicare or other federal health care programs honestly, with a good faith belief that a claim is appropriate and completely accurate, if it is later learned that the claim was improper or inaccurate for any reason, the health care provider may have an affirmative duty to return the money. Pursuant to 42 U.S.C. § 1320a-7b(3), it is a felony for any person or entity to conceal or fail to disclose information affecting the person or entity's "initial or continued right" to a benefit or payment already received, if the failure to disclose is done "with an intent fraudulently to secure such benefit or payment." Thus, if a health care provider submits a claim to Medicare and later receives information that the claim was improper in whole or in part, Section 1320a-7b(3) imposes an affirmative duty to disclose the inaccurate or improper bill to the Medicare program and to return any amounts to which the provider was not entitled.

In addition, the 1986 amendments to the False Claims Act extended civil liability to anyone who "knowingly makes, uses, or causes to be made or used, a false record or statement to conceal, avoid, or decrease an obligation to pay or transmit money or property to the Government."[238] Unlike Section 1320a-7b(3), this False Claims Act amendment requires an affirmative act of concealment to avoid a repayment obligation.[239] There has not been much case law interpreting either of

---

238   31 U.S.C. § 3729(a)(7).

239   *See Wilkins ex rel. United States v. Ohio*, 885 F. Supp. 1055 (S.D. Ohio 1995) (failure to report events that might result in obligations to the United States found insufficient for reverse false claims liability absent knowing false submission.)

these provisions to date,[240] but prosecutors are talking more and more about using these theories of recovery.

The most difficult issue facing providers and their counsel in dealing with these "reverse false claims" types of theories comes in deciding when, and under what circumstances, there may be an affirmative duty to investigate whether overpayments have been received. Putting aside the issue of what defenses may be available to reverse false claims charges once they have been brought in either the criminal or civil context, when providers and their counsel are dealing with a situation before it has come to the attention of the government, it appears quite clear that when providers discover clear overpayment situations, they should return the money.[241]

A more difficult situation arises when the provider receives information that, if investigated, may result in the discovery of overpayments. In this context, what is the provider's obligation? Is an internal investigation required? In making the decision, the provider should consider the following. Government enforcement authorities are likely to analyze the situation more strictly than the provider. They may seek to impose liability if they believe that the provider has remained deliberately ignorant of a situation which it should or could have known about with reasonable effort. If a reasonable person under the circumstances would or should know that receipt of an overpayment was likely, enforcement authorities would likely conclude that the provider has an affirmative duty to investigate. If the provider deliberately chooses not to investigate because the results may demonstrate an overpayment, many prosecutors and many *qui tam* relators would seek to impose civil or criminal false claims liability.

These considerations have important implications to the operations of a corporate compliance program. One of the required elements of an effective compliance program is a monitoring and auditing program. The compliance program must identify areas which expose the company to the risk of regulatory violations and test the company's compliance with legal requirements. When compliance programs are new, audits of past billings are more likely to identify errors and improprieties than are likely when a compliance program has been in place for several years. This can trigger obligations to repay overpayments that were previously unknown to the company.

Because of this risk, many companies, through their compliance programs, choose to conduct only "prospective" audits at first. By prospective audits we mean reviews of records of services that have not yet been billed. If errors are discovered

---

240 *See* John T. Boese, Civil False Claims and *Qui Tam* Actions II-(A)(7) (Aspen Law & Business 1995).

241 One situation in which overpayments or double payments frequently arises occurs when a Medicare beneficiary also has private insurance. When payments are received from both payors, the provider's systems should track the resulting "credit balances" by payor and return appropriate amounts to either Medicare or the private insurer.

related to unbilled claims, the errors can be corrected before the bill goes out and overpayment obligations do not arise.

If a company chooses to conduct "retrospective" audits of past billings, it should decide in advance that if a review of any claim reveals a billing error, the company will follow up with an analysis of whether or not there has been an overpayment. If there has been, the company should repay the money promptly. A failure to do so will expose the company to civil and criminal liability. In addition, employees who are aware of the situation become potential *qui tam* relators.

Another issue arises when individual claim reviews disclose mistakes. Must the company simply repay the claim in which the error has been found or must it extrapolate overpayments on all similar claims? The decision on this issue can involve very large sums of money depending on the volume of claims for the same type of service. For this reason, many providers who conduct retrospective reviews or audits choose sample sizes that are not large enough to be statistically significant. In this manner, the review or audit is applicable only to the specific claims and files reviewed and does not trigger broader repayment obligations.

In making a decision on this issue, however, the provider must be very careful about the selection of a sample size. It is possible that the government may view the sample as demonstrating sufficiently serious problems that a duty to conduct further investigation may arise. There are no clear cut answers to these questions. The company and its counsel should be very careful in making decisions about whether and to what extent repayment obligations may be triggered before embarking on an audit or internal investigation. Factors that should be considered are: (1) what information has already come to the attention of the company, and what does it indicate about practices in general as opposed to specific claims; (2) does negative information indicate that overpayments are likely; if so they should be calculated and repaid; (3) if intentional wrongdoing is discovered, the company must be prepared to take appropriate disciplinary action against the wrongdoer no matter what his or her position in the company might be; (4) if billing errors are discovered, the company should examine training and other information provided to the employees in the department(s) where the errors were made; (5) if there is an error in the training and the training error was widespread, rather than isolated to one or two individuals, there may be a duty to expand the audit to discover the scope of the errors made and the impact on company billings; and (6) such expansion of the audits may be required even if it is determined that the errors were inadvertent and unintentional.

Once a determination has been made that the company has received overpayments from a government health care program, and the nature and scope of the overpayments has been determined, the company must decide to whom to report the errors and repay the overpayment. There are a number of options depending on the circumstances. If the reason for the overpayment and its amount are relatively easy to determine, if the overpayments can be traced to specific patients, and if it can be determined that the billing error was not intentional, it is usually best to simply repay through the Medicare carrier or intermediary. If it can be stated truthfully, the overpayment should be returned with an explanation that it came about as a result of an inadvertent billing error or misunderstanding.

On the other hand, if it is determined that the error was intentional, for example, if a regional administrator sought to increase billings to Medicare fraudulently so he or she could reach incentives for a bonus, the company should consider making a formal "voluntary disclosure." The HHS OIG has refined and expanded the formal voluntary disclosure program it instituted in 1995 as part of Operation Restore Trust. In 1998, HHS OIG issued its "Provider Self-Disclosure Protocol."[242]

> "Unlike the earlier pilot program, there are no pre-disclosure requirements, applications for admission or preliminary qualifying characteristics that must be met. The Provider Self-Disclosure Protocol is open to all health care providers, whether individuals or entities. . . ."[243] By its own terms, the Provider Self-Disclosure Protocol "is intended to facilitate resolution of only matters that, in the provider's reasonable assessment, are potentially violative of Federal criminal, civil or administrative laws. Matters exclusively involving overpayments or errors that do not suggest that violations of law have occurred should be brought directly to the attention of the entity (e.g., a contractor such as a carrier or an intermediary) that processes claims and issues payment on behalf of the Government agency responsible for the particular Federal health care program (*e.g.*, HCFA for matters involving Medicare)."[244]

Providers are not legally required to comply with the Provider Self-Disclosure Protocol on any particular matter, but should be aware that if they initially choose to report an overpayment to their carrier or intermediary, the fraud control unit of the carrier or intermediary may refer the matter to OIG on their own initiative. The company should, therefore, carefully consider the nature and amount of any billing errors it discovers, as well as the likelihood that it will be reported to government enforcement authorities before making a final decision on self-reporting.

B. Conduct of Internal Investigations

There are many ways that information about potential improper billing practices can come to the attention of a company in the health care business. Some of the more frequent methods include: (1) a hotline report through the compliance program; (2) an internal audit or claim review through the compliance program; (3) allegations made by a terminated employee; (4) a *qui tam* complaint under the civil False Claims Act; (5) receipt of a civil investigative demand from the Department of Justice; (6) contacts with current or former employees by FBI or OIG investigators; or (7) the execution of a search warrant. If the existence of an investigation comes to the attention of a company through any of these methods, it is prudent for

---

242   A copy of the Provider Self-Disclosure Protocol is attached as Appendix 4.

243   HHS OIG Provider Self-Disclosure Protocol at 3.

244   *Id.*

the company to initiate an internal investigation to determine whether improper practices are occurring.

One of the first decisions a company facing an investigation must make is who should conduct the internal investigation. There are several possible choices, including: the Internal Audit Department; the Compliance Department; in-house counsel; or outside counsel. If the potential exposure can be determined before the investigation begins; it is clear that there is no criminal conduct by the company or its employees; and if it is clear that civil fraud penalties and administrative penalties will not be significant, the investigation can be safely done in-house by the Internal Audit or Compliance departments with oversight and guidance from the inside counsel's office. On the other hand, if the investigation involves potential criminal liability, large civil or administrative penalties or exclusion, it is generally in the company's interest to have the investigation conducted by outside attorneys and consultants.

Several reasons support using outside counsel to conduct an investigation. First, confidentiality of the nature and results of the investigation can be preserved through the use of the attorney-client and work product privileges.[245] Even if the ultimate decision is to disclose the findings, the timing and scope of the disclosure can be controlled by the company if the investigation is conducted by outside counsel. In addition, if billing and coding or other experts are needed to complete the investigation, their work will come under the attorney-client and work product privileges if they are retained by counsel as part of the process of providing legal advice.

Consultants retained directly by and supervised by the company may reach conclusions that the company does not want to disclose. Enforcement authorities know that health care companies frequently hire consultants and that consultant reports can provide a road map to a fraud case for prosecutors. As a result, one of the first items on government subpoenas to health care companies is usually a demand to produce all consultant reports and correspondence. If the consultant is retained by and supervised by outside counsel, any reports written are covered by the attorney-client and work product privilege unless and until the company chooses to make a disclosure.

In addition to the preservation of the confidentiality of internal communications, use of outside counsel will help maintain confidentiality of communications among parties with similar interests. For example, when companies are under investigation, it frequently occurs that individual employees may have interests that are potentially adverse to those of the company. For this reason, the company's counsel cannot also represent all employees. Depending on the law in specific jurisdictions, it is a common practice, and usually a good idea, for a company to indemnify employees for legal expenses related to an investigation of which the

---

245 *See* Chapter 3 on Attorney-Client Privilege.

company is a subject. While the employee may have the right to choose his or her own lawyer, it is prudent for the company's counsel to help identify potential counsel for employees who have the requisite experience necessary to handle a complex medical fraud investigation, and with whom the company's counsel has a good working relationship.

Once counsel for the employee is chosen, the parties can consider whether to enter into a Joint Defense Agreement. The Joint Defense Doctrine extends the confidentiality protections of the attorney-client privilege and work-product doctrine to protect communications between parties where the intent is to further the parties' common interests.[246] In order to obtain the protections of the Joint Defense Doctrine, the party asserting it must establish that: (1) the communication was made in the course of a joint defense effort; (2) the communication was designed to further the joint defense effort; and (3) the protections of the Doctrine have not been waived.[247] A joint defense agreement generally permits more sharing of information between parties and collaboration on strategy. It also enables the parties to reduce costs by dividing the work load. While joint defense agreements are generally beneficial, the parties must recognize that they may be prevented from communicating information learned through the joint defense process, and that they are difficult to enforce if one of the parties discloses information without authorization from the other parties.[248]

C. Parallel Proceedings

As described in the chapter on Parallel Proceedings,[249] there are special considerations which must be taken into account when a company under investigation faces potential criminal, civil and/or administrative liability. This is especially true for health care companies. As enforcement authorities begin to work together with more and more sharing of information, adverse effects can come from many directions. These directions include: DOJ; the FBI; HHS OIG; HCFA and its carriers and intermediaries; state Medicaid Fraud Control Units ("MFCU"); state health care administrators; private insurers and other third-party payors; Medicare and Medicaid fraud contractors; and *qui tam* relators and their counsel. These entities have the power to generate the criminal, civil and administrative penalties that have been described in this chapter. Lawyers who represent health care companies faced with an investigation by one of theses entities must advise his or her clients about the possibility that one or more additional entities will join in the investigation or follow up with a second investigation. Settlement negotiations must take

---

246 *See* Chapter 7.

247 *United States v. Bay State Ambulance and Hospital Rental Service, Inc.*, 874 F.2d 20, 29 (1st Cir. 1989); *United States v. Schwimmer*, 892 F.2d 237, 243 (2d Cir. 1989).

248 *See e.g., FDIC v. Cheng*, 1992 Fed. Sec. L. Rep. (CCH) par. 94, 211 (N.D. Tex. 1992).

249 *See* Chapter 6.

218   Corporate Fraud Investigations & Compliance Programs

into account all of the potential sources of liability, or the client will have no peace of mind that a case is actually over.

Reaching a resolution with all of the potential criminal, civil and administrative enforcement authorities is sometimes easier said than done. Consider the following two hypothetical examples.

In the first case, the state MFCU identified potential overpayments through a routine cost report audit. The MFCU notified its Medicare counterparts and the U.S. Attorney's Office. The company's counsel worked with the MFCU and convinced them not to bring criminal charges. Using an outside consultant, the company's counsel determined that there had been an overpayment and negotiated a civil resolution of that overpayment with the MFCU. Simultaneously, the company's counsel negotiated a waiver of the state Medicaid office's exclusion authority and a civil settlement with the local U.S. Attorney's Office. Through the U.S. Attorney, the company also negotiated a waiver of the HHS OIG's exclusion authority. This package resolution was reached because the company's counsel identified the potential sources of liability and worked cooperatively through the compliance program to resolve them all as part of a package settlement.

The second case involved allegations of Medicare and Medicaid billing fraud and forgeries of physician signatures on order forms. The company's counsel identified the potential sources of liability from government enforcement and regulatory authorities, and engaged in discussions with the MFCU, the U.S. Attorney's Office and OIG. The MFCU and U.S. Attorney's Office were convinced that wrongdoing discovered through an internal investigation conducted by the company's counsel was instigated by the former owners of the company. The MFCU and the U.S. Attorney granted immunity to the company and its employees in exchange for cooperation in the investigation of the former owners. This immunity was granted even though the wrongdoing continued after the company was acquired because the former owner was kept on as a manager. Once the immunity agreement was negotiated, the company's lawyers tried to negotiate an agreement with HHS OIG to waive its permissive exclusion authority as part of the exchange for cooperation. HHS OIG declined to enter into such an agreement at that time, stating that it did not have sufficient information to make an informed decision. OIG representatives stated that they would consider favorably any cooperation by the company but would not guarantee any result.

In the second situation, the company had to decide whether to withhold cooperation with the U.S. Attorney until the OIG had agreed to waive its exclusion authority or to take the risk that its cooperation would generate information that the OIG would later use to seek exclusion. In that case the timing of the negotiations did not permit the company' counsel to wrap up all potential liabilities into a single global agreement. After careful consideration, the company chose to go forward with the criminal immunity agreement and to cooperate in reliance on an assumption that the OIG would act in good faith and would not seek exclusion. In addition, there was potential liability to private insurers that could not be resolved prior to cooperation. In that case, the private insurer had not surfaced as a participant in the investigation. As time goes on, however, and exchanges of information between government agencies and private insurers increases, settlement negotiations are likely to become even more complicated.

There are no guarantees that global settlements can be reached on the timetable of the company under investigation. It is, therefore, incumbent on counsel for the company to consider and disclose to the client all of the possible ramifications of an investigation and not to rely entirely on negotiations with a single enforcement agency. The client will then be in a position to make an informed judgment on the best strategy for going forward.

XI. Conclusion

For the forseeable future, the health care industry will be under heavy scrutiny from a large array of public and private investigative forces. The current bias, particularly of government investigators, is to view billing errors as intentional fraud or the result of reckless practices. The result is that relationships between the industry and its regulators is frequently adversarial. As long as this remains the case, health care companies and their lawyers will have to be aware of and use the internal investigation tools and techniques described in this chapter and the other chapters of this book. In addition, we cannot stress enough the importance of an effective compliance program for health care companies. Good compliance programs bring many benefits at considerably less cost than a single government investigation. They help to identify problems before they come to the government's attention; they help to persuade the government that the company does not have the requisite intent to be charged with criminal violations; they can help to persuade government investigators that the company lacks the intent to be charged with civil fraud violations; they can help persuade the OIG and other regulators that exclusion from government health care programs is not warranted; and in the event of a criminal conviction, they can significantly reduce the penalties imposed.

CHAPTER 11:
ENVIRONMENTAL CRIMES & ENVIRONMENTAL COMPLIANCE

Federal authorities have made the investigation and prosecution of environmental crimes a national priority. The U.S. Department of Justice publicly stated that it intends to vigorously pursue criminal cases against those who violate environmental laws.[1] The Federal Bureau of Investigation ("FBI") identified the investigation of environmental crimes as one of its "national priorities." During 1997, for example, the FBI participated in 31 environmental crimes task forces nationwide; over 400 environmental crime investigations were underway.[2] Finally, the Environmental Protection Agency—Criminal Investigation Division ("EPA-CID"), has continued to increase in size and impact. During fiscal 1998, EPA-CID set a new record for defendants charged (350) and the number of criminal investigations begun (636). EPA-CID referred 266 criminal cases to the Department of Justice for prosecution.[3]

Prosecutors are increasingly charging not only the organization which committed an environmental offense, but also the corporation's officers and managers as well.[4] Penalties for environmental offenses have increased in severity over the years. Federal courts assessed over $90,000,000 in fines against environmental offenders in 1998 alone; $163,000,000 in 1997.[5] Convictions commonly result in significant terms of imprisonment.[6]

---

1   U.S. Dep't of Justice: Strategic Plan (1997—2002)

2   *Id.*

3   EPA Office of Enforcement and Compliance Assurance FY98 Accomplishments Report at 2. [herein after OECA 98 Report]

4   Gaynor Thomas, Bartman, *Criminal Enforcement of Environmental Laws*, 10 Colo. J. Int'l Envt'l L & Pol'y 39 (1999).

5   OECA 98 Report at 2; EPA Press Release, EPA Sets Records for Enforcement While Expanding Program for Industry to Disclose and Correct Violations, Dec. 22, 1997.

6   *See, e.g., Colorado v. Richard Ernest Newman & Thoro Products Co.,*(Dist. Ct., Jefferson County, Co. 1999). The defendants were convicted of dumping bulk quantities of chlorinated solvent into the water table for a 20-year period. In this joint state and federal case, the Court sentenced the company's president to 14 years in prison, fined the company $950,000 and placed the company on 10 years probation. (1999 WL 9310352.)

Given the increasing enforcement of environmental criminal laws, organizations subject to environmental regulation need to protect themselves against both civil and criminal liability. First, organizations and management need to understand the broad scope of environmental laws, and they need to know how those laws apply to them. To that end, we begin this chapter by explaining the chief environmental criminal statutes. Environmental crimes, however, are not limited to just environmental statutes. Prosecutors are increasingly charging traditional offenses together with environmental offenses. Hence, we will briefly review a number of those statutes as well.

Second, corporations and their employees need to know just how easy it is to commit an environmental offense. Though incorrectly characterized as "strict liability" offenses, such a label is not too far from the truth. A person can commit an environmental felony without intending to do so and without any awareness that their conduct violates the law. Indeed, in the Clean Water Act and Clean Air Act, the negligent conduct of an individual or organization can result in a criminal violation. Consequently, the second portion of this chapter will address the theories underlying environmental criminal liability.

Third, we will discuss the reasons why corporations should have environmental compliance programs. Both the Environmental Protection Agency ("EPA") and the Department of Justice ("DOJ") have offered significant incentives to regulated entities that operate environmental compliance programs.

I. Environmental Criminal Statutes

Overall, there are 18 environmental criminal statutes.[7] Of those 18, two statutes, the Clean Water Act and the Resources Conservation and Recovery Act, account for the majority of environmental crime prosecutions.[8] We will focus on the four chief statutes which prosecutors utilize to charge environmental crimes.

---

7   The Department of Justice Manual lists 18 statutes which it classifies as "environmental crimes": Federal Insecticide, Fungicide and Rodenticide Act, 7 U.S.C. §§ 136-136Y; Energy Supply and Environmental Coordination Act, 15 U.S.C. §§ 791-798; Toxic Substances Control Act, 15 U.S.C. §§ 2601-2692; Surface Mining Control and Reclamation Act, 30 U.S.C. §§ 1201-1328; Rivers and Harbors Appropriation Act, Refuse Act, 33 U.S.C. §§ 401-454; Clean Water Act, 33 U.S.C. §§ 1251-1387; Ocean Dumping Act, 33 U.S.C. §§ 1401-1445; Deep Water Port Act, 33 U.S.C. §§ 1501-1524; Act to Prevent Pollution from Ships, 33 U.S.C. §§ 1901-1912; Safe Drinking Water Act, 42 U.S.C. §§ 300F-300J-26; Atomic Energy Act, 42 U.S.C. §§ 2011-2296; Noise Control Act, 42 U.S.C. §§ 4901-4918; Resource Conservation and Recovery Act, 42 U.S.C. §§ 6901-6992K; Clean Air Act, 42 U.S.C. §§ 7401-7671G; Comprehensive Environmental Response, Compensation & Liability Act, 42 U.S.C. §§ 9601-9675; Emergency Planning & Community Right to Know Act, 42 U.S.C. §§ 11001-11050; Outer Continental Shelf Lands Act, 43 U.S.C. §§ 1331-1356; Federal Hazardous Materials Transportation Statute, 49 U.S.C. §§ 5101-5127. Vol. 4 *Dep't of Justice Manual* 5-11.000 Attachment.

8   Turner, *Mens Rea In Environmental Crime Prosecutions*, 23 Colum. J. Envtl. L. 217, 219 (1998).

A. Resource Conservation and Recovery Act (42 U.S.C. §§ 6901-6992k)

The Resource Conservation and Recovery Act ("RCRA") provides "cradle-to-grave" regulation of the generation, transportation, treatment, storage and disposal of hazardous waste. As a part of its regulatory scheme, RCRA mandates that individuals or organizations obtain a permit in order to transport, treat, store or dispose of hazardous waste.

RCRA imposes criminal penalties on individuals or organizations that knowingly:

- transport hazardous waste to a facility which does not have a RCRA permit;
- treat, store, or dispose of any hazardous waste without a permit or in violation of any material condition of a permit;
- omit material information or make false statements or representations in any application, label, manifest, or any other record or report that is filed, maintained or used to comply with RCRA;
- transport hazardous waste or used oil without a manifest;
- export hazardous waste without the consent of the receiving country or if the export violates an international treaty or agreement governing the transport, treatment, storage and disposal of hazardous waste.[9]

The case of *U.S. v. Kelley Technical Coatings, Inc.*,[10] provides a good example of a RCRA prosecution. In that case, the company was an industrial paint manufacturer, and it stored and disposed of hazardous waste at its plants. Though it generated a substantial amount of hazardous waste, the company did not store it properly but let it accumulate at its plant. Hundreds of drums containing hazardous waste accumulated over several years, but the company never applied for a permit to store or dispose of it on site. The company's vice president of manufacturing failed to take any action, though he was responsible for environmental policy compliance. Finally, the company's vice president arranged for a hazardous waste company to drain the company's accumulated waste from the drums on site. After the waste was drained, company employees then poured off rainwater from the drums and repeatedly spilled hazardous waste on the ground in the process. Both the company and its vice president were convicted of RCRA violations: the company was fined $225,000 and the vice president was sentenced to 21 months imprisonment.

Violating any of RCRA's criminal provisions will result in a felony conviction. Courts can impose fines of up to $50,000.00 per day for each violation and/or imprisonment of up to five years. RCRA provides even harsher penalties for anyone who knowingly places another in danger. A person who knowingly transports, treats, stores, disposes or exports hazardous waste and, in doing so, places another

---

9   42 U.S.C. § 6928(d).

10   157 F.3d 432 (6th Cir. 1998).

224 Corporate Fraud Investigations & Compliance Programs

person in eminent danger of death or serious bodily injury can be imprisoned for up to fifteen years. Corporations may be fined up to $1,000,000.00.[11]

B. Clean Water Act (33 U.S.C. §§ 1251-1387)

In passing the Clean Water Act ("CWA"), Congress sought to "restore and maintain the chemical, physical, and biological integrity of the nation's waters," and it established the "national goal" of eliminating the discharge of pollutants into navigable waters.[12] Pursuant to the CWA, the Environmental Protection Agency ("EPA") sets effluent standards on an industry-by-industry basis, and it determines water quality standards governing all contaminants in surface waters. The CWA makes it unlawful for any "person" to discharge any pollutant from a "point source" into any navigable waters of the United States without first obtaining a permit ("NPDES") regulating such discharges.[13]

The CWA provides broad criminal liability not only for "knowing" violations, but it applies to negligent conduct as well. It is a misdemeanor for any "person" to, among other things, *negligently* (a) discharge pollutants into the waters of the United States without a permit or in violation of any permit condition or requirement; (b) fail to provide notice when required of the discharge of any hazardous waste; (c) fail to monitor and maintain required reports of permitted discharges; and (d) negligently introduce in a sewer system or treatment wastes any pollutant or hazardous substances that the person knew or presumably should have known could cause personal injury or property damage.[14]

To "knowingly" violate any of the provisions listed above will result in a felony punishable by imprisonment for up to three years, and fines of up to $50,000 per violation.[15] As in RCRA, the CWA also punishes violators who knowingly endanger others when violating the CWA with prison terms of up to 15 years imprisonment and substantial fines.[16]

Corporations or individuals who "knowingly" make any material false statement or representation in any record required to be maintained by or submitted under the CWA may also be convicted of a felony punishable by up to two years in jail or fines up to $10,000.[17]

The CWA imposes criminal liabilities not only on corporations and their employees who knowingly or negligently violate its provisions, but also on any

---

11   42 U.S.C. § 6928(e).

12   33 U.S.C. § 1251(a).

13   33 U.S.C. § 1311.

14   33 U.S.C. § 1319(c)(1).

15   33 U.S.C. § 1319(c)(2).

16   33 U.S.C. § 1313 (c)(3).

17   33 U.S.C. § 1319(c)(4).

"responsible corporate officer."[18] The CWA does not define what is a responsible corporate officer. We will address the meaning of the concept in the next section below.

CWA prosecutions frequently involve not only violations alleging illegal discharges of hazardous pollutants into waters, but also attempts to fraudulently conceal such discharges. For example, the U.S. Attorney for the Western District of Pennsylvania recently charged the operator of a small waste water treatment plant in Youngsville, PA of violating the CWA. The waste water plant operator violated the CWA by discharging untreated sewage and waste sludge into a nearby creek. In addition, he covered up the fact that the plant was overloaded by tampering with flow monitoring equipment and filing false flow reports. The plant operator pled guilty, and faces imprisonment of up to 7 years and a $500,000 fine.[19]

C. Clean Air Act (42 U.S.C. §§ 7401-7671g)

The Clean Air Act ("CAA") is a complex and comprehensive law that seeks to protect the public by establishing air quality standards and regulating air omissions from area, stationary, and mobile sources. By enacting the CAA, Congress sought to set and achieve National Ambient Air Quality Standards for each state. The CAA also directed the states to develop state implementation plans to regulate industrial pollution in each state. Among its many aims, the CAA provides for the permitting of air pollution sources; the regulation of motor vehicle emissions; and numerous provisions designed to prevent deterioration of air quality from sources such as acid rain, stratospheric ozone depletions, and hazardous air pollutants.

The CAA imposes criminal penalties for "knowing" violations of its numerous provisions, administrative regulations and air quality standards, as well as CAA emission permits.[20] Violating the Act's provisions is a felony punishable by up to 5 years in prison and substantial fines. The CAA also contains a false statement prohibition. Prosecutors may charge any person who knowingly makes any false material statement or omits material information from any document required to be filed and maintained under the Act with a felony punishable by up to two years in jail.[21]

As with other environmental statutes, the CAA threatens increased punishment on violators whose air emissions place another person in imminent danger of death or serious bodily injury.[22] First, the CAA makes it a crime to negligently emit hazardous air pollutants and thereby negligently place another person in imminent danger of death or serious bodily injury. "Negligent endangerment" is a misdemeanor,

---

18   33 U.S.C. § 1319 (c)(6).

19   EPA Press Release, Pennsylvania Treatment Plan Operator Violates Clean Water Act, 8/26/99.

20   42 U.S.C. § 7413(c)

21   *Id.*

22   42 U.S.C. § 7413(c)(4).

punishable by up to one year in jail. Second, the penalties increase substantially if a person knowingly emits hazardous air pollutants that place another person in imminent danger. Knowing violations are subject to imprisonment by up to 15 years, and organizations can be fined up to $1,000,000.00 for each violation.[23]

As in the CWA, the CAA specifically provides that a "responsible corporate officer" is subject to the Act's criminal penalties along with individuals and organizations.[24]

The DOJ has brought relatively few CAA prosecutions.[25] Of those, federal authorities have brought a number of cases for violating federal asbestos regulations. For example, the U.S. Attorney's office in the Eastern District of Kentucky prosecuted the on-site supervisor and project manager who were overseeing the removal of asbestos containing material from a department store in Louisville, Kentucky. By improperly removing the asbestos in violation of federal regulations, the two individuals were sentenced to prison terms of 51 months and 10 months, respectively.[26]

The DOJ has also "cracked down" on illegal sales and imports of chloroflurocarbons ("CFCs") such as "freon." In 1997, DOJ indicted 39 defendants for CFC smuggling.[27]

D. Comprehensive Environmental Response, Compensation and Liability Act (42 U.S.C. §§ 9601-9675)

Congress enacted the Comprehensive Environmental Response, Compensation and Liability Act ("CERCLA" also known as the "Superfund" Act) primarily to control the "vast problems" associated with abandoned and inactive hazardous waste disposal sites.[28] CERCLA also regulates the uncontrolled (i.e., unpermitted) release of hazardous substances by requiring that federal and state authorities be notified when such a release occurs.[29]

CERCLA imposes criminal liability for three kinds of conduct: (a) the failure of any person "in charge" of a vessel or "facility" to give notice of an unpermitted release of hazardous substances as soon as they have knowledge of such release; (b) failing to notify the EPA of the existence of an unpermitted

---

23   42 U.S.C. § 7413(c)(5).

24   42 U.S.C. § 7413(c)(b).

25   Lachenmayr, Lockner, Olson, and Wolpert, *Environmental Crimes*, 35 Am. Crim. L. Rev. 597, 634 (Spring 1998).

26   *U.S. v. Barry Shurelds, et al.*, (Kentucky), OECA 98 Accomplishments Report at 76.

27   DOJ 1997 Annual Report at 63.

28   H.R. Rep. No. N6-1016, 22 (1980), *reprinted in* 1980 U.S.C.C.A.N. 619, 6125.

29   42 U.S.C. § 9603.

hazardous waste disposal site; and (c) knowingly destroying, disposing of, concealing or falsifying records.[30]

CERCLA punishes the knowing failure to notify authorities of the release of hazardous substances by up to three years in jail. The same sentence may also be imposed for destroying or falsifying records.[31] Failing to inform EPA of the existence of a hazardous waste site is a misdemeanor, and violators can be sentenced for up to one year in jail.[32]

CERCLA provides for the payment of rewards of up to $10,000.00 to any person who provides information resulting in the arrest and conviction of any person for violating CERCLA, including its provision for failing to report the spill of hazardous waste.[33]

E. Additional Environmental Criminal Statutes

Though less frequently used than the four chief criminal statutes listed above, DOJ has also brought environmental criminal prosecutions under the following statutes:

(a) The Toxic Substances Control Act ("TSCA"), 15 U.S.C. §§ 2601-2692, regulates chemical substances which present an unreasonable risk of injury to health or the environment. TSCA specifically regulates the use and disposal of polychlorinated biphenyls ("PCB's") in addition to other hazardous chemicals.[34] A willful or knowing violation of TSCA is punishable as a misdemeanor.[35]

(b) The Federal Insecticide, Fungicide, and Rodenticide Act ("FIFRA"), 7 U.S.C. §§ 136-136y, requires the registration of pesticides, prohibits the distribution and sale of any pesticide not registered, and provides that the EPA may limit the distribution, sale or use of unregistered pesticides. FFFRA provides for misdemeanors penalties for knowing violations.[36]

(c) The Rivers & Harbors Act of 1899, 33 U.S.C. §§ 401-467, imposes misdemeanor penalties on anyone who throws, discharges, or deposits "any refuse matter of any kind of description" into the navigable waters of the United States without a permit from the EPA. This Act is broader than the CWA as it is not limited to a "point source."

---

30   42 U.S.C. §§ 9603(b), (c) and (d).

31   42 U.S.C. §§ 9603(b) and (d).

32   42 U.S.C. § 9603(c).

33   42 U.S.C. § 9609(d).

34   15 U.S.C. § 2605(e)

35   15 U.S.C. § 2615(b).

36   7 U.S.C. §§ 136, 136j(b). FIFRA does impose felony liability to anyone who "with intent to defraud" reveals to third parties the product formulas acquired under the Act. 7 U.S.C. 136j(b)(3).

II. Nontraditional "Environmental" Crimes

Environmental criminal prosecutions often include more traditional crimes such as mail fraud, conspiracy, or false statements in addition to counts stating environmental criminal violations. According to DOJ, "[e]xperience has shown that cases involving violations of [environmental crimes] also may involve...other federal statues."[37] In turn, DOJ has specifically authorized environmental crime prosecutors to investigate and prosecute additional crimes that arise in environmental criminal investigations.[38]

For example, in *U.S. v. Eidson*,[39] the U. S. Attorney's Office for the Middle District of Florida prosecuted the owners of a used oil recycling and waste water disposal business not only for CWA criminal violations but also for mail fraud violations. In that case, the defendants violated the CWA by discharging used oil and other pollutants into local storm sewers. Defendants also lied to business customers to obtain their waste water disposal business. By doing so, the indictment charged the defendants with engaging in a scheme to defraud by falsely informing their perspective customers that they had proper licenses and permits to dispose of waste water. Moreover, federal prosecutors seek indictments on the most serious charge that they can prove. Environmental offenses, though felonies, are rarely the most serious offense. Consequently, if the conduct being investigated gives rise to more than just an environmental offense, prosecutors will charge not only the environmental offense but more traditional offenses such as the following:

A. Conspiracy to Commit Offense or to Defraud the United States, 18 U.S.C. § 371

The crime of conspiracy consists of an agreement between two or more persons either to "commit any offense against the United States" or "to defraud the United States." A conspirator is anyone who participates in the criminal plan or agreement, no matter how small their role is. The object of the conspiracy, the crime against the United States, can be any federal statute including environmental offenses such as CWA.

For example, in *U.S. v. Weitzenhoff*,[40] the Court upheld the conviction of the manager and assistant manager of a sewage treatment plant who conspired to violate the CWA by participating in a scheme to discharge sludge in violation of the plant's NPDES permit. Conspiracy is a felony punishable up to five years imprisonment, and violators can be subject to substantial fines.

---

37   Vol. 4 DOJ Manual 5-11.102.

38   *Id.*

39   108 F.3d 1336 (11th Cir. 1997).

40   35 F.3d 1275 (9th Cir. 1993).

B. False Statements, 18 U.S.C. § 1001

Section 1001 makes it a federal crime to knowingly and willfully make any materially false or fraudulent statement or representation, either oral or written, to any person or make or use any false writing or document known to contain a materially false statement or entry. The statute applies to false statements or documents that fall within the broad jurisdiction of the "executive, legislative, or judicial branch of the government of the United States." Violations of this statute are punishable by up to five years imprisonment. False statement prosecutions are frequently made in environmental cases. Perpetrators commonly submit false records such as monthly discharge reports or lab results to federal agencies or state agencies administering federal programs in order to cover up other violations.

C. Mail and Wire Fraud, 18 U.S.C. §§ 1341, 1343

Mail fraud and wire fraud are probably the most widely used federal criminal statutes. They apply to anyone who attempts to defraud another person and in so doing utilizes the mails, commercial interstate carriers such as FedEx, or uses the wires (faxes, telephones, radios, or television) for interstate or foreign communications. Mail and wire fraud are punishable by up to five years imprisonment along with substantial fines.

D. Money Laundering Control Act , 18 U.S.C. §§ 1956, 1957

Few people think of money laundering in conjunction with environmental crimes, and there are no reported cases where money laundering and environmental offenses have been charged together—yet. Given its severe penalties, however, prosecutors are increasingly including money laundering as the most severe offense in indictments of more traditional crimes such as mail fraud and wire fraud.[41] It is only a matter of time before money laundering is charged together with environmental offenses.

A person or organization commits money laundering when they utilize "the proceeds of some form of unlawful activity" to conduct a "financial transaction" with the intent either to promote the carrying on of "specified unlawful activity" or by engaging in a transaction intended to conceal or disguise the source and nature of the proceeds of the specified unlawful activity.[42] People often think of money laundering as an attempt to conceal illegal proceeds in a financial transaction, and the

---

41 Money laundering and fraud are very similar, and in some cases may be factually indistinguishable. Under the Federal Sentencing guidelines, the same fraudulent conduct, if charged as money laundering, is punished much more severely. For example, consider someone who steals $100,000 using the mail and deposits the money in a bank under a false name to avoid detection. If charged as fraud without any enhancements, the sentence would be roughly 10-16 months in prison. If charged as money laundering, the sentence would be 33-41 months in prison. *Compare* U.S.S.G. 2Fl.1 and 2S1.1.

42 18 U.S.C. § 1956 (a).

majority of reported cases reflect that. Money laundering also occurs when a person or corporation uses proceeds from an ongoing "unlawful activity" to keep the corporation operating.

For example, prosecutors could have charged the manager and the assistant manager of the sewage treatment plant in the *Weitzenhoff* case with money laundering. By discharging sewage sludge in violation of the plant's NPDES permit, the two defendants carried on "an unlawful" activity and in doing so billed customers for handling their waste. Under the Money Laundering Act, the receipt of customer payments may be characterized as "proceeds from an unlawful activity," *i.e.*, CWA violations. In turn, the defendants used those "proceeds" to continue operating the plant, which continued to discharge sludge in violation of the CWA. The ongoing CWA violations qualify as "specified unlawful activity" under the Money Laundering Act.[43] Thus, prosecutors could have charged the plant manager with using customer payments from CWA violations to operate the plant and "promote the carrying on" of additional CWA violations.

Offenders who commit money laundering can be sentenced to imprisonment for up to twenty years, and fined up to $500,000.00 or twice the value of the property involved in the transaction whichever is greater.

III. The Basis of Environmental Criminal Liability

There has been significant confusion as to how environmental criminal liability arises. What criminal intent must a person have to commit an environmental crime? Is it a strict liability offense? And who is liable? The corporate president, the managers, employees? Employees and businesses regulated by environmental laws need to know the answers to these questions to conduct their businesses lawfully.

To better understand the unique nature of environmental crimes, we will first briefly explain the distinguishing characteristic of traditional crime: the requirement of guilty knowledge. Second, we will show that environmental felonies have not entirely done away with the requirement that a perpetrator act willfully or possess guilty knowledge—but such a traditional characteristic has been substantially diluted. To commit an environmental a person must only have knowledge of the facts; they do not need to be aware that their conduct is illegal. Third, we will examine how a "responsible corporate official" can be criminally responsible for the conduct of another in CAA and CWA cases. As we will see, prosecuting "responsible corporate officers" for the *negligent* acts of subordinates is very similar to strict liability offenses.

Environmental criminal offenses differ markedly from traditional "common law" crimes. Historically, to commit a common law crime such as theft, fraud or murder, the perpetrator had to have what is known as "criminal intent" or "mens rea."

---

43   18 U.S.C. § 1956 (c)(7)(e).

Courts traditionally characterized this mental element of an offense with terms such as "guilty knowledge," "vicious will," "willfulness," and "scienter."[44] Essentially, a person had to be conscious that their conduct amounted to wrong doing.[45] To prove a person committed a crime, therefore, meant that the prosecutor had to show that the person acted intentionally and knew their conduct was wrong. As the Supreme Court observed:

> That an injury can amount to a crime only when inflicted by intention is . . . as universal and persistent in mature systems of law as belief in freedom of the human will and a consequent ability and duty of the normal individual to choose between good and evil.[46]

Though it has not entirely dispensed with *mens rea*, Congress has substantially diluted the amount of criminal intent necessary for proving criminal liability for environmental felony and most misdemeanor offenses.[47] To be convicted of a felony environmental offense under CWA, CAA, or RCRA, the prosecution must simply show the defendant had "knowledge" of the facts constituting the crime. To steal, you have to intend to take the property of another; to commit a fraud, you have to purposely make a false statement to another. A person who knowingly commits an environmental crime, however, *does not* have to have a guilty mind to commit a crime. Rather, they simply must be conscious of the facts that give rise to the offense. Clearly, by using the word "knowingly" in environmental criminal statutes, Congress "intended to provide a different and lesser standard [of *mens rea*]."[48] We examine what it means to "knowingly" commit an environmental offense below.

First, to knowingly violate an environmental offense, the perpetrator must have knowledge of each element of the offense. For example, in *U.S. v. Wilson*,[49] the jury convicted the defendant of violating the CWA by "knowingly discharging fill material and excavated dirt into wetlands on four separate parcels without a permit, in violation of the Clean Water Act."[50] The appellate court reversed the defendant's conviction because the district court failed to properly instruct the jury that they had to find that the defendant acted knowingly with regard to each element of the offense. To knowingly commit each element of a CWA violation, the prosecution must show:

> (1) that the defendant knew he was discharging a substance, eliminating a prosecution for accidental discharges;

---

44 *Morissette v. U.S.*, 342 U.S. 246, 252 (1952).

45 *Id.* at 251-52.

46 *Id.* at 250.

47 *U.S. v. Weitzenhoff*, 35 F.3d at 1293, Dissent From Order Rejecting Suggestion for Rehearing En Banc, ("dilution of traditional requirement of a criminal state of mind")

48 *U.S. v. Wilson*, 133 F.3d 251, 262 (4th Cir. 1997).

49 *Id.*

50 *Id.* at 251.

(2) that the defendant correctly identified the substance he was discharging, not mistaking it for a different, unprohibited substance;

(3) that the defendant knew the method or instrumentality used to discharge the pollutants;

(4) that the defendant knew the physical characteristics of the property into which the pollutant was discharged that identify it as a wetland, such as the presence of water and water-loving vegetation;

(5) that the defendant was aware of the facts establishing the link between the wetlands and waters of the United States; and

(6) that the defendant knew he did not have a permit.[51]

Second, to prove a CWA violation or any other environmental felony, the Government does not have to show that a defendant knew that his conduct was illegal.[52] Rather, the defendant need only "know the facts that make his conduct illegal."[53] For instance, in *Wilson* the Government did not need to show that when the defendant filled in the wetlands, the defendant "understood the legal consequences of those facts"—that he was breaking the law—or that the defendant was even aware of a law prohibiting that conduct.[54] A defendant cannot argue that her or she was mistaken or ignorant about the law.

For environmental offenses, courts have applied the "common law principle" that being ignorant of the law does not excuse its violation in environmental prosecutions.[55] This maxim, moreover, governs not only where a perpetrator was ignorant of an environmental statute, but also where the perpetrator was ignorant of the permit or material provisions of the permit.

For example, in *U.S. v. Sinskey,*[56] the Court rejected the defendant's argument in a CWA prosecution that to be convicted of knowingly violating a CWA permit the defendant had to be aware of the permit. In that case, the defendant, the plant manager of a slaughterhouse that was subject to a CWA permit, knowingly discharged water containing excess amounts of ammonia nitrogen. The defendant contended that to knowingly violate the permit, he had to be aware that his conduct violated the plant's NPDES permit. The court rejected the defendant's contention, and found that the "government was not required to prove that [defendant] knew that his acts violated either the CWA or the NPDES permit, but merely that he was

---

51   *Id*. at 264; *see also U.S. v. Ahmad*, 101 F.3d 386, 391 (5th Cir. 1996) which held that the Government must show knowledge of each element of the offense except for "purely jurisdictional elements" such as that the discharge was into a navigable water of the United States.

52   *Id* at 261.

53   *Id*. at 262, quoted in *Staples v. U.S.*, 511 U.S. 600, 605 (1994).

54   *Id*. at 264.

55   *Id*. at 261.

56   119 F.3d 712 (8th Cir. 1997).

aware of the conduct that resulted in the permit's violation."[57] Finding that defendant's ignorance of the law was not an excuse, the Court observed that anyone, such as defendant, dealing with "dangerous or obnoxious waste . . . must be presumed to be aware of the existence" of any applicable regulations and laws.[58]

Second, if a perpetrator is mistaken about the facts that constitute the environmental crime, then he does not have the requisite knowledge to have committed the offense. The case of *U.S. v. Ahmad*[59] illustrates this "mistake of fact" defense. In *Ahmad*, the prosecutor accused the owner of a convenience store and gas station of discharging gasoline, a pollutant, from one of his gasoline tanks without a permit. That tank had developed a water leak, and contained a substantial amount of water and, according to witnesses, a substantial amount of gasoline as well. When the defendant had the tank pumped, gasoline was pumped into a nearby storm sewer. While there was no dispute that gasoline was pumped out, the defendant argued at trial that he thought at the time he was pumping water. To convict the defendant, the jury had to find that the defendant had knowingly discharged a substance which he knew to be a pollutant. The Court reversed because the jury had not been asked to determine whether the defendant was mistaken about what he pumped out from the tank.

Third, the Government may establish a knowing environmental violation by using circumstantial as well as direct evidence, and that includes evidence that the offender turned a blind eye toward illegal conduct. For example, in *U.S. v. Hopkins*,[60] the appellate court upheld the conviction of a corporate vice president of a manufacturing company who had been charged with falsifying monitoring data and violating the company's NPDES permit. The defendant was responsible for ensuring compliance with the company's NPDES permit, and that permit required the company to test its waste water discharge. Company employees tampered with the testing so that the test results passed.

The defendant contended that he did know that employees had tampered with the monitoring test. The evidence showed, however, that the employees reported to him that they diluted or filtered test samples in order to get a satisfactory sample, and that the defendant replied "I know nothing, I hear nothing."[61] Though the defendant denied he had knowledge of the illegal conduct, the Court instructed the jury that they could find the defendant guilty if he was "willfully ignorant" of his employees' illegal conduct. If the defendant had been aware of a high probability

---

57   *Id.* at 715-16.

58   *Id.* at 716; *but see U.S. v. Johnson & Towers, Inc.*, 741 F.2d 662 (3rd Cir. 1984) wherein the Court held in a RCRA case involving the disposal of hazardous waste without a permit the Court found that the jury must find that each defendant had to know the corporation was required to have a permit and that it did not have a permit.

59   101 F.3d 386 (5th Cir. 1996).

60   53 F.3d 533 (2d Cir. 1995).

61   *Id.* at 536.

that the results were being tampered with and "consciously avoided confirming that fact," then the jury could find that the had knowledge of the illegal conduct.[62]

IV. Environmental Criminal Prosecutions Target the Responsible Corporate Official

Enforcement of environmental criminal laws has increased significantly over the last ten years.[63] Early on, federal prosecutors primarily targeted organizations for prosecution of environmental crimes.[64] More recently, federal prosecutors increasingly target not just a corporate offender for prosecution, but the corporate executives as well.[65] "Prosecution of individuals," observed one commentator, "now outnumbers prosecutions of corporations by a three to one margin."[66] When federal prosecutors investigate environmental crimes, their goal is to "identify, prosecute, and convict the highest ranking person responsible for the violation."[67]

Not surprisingly, two major environmental criminal statutes, the CAA and CWA, identify the "responsible corporate officer" as being specially subject to prosecution.[68] Neither statute, however, defines what is a responsible corporate officer. In turn, there has been some confusion as to whether a corporate executive or manager can be convicted of an environmental criminal offense simply by virtue of their position in the company as the "responsible corporate officer."

To obtain a better understanding of what is a "responsible corporate officer," we will first show how the legal concept initially arose in the context of prosecutions for strict liability crimes. Second, we will examine how the "responsible corporate officer" doctrine has been and should be applied in the environmental felony offenses. As we will see, prosecuting an individual as a responsible corporate officer does not dispense with the need to demonstrate that the defendant "knowingly" violated the statute. Third, we will show what it means to prosecute a responsible corporate officer for negligently violating the CWA or CAA. To be convicted of negligently violating an environmental offense is tantamount to being subject to strict liability.

---

62   *Id.* at 541-42.

63   Gaynor, Thomas, and Bartman, *Criminal Enforcement Environmental Laws*, 10 Colo. J. Int'l Envtl. L. & Policy 39 (1999).

64   Lachenmyer, Lockner, Olson, Wolpert, *Environmental Crimes*, 35 Am. Crim. L. Rev. 597, 667 (Spring 1998).

65   Comment, *Criminal Sanctions For Deterrence On Needed Weapons, But Self Initiate Auditing Is Even Better*, 55 Ohio St. L. J. 1181, 1186 (1994).

66   *Id.*

67   *Id.*

68   33 U.S.C. § 1319(c)(6); 42 U.S.C. § 7416(c)(6).

V. Responsible Corporate Officer and Strict Liability

The concept of criminal liability for a "responsible corporate officer" arose in the context of "strict liability" or "public welfare" offenses. In strict liability offenses, the prosecution does not have to show that the defendant was aware of or knew about the facts which give rise to the offense.[69] A strict liability offense consists only of "forbidden acts or omissions," and the defendant does not have to have any criminal intent.[70] If the facts giving rise to the offense occur, then the *responsible* defendant may be found guilty regardless of whether he knew about those facts or illegal conditions—or even if the defendant was mistaken about the facts. [71]

The Supreme Court developed the responsible corporate officer doctrine in two seminal strict liability cases: *U.S. v. Dotterweich* and *U.S. v. Park.* In *U.S. v. Dotterweich*,[72] the Supreme Court held a corporation's president strictly criminally liable for delivering misbranded drugs in interstate commerce in violation of the Federal Food, Drugs and Cosmetic Act. In that case, the defendant's corporation had shipped mislabeled drugs, but the defendant did not participate personally in the crime. As a result of his position in the "business process," he was prosecuted because he had a "responsible share" in furthering the corporation's illegal conduct.[73]

The Supreme Court next expanded on responsible corporate officer liability in another strict liability case, *U.S. v. Park.*[74] In *Park*, the defendant, a corporate president, was convicted of allowing his company's food shipments to be exposed to rodent contamination in violation of the Federal Food, Drug, and Cosmetic Act. The defendant did not have knowledge of the violation, but the Court found that he was a criminally responsible "person" under the Act. The Act, observed the Court, imposed a "duty on responsible corporate agents," who by virtue of their responsibility and authority in the corporation had a duty to "prevent or correct the prohibited condition."[75]

---

69   *Staples v. U.S.*, 511 U.S. 600, 607 n. 3 (1994).

70   *Morissette v. U.S.*, 342 U.S. 246, 253 (1952).

71   Strict liability crimes use criminal sanctions to enforce public health, safety and welfare regulations. *Morissette v. U.S.*, 342 U.S. 246, 255 (1952). Strict liability offenses often arise when a "defendant knows he is dealing with a dangerous device of a character that places him in a responsible relation to public danger...[and] the possibility of strict regulation." *Staples v. U.S.*, 511 U.S. at 618. The dangerous nature of the device or activity are "considered sufficient in themselves to place the defendant on notice of the likelihood of regulation and thus...excuse the need to prove *mens rea*." *U.S. v. Wilson*, 133 F.3d at 263. The criminal sanctions for strict liability offenses are usually "relatively small." *Morissette v. U.S.*, 342 U.S. at 256. Indeed, the Supreme Court has suggested that strict liability crimes may not be punishable as felonies. *Staples v. U.S.*, 511 U.S. at 618.

72   320 U.S. 277 (1943).

73   *Id.* at 284.

74   421 U.S. 658 (1975).

75   *Id.* at 673.

Courts interpret the "responsible corporate officer" provisions found in both the CAA and CWA in light of *Dotterweich* and *Park*.[76] A responsible corporate officer, explained the Ninth Circuit,

> is the person who has authority to control the corporation's activity that is causing the discharges. There is no requirement that the officer in fact exercise such authority or that the corporation expressly vest a duty in the officer to oversee the activity.[77]

The responsible corporate officer concept of *Dotterweich/Park*, however, is applied quite differently to CAA and CWA felonies.

First, as discussed above, felony violations of the CAA and CWA require that the defendant have knowledge of the discharge or emission and that the substance discharged or emitted was a pollutant.[78] Just because these statutes reference a "responsible corporate officer," that doctrine does not supersede the statutes' express requirement that the defendant have knowledge.[79]

For example, in *U.S. v. Iverson*,[80] a jury convicted the president and chairman of a company for CWA felony violations as a result of the company discharging chemical residue from drums into the storm sewer. The prosecution alleged that the company president was a responsible corporate officer, and it sought to prove that the president had the "authority and capacity to prevent the discharge of pollutants to the sewer system."[81] Notwithstanding the allegation that the president was a responsible corporate officer, to achieve a felony conviction the Government still "had to prove that the defendant knew that the discharges were pollutants."[82] The Government did this by showing that the defendant had in the past discharged the residual waste himself and ordered employees to do so, and that defendant was "sometimes present" when employees were "cleaning" drums.[83]

Second, though often referred to as "public welfare offenses," environmental felonies are not strict liability offenses due to their requirement of some criminal intent.[84] Several circuit courts, however, have characterized environmental crimes as "public welfare offenses."[85] As *Weitzenhoff* explained: that label may be accurate for CAA and CWA misdemeanors which require only negligent conduct to state an offense. The Supreme Court, however, has sought to avoid construing criminal

---

76   *U.S. v. Iverson*, 162 F.3d 1015, 1023 (9th Cir. 1998).

77   *Id*. at 1025.

78   *Id*. at 1027.

79   U.S. v. MacDonald & Waste Oil Co., 933 F.2d 35, 52 (1st Cir. 1991).

80   162 F.3d 1015 (9th Cir. 1998).

81   *Id*. at 1025.

82   *Id*. at 1026.

83   *Id*. at 1019.

84   *U.S. v. Ahmad*, 101 F.3d 386 (5th Cir. 1996).

85   *See, e.g., U.S. v. Weitzenhoff*, 35 F.3d 1275, 1284 (9th Cir. 1993); *U.S. v. Kelley Technical Coatings, Inc.*, 157 F.3d 432, 439 (6th Cir. 1998).

statutes to impose strict liability, and instead has interpreted most "public welfare statutes to require at least that the defendant know he is dealing with some dangerous or deleterious substance."[86] In addition, the Supreme Court has suggested that "punishing a violation as a felony is simply incompatible with the theory of a public welfare offense."[87]

VI. Negligent Violations of the CWA and CAA

As noted above, the CWA and the CAA (though more narrowly) impose misdemeanor liability for negligent violations of the act.[88] Negligent environmental crimes are essentially strict liability offenses. To prove a negligent violation of the CAA or CWA, the prosecutor does not have to show that the defendant knew that they were discharging a pollutant or emitting a hazardous substance. As in *Dotterweich* and *Park*, the defendant does not have to be aware of the facts that gave rise to the offense. The Government, moreover, does not have to show that the defendant acted recklessly or was grossly indifferent. Rather, to negligently violate the CAA means only the defendant must fail to use reasonable care in the performance of his duties.

The recent case of *U.S. v. Hanousek*,[89] illustrates the broad scope of environmental criminal liability for negligent conduct. In *Hanousek*, the Court upheld the conviction of a "railroad road master" for negligently violating the CWA, even though he did not commit the offense nor was he aware of the violation. According to his contract with the railroad, the defendant was responsible for the safe and efficient maintenance and construction of the track section that he supervised. Next to an area of the track known as Six Mile, defendant's company was quarrying rock. The quarrying also took place next to an oil pipeline that ran right next to the track. Prior to defendants supervising the track, workers had protected the pipeline from the quarrying operation by putting a platform along with sand and gravel over the pipeline. Once defendant begin supervising the work, however, he did not instruct any further precautions to be made to protect the pipeline.

One day, while the defendant was not present, a backhoe operator went to clear rocks that had fallen on the track. In so doing, he struck the pipeline, causing it to rupture and spill about 5,000 gallons of oil in a river that was approximately 200 feet away. Defendant was charged with negligently discharging oil into the navigable waters of the United States in violation of the CWA. Defendant contended that he was innocent because he didn't know anything about the CWA, should not be convicted on the basis on the negligent conduct of employees working at the site.

Characterizing the CWA as a "public welfare statute," the Court rejected the defendant's claim that was innocent because he was ignorant of the law. Next the Court

---

88   CAA, 42 U.S.C., § 7413(c)(4); CWA, 33 U.S.C. § 1319(c)(1).

89   176 F.3d 1116 (9th Cir. 1999).

Characterizing the CWA as a "public welfare statute," the Court rejected the defendant's claim that was innocent because he was ignorant of the law. Next the Court pointed out that by allowing heavy machinery to work around unprotected pipeline, the defendant knew he was working "dangerous device" which therefore placed him in "responsible relation to a public danger."[90] As in *Dotterweich* and *Park*, the defendant should have been aware of the possibility of strict regulations concerning possible spills, and taken measures to avoid it. Furthermore, the Court conceded that the defendant could not be convicted solely on the basis of the negligence of others working under him. Nevertheless, if determined that as a supervisor defendant had a duty to protect the pipeline from the negligent acts of others by instructing the pipeline be covered up with rock, gravel, and railroad as had been done previously. By failing to take measures to protect the pipe, "defendant's conduct had a direct and substantial connection to the discharge."[91]

As shown by *Hanousek*, criminal liability as a "responsible corporate officer" does not really differ from criminal liability arising from a corporate officer or managerial employee's negligent supervision. Neither person must have knowledge of the underlying facts to commit a misdemeanor violation. In turn, the law punishes both the responsible corporate officer doctrine and the negligent offender for their failure to act with reasonable care where there is a responsibility to do so.[92]

VII. Environmental Compliance Programs Are Essential for Avoiding Criminal Liability

Every company regulated under federal, state or local environmental laws should have an environmental compliance program and a plan requiring periodic environmental audits. As shown above, a person or corporation can violate environmental laws without ever being aware that what they are doing is illegal. Unlike many other laws, you cannot simply rely on rules of good moral conduct or pangs of conscious to protect you from environmental violations. Rather, to protect oneself, a corporation needs to conduct a comprehensive environmental audit to determine what environmental laws apply and whether any of the corporation's practices violate those laws. Once that determination is made, the corporation can then institute a compliance program to implement systems that will insure that the corporation and its employees continue to adhere to environmental laws and to adopt procedures in the event that violations occur.

There are several additional reasons why corporations should implement environmental compliance programs. First, the existence of a corporate compliance program may favorably impact the prosecution's decision on whether or not to

---

90   *Id.* at 1122.

91   *Id.* at 1124.

92   *See, e.g., U.S. v. Park*, 421 U.S. at 671 ("the Act imposes not only a positive duty to seek out and remedy violations when they occur, but also, and primarily, a duty to implement measures that will insure that violations will not occur.")

prosecute an environmental criminal violation. The Department of Justice ("DOJ") has issued a specific policy to "encourage self-auditing, self-policing, and voluntary disclosure of environmental violations."[93] The existence of an operating environmental program is one important mitigating factor that the DOJ looks at in deciding whether or not to exercise its prosecuting authority.[94] The DOJ will not give credit simply because an organization has a compliance program. Rather, to be given credit, a compliance program must be operational prior at the time any law enforcement investigation began and should have included a program of periodic audits.

In evaluating any compliance program, DOJ looks at the following areas to see if the program was truly operating:

> Was there a strong institutional policy to comply with all environmental requirements? Safeguards beyond those required by existing law been developed and implemented to prevent noncompliance from occurring? Were there regular procedures, including internal or external compliance, and management audits, to evaluate, detect, prevent and remedy circumstances like those that led to the noncompliance? What are the procedures and safeguards to insure the integrity of any audit conducted? Did the audit evaluate all sources of pollution (*i.e.*, all media), including the possibility of cross-media transfer of pollutants? Were the auditor's recommendation implemented in a timely fashion? Were adequate resources committed to the auditing program and to implementing its recommendations? Was environmental compliance a standard by which employee and corporate department performance was judged?[95]

Along with the existence of a compliance program, the DOJ will also consider an organization's cooperation in any investigation of an environmental violation as well as whether or not the corporation voluntary disclosed the violation.[96] To cooperate and disclose essentially means that the organization provide the Department with "all relevant information including the complete results of any internal or external investigations and the names of all potential witnesses." *Id.* If corporate personnel have caused environmental violations, the corporation cannot simply withhold the names of the perpetrators if it wishes to cooperate with the government. Indeed, DOJ will look to see whether at minimum the corporation has internally disciplined employees who violated company environmental compliance policies.

Second, the EPA has also issued a policy providing incentives to organizations that implement compliance programs; discover violations through the operations of those programs; disclose such violations; and seek to correct and prevent further

---

93   Factors and Decisions on Criminal Prosecutions for Environmental Violations in the Context of Significant Voluntary Compliance or Disclosure Efforts by the Violator, Vol. 4 Dep't of Justice Manual 5-11.104A.

94   *Id.*

95   *Id.*

96   *Id.*

violations in the future.[97] The EPA provides that "where violations are found through voluntary environmental audits or efforts that reflect to regulate entities due diligence, and are properly disclosed and expeditiously corrected, EPA will not seek gravity based penalties and will generally not recommend criminal prosecution against the regulated entity.[98] Much like the Department of Justice policy, EPA's "incentives for self-policing" also requires the good faith operation of an environmental auditor due diligence program, and the disclosure to EPA of violations found through that program.

Third, regardless of DOJ's or EPA's formal policies, the operation of a corporate compliance program may provide intangible benefits to keep the corporation from being prosecuted in the event of a violation. Although they may like us to think otherwise, the DOJ and federal investigative agencies do not have unlimited resources. They are selective in who they prosecute, and their decisions on who to prosecute often depend on the severity of the conduct at issue and how easily it is to obtain a conviction. Organizations that properly maintain compliance programs, however, are not good targets for prosecutors. Simply stated, if the organization has a *good* compliance program then it just does not look like a law breaker and does not have jury appeal. Indeed, in at least two cases, organizations have used their compliance programs in court to show that they were not liable for the crimes of their employees.[99] In short, the existence of a compliance program can help persuade a prosecutor to utilize his resources in more pressing cases and instead allow the civil process to address environmental violations.

For these reasons and other reasons explained throughout this text, having an environmental compliance program for companies subject to environmental laws is an absolute essential for maintaining a well run organization.

---

97   Environmental Protection Agency, Incentives for Self-Policing: Discovery, Disclosure, Correction and Prevention of Violations, [FRL-5400-1] (1996).

98   *Id.*

99   Note, *The Role of Corporate Compliance Programs in Determining Corporate Criminal Liability: A Suggested Approach*, 96 Colum. L. Rev. 1252 (June 1996). This Note discusses *United States v. Beusch*, 596 F.2d 871 (9th Cir. 1979) and *U.S. v. Basic Construction Company*, 711 F.2d 570, 572 (4th Cir.), *cert. denied*, 464 U.S. 956 (1983). In both cases, the Court allowed organizations accused of misconduct to introduce their compliance programs to show that they were not vicariously liable for the acts of their employees.

CHAPTER 12:
ENVIRONMENTAL CRIMINAL PROSECUTIONS IN THE MARITIME INDUSTRY

I. Background

Ships carry approximately 95% of the goods that are imported into or exported from the United States.[1] Shipping is an international business with billions of dollars invested in capital equipment and many more billions in annual revenues.[2] They thus present a large target for government enforcement actions, both criminal and civil.

While there are a number of pervasively regulated industries, few encounter as diverse a variety of legal regimes as does the maritime industry. Ships and shipping are subject to international law (primarily by means of conventions and related documents promulgated by the International Maritime Organization (IMO)),[3] flag state law,[4] port state law,[5] and coastal state law.[6]

---

[1] The total value of goods involved in the U.S. import and export trade in 1998 was approximately $1,594 billion. *U.S. Foreign Trade Highlights* (Office of Trade and Economic Analysis, U.S. Department of Commerce, 1999).

[2] *See*, Farthing & Brownrigg, *Farthing on International Shipping* (3d ed., LLP, London, 1997).

[3] The IMO is a specialized agency of the United Nations, headquartered in London, United Kingdom. As its name implies, it focuses on establishing international safety, environmental, and related standards for the marine industry.

[4] The flag state is the nation with which the vessel is registered. The flag state has the right and obligation to exercise its jurisdiction and control in administrative, technical, and social matters over vessels flying its flag. *See*, Article 94, 1982 United Nations Convention on the Law of the Sea.

[5] *See*, G. Kasoulides, *Port State Control and Jurisdiction* (Martinus Nijhoff Publishers, Dordrecht, The Netherlands 1993). For the authority of port states to enforce environmental laws and regulations against foreign vessels voluntarily in their ports or off-shore terminals, see Articles 218 and 219 of the 1982 United Nations Convention on the Law of the Sea.

[6] The major limitation on coastal state authority over passing vessels is the right of innocent passage through the territorial sea. *See*, Article 21, 1982 United Nations Convention on the Law of the Sea. For the authority of coastal states to enforce environmental laws and regulations against vessels passing through the territorial sea or the exclusive economic zone, see Article 220 of the Convention.

242 Corporate Fraud Investigations & Compliance Programs

Moreover, all shipping companies that enter U.S. territorial waters, whether domestic or foreign, are subject to the environmental and criminal laws of the United States. The threat to the maritime industry of enforcement action (both criminal and civil), particularly for environmental violations, has never been greater.[7]

For example, on July 21, 1999, the U.S. Department of Justice announced that Royal Caribbean Cruises Ltd. (RCCL), one of the world's largest cruise lines, had agreed to plead guilty to 21 felony counts for a variety of violations, including the dumping of waste oil and hazardous chemicals and lying to the U.S. Coast Guard. RCCL agreed to pay a record $18 million criminal fine for these offenses. If the agreement is accepted by the courts, RCCL will operate for the next five years under a court-supervised environmental compliance program. RCCL will also be required to disclose its internal investigation and assist the government in its prosecution of employees involved in the wrongdoing.

The legal proceedings occurred in areas where RCCL was charged with violating federal environmental laws: Miami, New York City, Los Angeles, Anchorage, St. Thomas (in the U.S. Virgin Islands) and San Juan, Puerto Rico. At the press conference announcing RCCL's agreement to plead guilty, U.S. Attorney General Janet Reno stated that "RCCL used our nation's waters as its dumping ground, even as it promoted itself as an environmentally 'green' company. This case will sound like a foghorn throughout the entire maritime industry." Coast Guard Vice Admiral James Card said: "Vigorous prosecution of flagrant violators is essential to ensure full compliance with the law." Further, Administrator Carol Browner of the U.S. Environmental Protection Agency (EPA) stated that "Companies that profit from polluting will be held accountable to the fullest extent of the law."[8]

This was not RCCL's first run-in with federal prosecutors. In June, 1998, RCCL pled guilty to substantially similar offenses in Miami and San Juan. In those earlier actions, RCCL was convicted on its plea of various offenses including conspiracy to violate the Clean Water Act[9] and presenting a false oil record book to the U.S. Coast Guard.[10] In addition to an $8 million fine and a $1 million payment to the National Fish and Wildlife Foundation, the company was required to institute a maritime compliance program. The compliance program, which was monitored by the court, included, among other things, the posting of environmental officers on each of the company's cruise ships and

---

7 Shuker, *Owners fear spill charges*, TradeWinds, page 23 (18 June 1999).

8 Press Releases of July 21, 1999, the U.S. Department of Justice, the U.S. Department of Transportation, and the Environmental Protection Agency. *See also, Royal Caribbean to Plead Guilty on Dumping Charges*, New York Times (July 21, 1999).

9 The Clean Water Act is otherwise known as the Federal Water Pollution Control Act.

10 Making a false statement or presenting a false document to a federal official who has responsibility in the matter covered by the statement or document is punishable under 18 U.S.C. § 1001.

Environmental training for all crewmembers.[11] The plea came only after the charges had been vigorously contested by RCCL based on, among other grounds, alleged noncompliance with international law by the federal government since at least some of the alleged discharges occurred on the high seas.[12]

II. Threat of Criminal Prosecution

A. Criminal Negligence and No-Fault Crimes

The average ship owner can easily grasp the criminal sanctions that are attached to actions such as the intentional dumping of oil and other pollutants into the water. Few, though, appreciate that, at least in the United States, criminal sanctions can (and sometimes do) attach to actions committed without any intent to cause harm.[13] Under the Clean Water Act[14] as amended by the Oil Pollution Act of 1990,[15] spills into the waters of the United States caused by ordinary negligence may result in criminal convictions for those involved.[16] Further, under the Refuse Act of 1899,[17] the mere discharge of oil or other material into U.S. waters is a criminal offense, even in the absence of negligence. Under the Migratory Bird Treaty Act,[18] if a migratory bird (and this includes the vast percentage of

---

11   See, *New York Times*, page 1 (January 3, 1999).

12   *See, United States v. Royal Caribbean Cruises, Ltd.*, 11 F. Supp. 1358 (S.D. Fla. 1998); *United States v. Royal Caribbean Cruises, Ltd.*, 30 F. Supp. 114 (D. P.R. 1997); *United States v. Royal Caribbean Cruises, Ltd.*, 24 F. Supp. 155 (D. P.R. 1997).

13   No-fault criminal prosecution for oil spills has recently become a threat in the United Kingdom, where the port of Milford Haven pled guilty to violation of the Water Resources Act, 1991 for the 1996 oil spill from the grounding of the M/V SEA EMPRESS. The port was fined £ 4 million. Criminal charges were also brought against the pilot of the tanker, but were dismissed following the port's acceptance of responsibility. *See, Environmental liability for parties where primary fault lies elsewhere*, Montaq Business Briefing (London), June 8, 1999; *Salvors balk at enviro-clean-up*, Environment Business (London), February 11, 1999; *Oil disaster port fined a record £ 4 m*, London Daily Mail, January 16, 1999.

14   33 U.S.C. § 1319.

15   Pub.L. 101-380, § 4301(c), 104 Stat. 537 (August 18, 1990).

16   In *United States v. Hanousek*, 176 F.3d 1116 (9th Cir. 1999), the criminal conviction of the defendant for violation of sections 1319 and 1321 of the Clean Water Act was upheld. The defendant was a roadmaster for an Alaskan railroad and supervised repairs to the railway adjacent to the Skagway River. The right of way was shared with a petroleum pipeline. The defendant negligently failed to ensure that the work crew maintained a protective barrier between the moving work site and the pipeline. A backhoe hit the pipeline in an unprotected area, spilling oil into the river. The defendant appealed his conviction, contending, among other things, that ordinary negligence was insufficient to sustain a criminal conviction. The appellate court held that the 1990 amendments to the FWPCA utilized the ordinary negligence standard in the criminal liability provision of the law.

17   The Rivers and Harbors Appropriation Act of 1899, c. 425, §§ 13, 16, 30 Stat. 1152 (March 3, 1899), codified at 33 U.S.C. §§ 407, 411.

18   Act of July 3, 1918, c. 128, 40 Stat. 755, codified at 16 U.S.C. §§ 703-712.

244 Corporate Fraud Investigations & Compliance Programs

birds located in the U.S.)[19] is injured or killed by spilled oil or a similar incident, those responsible for the incident may be criminally prosecuted, again even in the absence of negligence. As can be seen, any spilling of oil or other material into U.S. waters is a potential criminal event.[20]

These prosecutions are no longer isolated events for the maritime community. Commercial vessels operating in U.S. waters have recently become enforcement targets, particularly with regard to perceived violations of environmental statutes and regulations. In many cases, in addition to fines, the courts have imposed requirements on ship owners and operators to institute maritime compliance programs. The court-mandated compliance programs tend to be more onerous than ones that would have qualified the holder thereof for a downward adjustment of the sentence had the program been in place prior to the offense.

For example, the barge North Cape grounded off the coast of Rhode Island on January 19, 1996, after a fire broke out on the tug that was towing it. The barge spilled approximately 828,000 gallons of home heating oil. Subsequently, the corporate owner and several of its officials entered guilty pleas to criminal violations of the Refuse Act of 1899 and the Migratory Bird Treaty Act and to criminal negligence in failing to maintain written training records for the crewmembers and in failing to have a working anchor on the barge. Penalties imposed included criminal fines of $7 million, a donation of $1.5 million to the Nature Conservancy to purchase land in New Hampshire for a bird habitat, a commitment by the company to spend $1 million in safety upgrades for its vessels, and the establishment of a court-supervised compliance program.[21]

In another case, following a major oil spill from the barge Morris J. Berman, which grounded off San Juan, Puerto Rico, on January 7, 1994, the corporate owner and related companies were convicted on their guilty pleas to a violation of the Oil Pollution Act of 1990 and the Ports and Waterways Safety Act.[22] In addition to being assessed more than $85 million in clean-up costs, damages, and criminal fines, the company was placed on five years probation. One of the conditions of probation included the institution of a court-supervised environmental

---

19   The list of migratory birds is located at 50 CFR § 10.13. The alphabetical listing is eight pages in length.

20   Appendix 7 contains a brief discussion of some actions taken by the federal government under the Refuse Act and the Migratory Bird Treaty Act that demonstrate the breadth of these statutes that were written many years ago for originally narrow reasons.

21   *See*, Douglas Eklof, *Wake Up Call: Lessons Learned from the North Cape Pollution Incident*, Marine Log (November 1998). Interestingly, there were no statutes or regulations requiring the maintenance of written training records nor was the barge required to have an anchor, let alone an operable anchor. *See also*, *Providence (RI) Journal-Bulletin*, page 1A (November 1, 1998).

22   33 U.S.C. §§ 1221-1236.

compliance program.[23] Cases like this, including where owners and operators have been convicted of criminal offenses, have been increasing.[24]

B. Compliance Programs

A maritime compliance program provides protection not only with regard to no-fault and negligent offenses, but also for deliberate dumping and other intentional crimes committed by rogue employees. A maritime compliance program is designed specifically for a company in the maritime industry to take advantage of the provision in the Federal Sentencing Guidelines and the policy of the U.S. Department of Justice relating to compliance programs, which includes a potentially reduced sentence in the event of a conviction[25] and possible favorable consideration with regard to both the bringing of criminal indictments and the settling of charges.[26]

III. Oversight Programs Generally

For the maritime industry, there are four major programs that provide a shipowner and others with a systematic overview of the company's compliance with applicable safety, environmental, and other applicable laws and regulations. These programs partially overlap in their coverage, but have distinctly different purposes. The four programs are:

1. The International Safety Management (ISM) Code;

2. The ISO Quality Management Standard (ISO 9000 Series);

3. The ISO Environmental Management Standard (ISO 14001); and

4. A Maritime Compliance Program.

---

23 *New York Law Journal*, page 3 (December 26, 1997). For litigation surrounding this incident, see, *Commonwealth of Puerto Rico v. M/V Emily S*, 1998 A.M.C. 2726 (D. P.R. 1998); *Commonwealth of Puerto Rico v. M/V Emily S*, 1998 A.M.C. 2020 (D. P.R. 1998); *In re Metlife Capital Corp.*, 1998 A.M.C. 635 (1st Cir. 1997); *Commonwealth of Puerto Rico v. M/V Emily S*, 1995 A.M.C. 1025 (D. P.R. 1995).

24 A more complete list of some federal enforcement actions in the maritime sector, that have involved mandated compliance programs, is set forth in Appendix 8.

25 See, Martin, Implementing Effective Corporate Legal Compliance Programs, 11 Nat. Resources & Env't 14 (1997); Goldsmith, Policing Corporate Crime: The Dilemma of Internal Compliance Programs, 50 Vand. L. Rev. 1 (1997); Devine, The Draft Organization Sentencing Guidelines for Environmental Crimes, 20 Colum. J. Env. L. 249 (1995).

26 Warin, *Corporate Compliance Programs as a Component of Plea Agreements and Civil and Administrative Settlements*, 24 J. Corp. L. 71 (1998); Kowal, *Corporate Compliance Programs: A Shield Against Criminal Liability*, 53 Food & Drug L. J. 517 (1998).

246 Corporate Fraud Investigations & Compliance Programs

The first three programs (about which much has already been written)[27] will be briefly reviewed and they will then be compared with the Maritime Compliance Program.[28]

IV. ISM Code

The International Safety Management (ISM) Code[29] was adopted by the IMO in 1993[30] and was incorporated into the International Convention for the Safety of Life at Sea (SOLAS Convention) in 1994.[31] It went into effect for many ocean-going vessels (i.e., passenger ships, passenger high speed craft, oil tankers, chemical tankers, gas carriers, bulk carriers, and cargo high speed craft of 500 gross tons and greater) on July 1, 1998. On July 1, 2002, it will go into effect for most other ocean-going commercial vessels of 500 gross tons and greater.[32]

The objectives of the ISM Code are to improve safety of life at sea, to reduce the occurrence of human injury or loss of life, and to minimize environmental and property damage attributable to marine casualties. The ISM Code seeks to accomplish these objectives by encouraging the implementation of safety management systems (SMS's) by companies which own, manage, charter, or operate ships, with oversight by the national administrations. In the United States, the national administration for SOLAS matters is the U.S. Coast Guard. The ISM Code and a

---

27   For the ISM Code, see, Anderson, *ISM Code: A Practical Guide to the Legal and Insurance Implications* (LLP, Ltd., London 1998); Allen, *The ISM Code and Shipowner Records: Shared Safety Goals vs. Industry's Privacy Needs*, 11 U.S.F. Mar. L. J. 1 (1999); Poulos, *Legal Implications of the ISM Code: New Impediments to Sea Fever*, 9 U.S.F. Mar. L. J. 37 (1996).

For ISO 9000, *see*, Peach, *The ISO 9000 Handbook* (Irwin Professional Pub., 3d ed. 1996); Young, *An Overview of ISO 9000 Application to Drugs, Medical Devices, and Environmental Management Issues*, 49 Food & Drug L. J. 469 (1994); Scott, *Products Liability and Proper Implementation of ISO 9000*, 4 Prod. Liab. L. J. 5 (1992).

For ISO 14001, *see*, Woodside, *The ISO 14001 Implementation Manual* (McGraw Hill 1998); Davis, *ISO 14001: Meeting Business Goals through an Effective Environmental Management System* (Bureau of Business Practice 1998); Bell, *Practical Considerations in Implementing ISO 14001*, 3 Alb. L. Env. Outlook 11 (1997); Mathews, *The ISO 14001 Environmental Management System Standard: An Innovative Approach to Environmental Protection*, 2 Env. Law 817 (1996).

28   The requirements for an effective compliance program are set forth in Chapter 8. It is important to note that owners and operators of vessels that have instituted safety management systems in accordance with the ISM Code or have been certified under either ISO 9000 or ISO 14001 have taken many of the steps required for an effective maritime compliance program. Those steps will not have to be repeated in the development of a compliance program.

29   The full title is: *International Management Code for the Safe Operation of Ships and for Pollution Prevention*.

30   IMO Assembly Resolution A.741(18), adopted November 4, 1993.

31   Conference of Contracting Governments to the 1974 SOLAS Convention, held at London in May 1994. The ISM Code is now Chapter IX of the SOLAS Convention. *See also*, IMO Assembly Resolution A.788(19), adopted November 23, 1995.

32   SOLAS Convention, Regulation IX/2.

company's SMS focus on compliance with applicable international and flag state safety and environmental protection laws and regulations. The SMS usually does not address port state or coastal state rules regarding these issues. Neither the ISM Code nor the SMS address other rules that may be applicable to the company or the vessel, such as those relating to economic regulation.

V. ISO 9000

The International Organization for Standardization, which is known by the term ISO,[33] is a non-governmental organization headquartered in Geneva, Switzerland. It is a worldwide federation of national standards bodies from approximately 130 nations. Its mission is to promote the development of standardization and related activities in the world with a view to facilitating the international exchange of goods and services. ISO's work results in international agreements that are published as International Standards. It is expected that users will have more confidence in products and services that conform to International Standards. Assurance of conformity can be provided by audits carried out by independent bodies. The ISO 9000 series is a set of international quality standards and guidelines. It initially focused on quality management and quality assurance for the manufacturing sector, but was later expanded to address industry generally. Included within the ISO 9000 series are sector-specific quality requirements.[34] Except for the fact that it was promulgated outside the ISO system, the ISM Code might be seen, in some respects, as a maritime industry-specific quality requirement. There is no governmental requirement for a company to achieve ISO 9000 certification. A number of benefits, though, may result from this effort. It may fulfill various contractual requirements for quality assurance. It may provide certain marketing advantages, differentiating one company from another. It may assist in complying with various regulatory requirements. Finally, it may help the company in its quality development and risk management efforts. As a voluntary program, its breadth and detail are, in some measure, controlled by the company. To the extent that the ISO 9000 program adopted by a company addresses compliance with legal requirements, it may be limited, for instance, to domestic law or to specific legal issues, such as trademark and patent law.

VI. ISO 14001

The International Organization for Standardization followed up on its quality management standards by developing a series of standards relating to environmental management, known as the ISO 14000 series. The standards in this series address environmental management, auditing and related investigations, performance evaluation, labeling, life cycle assessment, etc. The principal standard in this series

---

33   ISO is derived from the Greek word "isos" meaning equal and which is the root of the prefix iso- as in isometric, isobar, and isotherm. It reflects the primary goal of the organization: the setting of standards or measures of equality.

34   *See, e.g.*, QS-9000 for the automotive industry.

is ISO 14001 relating to environmental management systems (EMS). Another concept that pervades the ISO 14000 series is sustainable development.

As is the case with the ISO 9000 series, achieving ISO 14001 certification is voluntary, but can further a number of company goals. In addition, since many environmental standards have been established by (and are enforced by) governments, achieving environmental management certification through the ISO system may reduce the likelihood of violation of government environmental standards. While government agencies do not equate ISO 14001 with regulatory compliance, they tend to recognize the value of achieving ISO 14001 certification.[35]

The ISO 14001 standard requires the establishment of a company environmental policy, the determination of the environmental aspects and impacts of the company's activities, the development of environmental objectives (and measurable targets toward those objectives), the implementation of programs to achieve those objectives, establishment of a corrective action program, and management review. The incorporation into the company's ISO 14001 program of legal and other outside environmental requirements is necessary if the program is to be meaningful. The key to a successful environmental management system is having documented procedures that are implemented and maintained so that achievement of environmental goals commensurate with the type and level of company operations are promoted. Adoption of the ISO 14001 standard, in conjunction with the safety management system of the ISM Code, can go hand-in-hand with the implementation of a maritime compliance program, since there are numerous overlaps.[36]

Increasingly raised is the vexing issue of the confidentiality of environmental audits conducted under the auspices of ISO 14001 or similar programs.[37] It is the policy of the U.S. Environmental Protection Agency (EPA) to encourage environmental audits.[38] To that end, it is the practice of the EPA "to refrain from *routine requests* for environmental audit reports."[39] (emphasis added). The EPA has not clarified what it means by routine requests and the circumstances under

---

35   *See, EPA Position Statement on Environmental Management Systems and ISO 14001*, located at 63 *Fed. Reg.* 12094 (March 12, 1998); *Code of Environmental Management Principles*, located at 61 *Fed. Reg.* 54062 (October 16, 1996).

36   *See*, Carr & Thomas, *Devising a Compliance Strategy under the ISO 14000 International Environmental Management Standards*, 15 Pace Env. L. Rev. 85 (1997).

37   *See*, Croutch, *Environmental Audits: Should a New Evidentiary Privilege be formulated or do Existing Privileges provide Adequate Protection?*, 46 Drake L. Rev. 425 (1997).

38   EPA Final Policy Statement, *Incentives for Self-Policing: Discovery, Disclosure, Correction and Prevention of Violations*, 60 *Fed. Reg.* 66706 (December 22, 1995). *See also*, EPA Notice of Final Policy, *Interim Policy on Compliance Incentives for Small Businesses*, 61 *Fed. Reg.* 27984 (June 3, 1996); EPA Request for Comments, *Environmental Enforcement and Compliance Assurance Activities*, 64 *Fed. Reg.* 10144 (March 2, 1999); EPA Policy Statement, *Evaluation of "Incentives for Self-Policing: Discovery, Disclosure, Correction and Prevention of Violations" Policy Statement, Proposed Revisions and Request for Public Comment*, 64 *Fed. Reg.* 26745 (May 17, 1999).

39   64 *Fed. Reg.* at 26746 (May 17, 1999).

which it would seek access to a company's environmental audit results. The U.S. Department of Justice has, on the other hand, made no such policy statement with regard to refraining from routine requests for environmental audit reports. Environmental audit reports are routinely sought by federal prosecutors during criminal investigations and prosecutions.

VII. Comparison: ISM Code, ISO 9000, ISO 14001, and Maritime Compliance Program

The ISM Code is the only one of the four oversight programs that is mandatory. With certain exceptions, the company that owns or operates a ship engaged in international commerce must develop and implement a safety management system in conformance with the ISM Code. The other programs are voluntary. A company can develop and implement these other programs if it determines that the benefits (both direct and indirect) outweigh the costs.

A significant distinction between a Maritime Compliance Program and the other three oversight programs is the element of discipline. As noted above, for a maritime compliance program to qualify under Department of Justice policy and under the Federal Sentencing Guidelines, it must contain a provision for the appropriate disciplining of individuals who act in manners contrary to the compliance program. The other oversight programs are silent on this issue.

As noted previously, the impact of the various oversight programs also varies widely. A vessel without a safety management system required under the ISM Code is effectively barred from international trade. Certification under either ISO 9000 or ISO 14001 can be an excellent marketing tool for a company, differentiating it from many of its competitors. Such certification has other advantages, as discussed above. In addition, a conscientiously applied program under ISO 9000 or ISO 14001 can address issues well beyond statutory and regulatory compliance and lead to significant business and environmental improvements outside the scope of the traditional command and control structures.[40]

The primary benefit of a maritime compliance program is realized when the federal government initiates enforcement action against the company or one of its vessels or employees. The U.S. Attorney may elect to forgo the enforcement action because the company had previously instituted an effective compliance program covering the law or regulation at issue. If the enforcement action goes forward despite the presence of an effective compliance program, the U.S. Attorney is more likely to agree to settlement on terms favorable to the company due to the presence of the compliance program. If the matter goes to trial despite the presence of an effective compliance program, the judgment will likely be more favorable to the company than it would have been if no compliance program was in place. Unfortunately,

---

40 *See* Appendix 8.

there are no guarantees regarding exactly what judicial benefits will accrue to a company that adopts a maritime compliance program.

The major practical benefit may be that the likelihood that a company with an effective maritime compliance program will encounter a federal enforcement action is decreased, because the education, training, feedback, and disciplinary elements of the program will significantly reduce the probability of a violation of federal law or regulation. Due particularly to the presence of the criminal negligence and no-fault crimes in federal law, even the most conscientious owner or operator can not discount the possibility of a federal enforcement action. A maritime compliance program may provide the only reasonably effective shield against this situation.

CHAPTER 13:
FORENSIC ACCOUNTING

In an internal fraud investigation, attorneys must gather evidence, evaluate and protect the evidence and assist the client in taking remedial measures. Many internal investigations however involve significant financial elements or, worse, financial fraud. As such, evidence to be gathered and evaluated may be financial, accounting, and transactional in nature. In those cases, many of the answers needed to solve the investigation may be buried within the financial documents. In fact, the documents often contain a treasure trove of information about transactional histories, involved parties and funds flow. Corporate fraud investigations are required for many types of matters including embezzlement of corporate assets, earnings manipulation, price fixing, mismanagement, program fraud, false claims, inventory shortages and purchasing fraud. All of these have at least one element in common; information critical to the discovery and resolution of the suspected fraudulent transaction is contained within documents, reports and records. As a consequence, engaging the assistance of a forensic accountant can be of great benefit in obtaining and analyzing the evidence.

But what is a forensic accountant? A forensic accountant is an accountant who has a specialized background to apply financial and investigative skills to gathering and reconstructing financial evidence and solving problems within the context of the rules of evidence and the legal system. The forensic accountant gets involved in many areas of practice where financial skills are needed to analyze and reconstruct documents and information, trace funds, locate assets, and interpret business transactions. To be of value to the attorney in the investigation, the forensic accountant must be knowledgeable about fraud schemes, as well as conducting fraud investigations.

A common misconception is that a forensic accountant is only needed to process information after the investigation is completed. In reality, forensic accounting is a valuable and often critical resource, not only in financial fraud investigations, but also in other fraud investigations as well. The investigating attorneys will generally engage the forensic accountants to assist them with the investigation. In order to properly plan an investigation, the forensic accountant should be part of the pre-planning process to assist the attorney in determining the scope and procedures of the investigation. The perspective and knowledge of the forensic accountant in the areas of transactional review, operational functions, funds movement, document analysis and document reconstruction provides an important element to the planning and the ultimate success of an investigation.

Moreover, with increased business complexities, voluminous accounting transactions, emphasis on earnings and an ever-increasing litigious environment, forensic accounting has become instrumental as an adjunct to the lawyer who is called in to conduct an internal investigation. The ability to determine and document what happened is a critical element of successful case development. Many of the successful and larger frauds have occurred because the perpetrators were able to utilize and manipulate accounting and financial transaction systems. Knowledge of systems, ways to manipulate systems and the ability to discover the existence and extent of systems manipulation are essential tools that the investigating attorney must have at his disposal.

An investigation also typically involves interviewing potential witnesses, gathering evidence and compiling the data collected in order to determine if a fraud or crime has been committed; then quantifying the amount of the loss. The attorney can look to the forensic accountant in searching for and gathering transactional and financial data and in analyzing and reconstructing it. This transactional and financial data is important to the attorney in getting the greatest value from the interview process, assembling adequate evidence and making the case. Ultimately, the forensic accountant will be able to synthesize all of the information and determine the extent of the loss or harm.

Forensic accounting is also frequently referred to as forensic auditing or investigative accounting. It is important that the "forensic accountant" have skills that go well beyond that of a financial auditor or the typical CPA. Lawyers sometimes fail to distinguish between a forensic accountant and an auditor. Typically, a financial auditor is engaged to audit the historical financial performance of a company and opine on whether its financial statements are fairly presented. The forensic accountant reconstructs data, gathers legally sufficient evidence, and assists in determining what financial documents will support or refute allegations of wrongdoing. An audit is more routine and broad in scope and typically involves reviewing documentation on a test basis in order to obtain a reasonable comfort level that, in fact, management has fairly presented the company's financial statements. In a financial audit, the test basis is designed from statistical sampling methods gauged upon materiality thresholds in risk assessments. However, for forensic purposes, these statistical sampling methods may fail to select financial transactions that are often the "key" in locating a source of fraudulent intent or behavior.

While it goes without saying that the forensic accountant must have a deep understanding of the principles and standards of accounting and auditing, other broader skills and knowledge are essential. The role of the forensic accountant is to search out fraud from the documents and records. As such, the forensic accountant must have an understanding of the motives behind fraud and the methods to manipulate accounting transactions and records in order to perpetrate fraud. In other words, be able to "step into the shoes" of the perpetrator. Additionally, in today's complex world, the forensic accountant must understand the rules of evidence, computers, legal principles, finance, banking, and fraud risks and vulnerabilities.

Frequently, gathering the facts and the story behind the facts is the most important and often difficult component of an investigation. When a fraud is suspected, the area of greatest exposure should first be defined by reviewing and understanding the control environment and profiling individuals with motivations to commit fraud. The most basic areas of fraud exposure involves "assets that are susceptible to theft" and "financial statement items susceptible to misstatement" but differ business to business depending on the industry and setting. Assets that are more liquid or readily accessible tend to be more prone to theft due to the ease with which they may be misappropriated or converted.

Once the areas most susceptible to fraud have been determined, the next stage of focus by the forensic accountant is on relationships within the company. These relationships could be strictly internal, or may be external relationships between company personnel and outside parties. In addition to understanding relationships, the forensic accountant should analyze possible motives of employees to commit fraud. In understanding motives, the forensic accountant has experience in understanding how items such as personal and financial status and life-style habits influence employee motivation.

What motivates individuals to commit fraud and engage in misconduct? In attempting to uncover and investigate fraud, often the relationships of individuals within a company are ignored and the focus is on the quantitative data alone. In addition to reviewing and analyzing quantitative data, employee lifestyle, personal relationships, abnormal behavior, cultural issues, business pressures and other "red flags" must be identified. In today's complex and mechanized world, many advanced forensic accountants have developed proprietary information technology tools for rapid and sophisticated data sorting and analysis. But even with these tools, ultimately it is the experience of the forensic accountant in reviewing and analyzing this output that makes the difference.

It goes without saying that companies and computer systems do not perpetrate fraud. Fraud is perpetrated by individuals that do not have adequate oversight or are in the position of decision making. These individuals may include, but obviously are not limited to, purchasing agents, accounts payable and receivable clerks, and financial executives. Depending on the company and the fraud, there are essentially three possible beneficiaries of fraud: (1) the company itself, (2) individuals in the company or (3) third parties. Each type of fraud has a common theme, but this is where the similarities end. Each requires a different set of tools to expose and prove the fraud. The experienced forensic accountant will customize the engagement techniques to best assist the lawyer and bring a greater chance of success.

The Company—Fraud perpetrated to benefit the company, commonly known as "management fraud", usually involves the manipulation of earnings in order to improve financial results. Management fraud can also be intended to manipulate the financial records in order to disguise the embezzlement of funds or misappropriation of assets. At times, it will also be used to create slush funds. The motives for this type of behavior are plentiful; healthier earnings reports, diversion of funds for illicit uses, the appearance of improved credit worthiness, masking covenant violations and other types of loan defaults, and hiding under-performing or non performing assets, among others.

When performing the initial review of the financial statements, the forensic accountant should look for unusual trends in financial ratios that may or may not be indicative of a problem. Simply reviewing the financial ratios on a macro level to determine the presence of fraud will not in itself allow a forensic accountant to draw any conclusions. Financial ratios should be compared to company specific historical data, economic data and industry trends to assess whether these accounts are reasonable or raise red flags. However, a detailed examination of the corporate culture, integrity system controls, overall environment, transactions, operating history and records is needed to uncover specific, fraudulent behavior.

The Individual—Individuals who commit fraud against the company have various motives for their actions and have access to a large variety of techniques and elaborate schemes to perpetrate fraud and attempt to cover the trail. Often, for example, the employee may be suffering from an economic hardship or may feel that the current salary is not adequate for their workload and believes that some additional compensation is due, albeit unilaterally decided by the employee.

A review and understanding of the business and control environment of a company by the forensic accountant is instrumental in devising a meaningful financial investigative work plan in situations where fraud is suspected. Often, areas of vulnerability are identified by control weaknesses. In many organizations, a high degree of responsibility is given to individuals who are trusted. It is believed that these people would never commit a fraudulent act against the company for personal gain. Companies with fewer personnel covering many tasks compromise a sound control environment with adequate segregation of duties and substitute trust as the enhancement for ensuring honesty. The absence of an adequate control environment will heighten the risk of losses from employees, including embezzlement, the creation of phantom employees[1] and fictitious vendors and the submission of fraudulent expenses, among others. The forensic accountant should not only review corporate financial records, but also the individual target's financial transactions to the extent they can be obtained.

The Third Party—Fraudulent transactions that fall into this category often involve collusion with company employees and are more difficult to detect. A simple example may involve an accounts payable clerk submitting payment requests to pay a third party for services not rendered; for his role in the fraud the accounts payable clerk receives a kickback. However, third party fraud will often be unassisted by

---

1   Using ghost payroll and false social security numbers.

company employees and may involve fraudulent misrepresentation by a vendor, fictitious or sub-par product delivery, excessive charges, fabricated construction change orders or other similar types of behavior.

Fraudulent vendor payments are often difficult to discover due to collusion, which allows the fraud to be more complex and clandestine. The forensic accountant can provide the knowledge about the scheme and review unusual relationships through vendor payment histories. When the investigating lawyer conducts interviews, the forensic accountant can provide valuable information from the financial and transactional evidence gathered.

I. The Forensic Accounting Process

In order to understand the uses of funds and any potential misapplication or misappropriation of funds, certain analysis should be performed. An understanding must be gained of the difference between the actual and the documented cash movements to identified and unidentified accounts. Fund movements must be mapped in order to determine the location and ownership of the assets, the individuals involved in their movement and additional areas to review for fraudulent transactions

An investigation should not overlook or fail to consider the movement of funds and other accounts that are off-book or off-balance sheet. Businesses that use these "accounts" can typically generate large sums of cash and avoid establishing a paper trail. Perpetrators can use off-book schemes for many purposes, including hiding financial interests, value stripping and others. In off-balance sheet schemes, it is difficult to identify the flow of funds, and often times the origin of the transaction, due to the lack of an audit trail. In the event that the origin can not be identified, the focus of the investigation may shift to the recipient of the funds and work backward in the flow of funds. The use of appropriate source documentation, coupled with reconstruction of the flow of funds, will often lead to non-congruent relationships between expenditures and receipts upon which the forensic accountant can more intensively search.

The difficulty in a financial fraud investigation is that no formula exists on how to detect fraud or where fraudulent acts may occur. Skilled perpetrators try to remain one step ahead by devising schemes that are more immune to detection. Quantitative investigative measures to uncover fraud can be employed to detect fraud, but the intuition and experience of the forensic accountant is an important factor. With the increase in electronic commerce, paper trails are rapidly becoming extinct. This switch to electronic commerce will no doubt increase the complexities of fraud investigations and result in a greater demand for the experienced forensic accountant.

Forensic accounting in fraud investigations encompasses more than financial analysis and reviewing audit trails. The application of financial fraud detection methods falls under the larger category of economic crimes. Trends developing in economic crimes have allowed the forensic accountant to expand the support role to law firms in assisting in criminal matters, insurance claims and computer crimes.

II. Computer Fraud

A particular economic crime in which the a paper trail hardly, if ever, exists is computer crime. The ever increasing electronic world and the heightened use of personal computers has technology intensive companies on alert for an increase in computer crime. Computer crimes can be investigated by determining where within the computation and or storage of data in the computer system the crime is being committed. The perpetrator can either influence the data being entered into the system, or manipulate the system to produce the desired results. In today's fast paced world of e-commerce, old-fashioned computer crime's newest cousin, cybercrime, is coming on strong. Perpetrators pirate developer's codes and use other software piracy techniques to steal intangible value. Economic espionage is no longer only what we read about in spy novels.

III. Accounting Conventions

With the growing globalization of business, the forensic accountant must not only have a knowledge of U.S. GAAP but also possess an understanding of accounting principles and acceptable practices in foreign countries when investigating fraudulent activities on an international level. International fraud is often more complex when U.S. accounting principles may not apply to a foreign company that is the target of fraudulent activity or itself suspected of fraudulent activity. Obviously, in addition to being familiar with U.S. GAAP, the forensic accountant must be familiar with colloquial accounting practices and must understand what are acceptable in particular foreign jurisdictions. Often times, large international accounting firms call upon their offices located in the specified countries of suspected fraudulent activity in order to tap their expertise regarding cultural differences and "creative accounting methodologies" typically employed in those countries.

The complexity involved in international fraud investigations can result from the lack of uniform international accounting procedures that are followed outside of U.S. GAAP. The forensic accountant's work is complicated by the conflicting authoritative accounting literature in the international arena. Not only is the forensic accountant burdened with understanding the fraudulent transaction, his efforts are further complicated by having to determine if the activity is indeed fraudulent based on local and accounting conventions within the respective country. What appears to be a clear case of the use of manipulation of earnings may well be an aggressive accounting method that is wholly accepted by the country's reporting requirements.

In addition to the forensic accountant possibly needing to understand the international accounting standards[2] (IAS) v. U.S. accounting and reporting standards,[3] the forensic accountant may be involved in an investigation where none of these standards applies. A noted research paper in *Accounting Horizons*[4] notes that some countries have their own very different financial accounting standards. This research paper concluded that on average the earnings determined under Chinese GAAP was 20-30% higher then earnings reported under IAS. Would some transactions and accounting for the transactions be fraudulent in one country, but not in another? Would the financial trail in one country lead you to believe that a fraud was perpetrated when viewed under the accounting standards microscope of another country?

IV. Money Laundering

Many investigations today involving international transactions relate to violations of money laundering laws. The United States provides very specific laws and sanctions relating to money laundering.[5] Potential money laundering violations can be a problem where U.S. banks permit their institution to be used to further a money laundering enterprise. Similar problems have arisen more recently when U.S. banks acquire overseas banks. In this event, it is prudent for the bank to engage counsel, who will in turn engage forensic accountants, to review the operations and accounts of the target bank to determine whether under U.S. laws the target may be engaging in money laundering activities. In that case, the U.S. bank could be held liable under U.S. laws.

As complex money laundering schemes capture more of the global business environment, forensic accountants must be aware of the developing trends and the technological advances in combating these complex money-laundering schemes. In a statement by Mary Lee Warren[6] to members of Congress, she outlined the recent trends. Such trends include the use of money service businesses, money orders and traveler's checks to circumvent the barriers that financial institutions have developed to prevent illicit cash proceeds from being deposited in United States financial institutions. Another trend is the conversion of illicit proceeds into exported goods. This involves, for example, the use of illicit proceeds laundered

---

2   International Accounting Standards, promulgated by International Accounting Standards Committee (IASC), a private international organization composed of 143 accounting bodies from 103 countries.

3   Generally Accepted Accounting Principles, promulgated by Financial Accounting Standards Board (FASB).

4   Chen, Charles J.P., Gul, Ferdinand A., Su, Xijia. "A Comparison of Reported Earnings Under Chinese GAAP vs. IAS: Evidence from the Shanghai Stock Exchange." *Accounting Horizons* 13 (1999): 91-111.

5   18 USC. §§ 1956 and 1957, Money Laundering Control Act of 1986.

6   Warren, Mary Lee. "Deputy Assistant Attorney General, Criminal Division, US Department of Justice." Address, Washington D.C., 15 Apr. 1999.

through foreign black market currency exchange systems to fund the smuggling of foreign goods later converted back into cash. This trend has increased recently using precious metals. Bulk cash movements are an increasing trend involving the use of large sums of U.S. currency concealed in goods for export. This scheme evades the U.S. reporting requirements on sums of currency greater than $10,000.[7] U.S. reporting requirements are also frequently circumvented by depositing large sums of cash in amounts of $10,000 or less.[8] This is known as smurfing or structuring.

An experienced forensic accountant should have extensive knowledge about the three steps that are considered when focusing on the laundering of illicit funds, placement, layering and integration.[9] The first step, placement, involves changing the money from the illegal activity to a less conspicuous form and coordinating the large sums of cash into a more manageable form. The second step, layering, involves the use of voluminous financial transactions that appear to be legitimate financial activity. These transactions often take the form of numerous wire transfers through several bank accounts in order to conceal the true origin of the funds. The final step of laundering illicit funds involves the integration of the illicit funds. This integration of laundered funds back into the global financial markets is made simple by the large variety of financial instruments such as bonds and securities. The forensic accountant is tasked with understanding the origin of the proceeds and the flow of funds. The problem lies in the volume of financial transactions in a typical money laundering scheme and the ability to determine legal from illicit transactions.

V. Government Investigations

In government investigations, counsel for the company will obviously be cognizant of the federal sentencing guidelines and will seek ways to minimize potential damage and fines.[10] As part of his strategy, counsel may consider making voluntary disclosures to the government. The forensic accountant's assistance in gathering evidence can help in determining the merits of voluntary disclosure. Whether or not voluntary disclosure is made, the forensic accountant should assist in challenging and testing the adequacy and sufficiency of the government's evidence, samples and tests. In either case, the economic fruits or harm of the activity needs to be quantified to properly gauge the level of the base fine.

---

7   The Currency and Foreign Transaction Reporting Act of 1970 , 31 USC §§ 5311-5314, 5316-5324, also known as the Bank Secrecy Act.

8   *Id.*

9   Richards, James, *Money Laundering; A Desk Reference For Law Enforcement and Financial Investigators* (1997): 43,49,70.

10   18 USC. §§ 3551-86 (1988); 28 USC. §§ 991-98 (1988).

APPENDICES

APPENDIX 1

JULY 28, 1997 OFFICE OF THE ATTORNEY GENERAL MEMO

Office of the Attorney General
Washington, D.C. 20530

July 28, 1997

**MEMORANDOM FOR ALL UNITED STATES ATTORNEYS
ALL ASSISTANT UNITED STATES ATTORNEYS
ALL LITIGATING DIVISIONS
ALL TRIAL ATTORNEYS**

FROM: **THE ATTORNEY GENERAL**

SUBJECT: **Coordination of Parallel Criminal, Civil, and Administrative Proceedings**

The key to the Department's federal white-collar crime enforcement effort is to use the Government's resources as efficiently and effectively as possible in order to punish offenders, recover damages, and prevent future misconduct. In recent years, we have pursued greater numbers of complex cases, in which the Government has been required to employ the full range of criminal, civil and administrative remedies and sanctions. The challenge requires greater cooperation, communication and teamwork between the criminal and civil prosecutors who are often conducting parallel investigations of the same offenders and matters. Although policies and procedures on parallel proceedings have been adopted by many of the United States Attorneys' offices, and Department components, I am issuing the following policy statement to clarify the Department's priorities and responsibilities in this new litigative environment.

We have experienced significant change in the way the Government fights white-collar crime. We have also experienced enormouse growth of affirmative civil enforcement (AC), and with additional ACE resources, annual recoveries have increased by hundreds of millions of dollars. Enforcement priorities encompass not only government procurement and health care fraud, but also consumer protection, the environment, tax, and securities fraud, which implicate a variety of civil, criminal, and regulatory remedies.

In order to maximize the efficient use of resources, it is essential that our attorneys consider whether there are investigative steps common to civil and criminal prosecutions, and to agency administrative actions, and that they discuss all significant issues that might have a bearing on the matter as a whole with their colleagues. When appropriate, criminal, civil, and administrative attorneys should coordinate an investigative strategy that includes prompt decisions on the merits of criminal and civil matters; sensitivity to grand jury secrecy, tax disclosure limitations and civil statutes of limitation; early computation and recovery of the full measure of the Government's losses; prevention of the dissipation of assets; global settlements; proper use of discovery, and compliance with the Double Jeopardy Clause. By bringing additional expertise to our efforts, expanding our arsenal of remedies, increasing program integrity and deterring future violations, we represent the full range of the Government's interests.

Accordingly, every United States Attorney's office and each Department Litigating Division should have a system for coordinating the criminal, civil and administrative aspects of all white-collar crime matters within the office. The system should contain management procedures to address issues of parallel proceedings including:

- timely assessment of the civil and administrative potential in all criminal case referrals, indictments, and declinations;

- timely assessment of the criminal potential in all civil case referrals and complaints;

- effective and timely communication with cognizant agency officials, including suspension and debarment authorities, to enable agencies to pursue available remedies;

- early and regular communication between civil and criminal attorneys regarding *qui tam* and other civil referrals, especially when the civil case is developing ahead of the criminal prosecution; and

- coordination, when appropriate with state and local authorities.

Consistent with our responsibility to make our enforcement efforts more efficient and effective, prosecutors should consult with the government attorneys on the civil side and appropriate agency officials regarding the investigative strategies to be used in their cases. With proper safeguards, evidence can be obtained without the grand jury by administrative subpoenas, search warrants and other means. Evidence can then be shared among the various personnel responsible for the matters. This information-sharing can provide a mechanism through which the Government can achieve a comprehensive settlement of all of the Government's various interests.

I welcome the participation of the various law enforcement agencies in this effort. I encourage those agencies and offices with investigatory responsibilities to recognize, through workplans and credit in the review process, accomplishments in the civil and administrative areas that arise from the work of their agents. I also encourage the United States Attorneys, Litigating Divisions and administrative agencies to similarly recognize those contributions.

To help offices in overcoming impediments to coordination that may arise from a lack of resources, experience or expertise, I also direct that appropriate staff in each office receive comprehensive training regarding parallel proceedings utilizing a course of instruction and training materials to be developed by the Council on White-Collar Crime and the Office of Legal Education.

APPENDIX 2

CHAPTER EIGHT—SENTENCING OF ORGANIZATIONS

Introductory Commentary

The guidelines and policy statements in this chapter apply when the convicted defendant is an organization. Organizations can act only through agents and, under federal criminal law, generally are vicariously liable for offenses committed by their agents. At the same time, individual agents are responsible for their own criminal conduct. Federal prosecutions of organizations therefore frequently involve individual and organizational co-defendants. Convicted individual agents of organizations are sentenced in accordance with the guidelines and policy statements in the preceding chapters. This chapter is designed so that the sanctions imposed upon organizations and their agents, taken together, will provide just punishment, adequate deterrence, and incentives for organizations to maintain internal mechanisms for preventing, detecting, and reporting criminal conduct.

This chapter reflects the following general principles: First, the court must, whenever practicable, order the organization to remedy any harm caused by the offense. The resources expended to remedy the harm should not be viewed as punishment, but rather as a means of making victims whole for the harm caused. Second, if the organization operated primarily for a criminal purpose or primarily by criminal means, the fine should be set sufficiently high to divest the organization of all its assets. Third, the fine range for any other organization should be based on the seriousness of the offense and the culpability of the organization. The seriousness of the offense generally will be reflected by the highest of the pecuniary gain, the pecuniary loss, or the amount in a guideline offense level fine table. Culpability generally will be determined by the steps taken by the organization prior to the offense to prevent and detect criminal conduct, the level and extent of involvement in or tolerance of the offense by certain personnel, and the organization's actions after an offense has been committed. Fourth, probation is an appropriate sentence for an organizational defendant when needed to ensure that another sanction will be fully implemented, or to ensure that steps will be taken within the organization to reduce the likelihood of future criminal conduct.

Historical Note: Effective November 1, 1991 (see Appendix C, amendment 422).

264 Corporate Fraud Investigations & Compliance Programs

PART A—GENERAL APPLICATION PRINCIPLES

§8A1.1. Applicability of Chapter Eight

This chapter applies to the sentencing of all organizations for felony and Class A misdemeanor offenses.

Commentary

Application Notes:

1. "Organization" means "a person other than an individual." 18 U.S.C. § 18. The term includes corporations, partnerships, associations, joint-stock companies, unions, trusts, pension funds, unincorporated organizations, governments and political subdivisions thereof, and non-profit organizations.

2. The fine guidelines in §§8C2.2 through 8C2.9 apply only to specified types of offenses. The other provisions of this chapter apply to the sentencing of all organizations for all felony and Class A misdemeanor offenses. For example, the restitution and probation provisions in Parts B and D of this chapter apply to the sentencing of an organization, even if the fine guidelines in §§8C2.2 through 8C2.9 do not apply.

Historical Note: Effective November 1, 1991 (see Appendix C, amendment 422).

§8A1.2. Application Instructions—Organizations

(a) Determine from Part B (Remedying Harm from Criminal Conduct) the sentencing requirements and options relating to restitution, remedial orders, community service, and notice to victims.

(b) Determine from Part C (Fines) the sentencing requirements and options relating to fines:

(1) If the organization operated primarily for a criminal purpose or primarily by criminal means, apply §8C1.1 (Determining the Fine—Criminal Purpose Organizations).

(2) Otherwise, apply §8C2.1 (Applicability of Fine Guidelines) to identify the counts for which the provisions of §§8C2.2 through 8C2.9 apply. For such counts:

(A) Refer to §8C2.2 (Preliminary Determination of Inability to Pay Fine) to determine whether an abbreviated determination of the guideline fine range may be warranted.

(B) Apply §8C2.3 (Offense Level) to determine the offense level from Chapter Two (Offense Conduct) and Chapter Three, Part D (Multiple Counts).

(C) Apply §8C2.4 (Base Fine) to determine the base fine.

(D) Apply §8C2.5 (Culpability Score) to determine the culpability score.

Appendix 2   265

(E) Apply §8C2.6 (Minimum and Maximum Multipliers) to determine the minimum and maximum multipliers corresponding to the culpability score.

(F) Apply §8C2.7 (Guideline Fine Range—Organizations) to determine the minimum and maximum of the guideline fine range.

(G) Refer to §8C2.8 (Determining the Fine Within the Range) to determine the amount of the fine within the applicable guideline range.

(H) Apply §8C2.9 (Disgorgement) to determine whether an increase to the fine is required.

For any count or counts not covered under §8C2.1 (Applicability of Fine Guidelines), apply §8C2.10 (Determining the Fine for Other Counts).

(3) Apply the provisions relating to the implementation of the sentence of a fine in Part C, Subpart 3 (Implementing the Sentence of a Fine).

(4) For grounds for departure from the applicable guideline fine range, refer to Part C, Subpart 4 (Departures from the Guideline Fine Range).

(c) Determine from Part D (Organizational Probation) the sentencing requirements and options relating to probation.

(d) Determine from Part E (Special Assessments, Forfeitures, and Costs) the sentencing requirements relating to special assessments, forfeitures, and costs.

Commentary

Application Notes:

1. Determinations under this chapter are to be based upon the facts and information specified in the applicable guideline. Determinations that reference other chapters are to be made under the standards applicable to determinations under those chapters.

2. The definitions in the Commentary to §1B1.1 (Application Instructions) and the guidelines and commentary in §§1B1.2 through 1B1.8 apply to determinations under this chapter unless otherwise specified. The adjustments in Chapter Three, Parts A (Victim-Related Adjustments), B (Role in the Offense), C (Obstruction), and E (Acceptance of Responsibility) do not apply. The provisions of Chapter Six (Sentencing Procedures and Plea Agreements) apply to proceedings in which the defendant is an organization. Guidelines and policy statements not referenced in this chapter, directly or indirectly, do not apply when the defendant is an organization; e.g., the policy statements in Chapter Seven (Violations of Probation and Supervised Release) do not apply to organizations.

3. The following are definitions of terms used frequently in this chapter:

(a) "Offense" means the offense of conviction and all relevant conduct under §1B1.3 (Relevant Conduct) unless a different meaning is specified or is otherwise clear from the context. The term "instant" is used in connection with "

offense," "federal offense," or "offense of conviction," as the case may be, to distinguish the violation for which the defendant is being sentenced from a prior or subsequent offense, or from an offense before another court (e.g., an offense before a state court involving the same underlying conduct).

(b) "High-level personnel of the organization" means individuals who have substantial control over the organization or who have a substantial role in the making of policy within the organization. The term includes: a director; an executive officer; an individual in charge of a major business or functional unit of the organization, such as sales, administration, or finance; and an individual with a substantial ownership interest. "High-level personnel of a unit of the organization" is defined in the Commentary to §8C2.5 (Culpability Score).

(c) "Substantial authority personnel" means individuals who within the scope of their authority exercise a substantial measure of discretion in acting on behalf of an organization. The term includes high-level personnel, individuals who exercise substantial supervisory authority (e.g., a plant manager, a sales manager), and any other individuals who, although not a part of an organization's management, nevertheless exercise substantial discretion when acting within the scope of their authority (e.g., an individual with authority in an organization to negotiate or set price levels or an individual authorized to negotiate or approve significant contracts). Whether an individual falls within this category must be determined on a case-by-case basis.

(d) "Agent" means any individual, including a director, an officer, an employee, or an independent contractor, authorized to act on behalf of the organization.

(e) An individual "condoned" an offense if the individual knew of the offense and did not take reasonable steps to prevent or terminate the offense.

(f) "Similar misconduct" means prior conduct that is similar in nature to the conduct underlying the instant offense, without regard to whether or not such conduct violated the same statutory provision. For example, prior Medicare fraud would be misconduct similar to an instant offense involving another type of fraud.

(g) "Prior criminal adjudication" means conviction by trial, plea of guilty (including an Alford plea), or plea of nolo contendere.

(h) "Pecuniary gain" is derived from 18 U.S.C. § 3571(d) and means the additional before- tax profit to the defendant resulting from the relevant conduct of the offense. Gain can result from either additional revenue or cost savings. For example, an offense involving odometer tampering can produce additional revenue. In such a case, the pecuniary gain is the additional revenue received because the automobiles appeared to have less mileage, i.e., the difference between the price received or expected for the automobiles with the apparent mileage and the fair market value of the automobiles with the actual mileage. An offense involving defense procurement fraud related to defective product testing can produce pecuniary gain resulting from cost savings. In such a case,

the pecuniary gain is the amount saved because the product was not tested in the required manner.

(i) "Pecuniary loss" is derived from 18 U.S.C. § 3571(d) and is equivalent to the term "loss" as used in Chapter Two (Offense Conduct). See Commentary to §§2B1.1 (Larceny, Embezzlement, and Other Forms of Theft), 2F1.1 (Fraud and Deceit), and definitions of "tax loss" in Chapter Two, Part T (Offenses Involving Taxation).

(j) An individual was "willfully ignorant of the offense" if the individual did not investigate the possible occurrence of unlawful conduct despite knowledge of circumstances that would lead a reasonable person to investigate whether unlawful conduct had occurred.

(k) An "effective program to prevent and detect violations of law" means a program that has been reasonably designed, implemented, and enforced so that it generally will be effective in preventing and detecting criminal conduct. Failure to prevent or detect the instant offense, by itself, does not mean that the program was not effective. The hallmark of an effective program to prevent and detect violations of law is that the organization exercised due diligence in seeking to prevent and detect criminal conduct by its employees and other agents. Due diligence requires at a minimum that the organization must have taken the following types of steps:

(1) The organization must have established compliance standards and procedures to be followed by its employees and other agents that are reasonably capable of reducing the prospect of criminal conduct.

(2) Specific individual(s) within high-level personnel of the organization must have been assigned overall responsibility to oversee compliance with such standards and procedures.

(3) The organization must have used due care not to delegate substantial discretionary authority to individuals whom the organization knew, or should have known through the exercise of due diligence, had a propensity to engage in illegal activities.

(4) The organization must have taken steps to communicate effectively its standards and procedures to all employees and other agents, e.g., by requiring participation in training programs or by disseminating publications that explain in a practical manner what is required.

(5) The organization must have taken reasonable steps to achieve compliance with its standards, e.g., by utilizing monitoring and auditing systems reasonably designed to detect criminal conduct by its employees and other agents and by having in place and publicizing a reporting system whereby employees and other agents could report criminal conduct by others within the organization without fear of retribution.

(6) The standards must have been consistently enforced through appropriate disciplinary mechanisms, including, as appropriate, discipline of individuals responsible for the failure to detect an offense. Adequate discipline of individuals responsible for an offense is a necessary component of enforcement; however, the form of discipline that will be appropriate will be case specific.

(7) After an offense has been detected, the organization must have taken all reasonable steps to respond appropriately to the offense and to prevent further similar offenses—including any necessary modifications to its program to prevent and detect violations of law.

The precise actions necessary for an effective program to prevent and detect violations of law will depend upon a number of factors. Among the relevant factors are:

(i) Size of the organization—The requisite degree of formality of a program to prevent and detect violations of law will vary with the size of the organization: the larger the organization, the more formal the program typically should be. A larger organization generally should have established written policies defining the standards and procedures to be followed by its employees and other agents.

(ii) Likelihood that certain offenses may occur because of the nature of its business—If because of the nature of an organization's business there is a substantial risk that certain types of offenses may occur, management must have taken steps to prevent and detect those types of offenses. For example, if an organization handles toxic substances, it must have established standards and procedures designed to ensure that those substances are properly handled at all times. If an organization employs sales personnel who have flexibility in setting prices, it must have established standards and procedures designed to prevent and detect price-fixing. If an organization employs sales personnel who have flexibility to represent the material characteristics of a product, it must have established standards and procedures designed to prevent fraud.

(iii) Prior history of the organization—An organization's prior history may indicate types of offenses that it should have taken actions to prevent. Recurrence of misconduct similar to that which an organization has previously committed casts doubt on whether it took all reasonable steps to prevent such misconduct.

An organization's failure to incorporate and follow applicable industry practice or the standards called for by any applicable governmental regulation weighs against a finding of an effective program to prevent and detect violations of law.

Historical Note: Effective November 1, 1991 (see Appendix C, amendment 422); November 1, 1997 (see Appendix C, amendment 546).

Appendix 2 269

PART B—REMEDYING HARM FROM CRIMINAL CONDUCT

Introductory Commentary

As a general principle, the court should require that the organization take all appropriate steps to provide compensation to victims and otherwise remedy the harm caused or threatened by the offense. A restitution order or an order of probation requiring restitution can be used to compensate identifiable victims of the offense. A remedial order or an order of probation requiring community service can be used to reduce or eliminate the harm threatened, or to repair the harm caused by the offense, when that harm or threatened harm would otherwise not be remedied. An order of notice to victims can be used to notify unidentified victims of the offense.

Historical Note: Effective November 1, 1991 (see Appendix C, amendment 422).

§8B1.1. Restitution—Organizations

(a) In the case of an identifiable victim, the court shall —

(1) enter a restitution order for the full amount of the victim's loss, if such order is authorized under 18 U.S.C. § 2248, § 2259, § 2264, § 2327, § 3663, or § 3663A; or

(2) impose a term of probation or supervised release with a condition requiring restitution for the full amount of the victim's loss, if the offense is not an offense for which restitution is authorized under 18 U.S.C. § 3663(a)(1) but otherwise meets the criteria for an order of restitution under that section.

(b) *Provided*, that the provisions of subsection (a) do not apply —

(1) when full restitution has been made; or

(2) in the case of a restitution order under § 3663; a restitution order under 18 U.S.C. § 3663A that pertains to an offense against property described in 18 U.S.C. § 3663A(c)(1)(A)(ii); or a condition of restitution imposed pursuant to subsection (a)(2) above, to the extent the court finds, from facts on the record, that (A) the number of identifiable victims is so large as to make restitution impracticable; or (B) determining complex issues of fact related to the cause or amount of the victim's losses would complicate or prolong the sentencing process to a degree that the need to provide restitution to any victim is outweighed by the burden on the sentencing process.

(c) If a defendant is ordered to make restitution to an identifiable victim and to pay a fine, the court shall order that any money paid by the defendant shall first be applied to satisfy the order of restitution.

(d) A restitution order may direct the defendant to make a single, lump sum payment, partial payments at specified intervals, in-kind payments, or a combination of payments at specified intervals and in-kind payments. See 18 U.S.C. § 3664(f)(3)(A). An in-kind payment may be in the form of (1) return of property; (2) replacement of property; or (3) if the victim agrees, services rendered to the victim or to a person or organization other than the victim. See 18 U.S.C. § 3664(f)(4).

(e) A restitution order may direct the defendant to make nominal periodic payments if the court finds from facts on the record that the economic circumstances of the defendant do not allow the payment of any amount of a restitution order, and do not allow for the payment of the full amount of a restitution order in the foreseeable future under any reasonable schedule of payments.

(f) Special Instruction

(1) This guideline applies only to a defendant convicted of an offense committed on or after November 1, 1997. Notwithstanding the provisions of §1B1.11 (Use of Guidelines Manual in Effect on Date of Sentencing), use the former §8B1.1 (set forth in Appendix C, amendment 571) in lieu of this guideline in any other case.

Commentary

Background: Section 3553(a)(7) of Title 18, United States Code, requires the court, "in determining the particular sentence to be imposed," to consider "the need to provide restitution to any victims of the offense." Orders of restitution are authorized under 18 U.S.C. §§ 2248, 2259, 2264, 2327, 3663, and 3663A. For offenses for which an order of restitution is not authorized, restitution may be imposed as a condition of probation.

Historical Note: Effective November 1, 1991 (see Appendix C, amendment 422); November 1, 1997 (see Appendix C, amendment 571).

§8B1.2. Remedial Orders—Organizations (Policy Statement)

(a) To the extent not addressed under §8B1.1 (Restitution—Organizations), a remedial order imposed as a condition of probation may require the organization to remedy the harm caused by the offense and to eliminate or reduce the risk that the instant offense will cause future harm.

(b) If the magnitude of expected future harm can be reasonably estimated, the court may require the organization to create a trust fund sufficient to address that expected harm.

Commentary

Background: The purposes of a remedial order are to remedy harm that has already occurred and to prevent future harm. A remedial order requiring corrective action by the organization may be necessary to prevent future injury from the instant offense, e.g., a product recall for a food and drug violation or a clean-up order for an environmental violation. In some cases in which a remedial order

Appendix 2

potentially may be appropriate, a governmental regulatory agency, e.g., the Environmental Protection Agency or the Food and Drug Administration, may have authority to order remedial measures. In such cases, a remedial order by the court may not be necessary. If a remedial order is entered, it should be coordinated with any administrative or civil actions taken by the appropriate governmental regulatory agency.

Historical Note: Effective November 1, 1991 (see Appendix C, amendment 422).

§8B1.3. Community Service—Organizations (Policy Statement)

Community service may be ordered as a condition of probation where such community service is reasonably designed to repair the harm caused by the offense.

Commentary

Background: An organization can perform community service only by employing its resources or paying its employees or others to do so. Consequently, an order that an organization perform community service is essentially an indirect monetary sanction, and therefore generally less desirable than a direct monetary sanction. However, where the convicted organization possesses knowledge, facilities, or skills that uniquely qualify it to repair damage caused by the offense, community service directed at repairing damage may provide an efficient means of remedying harm caused.

In the past, some forms of community service imposed on organizations have not been related to the purposes of sentencing. Requiring a defendant to endow a chair at a university or to contribute to a local charity would not be consistent with this section unless such community service provided a means for preventive or corrective action directly related to the offense and therefore served one of the purposes of sentencing set forth in 18 U.S.C. § 3553(a).

Historical Note: Effective November 1, 1991 (see Appendix C, amendment 422).

§8B1.4. Order of Notice to Victims—Organizations

Apply §5F1.4 (Order of Notice to Victims).

Historical Note: Effective November 1, 1991 (see Appendix C, amendment 422).

PART C—FINES

1. DETERMINING THE FINE—CRIMINAL PURPOSE ORGANIZATIONS

§8C1.1. Determining the Fine—Criminal Purpose Organizations

If, upon consideration of the nature and circumstances of the offense and the history and characteristics of the organization, the court determines that the organization operated primarily for a criminal purpose or primarily by criminal means, the

272 Corporate Fraud Investigations & Compliance Programs

fine shall be set at an amount (subject to the statutory maximum) sufficient to divest the organization of all its net assets. When this section applies, Subpart 2 (Determining the Fine—Other Organizations) and §8C3.4 (Fines Paid by Owners of Closely Held Organizations) do not apply.

Commentary

Application Note:

1. "Net assets," as used in this section, means the assets remaining after payment of all legitimate claims against assets by known innocent bona fide creditors.

Background: This guideline addresses the case in which the court, based upon an examination of the nature and circumstances of the offense and the history and characteristics of the organization, determines that the organization was operated primarily for a criminal purpose (e.g., a front for a scheme that was designed to commit fraud; an organization established to participate in the illegal manufacture, importation, or distribution of a controlled substance) or operated primarily by criminal means (e.g., a hazardous waste disposal business that had no legitimate means of disposing of hazardous waste). In such a case, the fine shall be set at an amount sufficient to remove all of the organization's net assets. If the extent of the assets of the organization is unknown, the maximum fine authorized by statute should be imposed, absent innocent bona fide creditors.

Historical Note: Effective November 1, 1991 (see Appendix C, amendment 422).

* * * * *

2. DETERMINING THE FINE—OTHER ORGANIZATIONS

§8C2.1. Applicability of Fine Guidelines

The provisions of §§8C2.2 through 8C2.9 apply to each count for which the applicable guideline offense level is determined under:

(a) §§2B1.1, 2B1.3, 2B2.3, 2B4.1, 2B5.3, 2B6.1;
§§2C1.1, 2C1.2, 2C1.4, 2C1.6, 2C1.7;
§§2D1.7, 2D3.1, 2D3.2;
§§2E3.1, 2E4.1, 2E5.1, 2E5.3;
§§2F1.1, 2F1.2;
§2G3.1;
§§2K1.1, 2K2.1;
§2L1.1;
§2N3.1;
§2R1.1;
§§2S1.1, 2S1.2, 2S1.3;
§§2T1.1, 2T1.4, 2T1.6, 2T1.7, 2T1.8, 2T1.9, 2T2.1, 2T2.2, 2T3.1; or

Appendix 2

(b) §§2E1.1, 2X1.1, 2X2.1, 2X3.1, 2X4.1, with respect to cases in which the offense level for the underlying offense is determined under one of the guideline sections listed in subsection (a) above.

Commentary

Application Notes:

1. If the Chapter Two offense guideline for a count is listed in subsection (a) or (b) above, and the applicable guideline results in the determination of the offense level by use of one of the listed guidelines, apply the provisions of §§8C2.2 through 8C2.9 to that count. For example, §§8C2.2 through 8C2.9 apply to an offense under §2K2.1 (an offense guideline listed in subsection (a)), unless the cross reference in that guideline requires the offense level to be determined under an offense guideline section not listed in subsection (a).

2. If the Chapter Two offense guideline for a count is not listed in subsection (a) or (b) above, but the applicable guideline results in the determination of the offense level by use of a listed guideline, apply the provisions of §§8C2.2 through 8C2.9 to that count. For example, where the conduct set forth in a count of conviction ordinarily referenced to §2N2.1 (an offense guideline not listed in subsection (a)) establishes §2F1.1 (Fraud and Deceit) as the applicable offense guideline (an offense guideline listed in subsection (a)), §§8C2.2 through 8C2.9 would apply because the actual offense level is determined under §2F1.1 (Fraud and Deceit).

Background: The fine guidelines of this subpart apply only to offenses covered by the guideline sections set forth in subsection (a) above. For example, the provisions of §§8C2.2 through 8C2.9 do not apply to counts for which the applicable guideline offense level is determined under Chapter Two, Part Q (Offenses Involving the Environment). For such cases, §8C2.10 (Determining the Fine for Other Counts) is applicable.

Historical Note: Effective November 1, 1991 (see Appendix C, amendment 422). Amended effective November 1, 1992 (see Appendix C, amendment 453); November 1, 1993 (see Appendix C, amendment 496).

§8C2.2. Preliminary Determination of Inability to Pay Fine

(a) Where it is readily ascertainable that the organization cannot and is not likely to become able (even on an installment schedule) to pay restitution required under §8B1.1 (Restitution—Organizations), a determination of the guideline fine range is unnecessary because, pursuant to §8C3.3(a), no fine would be imposed.

(b) Where it is readily ascertainable through a preliminary determination of the minimum of the guideline fine range (see §§8C2.3 through 8C2.7) that the organization cannot and is not likely to become able (even on an installment schedule) to pay such minimum guideline fine, a further determination of the guideline fine range is unnecessary. Instead, the court may use the preliminary determination and

274 Corporate Fraud Investigations & Compliance Programs

impose the fine that would result from the application of §8C3.3 (Reduction of Fine Based on Inability to Pay).

Commentary

Application Notes:

1. In a case of a determination under subsection (a), a statement that "the guideline fine range was not determined because it is readily ascertainable that the defendant cannot and is not likely to become able to pay restitution" is recommended.

2. In a case of a determination under subsection (b), a statement that "no precise determination of the guideline fine range is required because it is readily ascertainable that the defendant cannot and is not likely to become able to pay the minimum of the guideline fine range" is recommended.

Background: Many organizational defendants lack the ability to pay restitution. In addition, many organizational defendants who may be able to pay restitution lack the ability to pay the minimum fine called for by §8C2.7(a). In such cases, a complete determination of the guideline fine range may be a needless exercise. This section provides for an abbreviated determination of the guideline fine range that can be applied where it is readily ascertainable that the fine within the guideline fine range determined under §8C2.7 (Guideline Fine Range—Organizations) would be reduced under §8C3.3 (Reduction of Fine Based on Inability to Pay).

Historical Note: Effective November 1, 1991 (see Appendix C, amendment 422).

§8C2.3. Offense Level

(a) For each count covered by §8C2.1 (Applicability of Fine Guidelines), use the applicable Chapter Two guideline to determine the base offense level and apply, in the order listed, any appropriate adjustments contained in that guideline.

(b) Where there is more than one such count, apply Chapter Three, Part D (Multiple Counts) to determine the combined offense level.

Commentary

Application Notes:

1. In determining the offense level under this section, "defendant," as used in Chapter Two, includes any agent of the organization for whose conduct the organization is criminally responsible.

2. In determining the offense level under this section, apply the provisions of §§1B1.2 through 1B1.8. Do not apply the adjustments in Chapter Three, Parts A (Victim-Related Adjustments), B (Role in the Offense), C (Obstruction), and E (Acceptance of Responsibility).

Historical Note: Effective November 1, 1991 (see Appendix C, amendment 422).

§8C2.4. Base Fine

(a) The base fine is the greatest of:

(1) the amount from the table in subsection (d) below corresponding to the offense level determined under §8C2.3 (Offense Level); or

(2) the pecuniary gain to the organization from the offense; or

(3) the pecuniary loss from the offense caused by the organization, to the extent the loss was caused intentionally, knowingly, or recklessly.

(b) *Provided*, that if the applicable offense guideline in Chapter Two includes a special instruction for organizational fines, that special instruction shall be applied, as appropriate.

(c) *Provided, further*, that to the extent the calculation of either pecuniary gain or pecuniary loss would unduly complicate or prolong the sentencing process, that amount, i.e., gain or loss as appropriate, shall not be used for the determination of the base fine.

(d) Offense Level Fine Table

Offense Level	Amount
6 or less	$5,000
7	$7,500
8	$10,000
9	$15,000
10	$20,000
11	$30,000
12	$40,000
13	$60,000
14	$85,000
15	$125,000
16	$175,000
17	$250,000
18	$350,000
19	$500,000
20	$650,000
21	$910,000
22	$1,200,000
23	$1,600,000
24	$2,100,000

Offense Level	Amount
25	$2,800,000
26	$3,700,000
27	$4,800,000
28	$6,300,000
29	$8,100,000
30	$10,500,000
31	$13,500,000
32	$17,500,000
33	$22,000,000
34	$28,500,000
35	$36,000,000
36	$45,500,000
37	$57,500,000
38 or more	$72,500,000

Commentary

Application Notes:

1. "Pecuniary gain," "pecuniary loss," and "offense" are defined in the Commentary to §8A1.2 (Application Instructions—Organizations). Note that subsections (a)(2) and (a)(3) contain certain limitations as to the use of pecuniary gain and pecuniary loss in determining the base fine. Under subsection (a)(2), the pecuniary gain used to determine the base fine is the pecuniary gain to the organization from the offense. Under subsection (a)(3), the pecuniary loss used to determine the base fine is the pecuniary loss from the offense caused by the organization, to the extent that such loss was caused intentionally, knowingly, or recklessly.

2. Under 18 U.S.C. § 3571(d), the court is not required to calculate pecuniary loss or pecuniary gain to the extent that determination of loss or gain would unduly complicate or prolong the sentencing process. Nevertheless, the court may need to approximate loss in order to calculate offense levels under Chapter Two. See Commentary to §2B1.1 (Larceny, Embezzlement, and Other Forms of Theft). If loss is approximated for purposes of determining the applicable offense level, the court should use that approximation as the starting point for calculating pecuniary loss under this section.

3. In a case of an attempted offense or a conspiracy to commit an offense, pecuniary loss and pecuniary gain are to be determined in accordance with the principles stated in §2X1.1 (Attempt, Solicitation, or Conspiracy).

4. In a case involving multiple participants (i.e., multiple organizations, or the organization and individual(s) unassociated with the organization), the applicable offense level is to be determined without regard to apportionment of the gain from or loss caused by the offense. See §1B1.3 (Relevant Conduct). However, if the base fine is determined under subsections (a)(2) or (a)(3), the court may, as appropriate, apportion gain or loss considering the defendant's relative culpability and other pertinent factors. Note also that under §2R1.1(d)(1), the volume of commerce, which is used in determining a proxy for loss under §8C2.4(a)(3), is limited to the volume of commerce attributable to the defendant.

5. Special instructions regarding the determination of the base fine are contained in §§2B4.1 (Bribery in Procurement of Bank Loan and Other Commercial Bribery); 2C1.1 (Offering, Giving, Soliciting, or Receiving a Bribe; Extortion Under Color of Official Right); 2C1.2 (Offering, Giving, Soliciting, or Receiving a Gratuity); 2E5.1 (Offering, Accepting, or Soliciting a Bribe or Gratuity Affecting the Operation of an Employee Welfare or Pension Benefit Plan; Prohibited Payments or Lending of Money by Employer or Agent to Employees, Representatives, or Labor Organizations); 2R1.1 (Bid-Rigging, Price-Fixing or Market- Allocation Agreements Among Competitors); 2S1.1 (Laundering of Monetary Instruments); and 2S1.2 (Engaging in Monetary Transactions in Property Derived from Specified Unlawful Activity).

Background: Under this section, the base fine is determined in one of three ways: (1) by the amount, based on the offense level, from the table in subsection (d); (2) by the pecuniary gain to the organization from the offense; and (3) by the pecuniary loss caused by the organization, to the extent that such loss was caused intentionally, knowingly, or recklessly. In certain cases, special instructions for determining the loss or offense level amount apply. As a general rule, the base fine measures the seriousness of the offense. The determinants of the base fine are selected so that, in conjunction with the multipliers derived from the culpability score in §8C2.5 (Culpability Score), they will result in guideline fine ranges appropriate to deter organizational criminal conduct and to provide incentives for organizations to maintain internal mechanisms for preventing, detecting, and reporting criminal conduct. In order to deter organizations from seeking to obtain financial reward through criminal conduct, this section provides that, when greatest, pecuniary gain to the organization is used to determine the base fine. In order to ensure that organizations will seek to prevent losses intentionally, knowingly, or recklessly caused by their agents, this section provides that, when greatest, pecuniary loss is used to determine the base fine in such circumstances. Chapter Two provides special instructions for fines that include specific rules for determining the base fine in connection with certain types of offenses in which the calculation of loss or gain is difficult, e.g., price-fixing and money laundering. For these offenses, the special instructions tailor the base fine to circumstances that occur in connection with such offenses and that generally relate to the magnitude of loss or gain resulting from such offenses.

Historical Note: Effective November 1, 1991 (see Appendix C, amendment 422). Amended effective November 1, 1993 (see Appendix C, amendment 496); November 1, 1995 (see Appendix C, amendment 534).

§8C2.5. Culpability Score

(a) Start with **5** points and apply subsections (b) through (g) below.

(b) Involvement in or Tolerance of Criminal Activity

If more than one applies, use the greatest:

(1) If —

(A) the organization had 5,000 or more employees and

(i) an individual within high-level personnel of the organization participated in, condoned, or was willfully ignorant of the offense; or

(ii) tolerance of the offense by substantial authority personnel was pervasive throughout the organization; or

(B) the unit of the organization within which the offense was committed had 5,000 or more employees and

(i) an individual within high-level personnel of the unit participated in, condoned, or was willfully ignorant of the offense; or

(ii) tolerance of the offense by substantial authority personnel was pervasive throughout such unit,

add **5** organization points; or

(2) If —

(A) the had 1,000 or more employees and

(i) an individual within high-level personnel of the organization participated in, condoned, or was willfully ignorant of the offense; or

(ii) tolerance of the offense by substantial authority personnel was pervasive throughout the organization; or

(B) the unit of the organization within which the offense was committed had 1,000 or more employees and

(i) an individual within high-level personnel of the unit participated in, condoned, or was willfully ignorant of the offense; or

(ii) tolerance of the offense by substantial authority personnel was pervasive throughout such unit,

add **4** points; or

(3) If —

(A) the organization had 200 or more employees and

(i) an individual within high-level personnel of the organization participated in, condoned, or was willfully ignorant of the offense; or

(ii) tolerance of the offense by substantial authority personnel was pervasive throughout the organization; or

(B) the unit of the organization within which the offense was committed had 200 or more employees and

(i) an individual within high-level personnel of the unit participated in, condoned, or was willfully ignorant of the offense; or

(ii) tolerance of the offense by substantial authority personnel was pervasive throughout such unit,

add **3** points; or

(4) If the organization had 50 or more employees and an individual within substantial authority personnel participated in, condoned, or was willfully ignorant of the offense, add **2** points; or

(5) If the organization had 10 or more employees and an individual within substantial authority personnel participated in, condoned, or was willfully ignorant of the offense, add **1** point.

(c) Prior History

If more than one applies, use the greater:

(1) If the organization (or separately managed line of business) committed any part of the instant offense less than 10 years after (A) a criminal adjudication based on similar misconduct; or (B) civil or administrative adjudication(s) based on two or more separate instances of similar misconduct, add **1** point; or

(2) If the organization (or separately managed line of business) committed any part of the instant offense less than 5 years after (A) a criminal adjudication based on similar misconduct; or (B) civil or administrative adjudication(s) based on two or more separate instances of similar misconduct, add **2** points.

(d) Violation of an Order

If more than one applies, use the greater:

(1) (A) If the commission of the instant offense violated a judicial order or injunction, other than a violation of a condition of probation; or (B) if the organization (or separately managed line of business) violated a condition of probation by engaging in similar misconduct, i.e., misconduct similar to that for which it was placed on probation, add **2** points; or

(2) If the commission of the instant offense violated a condition of probation, add **1** point.

(e) Obstruction of Justice

If the organization willfully obstructed or impeded, attempted to obstruct or impede, or aided, abetted, or encouraged obstruction of justice during the investigation, prosecution, or sentencing of the instant offense, or, with knowledge thereof, failed to take reasonable steps to prevent such obstruction or impedance or attempted obstruction or impedance, add **3** points.

280 Corporate Fraud Investigations & Compliance Programs

(f) Effective Program to Prevent and Detect Violations of Law

If the offense occurred despite an effective program to prevent and detect violations of law, subtract **3** points.

Provided, that this subsection does not apply if an individual within high-level personnel of the organization, a person within high-level personnel of the unit of the organization within which the offense was committed where the unit had 200 or more employees, or an individual responsible for the administration or enforcement of a program to prevent and detect violations of law participated in, condoned, or was willfully ignorant of the offense. Participation of an individual within substantial authority personnel in an offense results in a rebuttable presumption that the organization did not have an effective program to prevent and detect violations of law.

Provided, further, that this subsection does not apply if, after becoming aware of an offense, the organization unreasonably delayed reporting the offense to appropriate governmental authorities.

(g) Self-Reporting, Cooperation, and Acceptance of Responsibility

If more than one applies, use the greatest:

(1) If the organization (A) prior to an imminent threat of disclosure or government investigation; and (B) within a reasonably prompt time after becoming aware of the offense, reported the offense to appropriate governmental authorities, fully cooperated in the investigation, and clearly demonstrated recognition and affirmative acceptance of responsibility for its criminal conduct, subtract **5** points; or

(2) If the organization fully cooperated in the investigation and clearly demonstrated recognition and affirmative acceptance of responsibility for its criminal conduct, subtract **2** points; or

(3) If the organization clearly demonstrated recognition and affirmative acceptance of responsibility for its criminal conduct, subtract **1** point.

Commentary

Application Notes:

1. "Substantial authority personnel," "condoned," "willfully ignorant of the offense," "similar misconduct," "prior criminal adjudication," and "effective program to prevent and detect violations of law," are defined in the Commentary to §8A1.2 (Application Instructions—Organizations).

2. For purposes of subsection (b), "unit of the organization" means any reasonably distinct operational component of the organization. For example, a large organization may have several large units such as divisions or subsidiaries, as well as many smaller units such as specialized manufacturing, marketing, or accounting operations within these larger units. For purposes of this definition, all of these types of units are encompassed within the term "unit of the organization."

3. "High-level personnel of the organization" is defined in the Commentary to §8A1.2 (Application Instructions—Organizations). With respect to a unit with 200 or more employees, "high-level personnel of a unit of the organization" means agents within the unit who set the policy for or control that unit. For example, if the managing agent of a unit with 200 employees participated in an offense, three points would be added under subsection (b)(3); if that organization had 1,000 employees and the managing agent of the unit with 200 employees were also within high-level personnel of the entire organization, four points (rather than three) would be added under subsection (b)(2).

4. Pervasiveness under subsection (b) will be case specific and depend on the number, and degree of responsibility, of individuals within substantial authority personnel who participated in, condoned, or were willfully ignorant of the offense. Fewer individuals need to be involved for a finding of pervasiveness if those individuals exercised a relatively high degree of authority. Pervasiveness can occur either within an organization as a whole or within a unit of an organization. For example, if an offense were committed in an organization with 1,000 employees but the tolerance of the offense was pervasive only within a unit of the organization with 200 employees (and no high-level personnel of the organization participated in, condoned, or was willfully ignorant of the offense), three points would be added under subsection (b)(3). If, in the same organization, tolerance of the offense was pervasive throughout the organization as a whole, or an individual within high-level personnel of the organization participated in the offense, four points (rather than three) would be added under subsection (b)(2).

5. A "separately managed line of business," as used in subsections (c) and (d), is a subpart of a for-profit organization that has its own management, has a high degree of autonomy from higher managerial authority, and maintains its own separate books of account. Corporate subsidiaries and divisions frequently are separately managed lines of business. Under subsection (c), in determining the prior history of an organization with separately managed lines of business, only the prior conduct or criminal record of the separately managed line of business involved in the instant offense is to be used. Under subsection (d), in the context of an organization with separately managed lines of business, in making the determination whether a violation of a condition of probation involved engaging in similar misconduct, only the prior misconduct of the separately managed line of business involved in the instant offense is to be considered.

6. Under subsection (c), in determining the prior history of an organization or separately managed line of business, the conduct of the underlying economic entity shall be considered without regard to its legal structure or ownership. For example, if two companies merged and became separate divisions and separately managed lines of business within the merged company, each division would retain the prior history of its predecessor company. If a company reorganized and became a new legal entity, the new company would retain the prior history of the predecessor company. In contrast, if one company purchased the physical assets but not the ongoing business of another company, the prior history of the company selling the physical assets would not be transferred to the company purchasing the assets. However, if an organization is acquired by another organization in response to solicitations by appropriate federal government officials, the prior history of the acquired organization shall not be attributed to the acquiring organization.

7. Under subsections (c)(1)(B) and (c)(2)(B), the civil or administrative adjudication(s) must have occurred within the specified period (ten or five years) of the instant offense.

8. Adjust the culpability score for the factors listed in subsection (e) whether or not the offense guideline incorporates that factor, or that factor is inherent in the offense.

9. Subsection (e) applies where the obstruction is committed on behalf of the organization; it does not apply where an individual or individuals have attempted to conceal their misconduct from the organization. The Commentary to §3C1.1 (Obstructing or Impeding the Administration of Justice) provides guidance regarding the types of conduct that constitute obstruction.

10. The second proviso in subsection (f) contemplates that the organization will be allowed a reasonable period of time to conduct an internal investigation. In addition, no reporting is required by this proviso if the organization reasonably concluded, based on the information then available, that no offense had been committed.

11. "Appropriate governmental authorities," as used in subsections (f) and (g)(1), means the federal or state law enforcement, regulatory, or program officials having jurisdiction over such matter. To qualify for a reduction under subsection (g)(1), the report to appropriate governmental authorities must be made under the direction of the organization.

12. To qualify for a reduction under subsection (g)(1) or (g)(2), cooperation must be both timely and thorough. To be timely, the cooperation must begin essentially at the same time as the organization is officially notified of a criminal investigation. To be thorough, the cooperation should include the disclosure of all pertinent information known by the organization. A prime test of whether the organization has disclosed all pertinent information is whether the information is sufficient for law enforcement personnel to identify the nature and extent of the offense and the individual(s) responsible for the criminal conduct. However, the cooperation to be measured is the cooperation of the organization itself, not the cooperation of individuals within the organization. If, because of the lack of cooperation of particular individual(s), neither the organization nor law enforcement personnel are able to identify the culpable individual(s) within the organization despite the organization's efforts to cooperate fully, the organization may still be given credit for full cooperation.

13. Entry of a plea of guilty prior to the commencement of trial combined with truthful admission of involvement in the offense and related conduct ordinarily will constitute significant evidence of affirmative acceptance of responsibility under subsection (g), unless outweighed by conduct of the organization that is inconsistent with such acceptance of responsibility. This adjustment is not intended to apply to an organization that puts the government to its burden of proof at trial by denying the essential factual elements of guilt, is convicted, and only then admits guilt and expresses remorse. Conviction by trial, however, does not automatically preclude an organization from consideration for such a reduction. In rare situations, an organization may clearly demonstrate an acceptance of responsibility for its criminal conduct even though it exercises its constitutional right to a trial. This may occur, for example, where an organization goes to trial to assert and preserve issues that do not relate to factual guilt (e.g., to make a constitutional challenge to a statute or a challenge to the applicability of a statute to its conduct). In each such instance, however, a determination that an organization has accepted responsibility will be based primarily upon pretrial statements and conduct.

14. In making a determination with respect to subsection (g), the court may determine that the chief executive officer or highest ranking employee of an organization should appear at sentencing in order to signify that the organization has clearly demonstrated recognition and affirmative acceptance of responsibility.

Background: The increased culpability scores under subsection (b) are based on three interrelated principles. First, an organization is more culpable when individuals who manage the organization or who have substantial discretion in acting for the organization participate in, condone, or are willfully ignorant of criminal conduct. Second, as organizations become larger and their managements become more professional, participation in, condonation of, or willful ignorance of criminal conduct by such management is increasingly a breach of trust or abuse of position. Third, as organizations increase in size, the risk of criminal conduct beyond that reflected in the instant offense also increases whenever management's tolerance of that offense is pervasive. Because of the continuum of sizes of organizations and professionalization of management, subsection (b) gradually increases the culpability score based upon the size of the organization and the level and extent of the substantial authority personnel involvement.

Historical Note: Effective November 1, 1991 (see Appendix C, amendment 422).

§8C2.6. Minimum and Maximum Multipliers

Using the culpability score from §8C2.5 (Culpability Score) and applying any applicable special instruction for fines in Chapter Two, determine the applicable minimum and maximum fine multipliers from the table below.

Culpability Score	Minimum Multiplier	Maximum Multiplier
10 or more	2.00	4.00
9	1.80	3.60
8	1.60	3.20
7	1.40	2.80
6	1.20	2.40
5	1.00	2.00
4	0.80	1.60
3	0.60	1.20
2	0.40	0.80
1	0.20	0.40
0 or less	0.05	0.20

Commentary

Application Note:

1. A special instruction for fines in §2R1.1 (Bid-Rigging, Price-Fixing or Market-Allocation Agreements Among Competitors) sets a floor for minimum and maximum multipliers in cases covered by that guideline.

Historical Note: Effective November 1, 1991 (see Appendix C, amendment 422).

§8C2.7. Guideline Fine Range—Organizations

(a) The minimum of the guideline fine range is determined by multiplying the base fine determined under §8C2.4 (Base Fine) by the applicable minimum multiplier determined under §8C2.6 (Minimum and Maximum Multipliers).

(b)The maximum of the guideline fine range is determined by multiplying the base fine determined under §8C2.4 (Base Fine) by the applicable maximum multiplier determined under §8C2.6 (Minimum and Maximum Multipliers).

Historical Note: Effective November 1, 1991 (see Appendix C, amendment 422).

§8C2.8. Determining the Fine Within the Range (Policy Statement)

(a) In determining the amount of the fine within the applicable guideline range, the court should consider:

(1) the need for the sentence to reflect the seriousness of the offense, promote respect for the law, provide just punishment, afford adequate deterrence, and protect the public from further crimes of the organization;

(2) the organization's role in the offense;

Appendix 2   285

(3) any collateral consequences of conviction, including civil obligations arising from the organization's conduct;

(4) any nonpecuniary loss caused or threatened by the offense;

(5) whether the offense involved a vulnerable victim;

(6) any prior criminal record of an individual within high-level personnel of the organization or high-level personnel of a unit of the organization who participated in, condoned, or was willfully ignorant of the criminal conduct;

(7) any prior civil or criminal misconduct by the organization other than that counted under §8C2.5(c);

(8) any culpability score under §8C2.5 (Culpability Score) higher than 10 or lower than 0;

(9) partial but incomplete satisfaction of the conditions for one or more of the mitigating or aggravating factors set forth in §8C2.5 (Culpability Score); and

(10) any factor listed in 18 U.S.C. § 3572(a).

(b) In addition, the court may consider the relative importance of any factor used to determine the range, including the pecuniary loss caused by the offense, the pecuniary gain from the offense, any specific offense characteristic used to determine the offense level, and any aggravating or mitigating factor used to determine the culpability score.

Commentary

Application Notes:

1. Subsection (a)(2) provides that the court, in setting the fine within the guideline fine range, should consider the organization's role in the offense. This consideration is particularly appropriate if the guideline fine range does not take the organization's role in the offense into account. For example, the guideline fine range in an antitrust case does not take into consideration whether the organization was an organizer or leader of the conspiracy. A higher fine within the guideline fine range ordinarily will be appropriate for an organization that takes a leading role in such an offense.

2. Subsection (a)(3) provides that the court, in setting the fine within the guideline fine range, should consider any collateral consequences of conviction, including civil obligations arising from the organization's conduct. As a general rule, collateral consequences that merely make victims whole provide no basis for reducing the fine within the guideline range. If criminal and civil sanctions are unlikely to make victims whole, this may provide a basis for a higher fine within the guideline fine range. If punitive collateral sanctions have been or will be imposed on the organization, this may provide a basis for a lower fine within the guideline fine range.

3. *Subsection (a)(4) provides that the court, in setting the fine within the guideline fine range, should consider any nonpecuniary loss caused or threatened by the offense. To the extent that nonpecuniary loss caused or threatened (e.g., loss of or threat to human life; psychological injury; threat to national security) by the offense is not adequately considered in setting the guideline fine range, this factor provides a basis for a higher fine within the range. This factor is more likely to be applicable where the guideline fine range is determined by pecuniary loss or gain, rather than by offense level, because the Chapter Two offense levels frequently take actual or threatened nonpecuniary loss into account.*

4. *Subsection (a)(6) provides that the court, in setting the fine within the guideline fine range, should consider any prior criminal record of an individual within high-level personnel of the organization or a unit of the organization. Since an individual within high-level personnel either exercises substantial control over the organization or a unit of the organization or has a substantial role in the making of policy within the organization or a unit of the organization, any prior criminal misconduct of such an individual may be relevant to the determination of the appropriate fine for the organization.*

5. *Subsection (a)(7) provides that the court, in setting the fine within the guideline fine range, should consider any prior civil or criminal misconduct by the organization other than that counted under §8C2.5(c). The civil and criminal misconduct counted under §8C2.5(c) increases the guideline fine range. Civil or criminal misconduct other than that counted under §8C2.5(c) may provide a basis for a higher fine within the range. In a case involving a pattern of illegality, an upward departure may be warranted.*

6. *Subsection (a)(8) provides that the court, in setting the fine within the guideline fine range, should consider any culpability score higher than ten or lower than zero. As the culpability score increases above ten, this may provide a basis for a higher fine within the range. Similarly, as the culpability score decreases below zero, this may provide a basis for a lower fine within the range.*

7. *Under subsection (b), the court, in determining the fine within the range, may consider any factor that it considered in determining the range. This allows for courts to differentiate between cases that have the same offense level but differ in seriousness (e.g., two fraud cases at offense level 12, one resulting in a loss of $21,000, the other $40,000). Similarly, this allows for courts to differentiate between two cases that have the same aggravating factors, but in which those factors vary in their intensity (e.g., two cases with upward adjustments to the culpability score under §8C2.5(c)(2) (prior criminal adjudications within 5 years of the commencement of the instant offense, one involving a single conviction, the other involving two or more convictions).*

Background: Subsection (a) includes factors that the court is required to consider under 18 U.S.C. §§ 3553(a) and 3572(a) as well as additional factors that the Commission has determined may be relevant in a particular case. A number of factors required for consideration under 18 U.S.C. § 3572(a) (e.g., pecuniary loss, the

*size of the organization) are used under the fine guidelines in this subpart to deter-
mine the fine range, and therefore are not specifically set out again in subsection
(a) of this guideline. In unusual cases, factors listed in this section may provide a
basis for departure.*

Historical Note: Effective November 1, 1991 (see Appendix C, amendment 422).

§8C2.9. Disgorgement

The court shall add to the fine determined under §8C2.8 (Determining the Fine
Within the Range) any gain to the organization from the offense that has not and
will not be paid as restitution or by way of other remedial measures.

Commentary

Application Note:

*1. This section is designed to ensure that the amount of any gain that has not and
will not be taken from the organization for remedial purposes will be added to the
fine. This section typically will apply in cases in which the organization has received gain from an offense but restitution or remedial efforts will not be required
because the offense did not result in harm to identifiable victims, e.g., money laundering, obscenity, and regulatory reporting offenses. Money spent or to be spent to
remedy the adverse effects of the offense, e.g., the cost to retrofit defective products, should be considered as disgorged gain. If the cost of remedial efforts made
or to be made by the organization equals or exceeds the gain from the offense, this
section will not apply.*

Historical Note: Effective November 1, 1991 (see Appendix C, amendment 422).

§8C2.10.Determining the Fine for Other Counts

For any count or counts not covered under §8C2.1 (Applicability of Fine Guidelines), the court should determine an appropriate fine by applying the provisions of
18 U.S.C. §§ 3553 and 3572. The court should determine the appropriate fine
amount, if any, to be imposed in addition to any fine determined under §8C2.8 (Determining the Fine Within the Range) and §8C2.9 (Disgorgement).

Commentary

*Background: The Commission has not promulgated guidelines governing the set-
ting of fines for counts not covered by §8C2.1 (Applicability of Fine Guidelines).
For such counts, the court should determine the appropriate fine based on the general statutory provisions governing sentencing. In cases that have a count or
counts not covered by the guidelines in addition to a count or counts covered by the
guidelines, the court shall apply the fine guidelines for the count(s) covered by the*

288   Corporate Fraud Investigations & Compliance Programs

guidelines, and add any additional amount to the fine, as appropriate, for the count(s) not covered by the guidelines.

Historical Note: Effective November 1, 1991 (see Appendix C, amendment 422).

* * * * *

3. IMPLEMENTING THE SENTENCE OF A FINE

§8C3.1. Imposing a Fine

(a) Except to the extent restricted by the maximum fine authorized by statute or any minimum fine required by statute, the fine or fine range shall be that determined under §8C1.1 (Determining the Fine—Criminal Purpose Organizations); §8C2.7 (Guideline Fine Range—Organizations) and §8C2.9 (Disgorgement); or §8C2.10 (Determining the Fine for Other Counts), as appropriate.

(b) Where the minimum guideline fine is greater than the maximum fine authorized by statute, the maximum fine authorized by statute shall be the guideline fine.

(c) Where the maximum guideline fine is less than a minimum fine required by statute, the minimum fine required by statute shall be the guideline fine.

Commentary

Background: This section sets forth the interaction of the fines or fine ranges determined under this chapter with the maximum fine authorized by statute and any minimum fine required by statute for the count or counts of conviction. The general statutory provisions governing a sentence of a fine are set forth in 18 U.S.C. § 3571.

When the organization is convicted of multiple counts, the maximum fine authorized by statute may increase. For example, in the case of an organization convicted of three felony counts related to a $200,000 fraud, the maximum fine authorized by statute will be $500,000 on each count, for an aggregate maximum authorized fine of $1,500,000.

Historical Note: Effective November 1, 1991 (see Appendix C, amendment 422).

§8C3.2. Payment of the Fine—Organizations

(a) If the defendant operated primarily for a criminal purpose or primarily by criminal means, immediate payment of the fine shall be required.

(b) In any other case, immediate payment of the fine shall be required unless the court finds that the organization is financially unable to make immediate payment or that such payment would pose an undue burden on the organization. If the court permits other than immediate payment, it shall require full payment at the earliest possible date, either by requiring payment on a date certain or by establishing an installment schedule.

Appendix 2 289

Commentary

Application Note:

1. When the court permits other than immediate payment, the period provided for payment shall in no event exceed five years. 18 U.S.C. § 3572(d).

Historical Note: Effective November 1, 1991 (see Appendix C, amendment 422).

§8C3.3. Reduction of Fine Based on Inability to Pay

(a) The court shall reduce the fine below that otherwise required by §8C1.1 (Determining the Fine—Criminal Purpose Organizations), or §8C2.7 (Guideline Fine Range—Organizations) and §8C2.9 (Disgorgement), to the extent that imposition of such fine would impair its ability to make restitution to victims.

(b) The court may impose a fine below that otherwise required by §8C2.7 (Guideline Fine Range—Organizations) and §8C2.9 (Disgorgement) if the court finds that the organization is not able and, even with the use of a reasonable installment schedule, is not likely to become able to pay the minimum fine required by §8C2.7 (Guideline Fine Range—Organizations) and §8C2.9 (Disgorgement).

Provided, that the reduction under this subsection shall not be more than necessary to avoid substantially jeopardizing the continued viability of the organization.

Commentary

Application Note:

1. For purposes of this section, an organization is not able to pay the minimum fine if, even with an installment schedule under §8C3.2 (Payment of the Fine—Organizations), the payment of that fine would substantially jeopardize the continued existence of the organization.

Background: Subsection (a) carries out the requirement in 18 U.S.C. § 3572(b) that the court impose a fine or other monetary penalty only to the extent that such fine or penalty will not impair the ability of the organization to make restitution for the offense; however, this section does not authorize a criminal purpose organization to remain in business in order to pay restitution.

Historical Note: Effective November 1, 1991 (see Appendix C, amendment 422).

§8C3.4. Fines Paid by Owners of Closely Held Organizations

The court may offset the fine imposed upon a closely held organization when one or more individuals, each of whom owns at least a 5 percent interest in the organization, has been fined in a federal criminal proceeding for the same offense conduct for which the organization is being sentenced. The amount of such offset shall not exceed the amount resulting from multiplying the total fines imposed on those individuals by those individuals' total percentage interest in the organization.

290 Corporate Fraud Investigations & Compliance Programs

Commentary

Application Notes:

1. For purposes of this section, an organization is closely held, regardless of its size, when relatively few individuals own it. In order for an organization to be closely held, ownership and management need not completely overlap.

2. This section does not apply to a fine imposed upon an individual that arises out of offense conduct different from that for which the organization is being sentenced.

Background: For practical purposes, most closely held organizations are the alter egos of their owner-managers. In the case of criminal conduct by a closely held corporation, the organization and the culpable individual(s) both may be convicted. As a general rule in such cases, appropriate punishment may be achieved by offsetting the fine imposed upon the organization by an amount that reflects the percentage ownership interest of the sentenced individuals and the magnitude of the fines imposed upon those individuals. For example, an organization is owned by five individuals, each of whom has a twenty percent interest; three of the individuals are convicted; and the combined fines imposed on those three equals $100,000. In this example, the fine imposed upon the organization may be offset by up to 60 percent of their combined fine amounts, i.e., by $60,000.

Historical Note: Effective November 1, 1991 (see Appendix C, amendment 422).

* * * * *

4. DEPARTURES FROM THE GUIDELINE FINE RANGE

Introductory Commentary

The statutory provisions governing departures are set forth in 18 U.S.C. § 3553(b). Departure may be warranted if the court finds "that there exists an aggravating or mitigating circumstance of a kind, or to a degree, not adequately taken into consideration by the Sentencing Commission in formulating the guidelines that should result in a sentence different from that described." This subpart sets forth certain factors that, in connection with certain offenses, may not have been adequately taken into consideration by the guidelines. In deciding whether departure is warranted, the court should consider the extent to which that factor is adequately taken into consideration by the guidelines and the relative importance or substantiality of that factor in the particular case.

To the extent that any policy statement from Chapter Five, Part K (Departures) is relevant to the organization, a departure from the applicable guideline fine range may be warranted. Some factors listed in Chapter Five, Part K that are particularly applicable to organizations are listed in this subpart. Other factors listed in Chapter Five, Part K may be applicable in particular cases. While this subpart lists factors that the Commission believes may constitute grounds for departure, the list is not exhaustive.

Historical Note: Effective November 1, 1991 (see Appendix C, amendment 422).

§8C4.1. Substantial Assistance to Authorities—Organizations (Policy Statement)

(a) Upon motion of the government stating that the defendant has provided substantial assistance in the investigation or prosecution of another organization that has committed an offense, or in the investigation or prosecution of an individual not directly affiliated with the defendant who has committed an offense, the court may depart from the guidelines.

(b) The appropriate reduction shall be determined by the court for reasons stated on the record that may include, but are not limited to, consideration of the following:

(1) the court's evaluation of the significance and usefulness of the organization's assistance, taking into consideration the government's evaluation of the assistance rendered;

(2) the nature and extent of the organization's assistance; and

(3) the timeliness of the organization's assistance.

Commentary

Application Note:

1. Departure under this section is intended for cases in which substantial assistance is provided in the investigation or prosecution of crimes committed by individuals not directly affiliated with the organization or by other organizations. It is not intended for assistance in the investigation or prosecution of the agents of the organization responsible for the offense for which the organization is being sentenced.

Historical Note: Effective November 1, 1991 (see Appendix C, amendment 422).

§8C4.2. Risk of Death or Bodily Injury (Policy Statement)

If the offense resulted in death or bodily injury, or involved a foreseeable risk of death or bodily injury, an upward departure may be warranted. The extent of any such departure should depend, among other factors, on the nature of the harm and the extent to which the harm was intended or knowingly risked, and the extent to which such harm or risk is taken into account within the applicable guideline fine range.

Historical Note: Effective November 1, 1991 (see Appendix C, amendment 422).

§8C4.3. Threat to National Security (Policy Statement)

If the offense constituted a threat to national security, an upward departure may be warranted.

Historical Note: Effective November 1, 1991 (see Appendix C, amendment 422).

§8C4.4. Threat to the Environment (Policy Statement)

If the offense presented a threat to the environment, an upward departure may be warranted.

Historical Note: Effective November 1, 1991 (see Appendix C, amendment 422).

§8C4.5. Threat to a Market (Policy Statement)

If the offense presented a risk to the integrity or continued existence of a market, an upward departure may be warranted. This section is applicable to both private markets (e.g., a financial market, a commodities market, or a market for consumer goods) and public markets (e.g., government contracting).

Historical Note: Effective November 1, 1991 (see Appendix C, amendment 422).

§8C4.6.Official Corruption (Policy Statement)

If the organization, in connection with the offense, bribed or unlawfully gave a gratuity to a public official, or attempted or conspired to bribe or unlawfully give a gratuity to a public official, an upward departure may be warranted.

Historical Note: Effective November 1, 1991 (see Appendix C, amendment 422).

§8C4.7. Public Entity (Policy Statement)

If the organization is a public entity, a downward departure may be warranted.

Historical Note: Effective November 1, 1991 (see Appendix C, amendment 422).

§8C4.8. Members or Beneficiaries of the Organization as Victims (Policy Statement)

If the members or beneficiaries, other than shareholders, of the organization are direct victims of the offense, a downward departure may be warranted. If the members or beneficiaries of an organization are direct victims of the offense, imposing a fine upon the organization may increase the burden upon the victims of the offense without achieving a deterrent effect. In such cases, a fine may not be appropriate. For example, departure may be appropriate if a labor union is convicted of embezzlement of pension funds.

Historical Note: Effective November 1, 1991 (see Appendix C, amendment 422).

§8C4.9. Remedial Costs that Greatly Exceed Gain (Policy Statement)

If the organization has paid or has agreed to pay remedial costs arising from the offense that greatly exceed the gain that the organization received from the offense, a downward departure may be warranted. In such a case, a substantial fine may not be necessary in order to achieve adequate punishment and deterrence. In deciding whether departure is appropriate, the court should consider the level and extent of substantial authority personnel involvement in the offense and the degree to which the loss exceeds the gain. If an individual within high-level personnel was involved in the offense, a departure would not be appropriate under this section. The lower the level and the more limited the extent of substantial authority personnel involvement in the offense, and the greater the degree to which remedial costs exceeded or will exceed gain, the less will be the need for a substantial fine to achieve adequate punishment and deterrence.

Historical Note: Effective November 1, 1991 (see Appendix C, amendment 422).

§8C4.10.Mandatory Programs to Prevent and Detect Violations of Law (Policy Statement)

If the organization's culpability score is reduced under §8C2.5(f) (Effective Program to Prevent and Detect Violations of Law) and the organization had implemented its program in response to a court order or administrative order specifically directed at the organization, an upward departure may be warranted to offset, in part or in whole, such reduction.

Historical Note: Effective November 1, 1991 (see Appendix C, amendment 422).

§8C4.11.Exceptional Organizational Culpability (Policy Statement)

If the organization's culpability score is greater than 10, an upward departure may be appropriate.

If no individual within substantial authority personnel participated in, condoned, or was willfully ignorant of the offense; the organization at the time of the offense had an effective program to prevent and detect violations of law; and the base fine is determined under §8C2.4(a)(1), §8C2.4(a)(3), or a special instruction for fines in Chapter Two (Offense Conduct), a downward departure may be warranted. In a case meeting these criteria, the court may find that the organization had exceptionally low culpability and therefore a fine based on loss, offense level, or a special Chapter Two instruction results in a guideline fine range higher than necessary to achieve the purposes of sentencing. Nevertheless, such fine should not be lower than if determined under §8C2.4(a)(2).

Historical Note: Effective November 1, 1991 (see Appendix C, amendment 422).

PART D—ORGANIZATIONAL PROBATION

Introductory Commentary

Section 8D1.1 sets forth the circumstances under which a sentence to a term of probation is required. Sections 8D1.2 through 8D1.5 address the length of the probation term, conditions of probation, and violations of probation conditions.

Historical Note: Effective November 1, 1991 (see Appendix C, amendment 422).

§8D1.1. Imposition of Probation—Organizations

(a) The court shall order a term of probation:

(1) if such sentence is necessary to secure payment of restitution (§8B1.1), enforce a remedial order (§8B1.2), or ensure completion of community service (§8B1.3);

(2) if the organization is sentenced to pay a monetary penalty (e.g., restitution, fine, or special assessment), the penalty is not paid in full at the time of sentencing, and restrictions are necessary to safeguard the organization's ability to make payments;

(3) if, at the time of sentencing, an organization having 50 or more employees does not have an effective program to prevent and detect violations of law;

(4) if the organization within five years prior to sentencing engaged in similar misconduct, as determined by a prior criminal adjudication, and any part of the misconduct underlying the instant offense occurred after that adjudication;

(5) if an individual within high-level personnel of the organization or the unit of the organization within which the instant offense was committed participated in the misconduct underlying the instant offense and that individual within five years prior to sentencing engaged in similar misconduct, as determined by a prior criminal adjudication, and any part of the misconduct underlying the instant offense occurred after that adjudication;

(6) if such sentence is necessary to ensure that changes are made within the organization to reduce the likelihood of future criminal conduct;

(7) if the sentence imposed upon the organization does not include a fine; or

(8) if necessary to accomplish one or more of the purposes of sentencing set forth in 18 U.S.C. § 3553(a)(2).

Commentary

Background: Under 18 U.S.C. § 3561(a), an organization may be sentenced to a term of probation. Under 18 U.S.C. § 3551(c), imposition of a term of probation is required if the sentence imposed upon the organization does not include a fine.

Historical Note: Effective November 1, 1991 (see Appendix C, amendment 422).

§8D1.2. Term of Probation—Organizations

(a) When a sentence of probation is imposed—

(1) In the case of a felony, the term of probation shall be at least one year but not more than five years.

(2) In any other case, the term of probation shall be not more than five years.

Commentary

Application Note:

1. Within the limits set by the guidelines, the term of probation should be sufficient, but not more than necessary, to accomplish the court's specific objectives in imposing the term of probation. The terms of probation set forth in this section are those provided in 18 U.S.C. § 3561(b).

Historical Note: Effective November 1, 1991 (see Appendix C, amendment 422).

§8D1.3. Conditions of Probation—Organizations

(a) Pursuant to 18 U.S.C. § 3563(a)(1), any sentence of probation shall include the condition that the organization not commit another federal, state, or local crime during the term of probation.

(b) Pursuant to 18 U.S.C. § 3563(a)(2), if a sentence of probation is imposed for a felony, the court shall impose as a condition of probation at least one of the following: (1) restitution, (2) notice to victims of the offense pursuant to 18 U.S.C. § 3555, or (3) an order requiring the organization to reside, or refrain from residing, in a specified place or area, unless the court finds on the record that extraordinary circumstances exist that would make such condition plainly unreasonable, in which event the court shall impose one or more other conditions set forth in 18 U.S.C. § 3563(b).

Note: Section 3563(a)(2) of Title 18, United States Code, provides that, absent unusual circumstances, a defendant convicted of a felony shall abide by at least one of the conditions set forth in 18 U.S.C. § 3563(b)(2), (b)(3), and (b)(13). Before the enactment of the Antiterrorism and Effective Death Penalty Act of 1996, those conditions were a fine ((b)(2)), an order of restitution ((b)(3)), and community service ((b)(13)). Whether or not the change was intended, the Act deleted the fine condition and renumbered the restitution and community service conditions in 18 U.S.C. § 3563(b), but failed to make a corresponding change in the referenced paragraphs under 18 U.S.C. § 3563(a)(2). Accordingly, the conditions now referenced are restitution ((b)(2)), notice to victims pursuant to 18 U.S.C. § 3555 ((b)(3)), and an order that the defendant reside, or refrain from residing, in a specified place or area ((b)(13)).

296 Corporate Fraud Investigations & Compliance Programs

(c) The court may impose other conditions that (1) are reasonably related to the nature and circumstances of the offense or the history and characteristics of the organization; and (2) involve only such deprivations of liberty or property as are necessary to effect the purposes of sentencing.

Historical Note: Effective November 1, 1991 (see Appendix C, amendment 422). Amended effective November 1, 1997 (see Appendix C, amendment 569).

§8D1.4. Recommended Conditions of Probation—Organizations (Policy Statement)

(a) The court may order the organization, at its expense and in the format and media specified by the court, to publicize the nature of the offense committed, the fact of conviction, the nature of the punishment imposed, and the steps that will be taken to prevent the recurrence of similar offenses.

(b) If probation is imposed under §8D1.1(a)(2), the following conditions may be appropriate to the extent they appear necessary to safeguard the organization's ability to pay any deferred portion of an order of restitution, fine, or assessment:

(1) The organization shall make periodic submissions to the court or probation officer, at intervals specified by the court, reporting on the organization's financial condition and results of business operations, and accounting for the disposition of all funds received.

(2) The organization shall submit to: (A) a reasonable number of regular or unannounced examinations of its books and records at appropriate business premises by the probation officer or experts engaged by the court; and (B) interrogation of knowledgeable individuals within the organization. Compensation to and costs of any experts engaged by the court shall be paid by the organization.

(3) The organization shall be required to notify the court or probation officer immediately upon learning of (A) any material adverse change in its business or financial condition or prospects, or (B) the commencement of any bankruptcy proceeding, major civil litigation, criminal prosecution, or administrative proceeding against the organization, or any investigation or formal inquiry by governmental authorities regarding the organization.

(4) The organization shall be required to make periodic payments, as specified by the court, in the following priority: (1) restitution; (2) fine; and (3) any other monetary sanction.

(c) If probation is ordered under §8D1.1(a)(3), (4), (5), or (6), the following conditions may be appropriate:

(1) The organization shall develop and submit to the court a program to prevent and detect violations of law, including a schedule for implementation.

(2) Upon approval by the court of a program to prevent and detect violations of law, the organization shall notify its employees and shareholders of its criminal

behavior and its program to prevent and detect violations of law. Such notice shall be in a form prescribed by the court.

(3) The organization shall make periodic reports to the court or probation officer, at intervals and in a form specified by the court, regarding the organization's progress in implementing the program to prevent and detect violations of law. Among other things, such reports shall disclose any criminal prosecution, civil litigation, or administrative proceeding commenced against the organization, or any investigation or formal inquiry by governmental authorities of which the organization learned since its last report.

(4) In order to monitor whether the organization is following the program to prevent and detect violations of law, the organization shall submit to: (A) a reasonable number of regular or unannounced examinations of its books and records at appropriate business premises by the probation officer or experts engaged by the court; and (B) interrogation of knowledgeable individuals within the organization. Compensation to and costs of any experts engaged by the court shall be paid by the organization.

Commentary

Application Notes:

1. In determining the conditions to be imposed when probation is ordered under §8D1.1(a)(3) through (6), the court should consider the views of any governmental regulatory body that oversees conduct of the organization relating to the instant offense. To assess the efficacy of a program to prevent and detect violations of law submitted by the organization, the court may employ appropriate experts who shall be afforded access to all material possessed by the organization that is necessary for a comprehensive assessment of the proposed program. The court should approve any program that appears reasonably calculated to prevent and detect violations of law, provided it is consistent with any applicable statutory or regulatory requirement.

Periodic reports submitted in accordance with subsection (c)(3) should be provided to any governmental regulatory body that oversees conduct of the organization relating to the instant offense.

Historical Note: Effective November 1, 1991 (see Appendix C, amendment 422).

§8D1.5. Violations of Conditions of Probation—Organizations (Policy Statement)

Upon a finding of a violation of a condition of probation, the court may extend the term of probation, impose more restrictive conditions of probation, or revoke probation and resentence the organization.

Commentary

Application Note:

1. In the event of repeated, serious violations of conditions of probation, the appointment of a master or trustee may be appropriate to ensure compliance with court orders.

Historical Note: Effective November 1, 1991 (see Appendix C, amendment 422).

PART E—SPECIAL ASSESSMENTS, FORFEITURES, AND COSTS

§8E1.1. Special Assessments—Organizations

A special assessment must be imposed on an organization in the amount prescribed by statute.

Commentary

Application Notes:

1. This guideline applies if the defendant is an organization. It does not apply if the defendant is an individual. See §5E1.3 for special assessments applicable to individuals.

2. The following special assessments are provided by statute (see 18 U.S.C. § 3013):

For Offenses Committed By Organizations On Or After April 24, 1996:

(A) $400, if convicted of a felony;

(B) $125, if convicted of a Class A misdemeanor;

(C) $50, if convicted of a Class B misdemeanor; or

(D) $25, if convicted of a Class C misdemeanor or an infraction.

For Offenses Committed By Organizations On Or After November 18, 1988 But Prior To April 24, 1996:

(E) $200, if convicted of a felony;

(F) $125, if convicted of a Class A misdemeanor;

(G) $50, if convicted of a Class B misdemeanor; or

(H) $25, if convicted of a Class C misdemeanor or an infraction.

For Offenses Committed By Organizations Prior To November 18, 1988:

(I) $200, if convicted of a felony;

(J) $100, if convicted of a misdemeanor.

3. A special assessment is required by statute for each count of conviction.

Background: Section 3013 of Title 18, United States Code, added by The Victims of Crimes Act of 1984, Pub. L. No. 98-473, Title II, Chap. XIV, requires courts to impose special assessments on convicted defendants for the purpose of funding the Crime Victims Fund established by the same legislation.

Historical Note: Effective November 1, 1991 (see Appendix C, amendment 422); November 1, 1997 (see Appendix C, amendment 573).

§8E1.2.Forfeiture—Organizations

Apply §5E1.4 (Forfeiture).

Historical Note: Effective November 1, 1991 (see Appendix C, amendment 422).

§8E1.3. Assessment of Costs—Organizations

As provided in 28 U.S.C. § 1918, the court may order the organization to pay the costs of prosecution. In addition, specific statutory provisions mandate assessment of costs.

Historical Note: Effective November 1, 1991 (see Appendix C, amendment 422).

APPENDIX 3

31 U.S.C. § 3729 THROUGH U.S.C. § 3733

[Laws in effect as of January 6, 1997]
[Document not affected by Public Laws enacted between January 6, 1997
and November 30, 1998]

TITLE 31—MONEY AND FINANCE
SUBTITLE III—FINANCIAL MANAGEMENT
CHAPTER 37—CLAIMS
SUBCHAPTER III—CLAIMS AGAINST THE UNITED STATES
GOVERNMENT

Sec. 3729. False claims

(a) Liability for Certain Acts.—Any person who—

(1) knowingly presents, or causes to be presented, to an officer or employee of the United States Government or a member of the Armed Forces of the United States a false or fraudulent claim for payment or approval;

(2) knowingly makes, uses, or causes to be made or used, a false record or statement to get a false or fraudulent claim paid or approved by the Government;

(3) conspires to defraud the Government by getting a false or fraudulent claim allowed or paid;

(4) has possession, custody, or control of property or money used, or to be used, by the Government and, intending to defraud the Government or willfully to conceal the property, delivers, or causes to be delivered, less property than the amount for which the person receives a certificate or receipt;

(5) authorized to make or deliver a document certifying receipt of property used, or to be used, by the Government and, intending to defraud the Government, makes or delivers the receipt without completely knowing that the information on the receipt is true;

(6) knowingly buys, or receives as a pledge of an obligation or debt, public property from an officer or employee of the Government, or a member of the Armed Forces, who lawfully may not sell or pledge the property; or

(7) knowingly makes, uses, or causes to be made or used, a false record or statement to conceal, avoid, or decrease an obligation to pay or transmit money or property to the Government,

is liable to the United States Government for a civil penalty of not less than $5,000 and not more than $10,000, plus 3 times the amount of damages which the Government sustains because of the act of that person, except that if the court finds that—

(A) the person committing the violation of this subsection furnished officials of the United States responsible for investigating false claims violations with all information known to such person about the violation within 30 days after the date on which the defendant first obtained the information;

(B) such person fully cooperated with any Government investigation of such violation; and

(C) at the time such person furnished the United States with the information about the violation, no criminal prosecution, civil action, or administrative action had commenced under this title with respect to such violation, and the person did not have actual knowledge of the existence of an investigation into such violation;

the court may assess not less than 2 times the amount of damages which the Government sustains because of the act of the person. A person violating this subsection shall also be liable to the United States Government for the costs of a civil action brought to recover any such penalty or damages.

(b) Knowing and Knowingly Defined.—For purposes of this section, the terms "knowing" and "knowingly" mean that a person, with respect to information—

(1) has actual knowledge of the information;

(2) acts in deliberate ignorance of the truth or falsity of the information; or

(3) acts in reckless disregard of the truth or falsity of the information,

and no proof of specific intent to defraud is required.

(c) Claim Defined.—For purposes of this section, "claim" includes any request or demand, whether under a contract or otherwise, for money or property which is made to a contractor, grantee, or other recipient if the United States Government provides any portion of the money or property which is requested or demanded, or if the Government will reimburse such contractor, grantee, or other recipient for any portion of the money or property which is requested or demanded.

(d) Exemption From Disclosure.—Any information furnished pursuant to subparagraphs (A) through (C) of subsection (a) shall be exempt from disclosure under section 552 of title 5.

(e) Exclusion.—This section does not apply to claims, records, or statements made under the Internal Revenue Code of 1986.

(Pub. L. 97-258, Sept. 13, 1982, 96 Stat. 978; Pub. L. 99-562, Sec. 2, Oct. 27, 1986, 100 Stat. 3153; Pub. L. 103-272, Sec. 4(f)(1)(O), July 5, 1994, 108 Stat. 1362.)

Appendix 3

Historical and Revision Notes

Revised Section	Source (U.S. Code)	Source (Statutes at Large)
3729	31:231.	R.S. Sec. 3490.

In the section, before clause (1), the words "a member of an armed force of the United States" are substituted for "in the military or naval forces of the United States, or in the militia called into or actually employed in the service of the United States" and "military or naval service" for consistency with title 10. The words "is liable" are substituted for "shall forfeit and pay" for consistency. The words "civil action" are substituted for "suit" for consistency in the revised title and with other titles of the United States Code. The words "and such forfeiture and damages shall be sued for in the same suit" are omitted as unnecessary because of rules 8 and 10 of the Federal Rules of Civil Procedure (28 App. U.S.C.). In clauses (1)-(3), the words "false or fraudulent" are substituted for "false, fictitious, or fraudulent" and "Fraudulent or fictitious" to eliminate unnecessary words and for consistency. In clause (1), the words "presents, or causes to be presented" are substituted for "shall make or cause to be made, or present or cause to be presented" for clarity and consistency and to eliminate unnecessary words. The words "officer or employee of the Government or a member of an armed force" are substituted for "officer in the civil, military, or naval service of the United States" for consistency in the revised title and with other titles of the Code. The words "upon or against the Government of the United States, or any department of the United States, or any department or officer thereof" are omitted as surplus. In clause (2), the word "knowingly" is substituted for "knowing the same to contain any fraudulent or fictitious statement or entry" to eliminate unnecessary words. The words "record or statement" are substituted for "bill, receipt, voucher, roll, account, claim, certificate, affidavit, or deposition" for consistency in the revised title and with other titles of the Code. In clause (3), the words "conspires to" are substituted for "enters into any agreement, combination, or conspiracy" to eliminate unnecessary words. The words "of the United States, or any department or officer thereof" are omitted as surplus. In clause (4), the words "charge", "or other", and "to any other person having authority to receive the same" are omitted as surplus. In clause (5), the words "document certifying receipt" are substituted for "certificate, voucher, receipt, or other paper certifying the receipt" to eliminate unnecessary words. The words "arms, ammunition, provisions, clothing, or other", "to any other person", and "the truth of" are omitted as surplus. In clause (6), the words "arms, equipments, ammunition, clothes, military stores, or other" are omitted as surplus. The words "member of an armed force" are substituted for "soldier, officer, sailor, or other person called into or employed in the military or naval service" for consistency with title 10. The words "such soldier, sailor, officer, or other person" are omitted as surplus.

References in Text

The Internal Revenue Code of 1986, referred to in subsec. (e), is classified generally to Title 26, Internal Revenue Code.

Amendments

1994—Subsec. (e). Pub. L. 103-272 substituted "1986" for "1954".

1986—Subsec. (a). Pub. L. 99-562, Sec. 2(1), designated existing provisions as subsec. (a), inserted subsec. heading, and substituted "Any person who" for "A person not a member of an armed force of the United States is liable to the United States Government for a civil penalty of $2,000, an amount equal to 2 times the amount of damages the Government sustains because of the act of that person, and costs of the civil action, if the person" in introductory provisions.

Subsec. (a)(1). Pub. L. 99-562, Sec. 2(2), substituted "United States Government or a member of the Armed Forces of the United States" for "Government or a member of an armed force".

Subsec. (a)(2). Pub. L. 99-562, Sec. 2(3), inserted "by the Government" after "approved".

Subsec. (a)(4). Pub. L. 99-562, Sec. 2(4), substituted "control of property" for "control of public property" and "by the Government" for "in an armed force".

Subsec. (a)(5). Pub. L. 99-562, Sec. 2(5), substituted "by the Government" for "in an armed force" and "true;" for "true; or".

Subsec. (a)(6). Pub. L. 99-562, Sec. 2(6), substituted "an officer or employee of the Government, or a member of the Armed Forces," for "a member of an armed force" and "property; or" for "property."

Subsec. (a)(7). Pub. L. 99-562, Sec. 2(7), added par. (7).

Subsecs. (b) to (e). Pub. L. 99-562, Sec. 2(7), added subsecs. (b) to (e).

Increased Penalties for False Claims in Defense Procurement Pub. L. 99-145, title IX, Sec. 931(b), Nov. 8, 1985, 99 Stat. 699, provided that: "Notwithstanding section 3729 of title 31, United States Code, the amount of the liability under that section in the case of a person who makes a false claim related to a contract with the Department of Defense shall be a civil penalty of $2,000, an amount equal to three times the amount of the damages the Government sustains because of the act of the person, and costs of the civil action."

[Section 931(c) of Pub. L. 99-145 provided that section 931(b) is applicable to claims made or presented on or after Nov. 8, 1985.]

Section Referred to in Other Sections

This section is referred to in sections 3730, 3731, 3732, 3733 of this title; title 10 section 2324; title 20 section 1078-9; title 41 section 256.

Sec. 3730. Civil actions for false claims

(a) Responsibilities of the Attorney General.—The Attorney General diligently shall investigate a violation under section 3729. If the Attorney General finds that a person has violated or is violating section 3729, the Attorney General may bring a civil action under this section against the person.

(b) Actions by Private Persons.—

(1) A person may bring a civil action for a violation of section 3729 for the person and for the United States Government. The action shall be brought in the name of the Government. The action may be dismissed only if the court and the Attorney General give written consent to the dismissal and their reasons for consenting.

(2) A copy of the complaint and written disclosure of substantially all material evidence and information the person possesses shall be served on the Government pursuant to Rule 4(d)(4) of the Federal Rules of Civil Procedure. The complaint shall be filed in camera, shall remain under seal for at least 60 days, and shall not be served on the defendant until the court so orders. The Government may elect to intervene and proceed with the action within 60 days after it receives both the complaint and the material evidence and information.

(3) The Government may, for good cause shown, move the court for extensions of the time during which the complaint remains under seal under paragraph (2). Any such motions may be supported by affidavits or other submissions in camera. The defendant shall not be required to respond to any complaint filed under this section until 20 days after the complaint is unsealed and served upon the defendant pursuant to Rule 4 of the Federal Rules of Civil Procedure.

(4) Before the expiration of the 60-day period or any extensions obtained under paragraph (3), the Government shall—

(A) proceed with the action, in which case the action shall be conducted by the Government; or

(B) notify the court that it declines to take over the action, in which case the person bringing the action shall have the right to conduct the action.

(5) When a person brings an action under this subsection, no person other than the Government may intervene or bring a related action based on the facts underlying the pending action.

(c) Rights of the Parties to Qui Tam Actions.—

(1) If the Government proceeds with the action, it shall have the primary responsibility for prosecuting the action, and shall not be bound by an act of the person bringing the action. Such person shall have the right to continue as a party to the action, subject to the limitations set forth in paragraph (2).

(2)(A) The Government may dismiss the action notwithstanding the objections of the person initiating the action if the person has been notified by the

Government of the filing of the motion and the court has provided the person with an opportunity for a hearing on the motion.

(B) The Government may settle the action with the defendant notwithstanding the objections of the person initiating the action if the court determines, after a hearing, that the proposed settlement is fair, adequate, and reasonable under all the circumstances. Upon a showing of good cause, such hearing may be held in camera.

(C) Upon a showing by the Government that unrestricted participation during the course of the litigation by the person initiating the action would interfere with or unduly delay the Government's prosecution of the case, or would be repetitious, irrelevant, or for purposes of harassment, the court may, in its discretion, impose limitations on the person's participation, such as—

(i) limiting the number of witnesses the person may call;

(ii) limiting the length of the testimony of such witnesses;

(iii) limiting the person's cross-examination of witnesses; or

(iv) otherwise limiting the participation by the person in the litigation.

(D) Upon a showing by the defendant that unrestricted participation during the course of the litigation by the person initiating the action would be for purposes of harassment or would cause the defendant undue burden or unnecessary expense, the court may limit the participation by the person in the litigation.

(3) If the Government elects not to proceed with the action, the person who initiated the action shall have the right to conduct the action. If the Government so requests, it shall be served with copies of all pleadings filed in the action and shall be supplied with copies of all deposition transcripts (at the Government's expense). When a person proceeds with the action, the court, without limiting the status and rights of the person initiating the action, may nevertheless permit the Government to intervene at a later date upon a showing of good cause.

(4) Whether or not the Government proceeds with the action, upon a showing by the Government that certain actions of discovery by the person initiating the action would interfere with the Government's investigation or prosecution of a criminal or civil matter arising out of the same facts, the court may stay such discovery for a period of not more than 60 days. Such a showing shall be conducted in camera. The court may extend the 60-day period upon a further showing in camera that the Government has pursued the criminal or civil investigation or proceedings with reasonable diligence and any proposed discovery in the civil action will interfere with the ongoing criminal or civil investigation or proceedings.

(5) Notwithstanding subsection (b), the Government may elect to pursue its claim through any alternate remedy available to the Government, including any administrative proceeding to determine a civil money penalty. If any such alternate remedy is pursued in another proceeding, the person initiating the action

shall have the same rights in such proceeding as such person would have had if the action had continued under this section. Any finding of fact or conclusion of law made in such other proceeding that has become final shall be conclusive on all parties to an action under this section. For purposes of the preceding sentence, a finding or conclusion is final if it has been finally determined on appeal to the appropriate court of the United States, if all time for filing such an appeal with respect to the finding or conclusion has expired, or if the finding or conclusion is not subject to judicial review.

(d) Award to Qui Tam Plaintiff.—

(1) If the Government proceeds with an action brought by a person under subsection (b), such person shall, subject to the second sentence of this paragraph, receive at least 15 percent but not more than 25 percent of the proceeds of the action or settlement of the claim, depending upon the extent to which the person substantially contributed to the prosecution of the action. Where the action is one which the court finds to be based primarily on disclosures of specific information (other than information provided by the person bringing the action) relating to allegations or transactions in a criminal, civil, or administrative hearing, in a congressional, administrative, or Government[1] Accounting Office report, hearing, audit, or investigation, or from the news media, the court may award such sums as it considers appropriate, but in no case more than 10 percent of the proceeds, taking into account the significance of the information and the role of the person bringing the action in advancing the case to litigation. Any payment to a person under the first or second sentence of this paragraph shall be made from the proceeds. Any such person shall also receive an amount for reasonable expenses which the court finds to have been necessarily incurred, plus reasonable attorneys' fees and costs. All such expenses, fees, and costs shall be awarded against the defendant.

(2) If the Government does not proceed with an action under this section, the person bringing the action or settling the claim shall receive an amount which the court decides is reasonable for collecting the civil penalty and damages. The amount shall be not less than 25 percent and not more than 30 percent of the proceeds of the action or settlement and shall be paid out of such proceeds. Such person shall also receive an amount for reasonable expenses which the court finds to have been necessarily incurred, plus reasonable attorneys' fees and costs. All such expenses, fees, and costs shall be awarded against the defendant.

(3) Whether or not the Government proceeds with the action, if the court finds that the action was brought by a person who planned and initiated the violation of section 3729 upon which the action was brought, then the court may, to the extent the court considers appropriate, reduce the share of the proceeds of the action which the person would otherwise receive under paragraph (1) or (2) of this subsection, taking into account the role of that person in advancing the case to

---

1   So in original. Probably should be "General".

litigation and any relevant circumstances pertaining to the violation. If the person bringing the action is convicted of criminal conduct arising from his or her role in the violation of section 3729, that person shall be dismissed from the civil action and shall not receive any share of the proceeds of the action. Such dismissal shall not prejudice the right of the United States to continue the action, represented by the Department of Justice.

(4) If the Government does not proceed with the action and the person bringing the action conducts the action, the court may award to the defendant its reasonable attorneys' fees and expenses if the defendant prevails in the action and the court finds that the claim of the person bringing the action was clearly frivolous, clearly vexatious, or brought primarily for purposes of harassment.

(e) Certain Actions Barred.—

(1) No court shall have jurisdiction over an action brought by a former or present member of the armed forces under subsection (b) of this section against a member of the armed forces arising out of such person's service in the armed forces.

(2)(A) No court shall have jurisdiction over an action brought under subsection (b) against a Member of Congress, a member of the judiciary, or a senior executive branch official if the action is based on evidence or information known to the Government when the action was brought.

(B) For purposes of this paragraph, "senior executive branch official" means any officer or employee listed in paragraphs (1) through (8) of section 101(f) of the Ethics in Government Act of 1978 (5 U.S.C. App.).

(3) In no event may a person bring an action under subsection (b) which is based upon allegations or transactions which are the subject of a civil suit or an administrative civil money penalty proceeding in which the Government is already a party.

(4)(A) No court shall have jurisdiction over an action under this section based upon the public disclosure of allegations or transactions in a criminal, civil, or administrative hearing, in a congressional, administrative, or Government[2] Accounting Office report, hearing, audit, or investigation, or from the news media, unless the action is brought by the Attorney General or the person bringing the action is an original source of the information.

(B) For purposes of this paragraph, "original source" means an individual who has direct and independent knowledge of the information on which the allegations are based and has voluntarily provided the information to the Government before filing an action under this section which is based on the information.

(f) Government Not Liable for Certain Expenses.—The Government is not liable for expenses which a person incurs in bringing an action under this section.

---

2   So in original. Probably should be "General".

Appendix 3

(g) Fees and Expenses to Prevailing Defendant.—In civil actions brought under this section by the United States, the provisions of section 2412(d) of title 28 shall apply.

(h) Any employee who is discharged, demoted, suspended, threatened, harassed, or in any other manner discriminated against in the terms and conditions of employment by his or her employer because of lawful acts done by the employee on behalf of the employee or others in furtherance of an action under this section, including investigation for, initiation of, testimony for, or assistance in an action filed or to be filed under this section, shall be entitled to all relief necessary to make the employee whole. Such relief shall include reinstatement with the same seniority status such employee would have had but for the discrimination, 2 times the amount of back pay, interest on the back pay, and compensation for any special damages sustained as a result of the discrimination, including litigation costs and reasonable attorneys' fees. An employee may bring an action in the appropriate district court of the United States for the relief provided in this subsection.

(Pub. L. 97-258, Sept. 13, 1982, 96 Stat. 978; Pub. L. 99-562, Secs. 3, 4, Oct. 27, 1986, 100 Stat. 3154, 3157; Pub. L. 100-700, Sec. 9, Nov. 19, 1988, 102 Stat. 4638; Pub. L. 101-280, Sec. 10(a), May 4, 1990, 104 Stat. 162; Pub. L. 103-272, Sec. 4(f)(1)(P), July 5, 1994, 108 Stat. 1362.)

Historical and Revision Notes

Revised Section	Source (U.S. Code)	Source (Statutes at Large)
3730(a)	31:233.	R.S. Sec. 3492.
3730(b)(1)	31:232(A), (B)(less words between 3d and 4th commas).	R.S. Sec. 3491(A)-(E); restated Dec. 23, 1943, ch. 377, Sec. 1, 57 Stat. 608; June 11, 1960, Pub. L. 86-507, Sec.1(28), (29), 74 Stat. 202.
3730(b)(2)	31:232(C)(1st-3d sentences, 5th sentence proviso).	
3730(b)(3)	31:232(C)(4th sentence, 5th sentence less proviso).	
3730(b)(4)	31:232(C)(last sentence), (D).	
3730(c)(1)	31:232(E)(1).	
3730(c)(2)	31:232(E)(2)(less proviso).	
3730(d)	31:232(B)(words between 3d and 4th commas), (E)(2)(proviso).	

In the section, the words "civil action" are substituted for "suit" for consistency in the revised title and with other titles of the United States Code.

In subsection (a), the words "Attorney General" are substituted for "several district attorneys of the United States [subsequently changed to 'United States attorneys' because of section 1 of the Act of June 25, 1948 (ch. 646, 62 Stat. 909)] for the respective districts, for the District of Columbia, and for the several Territories" because of 28:509. The words "by persons liable to such suit" are omitted as surplus. The words "and found within their respective districts or Territories" are omitted because of the restatement. The words "If the Attorney General finds that a person has violated or is violating section 3729, the Attorney General may bring a civil action under this section against the person" are substituted for "and to cause them to be proceeded against in due form of law for the recovery of such forfeiture and damages" for clarity and consistency. The words "as the district judge may order" are omitted as surplus. The words "of the Attorney General" are substituted for "the person bringing the suit" for consistency in the section.

In subsection (b)(1), the words "Except as hereinafter provided" are omitted as unnecessary. The words "for a violation of section 3729 of this title" are added because of the restatement. The words "and carried on", "several" and "full power and" are omitted as surplus.

The words "of the action" are substituted for "to hear, try, and determine such suit" to eliminate unnecessary words. The words "Trial is in the judicial district within whose jurisdictional limits the person charged with a violation is found or the violation occurs" are substituted for "within whose jurisdictional limits the person doing or committing such act shall be found, shall wheresoever such act may have been done or committed" for consistency in the revised title and with other titles of the Code. The words "withdrawn or" and "judge of the" are omitted as surplus. The words "Attorney General" are substituted for "district attorney [subsequently changed to 'United States attorneys' because of section 1 of the Act of June 25, 1948 (ch. 646, 62 Stat. 909)], first filed in the case" because of 28:509.

In subsection (b)(2), before clause (A), the words "bill of", "Whenever any such suit shall be brought by any person under clause (B) of this section" and "to the effective prosecution of such suit or" are omitted as surplus. The words "served on the Government under rule 4 of the Federal Rules of Civil Procedure (28 App. U.S.C.)" are substituted for "notice . . . shall be given to the United States by serving upon the United States Attorney for the district in which such suit shall have been brought . . . and by sending, by registered mail, or by certified mail, to the Attorney General of the United States at Washington, District of Columbia" because of 28:509 and to eliminate unnecessary words. The words "proceed with the action" are added for clarity. Clause (A) is substituted for "shall fail, or decline in writing to the court, during said period of sixty days to enter any such suit" for clarity and consistency. In clause (B), the words "a period of" and "therein" are omitted as surplus.

In subsection (b)(3), the words "within said period" are omitted as surplus. The words "proceeds with the action" are substituted for "shall enter appearance in such suit" for consistency. The words "In carrying on such suit" and "and may proceed in all respects as if it were instituting the suit" are omitted as surplus.

In subsection (b)(4), the words "Unless the Government proceeds with the action" are added because of the restatement. The words "shall dismiss an action brought by the person on discovering" are substituted for "shall have no jurisdiction to proceed with any such suit . . . or pending suit . . . whenever it shall be made to appear that" to eliminate unnecessary words. The words "or any agency, officer, or employee thereof" are omitted as unnecessary. The text of 31:232(C)(last sentence proviso) and (D) is omitted as executed.

In subsection (c), the words "herein provided", "fair and . . . compensation to such person", and "involved therein, which shall be collected" are omitted as surplus.

In subsection (c)(2), the words "whether heretofore or hereafter brought" are omitted as unnecessary. The words "bringing the action or settling the claim" are substituted for "who brought such suit and prosecuted it to final judgment, or to settlement" for clarity and consistency. The words "as provided in clause (B) of this section" are omitted as unnecessary. The words "the civil penalty" are substituted for "forfeiture" for clarity and consistency. The words "to his own use", "the court may", and "to be allowed and taxed according to any provision of law or rule of court in force, or that shall be in force in suits between private parties in said court" are omitted as surplus.

Subsection (d) is substituted for 31:232(B)(words between 3d and 4th commas) and (E)(2)(proviso) to eliminate unnecessary words.

References in Text

The Federal Rules of Civil Procedure, referred to in subsec. (b)(2), (3), are set out in the Appendix to Title 28, Judiciary and Judicial Procedure.

Section 101(f) of the Ethics in Government Act of 1978, referred to in subsec. (e)(2)(B), is section 101(f) of Pub. L. 95-521, title I, Oct. 26, 1978, 92 Stat. 1824, as amended, which was set out in the Appendix to Title 5, Government Organization and Employees.

Amendments

1994—Subsec. (e)(2)(B). Pub. L. 103-272 substituted "paragraphs (1) through (8)" for "section paragraphs (1) through (8)".

1990—Subsec. (e)(2)(B). Pub. L. 101-280 substituted "paragraphs (1) through (8) of section 101(f)" for "201(f)".

1988—Subsec. (c)(4). Pub. L. 100-700, Sec. 9(b)(1), which directed amendment of section 3730 of title 28 by substituting "with the action" for "with action" in subsec. (c)(4), was executed to subsec. (c)(4) of this section as the probable intent of Congress.

Subsec. (d)(3). Pub. L. 100-700, Sec. 9(a)(1), (2), added par. (3).

Former par. (3) redesignated (4).

Subsec. (d)(4). Pub. L. 100-700, Sec. 9(b)(2), which directed amendment of section 3730 of title 28 by substituting "claim of the person bringing the action" for "claim of the person bringing the actions" in subsec. (d)(4), was executed to subsec. (d)(4) of this section as the probable intent of Congress.

Pub. L. 100-700, Sec. 9(a)(1), redesignated former par. (3) as (4).

1986—Pub. L. 99-562, Sec. 3, amended section generally, revising and expanding provisions of subsecs. (a) to (c), adding subsecs. (d) and (e), redesignating former subsec. (d) as (f), and adding subsec. (g).

Subsec. (h). Pub. L. 99-562, Sec. 4, added subsec. (h).

Effective Date of 1990 Amendment

Section 10(c) of Pub. L. 101-280 provided that: "The amendments made by subsections (a) and (b) [amending this section and section 2397a of Title 10, Armed Forces] shall take effect on January 1, 1991."

Federal Rules of Civil Procedure

Costs, see rule 54, Title 28, Appendix, Judiciary and Judicial Procedure.

Section Referred to in Other Sections

This section is referred to in sections 3731, 3732, 3733 of this title.

Sec. 3731. False claims procedure

(a) A subpena requiring the attendance of a witness at a trial or hearing conducted under section 3730 of this title may be served at any place in the United States.

(b) A civil action under section 3730 may not be brought—

(1) more than 6 years after the date on which the violation of section 3729 is committed, or

(2) more than 3 years after the date when facts material to the right of action are known or reasonably should have been known by the official of the United States charged with responsibility to act in the circumstances, but in no event more than 10 years after the date on which the violation is committed,

whichever occurs last.

(c) In any action brought under section 3730, the United States shall be required to prove all essential elements of the cause of action, including damages, by a preponderance of the evidence.

(d) Notwithstanding any other provision of law, the Federal Rules of Criminal Procedure, or the Federal Rules of Evidence, a final judgment rendered in favor of the United States in any criminal proceeding charging fraud or false statements, whether upon a verdict after trial or upon a plea of guilty or nolo contendere, shall estop the defendant from denying the essential elements of the offense in any action which involves the same transaction as in the criminal proceeding and which is brought under subsection (a) or (b) of section 3730.

Appendix 3

(Pub. L. 97-258, Sept. 13, 1982, 96 Stat. 979; Pub. L. 99-562, Sec. 5, Oct. 27, 1986, 100 Stat. 3158.)

Historical and Revision Notes

Revised Section	Source (U.S. Code)	Source (Statutes at Large)
3731(a)	31:232(F).	R.S. Sec. 3491(F); added Nov. 2, 1978, Pub. L. 95-582, Sec. 1, 92 Stat. 2479.
3731(b)	31:235.	R.S. Sec. 3494.

In subsection (b), the words "A civil action under section 3730 of this title" are substituted for "Every such suit" for clarity.

References in Text

The Federal Rules of Criminal Procedure, referred to in subsec. (d), are set out in the Appendix to Title 18, Crimes and Criminal Procedure.

The Federal Rules of Evidence, referred to in subsec. (d), are set out in the Appendix to Title 28, Judiciary and Judicial Procedure.

Amendments

1986—Subsecs. (b) to (d). Pub. L. 99-562 added subsecs. (b) to (d) and struck out former subsec. (b) which read as follows: "A civil action under section 3730 of this title must be brought within 6 years from the date the violation is committed."

Section Referred to in Other Sections

This section is referred to in section 3733 of this title.

Sec. 3732. False claims jurisdiction

(a) Actions Under Section 3730.—Any action under section 3730 may be brought in any judicial district in which the defendant or, in the case of multiple defendants, any one defendant can be found, resides, transacts business, or in which any act proscribed by section 3729 occurred. A summons as required by the Federal Rules of Civil Procedure shall be issued by the appropriate district court and served at any place within or outside the United States.

(b) Claims Under State Law.—The district courts shall have jurisdiction over any action brought under the laws of any State for the recovery of funds paid by a State or local government if the action arises from the same transaction or occurrence as an action brought under section 3730.

(Added Pub. L. 99-562, Sec. 6(a), Oct. 21, 1986, 100 Stat. 3158.)

314 Corporate Fraud Investigations & Compliance Programs

References in Text

The Federal Rules of Civil Procedure, referred to in subsec. (a), are set out in the Appendix to Title 28, Judiciary and Judicial Procedure.

Section Referred to in Other Sections

This section is referred to in section 3733 of this title; title 20 section 1078-9.

Sec. 3733. Civil investigative demands

(a) In General.—

(1) Issuance and service.—Whenever the Attorney General has reason to believe that any person may be in possession, custody, or control of any documentary material or information relevant to a false claims law investigation, the Attorney General may, before commencing a civil proceeding under section 3730 or other false claims law, issue in writing and cause to be served upon such person, a civil investigative demand requiring such person—

(A) to produce such documentary material for inspection and copying,

(B) to answer in writing written interrogatories with respect to such documentary material or information,

(C) to give oral testimony concerning such documentary material or information, or

(D) to furnish any combination of such material, answers, or testimony.

The Attorney General may not delegate the authority to issue civil investigative demands under this subsection. Whenever a civil investigative demand is an express demand for any product of discovery, the Attorney General, the Deputy Attorney General, or an Assistant Attorney General shall cause to be served, in any manner authorized by this section, a copy of such demand upon the person from whom the discovery was obtained and shall notify the person to whom such demand is issued of the date on which such copy was served.

(2) Contents and deadlines.—

(A) Each civil investigative demand issued under paragraph (1) shall state the nature of the conduct constituting the alleged violation of a false claims law which is under investigation, and the applicable provision of law alleged to be violated.

(B) If such demand is for the production of documentary material, the demand shall—

(i) describe each class of documentary material to be produced with such definiteness and certainty as to permit such material to be fairly identified;

(ii) prescribe a return date for each such class which will provide a reasonable period of time within which the material so demanded may be assembled and made available for inspection and copying; and

(iii) identify the false claims law investigator to whom such material shall be made available.

(C) If such demand is for answers to written interrogatories, the demand shall—

(i) set forth with specificity the written interrogatories to be answered;

(ii) prescribe dates at which time answers to written interrogatories shall be submitted; and

(iii) identify the false claims law investigator to whom such answers shall be submitted.

(D) If such demand is for the giving of oral testimony, the demand shall—

(i) prescribe a date, time, and place at which oral testimony shall be commenced;

(ii) identify a false claims law investigator who shall conduct the examination and the custodian to whom the transcript of such examination shall be submitted;

(iii) specify that such attendance and testimony are necessary to the conduct of the investigation;

(iv) notify the person receiving the demand of the right to be accompanied by an attorney and any other representative; and

(v) describe the general purpose for which the demand is being issued and the general nature of the testimony,   including the primary areas of inquiry, which will be taken pursuant to the demand.

(E) Any civil investigative demand issued under this section which is an express demand for any product of discovery shall not be returned or returnable until 20 days after a copy of such demand has been served upon the person from whom the discovery was obtained.

(F) The date prescribed for the commencement of oral testimony pursuant to a civil investigative demand issued under this section shall be a date which is not less than seven days after the date on which demand is received, unless the Attorney General or an Assistant Attorney General designated by the Attorney General determines that exceptional circumstances are present which warrant the commencement of such testimony within a lesser period of time.

(G) The Attorney General shall not authorize the issuance under this section of more than one civil investigative demand for oral testimony by the same person unless the person requests otherwise or unless the Attorney General, after investigation, notifies that person in writing that an additional demand

Corporate Fraud Investigations & Compliance Programs

for oral testimony is necessary. The Attorney General may not, notwithstanding section 510 of title 28, authorize the performance, by any other officer, employee, or agency, of any function vested in the Attorney General under this subparagraph.

(b) Protected Material or Information.—

(1) In general.—A civil investigative demand issued under subsection (a) may not require the production of any documentary material, the submission of any answers to written interrogatories, or the giving of any oral testimony if such material, answers, or testimony would be protected from disclosure under—

(A) the standards applicable to subpoenas or subpoenas duces tecum issued by a court of the United States to aid in a grand jury investigation; or

(B) the standards applicable to discovery requests under the Federal Rules of Civil Procedure, to the extent that the application of such standards to any such demand is appropriate and consistent with the provisions and purposes of this section.

(2) Effect on other orders, rules, and laws.—Any such demand which is an express demand for any product of discovery supersedes any inconsistent order, rule, or provision of law (other than this section) preventing or restraining disclosure of such product of discovery to any person. Disclosure of any product of discovery pursuant to any such express demand does not constitute a waiver of any right or privilege which the person making such disclosure may be entitled to invoke to resist discovery of trial preparation materials.

(c) Service; Jurisdiction.—

(1) By whom served.—Any civil investigative demand issued under subsection (a) may be served by a false claims law investigator, or by a United States marshal or a deputy marshal, at any place within the territorial jurisdiction of any court of the United States.

(2) Service in foreign countries.—Any such demand or any petition filed under subsection (j) may be served upon any person who is not found within the territorial jurisdiction of any court of the United States in such manner as the Federal Rules of Civil Procedure prescribe for service in a foreign country. To the extent that the courts of the United States can assert jurisdiction over any such person consistent with due process, the United States District Court for the District of Columbia shall have the same jurisdiction to take any action respecting compliance with this section by any such person that such court would have if such person were personally within the jurisdiction of such court.

(d) Service Upon Legal Entities and Natural Persons.—

(1) Legal entities.—Service of any civil investigative demand issued under subsection (a) or of any petition filed under subsection (j) may be made upon a partnership, corporation, association, or other legal entity by—

Appendix 3 317

(A) delivering an executed copy of such demand or petition to any partner, executive officer, managing agent, or general agent of the partnership, corporation, association, or entity, or to any agent authorized by appointment or by law to receive service of process on behalf of such partnership, corporation, association, or entity;

(B) delivering an executed copy of such demand or petition to the principal office or place of business of the partnership, corporation, association, or entity; or

(C) depositing an executed copy of such demand or petition in the United States mails by registered or certified mail, with a return receipt requested, addressed to such partnership, corporation, association, or entity at its principal office or place of business.

(2) Natural persons.—Service of any such demand or petition may be made upon any natural person by—

(A) delivering an executed copy of such demand or petition to the person; or

(B) depositing an executed copy of such demand or petition in the United States mails by registered or certified mail, with a return receipt requested, addressed to the person at the person's residence or principal office or place of business.

(e) Proof of Service.—A verified return by the individual serving any civil investigative demand issued under subsection (a) or any petition filed under subsection (j) setting forth the manner of such service shall be proof of such service. In the case of service by registered or certified mail, such return shall be accompanied by the return post office receipt of delivery of such demand.

(f) Documentary Material.—

(1) Sworn certificates.—The production of documentary material in response to a civil investigative demand served under this section shall be made under a sworn certificate, in such form as the demand designates, by—

(A) in the case of a natural person, the person to whom the demand is directed, or

(B) in the case of a person other than a natural person, a person having knowledge of the facts and circumstances relating to such production and authorized to act on behalf of such person.

The certificate shall state that all of the documentary material required by the demand and in the possession, custody, or control of the person to whom the demand is directed has been produced and made available to the false claims law investigator identified in the demand.

(2) Production of materials.—Any person upon whom any civil investigative demand for the production of documentary material has been served under this section shall make such material available for inspection and copying to the false

claims law investigator identified in such demand at the principal place of business of such person, or at such other place as the false claims law investigator and the person thereafter may agree and prescribe in writing, or as the court may direct under subsection (j)(1). Such material shall be made so available on the return date specified in such demand, or on such later date as the false claims law investigator may prescribe in writing. Such person may, upon written agreement between the person and the false claims law investigator, substitute copies for originals of all or any part of such material.

(g) Interrogatories.—Each interrogatory in a civil investigative demand served under this section shall be answered separately and fully in writing under oath and shall be submitted under a sworn certificate, in such form as the demand designates, by—

(1) in the case of a natural person, the person to whom the demand is directed, or

(2) in the case of a person other than a natural person, the person or persons responsible for answering each interrogatory.

If any interrogatory is objected to, the reasons for the objection shall be stated in the certificate instead of an answer. The certificate shall state that all information required by the demand and in the possession, custody, control, or knowledge of the person to whom the demand is directed has been submitted. To the extent that any information is not furnished, the information shall be identified and reasons set forth with particularity regarding the reasons why the information was not furnished.

(h) Oral Examinations.—

(1) Procedures.—The examination of any person pursuant to a civil investigative demand for oral testimony served under this section shall be taken before an officer authorized to administer oaths and affirmations by the laws of the United States or of the place where the examination is held. The officer before whom the testimony is to be taken shall put the witness on oath or affirmation and shall, personally or by someone acting under the direction of the officer and in the officer's presence, record the testimony of the witness. The testimony shall be taken stenographically and shall be transcribed. When the testimony is fully transcribed, the officer before whom the testimony is taken shall promptly transmit a copy of the transcript of the testimony to the custodian. This subsection shall not preclude the taking of testimony by any means authorized by, and in a manner consistent with, the Federal Rules of Civil Procedure.

(2) Persons present.—The false claims law investigator conducting the examination shall exclude from the place where the examination is held all persons except the person giving the testimony, the attorney for and any other representative of the person giving the testimony, the attorney for the Government, any person who may be agreed upon by the attorney for the Government and the person giving the testimony, the officer before whom the testimony is to be taken, and any stenographer taking such testimony.

Appendix 3 319

(3) Where testimony taken.—The oral testimony of any person taken pursuant to a civil investigative demand served under this section shall be taken in the judicial district of the United States within which such person resides, is found, or transacts business, or in such other place as may be agreed upon by the false claims law investigator conducting the examination and such person.

(4) Transcript of testimony.—When the testimony is fully transcribed, the false claims law investigator or the officer before whom the testimony is taken shall afford the witness, who may be accompanied by counsel, a reasonable opportunity to examine and read the transcript, unless such examination and reading are waived by the witness. Any changes in form or substance which the witness desires to make shall be entered and identified upon the transcript by the officer or the false claims law investigator, with a statement of the reasons given by the witness for making such changes. The transcript shall then be signed by the witness, unless the witness in writing waives the signing, is ill, cannot be found, or refuses to sign. If the transcript is not signed by the witness within 30 days after being afforded a reasonable opportunity to examine it, the officer or the false claims law investigator shall sign it and state on the record the fact of the waiver, illness, absence of the witness, or the refusal to sign, together with the reasons, if any, given therefor.

(5) Certification and delivery to custodian.—The officer before whom the testimony is taken shall certify on the transcript that the witness was sworn by the officer and that the transcript is a true record of the testimony given by the witness, and the officer or false claims law investigator shall promptly deliver the transcript, or send the transcript by registered or certified mail, to the custodian.

(6) Furnishing or inspection of transcript by witness.—Upon payment of reasonable charges therefor, the false claims law investigator shall furnish a copy of the transcript to the witness only, except that the Attorney General, the Deputy Attorney General, or an Assistant Attorney General may, for good cause, limit such witness to inspection of the official transcript of the witness' testimony.

(7) Conduct of oral testimony.—

(A) Any person compelled to appear for oral testimony under a civil investigative demand issued under subsection (a) may be accompanied, represented, and advised by counsel. Counsel may advise such person, in confidence, with respect to any question asked of such person. Such person or counsel may object on the record to any question, in whole or in part, and shall briefly state for the record the reason for the objection. An objection may be made, received, and entered upon the record when it is claimed that such person is entitled to refuse to answer the question on the grounds of any constitutional or other legal right or privilege, including the privilege against self-incrimination. Such person may not otherwise object to or refuse to answer any question, and may not directly or through counsel otherwise interrupt the oral examination. If such person refuses to answer any question, a petition may be filed in the district court of the United States under subsection (j)(1) for an order compelling such person to answer such question.

(B) If such person refuses to answer any question on the grounds of the privilege against self-incrimination, the testimony of such person may be compelled in accordance with the provisions of part V of title 18.

(8) Witness fees and allowances.—Any person appearing for oral testimony under a civil investigative demand issued under subsection (a) shall be entitled to the same fees and allowances which are paid to witnesses in the district courts of the United States.

(i) Custodians of Documents, Answers, and Transcripts.—

(1) Designation.—The Attorney General shall designate a false claims law investigator to serve as custodian of documentary material, answers to interrogatories, and transcripts of oral testimony received under this section, and shall designate such additional false claims law investigators as the Attorney General determines from time to time to be necessary to serve as deputies to the custodian.

(2) Responsibility for materials; disclosure.—

(A) A false claims law investigator who receives any documentary material, answers to interrogatories, or transcripts of oral testimony under this section shall transmit them to the custodian. The custodian shall take physical possession of such material, answers, or transcripts and shall be responsible for the use made of them and for the return of documentary material under paragraph (4).

(B) The custodian may cause the preparation of such copies of such documentary material, answers to interrogatories, or transcripts of oral testimony as may be required for official use by any false claims law investigator, or other officer or employee of the Department of Justice, who is authorized for such use under regulations which the Attorney General shall issue. Such material, answers, and transcripts may be used by any such authorized false claims law investigator or other officer or employee in connection with the taking of oral testimony under this section.

(C) Except as otherwise provided in this subsection, no documentary material, answers to interrogatories, or transcripts of oral testimony, or copies thereof, while in the possession of the custodian, shall be available for examination by any individual other than a false claims law investigator or other officer or employee of the Department of Justice authorized under subparagraph (B). The prohibition in the preceding sentence on the availability of material, answers, or transcripts shall not apply if consent is given by the person who produced such material, answers, or transcripts, or, in the case of any product of discovery produced pursuant to an express demand for such material, consent is given by the person from whom the discovery was obtained. Nothing in this subparagraph is intended to prevent disclosure to the

Congress, including any committee or subcommittee of the Congress, or to any other agency of the United States for use by such agency in furtherance of its statutory responsibilities. Disclosure of information to any such other agency shall be allowed only upon application, made by the Attorney General to a United States district court, showing substantial need for the use of the information by such agency in furtherance of its statutory responsibilities.

(D) While in the possession of the custodian and under such reasonable terms and conditions as the Attorney General shall prescribe—

(i) documentary material and answers to interrogatories shall be available for examination by the person who produced such material or answers, or by a representative of that person authorized by that person to examine such material and answers; and

(ii) transcripts of oral testimony shall be available for examination by the person who produced such testimony, or by a representative of that person authorized by that person to examine such transcripts.

(3) Use of material, answers, or transcripts in other proceedings.—Whenever any attorney of the Department of Justice has been designated to appear before any court, grand jury, or Federal agency in any case or proceeding, the custodian of any documentary material, answers to interrogatories, or transcripts of oral testimony received under this section may deliver to such attorney such material, answers, or transcripts for official use in connection with any such case or proceeding as such attorney determines to be required. Upon the completion of any such case or proceeding, such attorney shall return to the custodian any such material, answers, or transcripts so delivered which have not passed into the control of such court, grand jury, or agency through introduction into the record of such case or proceeding.

(4) Conditions for return of material.—If any documentary material has been produced by any person in the course of any false claims law investigation pursuant to a civil investigative demand under this section, and—

(A) any case or proceeding before the court or grand jury arising out of such investigation, or any proceeding before any Federal agency involving such material, has been completed, or

(B) no case or proceeding in which such material may be used has been commenced within a reasonable time after completion of the examination and analysis of all documentary material and other information assembled in the course of such investigation,

the custodian shall, upon written request of the person who produced such material, return to such person any such material (other than copies furnished to the false claims law investigator under subsection (f)(2) or made for the Department of Justice under paragraph (2)(B)) which has not passed into the control of any court, grand jury, or agency through introduction into the record of such case or proceeding.

(5) Appointment of successor custodians.—In the event of the death, disability, or separation from service in the Department of Justice of the custodian of any documentary material, answers to interrogatories, or transcripts of oral testimony produced pursuant to a civil investigative demand under this section, or in the event of the official relief of such custodian from responsibility for the custody and control of such material, answers, or transcripts, the Attorney General shall promptly—

(A) designate another false claims law investigator to serve as custodian of such material, answers, or transcripts, and

(B) transmit in writing to the person who produced such material, answers, or testimony notice of the identity and address of the successor so designated.

Any person who is designated to be a successor under this paragraph shall have, with regard to such material, answers, or transcripts, the same duties and responsibilities as were imposed by this section upon that person's predecessor in office, except that the successor shall not be held responsible for any default or dereliction which occurred before that designation.

(j) Judicial Proceedings.—

(1) Petition for enforcement.—Whenever any person fails to comply with any civil investigative demand issued under subsection (a), or whenever satisfactory copying or reproduction of any material requested in such demand cannot be done and such person refuses to surrender such material, the Attorney General may file, in the district court of the United States for any judicial district in which such person resides, is found, or transacts business, and serve upon such person a petition for an order of such court for the enforcement of the civil investigative demand.

(2) Petition to modify or set aside demand.—

(A) Any person who has received a civil investigative demand issued under subsection (a) may file, in the district court of the United States for the judicial district within which such person resides, is found, or transacts business, and serve upon the false claims law investigator identified in such demand a petition for an order of the court to modify or set aside such demand. In the case of a petition addressed to an express demand for any product of discovery, a petition to modify or set aside such demand may be brought only in the district court of the United States for the judicial district in which the proceeding in which such discovery was obtained is or was last pending. Any petition under this subparagraph must be filed—

(i) within 20 days after the date of service of the civil investigative demand, or at any time before the return date specified in the demand, whichever date is earlier, or

(ii) within such longer period as may be prescribed in writing by any false claims law investigator identified in the demand.

(B) The petition shall specify each ground upon which the petitioner relies in seeking relief under subparagraph (A), and may be based upon any failure of the demand to comply with the provisions of this section or upon any constitutional or other legal right or privilege of such person. During the pendency of the petition in the court, the court may stay, as it deems proper, the running of the time allowed for compliance with the demand, in whole or in part, except that the person filing the petition shall comply with any portions of the demand not sought to be modified or set aside.

(3) Petition to modify or set aside demand for product of discovery.—

(A) In the case of any civil investigative demand issued under subsection (a) which is an express demand for any product of discovery, the person from whom such discovery was obtained may file, in the district court of the United States for the judicial district in which the proceeding in which such discovery was obtained is or was last pending, and serve upon any false claims law investigator identified in the demand and upon the recipient of the demand, a petition for an order of such court to modify or set aside those portions of the demand requiring production of any such product of discovery. Any petition under this subparagraph must be filed—

(i) within 20 days after the date of service of the civil investigative demand, or at any time before the return date specified in the demand, whichever date is earlier, or

(ii) within such longer period as may be prescribed in writing by any false claims law investigator identified in the demand.

(B) The petition shall specify each ground upon which the petitioner relies in seeking relief under subparagraph (A), and may be based upon any failure of the portions of the demand from which relief is sought to comply with the provisions of this section, or upon any constitutional or other legal right or privilege of the petitioner. During the pendency of the petition, the court may stay, as it deems proper, compliance with the demand and the running of the time allowed for compliance with the demand.

(4) Petition to require performance by custodian of duties.—At any time during which any custodian is in custody or control of any documentary material or answers to interrogatories produced, or transcripts of oral testimony given, by any person in compliance with any civil investigative demand issued under subsection (a), such person, and in the case of an express demand for any product of discovery, the person from whom such discovery was obtained, may file, in the district court of the United States for the judicial district within which the office of such custodian is situated, and serve upon such custodian, a petition for an order of such court to require the performance by the custodian of any duty imposed upon the custodian by this section.

(5) Jurisdiction.—Whenever any petition is filed in any district court of the United States under this subsection, such court shall have jurisdiction to hear and

determine the matter so presented, and to enter such order or orders as may be required to carry out the provisions of this section. Any final order so entered shall be subject to appeal under section 1291 of title 28. Any disobedience of any final order entered under this section by any court shall be punished as a contempt of the court.

(6) Applicability of federal rules of civil procedure.—The Federal Rules of Civil Procedure shall apply to any petition under this subsection, to the extent that such rules are not inconsistent with the provisions of this section.

(k) Disclosure Exemption.—Any documentary material, answers to written interrogatories, or oral testimony provided under any civil investigative demand issued under subsection (a) shall be exempt from disclosure under section 552 of title 5.

(l) Definitions.—For purposes of this section—

(1) the term "false claims law" means—

(A) this section and sections 3729 through 3732; and

(B) any Act of Congress enacted after the date of the enactment of this section which prohibits, or makes available to the United States in any court of the United States any civil remedy with respect to, any false claim against, bribery of, or corruption of any officer or employee of the United States;

(2) the term "false claims law investigation" means any inquiry conducted by any false claims law investigator for the purpose of ascertaining whether any person is or has been engaged in any violation of a false claims law;

(3) the term "false claims law investigator" means any attorney or investigator employed by the Department of Justice who is charged with the duty of enforcing or carrying into effect any false claims law, or any officer or employee of the United States acting under the direction and supervision of such attorney or investigator in connection with a false claims law investigation;

(4) the term "person" means any natural person, partnership, corporation, association, or other legal entity, including any State or political subdivision of a State;

(5) the term "documentary material" includes the original or any copy of any book, record, report, memorandum, paper, communication, tabulation, chart, or other document, or data compilations stored in or accessible through computer or other information retrieval systems, together with instructions and all other materials necessary to use or interpret such data compilations, and any product of discovery;

(6) the term "custodian" means the custodian, or any deputy custodian, designated by the Attorney General under subsection (i)(1); and

(7) the term "product of discovery" includes—

(A) the original or duplicate of any deposition, interrogatory, document, thing, result of the inspection of land or other property, examination, or admission, which is obtained by any method of discovery in any judicial or administrative proceeding of an adversarial nature;

(B) any digest, analysis, selection, compilation, or derivation of any item listed in subparagraph (A); and

(C) any index or other manner of access to any item listed in subparagraph (A).

(Added Pub. L. 99-562, Sec. 6(a), Oct. 27, 1986, 100 Stat. 3159.)

References in Text

The Federal Rules of Civil Procedure, referred to in subsecs. (b)(1)(B), (c)(2), (h)(1), and (j)(6), are set out in the Appendix to Title 28, Judiciary and Judicial Procedure.

The date of enactment of this section, referred to in subsec. (l)(1)(B), is the date of enactment of Pub. L. 99-562, which was approved Oct. 27, 1986.

Section Referred to in Other Sections

This section is referred to in title 20 section 1078-9.

APPENDIX 4

PROVIDER SELF-DISCLOSURE PROTOCOL

Office of Inspector General
Department of Health and Human Services

I. INTRODUCTION

The Office of Inspector General (OIG) of the United States Department of Health and Human Services (HHS) relies heavily upon the health care industry to help identify and resolve matters that adversely affect the Federal health care programs (as defined in 42 U.S.C. § 1320a-7b(f)). OIG believes that, as participants in the Federal health care programs, health care providers have an ethical and legal duty to ensure the integrity of their dealings with these programs. This duty includes an obligation to take measures, such as instituting a compliance program, to detect and prevent fraudulent, abusive and wasteful activities. It also encompasses the need to implement specific procedures and mechanisms to examine and resolve instances of non-compliance with program requirements. Whether as a result of voluntary self-assessment or in response to external forces, health care providers must be prepared to investigate such instances, assess the potential losses suffered by the Federal health care programs, and make full disclosure to the appropriate authorities. To encourage providers to make voluntary disclosures, OIG issues this Provider Self-disclosure Protocol (Protocol).

The concept of voluntary self-disclosure is not new to OIG. For many years, OIG has worked informally with providers and suppliers that came forward to cooperate with OIG to resolve billing, marketing or quality of care problems. In 1995, as part of the Operation Restore Trust (ORT) initiative, HHS and the Department of Justice (DOJ) announced a pilot voluntary disclosure program, which embraced OIG's longstanding policy favoring voluntary self-disclosure. The demonstration program was developed in coordination with representatives of OIG, DOJ, various United States Attorneys' Offices, the Federal Bureau of Investigation and the Health Care Financing Administration (HCFA). The pilot program was limited to five States (New York, Florida, Illinois, Texas and California) and four different types of providers (home health agencies, skilled nursing facilities, durable medical equipment suppliers, and hospice providers). It gave those qualifying entities a formal mechanism for disclosing and seeking the resolution of matters relating to the Medicare and Medicaid programs. In 1997, the pilot voluntary disclosure program was concluded. While there was limited participation in the pilot, OIG gained valuable insight into the variables influencing the decision to make a disclosure to the Government.

OIG believes it must continue encouraging the health care industry to conduct voluntary self-evaluations and providing viable opportunities for self-disclosure. By establishing this Protocol, OIG renews its commitment to promote an environment of openness and cooperation. The Protocol has no rigid requirements or limitations. Rather, it provides OIG's views on what are the appropriate elements of an effective investigative and audit working plan to address instances of non-compliance. Providers that follow the Protocol expedite OIG's verification process and thus diminish the time it takes before the matter can be formally resolved. Failure to conform to each element of the Protocol is not necessarily fatal to the provider's disclosure, but will likely delay the resolution of the matter.

OIG's principal purpose in producing the Protocol is to provide guidance to health care providers that decide voluntarily to disclose irregularities in their dealings with the Federal health care programs. Because a provider's disclosure can involve anything from a simple error to outright fraud, OIG cannot reasonably make firm commitments as to how a particular disclosure will be resolved or the specific benefit that will enure to the disclosing entity. In our experience, however, opening lines of communication with, and making full disclosure to, the investigative agency at an early stage generally benefits the individual or company. In short, the Protocol can help a health care provider initiate with OIG a dialogue directed at resolving its potential liabilities.

The decision to follow OIG's suggested Protocol rests exclusively with the provider. While OIG can offer only limited guidance on what is inherently a case-specific judgement, there are several considerations that should influence the decision. First, a provider that uncovers an ongoing fraud scheme within its organization immediately should contact OIG, but should *not* follow the Protocol's suggested steps to investigate or quantify the scope of the problem. If the provider follows the Protocol in this type of situation without prior consultation with OIG, there is a substantial risk that the Government's subsequent investigation will be compromised.

Second, OIG anticipates that a provider will apply the Protocol's suggested steps only after an initial assessment substantiates there is a problem with non-compliance with program requirements. The initial identification of potential risk areas should be less intensive and need not conform to the Protocol's suggested procedures. Similarly, when OIG conducts a national review of a particular billing practice, providers should consider the option of conducting a limited assessment of the practice under OIG review, rather than incur the expense of a comprehensive audit. In such cases, an audit that conforms to the Protocol's guidelines may be appropriate only in instances where a preliminary assessment suggests the provider has in fact engaged in the practices under OIG scrutiny.

II. THE PROVIDER SELF-DISCLOSURE PROTOCOL

Unlike the earlier pilot program, there are no pre-disclosure requirements, applications for admission or preliminary qualifying characteristics that must be met. The

Provider Self-disclosure Protocol is open to all health care providers, whether individuals or entities, and is not limited to any particular industry, medical specialty or type of service. While no written agreement setting out the terms of the self-assessment will be required, OIG expects the commitment of the health care provider to disclose specific information and engage in specific self-evaluative steps relating to the disclosed matter. In contrast to the pilot disclosure program, the fact that a disclosing health care provider is already subject to Government inquiry (including investigations, audits or routine oversight activities) will not automatically preclude a disclosure. The disclosure, however, must be made in good faith. OIG will not continue to work with a provider that attempts to circumvent an ongoing inquiry or fails to fully cooperate in the self-disclosure process. In short, OIG will continue its practice of working with providers that are the subject of an investigation or audit, provided that the collaboration does not interfere with the efficient and effective resolution of the inquiry.

The Provider Self-disclosure Protocol is intended to facilitate the resolution of only matters that, in the provider's reasonable assessment, are potentially violative of Federal criminal, civil or administrative laws. Matters exclusively involving overpayments or errors that do not suggest that violations of law have occurred should be brought directly to the attention of the entity (*e.g.*, a contractor such as a carrier or an intermediary) that processes claims and issues payment on behalf of the Government agency responsible for the particular Federal health care program (*e.g.*, HCFA for matters involving Medicare). The program contractors are responsible for processing the refund and will review the circumstances surrounding the initial overpayment. If the contractor concludes that the overpayment raises concerns about the integrity of the provider, the matter may be referred to OIG. Accordingly, the provider's initial decision of where to refer a matter involving non-compliance with program requirements should be made carefully.

OIG is not bound by any findings made by the disclosing provider under the Provider Self-disclosure Protocol and is not obligated to resolve the matter in any particular manner. Nevertheless, OIG will work closely with providers that structure their disclosures in accordance with the Provider Self-disclosure Protocol in an effort to coordinate any investigatory steps or other activities necessary to reach an effective and prompt resolution. It is important to note that, upon review of the provider's disclosure submission and/or reports, OIG may conclude that the disclosed matter warrants a referral to DOJ for consideration under its civil and/or criminal authorities. Alternatively, the provider may request the participation of a representative of DOJ or a local United States Attorney's Office in settlement discussions in order to resolve potential liability under the False Claims Act or other laws. In either case, OIG will report on the provider's involvement and level of cooperation throughout the disclosure process to any other Government agencies affected by the disclosed matter.

III. VOLUNTARY DISCLOSURE SUBMISSION

The disclosing provider will be expected to make a submission as follows:

A. EFFECTIVE DISCLOSURE: The disclosure must be made in writing and must be submitted to the Assistant Inspector General for Investigative Operations, Office of Inspector General, Department of Health and Human Services, 330 Independence Avenue, SW, Cohen Building, Room 5409, Washington, DC 20201. Submissions by telecopier, facsimile or other electronic media will not be accepted.

B. BASIC INFORMATION: The submission should include the following:

1. The name, address, provider identification number(s) and tax identification number(s) of the disclosing health care provider. If the provider is an entity that is owned, controlled or is otherwise part of a system or network, include a description or diagram describing the pertinent relationships and the names and addresses of any related entities, as well as any affected corporate divisions, departments or branches. Additionally, provide the name and address of the disclosing entity's designated representative for purposes of the voluntary disclosure.

2. Indicate whether the provider has knowledge that the matter is under current inquiry by a Government agency or contractor. If the provider has knowledge of a pending inquiry, identify any such Government entity or individual representatives involved. The provider must also disclose whether it is under investigation or other inquiry for any other matters relating to a Federal health care program and provide similar information relating to those other matters.

3. A full description of the nature of the matter being disclosed, including the type of claim, transaction or other conduct giving rise to the matter, the names of entities and individuals believed to be implicated and an explanation of their roles in the matter, and the relevant periods involved.

4. The type of health care provider implicated and any provider billing numbers associated with the matter disclosed. Include the Federal health care programs affected, including Government contractors such as carriers, intermediaries and other third-party payers.

5. The reasons why the disclosing provider believes that a violation of Federal criminal, civil or administrative law may have occurred.

6. A certification by the health care provider or, in the case of an entity, an authorized representative on behalf of the disclosing entity stating that, to the best of the individual's knowledge, the submission contains truthful information and is based on a good faith effort to bring the matter to the Government's attention for the purpose of resolving any potential liabilities to the Government.

C. SUBSTANTIVE INFORMATION: As part of its participation in the disclosure process, the disclosing health care provider will be expected to conduct an internal investigation and a self-assessment, and then report its findings to OIG. The internal review may occur after the initial disclosure of the matter. OIG will generally agree, for a reasonable period of time, to forego an investigation of the matter if the provider agrees that it will conduct the review in accordance with the Internal Investigation Guidelines and the Self-Assessment Guidelines set forth below.

IV. INTERNAL INVESTIGATION GUIDELINES

All disclosures to OIG under the Provider Self-disclosure Protocol should include a report based on an internal investigation conducted by the health care provider. While a provider is free to discuss its preliminary findings with OIG prior to completion of its investigation, the matter cannot be resolved until a comprehensive assessment has been completed pursuant to the following guidelines:

A. NATURE AND EXTENT OF THE IMPROPER OR ILLEGAL PRACTICE: A voluntary disclosure report should demonstrate that a full examination of the practice has been conducted. The report should contain a written narrative that:

1. identifies the potential causes of the incident or practice (*e.g.*, intentional conduct, lack of internal controls, circumvention of corporate procedures or Government regulations);

2. describes the incident or practice in detail, including how the incident or practice arose and continued;

3. identifies the division, departments, branches or related entities involved and/or affected;

4. identifies the impact on, and risks to, health, safety, or quality of care posed by the matter disclosed, with sufficient information to allow OIG to assess the immediacy of the impact and risks, the steps that should be taken to address them, as well as the measures taken by the disclosing entity;

5. delineates the period during which the incident or practice occurred;

6. identifies the corporate officials, employees or agents who knew of, encouraged, or participated in, the incident or practice and any individuals who may have been involved in detecting the matter;

7. identifies the corporate officials, employees or agents who should have known of, but failed to detect, the incident or practice based on their job responsibilities; and

8. estimates the monetary impact of the incident or practice upon the Federal health care programs, pursuant to the Self-Assessment Guidelines below.

B. DISCOVERY AND RESPONSE TO THE MATTER: The internal investigation report should relate the circumstances under which the disclosed matter was discovered and fully document the measures taken upon discovery to address the problem and prevent future abuses. In this regard, the report should:

1. Describe how the incident or practice was identified, and the origin of the information that led to its discovery.

2. Describe the entity's efforts to investigate and document the incident or practice (*e.g.*, use of internal or external legal, audit or consultative resources).

3. Describe in detail the chronology of the investigative steps taken in connection with the entity's internal inquiry into the disclosed matter including the following:

a. a list of all individuals interviewed, including each individual's business address and telephone number, and their positions and titles in the relevant entities during both the relevant period and at the time the disclosure is being made. For all individuals interviewed, provide the dates of those interviews and the subject matter of each interview, as well as summaries of the interview. The health care provider will be responsible for advising the individual to be interviewed that the information the individual provides may, in turn, be provided to OIG. Additionally, include a list of those individuals who refused to be interviewed and provide the reasons cited;

b. a description of files, documents, and records reviewed with sufficient particularity to allow their retrieval, if necessary; and

c. a summary of auditing activity undertaken and a summary of the documents relied upon in support of the estimation of losses. These documents and information must accompany the report, unless the calculation of losses is undertaken pursuant to the Self-Assessment Guidelines, which contain specific reporting requirements;

4. Describe the actions by the health care provider to stop the inappropriate conduct.

5. Describe any related health care businesses affected by the inappropriate conduct in which the health care provider is involved, all efforts by the health care provider to prevent a recurrence of the incident or practice in the affected division as well as in any related health care entities (*e.g.*, new accounting or internal control procedures, increased internal audit efforts, increased supervision by higher management or through training).

6. Describe any disciplinary action taken against corporate officials, employees and agents as a result of the disclosed matter.

7. Describe appropriate notices, if applicable, provided to other Government agencies, (*e.g.*, Securities and Exchange Commission and Internal Revenue Service) in connection with the disclosed matter.

Appendix 4 333

C. The internal investigation report must include a certification by the health care provider, or in the case of an entity an authorized representative on behalf of the disclosing health care provider, indicating that, to the best of the individual's knowledge, the internal investigation report contains truthful information and is based on a good faith effort to assist OIG in its inquiry and verification of the disclosed matter.

V. SELF-ASSESSMENT GUIDELINES

To estimate the monetary impact of the disclosed matter, the health care provider also should conduct an internal financial assessment and prepare a report of its findings. This self-assessment may be performed at the same time as the internal investigation, or commenced after the scope of the non-compliance with program requirements has been established. In either case, OIG will verify a provider's calculation of Federal health care program losses and it is strongly recommended that, at a minimum, the review conform to the following guidelines:

A. APPROACH: The self-assessment should consist of a review of either: (1) all of the claims affected by the disclosed matter for the relevant period; or (2) a statistically valid sample of the claims that can be projected to the population of claims affected by the matter for the relevant period. This determination should be based on the size of the population believed to be implicated, the variance of characteristics to be reviewed, the cost of the self-assessment, the available resources, the estimated duration of the review, and other factors as appropriate.

B. BASIC INFORMATION: Regardless of which of these two approaches is used, the disclosing provider should submit to OIG a work plan describing the self-assessment process. OIG will review the proposal and, where appropriate, provide comments on the plan in a timely manner. At its option, OIG may choose to carry out any necessary activities at any stage of the review to verify that the process is undertaken correctly and to validate the review findings. While OIG is not obligated to accept the results of a provider's self-assessment, findings based upon procedures which conform to the Protocol will be given substantial weight in determining any program overpayments. In addition, OIG will use the validated provider self-assessment report in preparing a recommendation to DOJ for resolution of the provider's False Claims Act or other liability. Among the issues that should be addressed in the plan are the following:

1. Review Objective: There should be a statement clearly articulating the objective of the review and the review procedure or combination of procedures applied to achieve the objective.

2. Review Population: The plan should identify the population, which is the group about which information is needed. In addition, there should be an explanation of the methodology used to develop the population and the basis for this determination.

3. Sources of Data: The plan should provide a full description of the source of the information upon which the review will be based, including the legal or other standards to be applied, the sources of payment data and the documents that will be relied upon (*e.g.*, employment contracts, rental agreements, etc.).

4. Personnel Qualifications: The plan should identify the names and titles of those individuals involved in any aspect of the self-assessment, including statisticians, accountants, auditors, consultants and medical reviewers, and describe their qualifications.

C. SAMPLE ELEMENTS: If the provider, in consultation with OIG, determines that the financial review will be based upon a sample, the work plan should also include the sampling plan as follows:

1. Sampling Unit: The plan should define the sampling unit, which is any of the designated elements that comprise the population of interest.

2. Sampling Frame: The plan should identify the sampling frame, which is the totality of the sampling units from which the sample will be selected. In addition, the plan should document how the audit population differs from the sampling frame and what effect this difference has on conclusions reached as a result of the audit.

3. Sample Size: The size of the sample must be determined through the use of a probe sample. Accordingly, the plan should include a description of both the probe sample and the full sample. At a minimum, the full sample must be designed to generate an estimate with a ninety (90) percent level of confidence and a precision of twenty-five (25) percent. The probe sample must contain at least thirty (30) sample units and cannot be used as part of the full sample.

4. Random Numbers: Both the probe sample and the sample must be selected through random numbers. The source of the random numbers used must be shown in the sampling plans. OIG strongly recommends the use of its Office of Audit Services' Statistical Sampling Software, also known as "RAT-STATS," which is currently available free of charge through the "internet" at "*www.hhs.gov/progorg/oas/ratstat.html*".

5. Sample Design: Unless the disclosing provider demonstrates the need to use a different sample design, the self-assessment should use simple random sampling. If necessitated, the provider may use stratified or multistage sampling. Details about the strata, stages and clusters should be included in the description of the audit plan.

6. Estimate of Review Time per Sample Item: The plan should estimate the time expended to locate the sample items and the staff hours expended to review a sample item.

7. Characteristics Measure by the Sample: The sampling plan should identify the characteristics used for testing each sample item. For example, in a sample drawn to estimate the value of overpayments due to duplicate payments,

the characteristics under consideration are the conditions that must exist for a sample item to be a duplicate. The amount of the duplicate payment is the measurement of the overpayment. The sampling plan must also contain the decision rules for determining whether a sample item entirely meets the criterion for having characteristics or only partially meets the criterion.

8. Missing Sample Items: The sampling plan must include a discussion of how missing sample items were handled and the rationale.

9. Other Evidence: Although sample results should stand on their own in terms of validity, sample results may be combined with other evidence in arriving at specific conclusions. If appropriate, indicate what other substantiating or corroborating evidence was developed.

10. Estimation Methodology: Because the general purpose of the review is to estimate the monetary losses to the Federal health care programs, the methodology to be used must be variables sampling using the difference estimator. To estimate the amount implicated in the disclosed matter, the provider must use the mean point estimate. The statistical estimates must be reported using a ninety (90) percent confidence level. The use of RAT-STATS to calculate the estimates is strongly recommended.

11. Reporting Results: The sampling plan should indicate how the results will be reported at the conclusion of the review. In preparing the report, enough details must be provided to clearly indicate what estimates are reported.

D. CERTIFICATION: Upon completion of the self-assessment, the disclosing health care provider, or in the case of an entity its authorized representative, must submit to OIG a certification stating that, to the best of the individual's knowledge, the report contains truthful information and is based on a good faith effort to assist OIG in its inquiry and verification of the disclosed matter.

VI. OIG's VERIFICATION

Upon receipt of a health care provider's disclosure submission, OIG will begin its verification of the disclosure information. The extent of OIG's verification effort will depend, in large part, upon the quality and thoroughness of the internal investigative and self-assessment reports. Matters uncovered during the verification process, which are outside of the scope of the matter disclosed to OIG, may be treated as new matters outside the Provider Self-disclosure Protocol.

To facilitate OIG's verification and validation processes, OIG must have access to all audit work papers and other supporting documents without the assertion of privileges or limitations on the information produced. In the normal course of verification, OIG will not request production of written communications subject to the attorney-client privilege. There may be documents or other materials, however, that may be covered by the work product doctrine, but which OIG believes are critical to resolving the disclosure. OIG is prepared to discuss with provider's counsel ways to gain access to the underlying information without the need to waive the protections provided by an appropriately asserted claim of privilege.

VII. PAYMENTS

Because of the need to verify the information provided by a disclosing health provider, OIG will not accept payments of presumed overpayments determined by the health care provider prior to the completion of OIG's inquiry. However, the provider is encouraged to place the overpayment amount in an interest-bearing escrow account to minimize further losses. While the matter is under OIG inquiry, the disclosing provider must refrain from making payment relating to the disclosed matter to the Federal health care programs or their contractors without OIG's prior consent. If OIG consents, the disclosing provider will be required to agree in writing that the acceptance of the payment does not constitute the Government's agreement as to the amount of losses suffered by the programs as a result of the disclosed matter, and does not affect in any manner the Government's ability to pursue criminal, civil or administrative remedies or to obtain additional fines, damages or penalties for the matters disclosed.

VIII. COOPERATION AND REMOVAL FROM THE PROVIDER SELF-DISCLOSURE PROTOCOL

The disclosing entity's diligent and good faith cooperation throughout the entire process is essential. Accordingly, OIG expects to receive documents and information from the entity that relate to the disclosed matter without the need to resort to compulsory methods. If a provider fails to work in good faith with OIG to resolve the disclosed matter, that lack of cooperation will be considered an aggravating factor when OIG assesses the appropriate resolution of the matter. Similarly, the intentional submission of false or otherwise untruthful information, as well as the intentional omission of relevant information, will be referred to DOJ or other Federal agencies and could, in itself, result in criminal and/or civil sanctions, as well as exclusion from participation in the Federal health care programs.

APPENDIX 5

U.S. DEPARTMENT OF JUSTICE POLICY STATEMENT

Factors in Decisions on Criminal Prosecutions for Environmental Violations in the Context of Significant Voluntary Compliance or Disclosure Efforts by the Violator

I. Introduction

It is the policy of the Department of Justice to encourage self-auditing, self-policing and voluntary disclosure of environmental violations by the regulated community by indicating that these activities are viewed as mitigating factors in the Department's exercise of criminal environmental enforcement discretion. This document is intended to describe the factors that the Department of Justice considers in deciding whether to bring a criminal prosecution for a violation of an environmental statute, so that such prosecutions do not create a disincentive to or undermine the goal of encouraging critical self-auditing, self-policing, and voluntary disclosure. It is designed to give federal prosecutors direction concerning the exercise of prosecutorial discretion in environmental criminal cases and to ensure that such discretion is exercised consistently nationwide. It is also intended to give the regulated community a sense of how the federal government exercises its criminal prosecutorial discretion with respect to such factors as the defendant's voluntary disclosure of violations, cooperation with the government in investigating the violations, use of environmental audits and other procedures to ensure compliance with all applicable environmental laws and regulations, and use of measures to remedy expeditiously and completely any violations and the harms caused thereby.

This guidance and the examples contained herein provide a framework for the determination of whether a particular case presents the type of circumstances in which lenience would be appropriate.

II. Factors to be Considered

Where the law and evidence would otherwise be sufficient for prosecution, the attorney for the Department should consider the factors contained herein, to the extent they are applicable, along with any other relevant factors, in determining whether and how to prosecute. It must be emphasized that these are examples of the types of factors which could be relevant. They do not constitute a definitive recipe or checklist of requirements. They merely illustrate some of the types of information which is relevant to our exercise of prosecutorial discretion.

It is unlikely that any one factor will be dispositive in any given case. All relevant factors are considered and given the weight deemed appropriate in the particular

338 Corporate Fraud Investigations & Compliance Programs

case. *See, Federal Principles of Prosecution* (U.S. Dept. of Justice, 1980), Comment to Part A.2; Part B.3.

A. Voluntary Disclosure

The attorney for the Department should consider whether the person[1] made a voluntary, timely and complete disclosure of the matter under investigation. Consideration should be given to whether the person came forward promptly after discovering the noncompliance, and to the quantity and quality of information provided. Particular consideration should be given to whether the disclosure substantially aided the government's investigatory process, and whether it occurred before a law enforcement or regulatory authority (federal, state or local authority) had already obtained knowledge regarding noncompliance. A disclosure is not considered to be "voluntary" if that disclosure is already specifically required by law, regulation, or permit.[2]

B. Cooperation

The attorney for the Department should consider the degree and timeliness of cooperation by the person. Full and prompt cooperation is essential, whether in the context of a voluntary disclosure or after the government has independently learned of a violation. Consideration should be given to the violator's willingness to make all relevant information (including the complete results of any internal or external investigation and the names of all potential witnesses) available to government investigators and prosecutors. Consideration should also be a given to the extent and quality of the violator's assistance to the government's investigation.

C. Preventive Measures and Compliance Programs

The attorney for the Department should consider the existence and scope of any regularized, intensive, and comprehensive environmental compliance program; such a program may include an environmental compliance or management audit. Particular consideration should be given to whether the compliance or audit program includes sufficient measures to identify and prevent future noncompliance, and whether the program was adopted in good faith in a timely manner.

Compliance programs may vary but the following questions should be asked in evaluating any program: Was there a strong institutional policy to comply with all

---

[1] As used in this document, the terms "person" and "violator" are intended to refer to business and nonprofit entities as well as individuals.

[2] For example, any person in charge of a vessel or of an on shore facility or an offshore facility is required to notify the appropriate agency of the United States Government of any discharge of oil or a hazardous substance into or upon *inter alia* the navigable waters of the United States. Section 311 (b)(5) of the Clean Water Act, 33 U.S.C. § 1321(b)(5), as amended by the Oil Pollution Act of 1990, Pub. L. 101-380, § 4301(a), 104 Stat. 485, 533 (1990).

environmental requirements? Had safeguards beyond those required by existing law been developed and implemented to prevent noncompliance from occurring? Were there regular procedures, including internal or external compliance and management audits, to evaluate, detect, prevent and remedy circumstances like those that led to the noncompliance? Were there procedures and safeguards to ensure the integrity of any audit conducted? Did the audit evaluate all sources of pollution (i.e., all media), including the possibility of cross-media transfers of pollutants? Were the auditor's recommendations implemented in a timely fashion? Were adequate resources committed to the auditing program and to implementing its recommendations? Was environmental compliance a standard by which employee and corporate departmental performance was judged?

D. Additional Factors Which May Be Relevant

1. Pervasiveness of Noncompliance

Pervasive noncompliance may indicate systemic or repeated participation in or condonation of criminal behavior. It may also indicate the lack of a meaningful compliance program. In evaluating this factor, the attorney for the Department should consider, among other things, the number and level of employees participating in the unlawful activities and the obviousness, seriousness, duration, history, and frequency of noncompliance.

2. Internal Disciplinary Action

Effective internal disciplinary action is crucial to any compliance program. The attorney for the Department should consider whether there was an effective system of discipline for employees who violated company environmental compliance policies. Did the disciplinary system establish an awareness in other employees that unlawful conduct would not be condoned?

3. Subsequent Compliance Efforts

The attorney for the Department should consider the extent of any efforts to remedy any ongoing noncompliance. The promptness and completeness of any action taken to remove the source of the noncompliance and to lessen the environmental harm resulting from the noncompliance should be considered. Considerable weight should be given to prompt, good-faith efforts to reach environmental compliance agreements with federal or state authorities, or both. Full compliance with such agreements should be a factor in any decision whether to prosecute.

III. Application of These Factors to Hypothetical Examples[3]

These examples are intended to assist federal prosecutors in their exercise of discretion in evaluating environmental cases. The situations facing prosecutors, of course, present a wide variety of fact patterns. Therefore, in a given case, some of the criteria may be satisfied while others may not. Moreover, satisfaction of various criteria may be a matter of degree. Consequently, the effect of a given mix of factors also is a matter of degree. In the ideal situation, if a company fully meets all of the criteria, the result may be a decision not to prosecute that company criminally. Even if satisfaction of the criteria is not complete, still the company may benefit in terms of degree of enforcement response by the government. The following hypothetical examples are intended to illustrate the operation of these guidelines.

Example 1:

This is the ideal case in terms of criteria satisfaction and consequent prosecution leniency.

1. Company A regularly conducts a comprehensive audit of its compliance with environmental requirements.

2. The audit uncovers information about employees' disposing of hazardous wastes by dumping them in an unpermitted location.

3. An internal company investigation confirms the audit information. (Depending upon the nature of the audit, this follow-up investigation may be unnecessary.)

4. Prior to the violations the company had a sound compliance program, which included clear policies, employees training, and a hotline for suspected violations.

5. As soon as the company confirms the violations, it discloses all pertinent information to the appropriate government agency; it undertakes compliance planning with that agency; and it carries out satisfactory remediation measures.

6. The company also undertakes to correct any false information previously submitted to the government in relation to the violations.

7. Internally the company disciplines the employees actually involved in the violations, including any supervisor who was lax in preventing or detecting the activity. Also, the company reviews its compliance program to determine how the violations slipped by and corrects the weaknesses found by that review.

---

3 While this policy applies to both individual and organizational violators, these examples focus particularly upon situations involving organizations.

Appendix 5 341

8. The company discloses to the government the names of the employees actually responsible for the violations, and it cooperates with the government by providing documentation necessary to the investigation of those persons.

Under these circumstances Company A would stand a good chance of being favorably considered for prosecutorial leniency, to the extent of not being criminally prosecuted at all. The degree of any leniency, however, may turn upon other relevant factors not specifically dealt with in these guidelines.[4]

Example 2:

At the opposite end of the scale is Company Z, which meets few of the criteria. The likelihood of prosecutorial leniency, therefore, is remote. Company Z's circumstances may include any of the following:

1. Because an employee has threatened to report a violation to federal authorities, the company is afraid that investigators may begin looking at it. An audit is undertaken, but it focuses only upon the particular violation, ignoring the possibility that the violation may be indicative of widespread activities in the organization.

2. After completing the audit, Company Z reports the violations discovered to the government.

3. The company had a compliance program, but it was effectively no more than a collection of paper. No effort is made to disseminate its content, impress upon employees its significance, train employees in its application, or oversee its implementation.

4. Even after "discovery" of the violation the company makes no effort to strengthen its compliance procedures.

5. The company makes no effort to come to terms with regulators regarding its violations. It resists any remedial work and refuses to pay any monetary sanctions.

6. Because of the non-compliance, information submitted to regulators over the years has been materially inaccurate, painting a substantially false picture of the company's true compliance situation. The company fails to take any steps to correct that inaccuracy.

7. The company does not cooperate with prosecutors in identifying those employees (including managers) who actually were involved in the violation, and it resists disclosure of any documents relating either to the violations or to the responsible employees.

---

4   For example, if the company had a long history of noncompliance, the compliance audit was done only under pressure from regulators, and a timely audit would have ended the violations much sooner, those circumstances would be considered.

In these circumstances leniency is unlikely. The only positive action is the so-called audit, but that was so narrowly focused as to be of questionable value, and it was undertaken only to head off a possible criminal investigation. Otherwise, the company demonstrated no good faith either in terms of compliance efforts or in assisting the government in obtaining a full understanding of the violation and discovering its sources.

Nonetheless, these factors do not assure a criminal prosecution of Company Z. As with Company A, above, other circumstances may be present which affect the balance struck by prosecutors. For example, the effect of the violation (because of substance, duration, or amount) may be such that prosecutors would not consider it to be an appropriate criminal case. Administrative or civil proceedings may be considered a more appropriate response.

Other examples:

Between these extremes there is a range of possibilities. The presence, absence, or degree of any criterion may affect the prosecution's exercise of discretion. Below are some examples of such effects:

1. In a situation otherwise similar to that of Company A, above, Company B performs an audit that is very limited in scope and probably reflects no more than an effort to avoid prosecution. Despite that background, Company B is cooperative in terms of both bringing itself into compliance and providing information regarding the crime and its perpetrators. The result could be any of a number of outcomes, including prosecution of a lesser charge or a decision to prosecute the individuals rather than the company.

2. Again the situation is similar to Company A's, but Company C refuses to reveal any information regarding the individual violators. The likelihood of the government's prosecuting the company is substantially increased.

3. In another situation similar to Company A's, Company D chooses to "sit on" the audit and take corrective action without telling the government. The government learns of the situation months or years after the fact.

A complicating fact here is that environmental regulatory programs are self policing: they include a substantial number of reporting requirements. If reports which in fact presented false information are allowed to stand uncorrected, the reliability of this system is undermined. They also may lead to adverse and unfair impacts upon other members of the regulated community. For example, Company D failed to report discharges of X contaminant into a municipal sewer system, discharges that were terminated as a result of an audit. The sewer authority, though, knowing only that there have been excessive loadings of X, but not knowing that Company D was a source, tightens limitations upon all known sources of X. Thus, all of those sources incur additional treatment expenses, but Company D is unaffected. Had Company D revealed its audit results, the other companies would not have suffered unnecessary expenses.

In some situations, moreover, failure to report is a crime. *See, e.g.*, 33 U.S.C. § 1321(b)(5) and 42 U.S.C. § 9603(b). To illustrate the effect of this factor, consider Company E, which conducts a thorough audit and finds that hazardous wastes have been disposed of by dumping them on the ground. The company cleans up the area and tightens up its compliance program, but does not reveal the situation to regulators. Assuming that a reportable quantity of a hazardous substance was released, the company was under a legal obligation under 42 U.S.C. § 9603(b) to report that release as soon as it had knowledge of it, thereby allowing regulators the opportunity to assure proper clean up. Company E's knowing failure to report the release upon learning of it is itself a felony.

In the cases of both Company D and Company E, consideration would be given by prosecutors for remedial efforts; hence prosecution of fewer or lesser charges might result. However, because Company D's silence adversely affected others who are entitled to fair regulatory treatment and because Company E deprived those legally responsible for evaluation cleanup needs of the ability to carry out their functions, the likelihood of their totally escaping criminal prosecution is significantly reduced.

4. Company F's situation is similar to that of Company B. However, with regard to the various violations shown by the audit, it concentrates upon correcting only the easier, less expensive, less significant among them. Its lackadaisical approach to correction does not make it a strong candidate for leniency.

5. Company G is similar to Company D in that it performs an audit and finds violations, but does not bring them to the government's attention. Those violations do not involve failures to comply with reporting requirements. The company undertakes a program of gradually correcting its violations. When the government learns of the situation, Company G still has not remedied its most significant violations, but claims that it certainly planned to get to them. Company G could receive some consideration for its efforts, but its failure to disclose and the slowness of its remedial work probably mean that it cannot expect a substantial degree of leniency.

6. Comprehensive audits are considered positive efforts toward good faith compliance. However, such audits are not indispensable to enforcement leniency. Company H's situation is essentially identical to that of Company A, except for the fact that it does not undertake a comprehensive audit. It does not have a formal audit program, but, as a part of its efforts to ensure compliance, does realize that it is committing an environmental violation. It thereafter takes steps otherwise identical to those of Company A in terms of compliance efforts and cooperation. Company H is also a likely candidate for leniency, including possibly no criminal prosecution.

In sum, mitigating efforts made by the regulated community will be recognized and evaluated. The greater the showing of good faith, the more likely it will be met with leniency. Conversely, the less good faith shown, the less likely that prosecutorial discretion will tend toward leniency.

IV. Nature of this Guidance

This guidance explains the current general practice of the Department in making criminal prosecutive and other decisions after giving consideration to the criteria described above, as well as any other criteria that are relevant to the exercise of criminal prosecutorial discretion in a particular case. This discussion is an expression of, and in no way departs from, the long tradition of exercising prosecutorial discretion. The decision to prosecute "generally rests entirely in [the prosecutor's] discretion." *Bordenkircher v. Hayes*, 434 U.S. 357, 364 (1978).[5] This discretion is especially firmly held by the criminal prosecutor.[6] The criteria set forth above are intended only as internal guidance to Department of Justice attorneys. They are not intended to, do not, and may not be relied upon to create a right or benefit, substantive or procedural, enforceable at law by a party to litigation with the United States, nor do they in any way limit the lawful litigative prerogatives, including civil enforcement actions, of the Department of Justice or the Environmental Protection Agency. They are provided to guide the effective use of limited enforcement resources, and do not derive from, find their basis in, nor constitute any legal requirement, whether constitutional, statutory, or otherwise, to forego or modify any enforcement action or the use of any evidentiary material. *See, Principles of Federal Prosecution* (U.S. Dept. of Justice, 1980) p.4; *United States Attorneys' Manual* (U.S. Dept. of Justice, 1986) 1-1,000.

Dated: July 1, 1991

---

5   Although some statutes have occasionally been held to require civil enforcement actions, *see, e.g., Dunlop v. Bachowski*, 421 U.S. 560 (1975), those are unusual cases, and the general rule is that both civil and criminal enforcement is at the enforcement agency's discretion where not prescribed by law. *Heckler v. Chaney*, 470 U.S. 821, 830-35 (1985); *Cutler v. Hayes*, 818 F.2d 879, 893 (D.C. Cir. 1987) (decisions not to enforce are not reviewable unless the statute provides an "inflexible mandate").

6   *Newman v. United States*, 382 F.2d 479, 480 (D.C. Cir. 1967).

APPENDIX 6

ENVIRONMENTAL PROTECTION AGENCY POLICY STATEMENT

Incentives for Self-Policing:
Discovery, Disclosure, Correction and Prevention of Violations

A. Purpose

This policy is designed to enhance protection of human health and the environment by encouraging regulated entities to voluntarily discover, disclose, correct and prevent violations of federal environmental requirements.

B. Definitions

For purposes of this policy, the following definitions apply:

"Environmental Audit" has the definition given to it in EPA's 1986 audit policy on environmental auditing, *i.e.*, "a systematic, documented, periodic and objective review by regulated entities of facility operations and practices related to meeting environmental requirements."

"Due Diligence" encompasses the regulated entity's systematic efforts, appropriate to the size and nature of its business, to prevent, detect and correct violations through all of the following:

(a) Compliance policies, standards and procedures that identify how employees and agents are to meet the requirements of laws, regulations, permits and other sources of authority for environmental requirements;

(b) Assignment of overall responsibility for overseeing compliance with policies, standards, and procedures, and assignment of specific responsibility for assuring compliance at each facility or operation;

(c) Mechanisms for systematically assuring that compliance policies, standards and procedures are being carried out, including monitoring and auditing systems reasonably designed to detect and correct violations, periodic evaluation of the overall performance of the compliance management system, and a means for employees or agents to report violations of environmental requirements without fear of retaliation;

(d) Efforts to communicate effectively the regulated entity's standards and procedures to all employees and other agents;

(e) Appropriate incentives to managers and employees to perform in accordance with the compliance policies, standards and procedures, including consistent enforcement through appropriate disciplinary mechanisms; and

346 Corporate Fraud Investigations & Compliance Programs

(f) Procedures for the prompt and appropriate correction of any violations, and any necessary modifications to the regulated entity's program to prevent future violations.

"Environmental audit report" means the analysis, conclusions, and recommendations resulting from an environmental audit, but does not include data obtained in, or testimonial evidence concerning, the environmental audit.

"Gravity-based penalties" are that portion of a penalty over and above the economic benefit., *i.e.*, the punitive portion of the penalty, rather than that portion representing a defendant's economic gain from non-compliance. (For further discussion of this concept, see "A Framework for Statute-Specific Approaches to Penalty Assessments," #GM-22, 1980, U.S. EPA General Enforcement Policy Compendium).

"Regulated entity" means any entity, including a federal, state or municipal agency or facility, regulated under federal environmental laws.

C. Incentives for Self-Policing

1. No Gravity-Based Penalties

Where the regulated entity establishes that it satisfies all of the conditions of Section D of the policy, EPA will not seek gravity-based penalties for violations of federal environmental requirements.

2. Reduction of Gravity-Based Penalties by 75%

EPA will reduce gravity-based penalties for violations of federal environmental requirements by 75% so long as the regulated entity satisfies all of the conditions of Section D(2) through D(9) below.

3. No Criminal Recommendations

(a) EPA will not recommend to the Department of Justice or other prosecuting authority that criminal charges be brought against a regulated entity where EPA determines that all of the conditions in Section D are satisfied, so long as the violation does not demonstrate or involve:

(i) a prevalent management philosophy or practice that concealed or condoned environmental violations; or

(ii) high-level corporate officials' or managers' conscious involvement in, or willful blindness to, the violations.

(b) Whether or not EPA refers the regulated entity for criminal prosecution under this section, the Agency reserves the right to recommend prosecution for the criminal acts of individual managers or employees under existing policies guiding the exercise of enforcement discretion.

4. No Routine Request for Audits

EPA will not request or use an environmental audit report to initiate a civil or criminal investigation of the entity. For example, EPA will not request an environmental audit report in routine inspections. If the Agency has independent reason to believe that a violation has occurred, however, EPA may seek any information relevant to identifying violations or determining liability or extent of harm.

D. Conditions

1. Systematic Discovery

The violation was discovered through:

(a) an environmental audit; or

(b) an objective, documented, systematic procedure or practice reflecting the regulated entity's due diligence in preventing, detecting, and correcting violations The regulated entity must provide accurate and complete documentation to the Agency as to how it exercises due diligence to prevent, detect and correct violations according to the criteria for due diligence outlined in Section B. EPA may require as a condition of penalty mitigation that a description of the regulated entity's due diligence efforts be made publicly available.

2. Voluntary Discovery

The violation was identified voluntarily, and not through a legally mandated monitoring or sampling requirement prescribed by statute, regulation, permit, judicial or administrative order, or consent agreement. For example, the policy does not apply to:

(a) emissions violations detected through a continuous emissions monitor (or alternative monitor established in a permit) where any such monitoring is required;

(b) violations of National Pollutant Discharge Elimination System (NPDES) discharge limits detected through required sampling or monitoring;

(c) violations discovered through a compliance audit required to be performed by the terms of a consent order or settlement agreement.

3. Prompt Disclosure

The regulated entity fully discloses a specific violation within 10 days (or such shorter period provided by law) after it has discovered that the violation has occurred, or may have occurred, in writing to EPA.

4. Discovery and Disclosure Independent of Government or Third Party Plaintiff

The violation must also be identified and disclosed by the regulated entity prior to:

(a) the commencement of a federal, state or local agency inspection or investigation, or the issuance by such agency of an information request to the regulated entity;

(b) notice of a citizen suit;

(c) the filing of a complaint by a third party;

(d) the reporting of the violation to EPA (or other government agency) by a "whistleblower" employee, rather than by one authorized to speak on behalf of the regulated entity; or

(e) imminent discovery of the violation by a regulatory agency.

5. Correction and Remediation

The regulated entity corrects the violation within 60 days, certifies in writing that violations have been corrected, and takes appropriate measures as determined by EPA to remedy any environmental or human harm due to the violation. If more than 60 days will be needed to correct the violation(s), the regulated entity must so notify EPA in writing before the 60-day period has passed. Where appropriate, EPA may require that to satisfy conditions 5 and 6, a regulated entity enter into a publicly available written agreement, administrative consent order or judicial consent decree, particularly where compliance or remedial measures are complex or a lengthy schedule for attaining and maintaining compliance or remediating harm is required.

6. Prevent Recurrence

The regulated entity agrees in writing to take steps to prevent a recurrence of the violation, which may include improvements to its environmental auditing or due diligence efforts.

7. No Repeat Violations

The specific violation (or closely related violation) has not occurred previously within the past three years at the same facility, or is not part of a pattern of federal, state or local violations by the facility's parent organization (if any), which have occurred within the past five years. For the purposes of this section, a violation is:

(a) any violation of federal, state or local environmental law identified in a judicial or administrative order, consent agreement or order, complaint, or notice of violation, conviction or plea agreement; or

(b) any act or omission for which the regulated entity has previously received penalty mitigation from EPA or a state or local agency.

8. Other Violations Excluded

The violation is not one which (i) resulted in serious actual harm, or may have presented an imminent and substantial endangerment to, human health or the environment, or (ii) violates the specific terms of any judicial or administrative order, or consent agreement.

9. Cooperation

The regulated entity cooperates as requested by EPA and provides such information as is necessary and requested by EPA to determine applicability of this policy. Cooperation includes, at a minimum, providing all requested documents and access to employees and assistance in investigating the violation, any noncompliance problems related to the disclosure, and any environmental consequences related to the violations.

E. Economic Benefit

EPA will retain its full discretion to recover any economic benefit gained as a result of noncompliance to preserve a ``level playing field'' in which violators do not gain a competitive advantage over regulated entities that do comply. EPA may forgive the entire penalty for violations which meet conditions 1 through 9 in section D and, in the Agency's opinion, do not merit any penalty due to the insignificant amount of any economic benefit.

F. Effect on State Law, Regulation or Policy

EPA will work closely with states to encourage their adoption of policies that reflect the incentives and conditions outlined in this policy. EPA remains firmly opposed to statutory environmental audit privileges that shield evidence of environmental violations and undermine the public's right to know, as well as to blanket immunities for violations that reflect criminal conduct, present serious threats or actual harm to health and the environment, allow noncomplying companies to gain an economic advantage over their competitors, or reflect a repeated failure to comply with federal law. EPA will work with states to address any provisions of state audit privilege or immunity laws that are inconsistent with this policy, and which may prevent a timely and appropriate response to significant environmental violations. The Agency reserves its right to take necessary actions to protect public health or the environment by enforcing against any violations of federal law.

G. Applicability

(1) This policy applies to the assessment of penalties for any violations under all of the federal environmental statutes that EPA administers, and supersedes any inconsistent provisions in media-specific penalty or enforcement policies and EPA's 1986 Environmental Auditing Policy Statement.

(2) To the extent that existing EPA enforcement policies are not inconsistent, they will continue to apply in conjunction with this policy. However, a regulated entity that has received penalty mitigation for satisfying specific conditions under this

policy may not receive additional penalty mitigation for satisfying the same or similar conditions under other policies for the same violation(s), nor will this policy apply to violations which have received penalty mitigation under other policies.

(3) This policy sets forth factors for consideration that will guide the Agency in the exercise of its prosecutorial discretion. It states the Agency's views as to the proper allocation of its enforcement resources. The policy is not final agency action, and is intended as guidance. It does not create any rights, duties, obligations, or defenses, implied or otherwise, in any third parties.

(4) This policy should be used whenever applicable in settlement negotiations for both administrative and civil judicial enforcement actions. It is not intended for use in pleading, at hearing or at trial. The policy may be applied at EPA's discretion to the settlement of administrative and judicial enforcement actions instituted prior to, but not yet resolved, as of the effective date of this policy.

H. Public Accountability

(1) Within 3 years of the effective date of this policy, EPA will complete a study of the effectiveness of the policy in encouraging:

(a) changes in compliance behavior within the regulated community, including improved compliance rates;

(b) prompt disclosure and correction of violations, including timely and accurate compliance with reporting requirements;

(c) corporate compliance programs that are successful in preventing violations, improving environmental performance, and promoting public disclosure;

(d) consistency among state programs that provide incentives for voluntary compliance.

EPA will make the study available to the public.

(2) EPA will make publicly available the terms and conditions of any compliance agreement reached under this policy, including the nature of the violation, the remedy, and the schedule for returning to compliance.

I. Effective Date

This policy is effective January 22, 1996.

Dated: December 18, 1995.
Steven A. Herman,
Assistant Administrator for Enforcement and Compliance Assurance.

Published at 60 Fed. Reg. 66706 (December 22, 1995).
The Federal Register Document also includes an extensive explanation of the policy. In 1999, the Environmental Protection Agency proposed a number of revisions to the Policy Statement and sought public comment on those proposed revisions. 64 Fed. Reg. 26745 (May 17, 1999).

APPENDIX 7

EXAMPLES OF NO-FAULT ENVIRONMENTAL CRIMES

1. The accidental discharge of commercially valuable gasoline into a river was within the ban established by the Refuse Act of 1899 against the deposit of "refuse" in navigable waters. The gasoline became waste upon its entry into the water. The dissent argued that the majority decision was contrary to the principle that criminal statutes are to be narrowly construed.[1]

2. The discharge of oil onto the ground in such close proximity to the water that the oil could flow into the navigable water of the United States by gravity alone constituted a violation of the Refuse Act of 1899 if the oil eventually reached the water.[2]

3. The motion of the FMC Corporation to dismiss criminal charges for violation of the Migratory Bird Treaty Act was denied by a federal judge in the case. The company operated a facility in upstate New York. Waste water from the facility was stored in a lagoon. The company had a permit to discharge waste water from the lagoon into a nearby stream from whence it entered Lake Ontario. During a routine monitoring inspection, state officials found several dead migratory birds in or near the lagoon. The judge ruled that the motion to dismiss was premature, although expressing concern about the absence of an intent element in this criminal statute. In his decision, the judge asked the following rhetorical question: "Migratory birds are killed by many accidental means, such as jet airplanes, air pollution and windows of tall buildings. Their nests and eggs are destroyed in clearing land for housing, recreation and highways. Can the Government charge land developers and high rise building constructors with the deaths of birds under the statute?"[3]

4. On appeal, the appellate court upheld the conviction of FMC for violation of the Migratory Bird Treaty Act, but not without concern regarding the broad language and strict liability of that law. The court stated: "Certainly construction [of the Migratory Bird Treaty Act] that would bring every killing within the statute, such as deaths caused by automobiles, airplanes, plate glass modern office buildings or picture windows in residential dwellings into which birds fly, would offend reason and common sense. . . . Such situations properly can be left to the sound discretion of prosecutors and the courts."[4]

5. The Ralston Purina Company pled guilty to violations of the Comprehensive Environmental Response, Compensation, and Liability Act (CERCLA), the Clean

---

1   *United States v. Standard Oil Company*, 384 U.S. 224 (1966).

2   *United States v. Esso Standard Oil Co. of Puerto Rico*, 375 F.2d 621 (3d. Cir. 1967).

3   *United States v. FMC Corporation*, 428 F. Supp. 615 (W.D.N.Y. 1977).

4   *United States v. FMC Corp.*, 572 F.2d 902, 905 (2d. Cir. 1978).

352　　　Corporate Fraud Investigations & Compliance Programs

Water Act, and the Refuse Act of 1899 and was fined $62,500. The violations resulted from the release of hexane into the Ohio River from the company's soybean-extraction plant in Louisville, Kentucky.[5]

6. Ashland Oil, Inc. was charged with criminal negligence and violations of the Clean Water Act and the Refuse Act of 1899 as a result of the oil storage tank collapse near Pittsburgh that spilled 713,000 gallons of oil into the Ohio River. Ashland noted that the Justice Department's decision to go forward with a criminal prosecution is contrary to its usual policy to pursue criminal violations only in instances of deliberate acts. "Such a departure from established practices impairs rather than promotes environmental compliance," the company said.[6]

7. The owner of the M/V WORLD PRODIGY pled guilty to negligent violation of the Clean Water Act and agreed to pay a $1 million fine. The master of the tanker also pled guilty and agreed to pay a $10,000 fine. As part of the settlement, the federal prosecutor dropped charges under the Refuse Act and agreed to not seek jail time for the master. Meanwhile, the state of Rhode Island announced that it was preparing to pursue criminal charges of its own against the master for water pollution and for failing to have a pilot on board the vessel when it grounded in Narragansett Bay on June 23, 1989, spilling nearly 300,000 gallons of oil.[7]

8. The March 24, 1989, oil spill into Prince William Sound, Alaska, from the M/V EXXON VALDEZ engendered a high level of activity by the federal government under the Refuse Act of 1899 and the Migratory Bird Treaty Act. That spill marks the commencement of the current frequent use of those statutes by federal prosecutors against the maritime industry.

> a. A Justice Department Press Conference was held concerning the criminal indictment of Exxon for the oil spill from the M/V EXXON VALDEZ, including strict liability charges under the Refuse Act and the Migratory Bird Treaty Act. Attorney General Richard Thornburgh said, among other things: "By pursuing criminal charges in this case, the federal government is sending a strong signal that environmental crimes will not be tolerated. Firms which violate the environmental laws will face tough prosecution in the federal courts. We intend to see that the environmental laws are fully and strictly enforced."[8]

> b. An article entitled *Exxon Indictment Unusual in Many Ways, Experts Say; Litigation: The Size of Possible Fines and the Use of Seldom-Used Provisions of Federal Statutes Make Some Suspect a Settlement is Being Sought* discussed probable motives of the federal prosecutors in filing criminal charges

---

5　　*Chemical Week* (January 13, 1982).

6　　*Oil & Gas Journal* (September 26, 1988). The spill eventually cost Ashland Oil over $32 million, including federal criminal fines in the amount of $2.25 million and state costs and penalties of $4.6 million. New York Times, page 25 (November 23, 1989).

7　　*Journal of Commerce* (August 23, 1989).

8　　*Federal News Service* (February 27, 1990).

against Exxon in the EXXON VALDEZ oil spill for alleged violation of the Refuse Act, the Migratory Bird Treaty Act, the Clean Water Act, the Ports and Waterways Safety Act, and the Dangerous Cargo Act, as well as use of the Alternative Fines Act.[9]

c. Exxon was charged with violations of the Dangerous Cargo Act, the Ports and Waterways Safety Act, the Clean Water Act, the Refuse Act of 1899, and the Migratory Bird Treaty Act as a result of the EXXON VALDEZ oil spill. The five count criminal indictment could result in fines totaling more than $700 million.[10]

d. An article entitled *Exxon paying the high cost of injustice* discusses the implications of criminal statutes, such as the Refuse Act and the Migratory Bird Treaty Act, that lack an intent requirement. The article contends that these two statutes were originally intended to address the intentional dumping of waste and hunting without a license respectively. It notes that the Justice Department voluntarily dropped its original felony charge against Exxon that the company had 'willfully and knowingly' entrusted the M/V EXXON VALDEZ to employees not capable or competent to steer it.[11]

e. Exxon pled guilty to violating the Migratory Bird Treaty Act and Exxon Shipping Company pled guilty to violating the Clean Water Act, the Refuse Act of 1899, and the Migratory Bird Treaty Act in a settlement with the federal government of charges arising from the EXXON VALDEZ oil spill. Exxon agreed to pay criminal fines of $150 million, civil damages of $900 million, and restoration damages of $100 million. Clean-up costs and third party damages were not addressed in the settlement.[12]

f. The criminal sentence of Joseph Hazelwood to 1,000 hours of community service was upheld by the Alaska Court of Appeals. Hazelwood had been convicted of negligently spilling oil into state waters following the grounding of the tanker EXXON VALDEZ in Prince William Sound in 1989.[13]

9. Shell Oil Pipeline Co. pled guilty to a violation of the Refuse Act and agreed to pay $200,00 in fines and an additional $8 million in restitution and settlements in connection with an 860,000 gallon spill into the Mississippi, Gasconade, and Missouri Rivers in 1988. The spill was the result of a rupture in a crude oil pipeline.[14]

10. An oil field saltwater disposal company, B & E, Inc., paid a $25,000 criminal fine for violation of the Migratory Bird Treaty Act by disposal of oil field saltwater in New Mexico. The fine was assessed by the EPA despite the fact that B & E had

---

9   *Los Angeles Times* (March 2, 1990).

10   *Oil & Gas Journal* (March 5, 1990).

11   *Houston Chronicle* (October 3, 1991).

12   *Oil Daily* (October 9, 1991).

13   *Washington Post* (July 5, 1998).

14   *St. Louis Post-Dispatch* (February 3, 1992).

permits from the federal Bureau of Land Management and the state Oil Conservation Division authorizing such disposal.[15]

11. Criminal fines totaling $1.5 million were imposed on Unocal as a result of the long-term leak of diluent from its pipeline at the Guadalupe oil field in San Luis Obispo County, California. The plea agreement also included a three-year probation period and a mandatory environmental training program for Unocal employees.[16]

12. A ship salvage company in Baltimore, Maryland, and the company president were convicted of violation of the Refuse Act of 1899, the Clean Water Act, and other criminal statutes for actions related to the scrapping of two former navy vessels. Among other things, the company and the president were convicted of discharging oil, construction debris, paint chips, metal fragments, insulation materials, and other pollutants into the local river. The president was sentenced to 30 months in prison and a $50,000 fine. The company was fined $50,000.[17]

13. Shell Oil Company has agreed to pay a $20,000 criminal fine for violation of the Migratory Bird Treaty Act at its Wood River Refining facility, near Wood River, Illinois. At least 40 migratory birds died after landing on the facility's exposed oil waste impoundments.[18]

---

15 *Oil & Gas Journal* (July 5, 1993).

16 *Oil Daily* (March 18, 1994).

17 *Washington Post* (February 15, 1998).

18 *M2 Communications Ltd.* (March 31, 1998).

APPENDIX 8

COMPARISON: ISM CODE, ISO 9000, ISO 14001, AND MARITIME COMPLIANCE PROGRAM

For the maritime industry, there are four major programs that provide a shipowner and others with a systematic overview of the company's compliance with applicable safety, environmental, and other applicable laws and regulations. These programs overlap in many coverage areas, but have distinctly different purposes. The following table illustrates the areas of significant duplication and uniqueness among these programs.

Comparison Table

	ISM Code	ISO 9000	ISO 14001	MCP
A. Jurisdictions Covered				
1. Flag State	X	X	X	
2. International	X	X	X	X
3. U.S. (for non-U.S. vessels)				X
B. Subject Areas				
1. Safety Regulation	X	X		X
2. Environment Regulation	X		X	X
3. Economic Regulation		X		X
4. Miscellaneous		X	X	
C. Elements				
1. Compliance Standards and Procedures	X	X	X	X
2. High-Level Individual	X	X	X	X
3. No delegation to one with propensity to engage in illegal acts				X
4. Training and Education	X	X	X	X
5. Monitoring and Auditing	X	X	X	X
6. Disciplinary Action				X
7. Remedial Action	X	X	X	X

Note: The presence of X's in two or more columns of the same roll does not necessarily mean that the items in the two programs are exactly equivalent. It merely means that the items are substantially the same and that it should not be difficult to develop one program to address both requirements. Likewise, the absence of an X in a column does not signify that the program could not accommodate the particular item. It merely means that the program does not sufficiently address the issue to provide for its adequate development without additional work or effort.

LIST OF SOURCES OF ADDITIONAL INFORMATION

SOURCES

Bennett, Rauh and Kriegel, *The Role of Internal Investigations in Defending Against Charges of Corporate Misconduct*, 763 PLI/Corp. 31 (Jan. 1992)

Black, *Internal Corporate Investigations*, Volume C5, Business Law Monographs (1998)

Zornow and Obermaier, *Representation of the Corporation and Its Employees in Internal and Government Investigations*, published in *How to Handle Internal Investigations and Establish Successful Compliance Programs* (PLI, 1992)

Defense of Businesses, Individual Officers and Employees in Corporate Criminal Investigations, 19 Pub. Con. L.J. 648 (1990)

Anton R. Valukas and Robert R. Stauffer, *Internal Investigations of Corporate Misconduct*, Vol. 6, No. 2, Feb. 1992.

Lawrence B. Pedowitz, Carol Miller, *Confronting the Criminal Investigation*, 161 PLI/Crim. 133 (1991)

Brad D. Brian and Barry F. McNeil, (editors) *Internal Corporate Investigations, Conducting Them, Protecting Them*, (Litigation Section, ABA 1992)

Richard M. Cooper, "Is It Always Smart for a Company to Let Employees Take the Rap?," *Business Crimes Bulletin,*, Vol. 4, No. 9, Oct. 1997

Rakoff Blumkin & Sauber, *Corporate Sentencing Guidelines: Compliance and Mitigation*, Law Journal Seminars-Press (1998)

Edna Selan Epstein, *The Attorney-Client Privilege and the Work-Product Doctrine*, (3d ed., Litigation Section, ABA, 1997)